Children born of war in the twentieth century

Manchester University Press

Children born of war in the twentieth century

Sabine Lee

Manchester University Press

Copyright © Sabine Lee 2017

The right of Sabine Lee to be identified as the author of this work has been asserted by her in accordance with the Copyright, Designs and Patents Act 1988.

Published by Manchester University Press
Altrincham Street, Manchester M1 7JA, UK
www.manchesteruniversitypress.co.uk

British Library Cataloguing-in-Publication Data is available

ISBN 978 1 5261 0458 8 *hardback*
ISBN 978 1 5261 0459 5 *paperback*

First published by Manchester University Press in hardback 2017

This edition first published 2019

The publisher has no responsibility for the persistence or accuracy of URLs for any external or third-party internet websites referred to in this book, and does not guarantee that any content on such websites is, or will remain, accurate or appropriate.

Typeset by Servis Filmsetting Ltd, Stockport, Cheshire

Contents

List of figures and tables	*page* vi
Acknowledgements	vii
List of abbreviations	x
1 Children born of war: an introduction	1
2 Children born of war: who are they? Experiences of children, mothers, families and post-conflict communities	21
3 Children born of war during and after the Second World War	51
4 *Bui Doi*: the children of the Vietnam War	112
5 Bosnia: a new dimension of genocidal rape and its children	151
6 African conflicts	187
7 Unintended consequences …	226
Epilogue: Children born of war: lessons learnt?	244
Bibliography	249
Index	286

Figures and tables

Figures

3.1	Conceptualisation of factors affecting life courses of children born of war	68
3.2	Significant factors in the assessment of the psychosocial impact of being a child born of war	69
3.3	Knut Weise, *Distelblüten* © Knut Weise, used with permission	88
3.4	Knut Weise, *Schattenkinder* © Knut Weise, used with permission	90
4.1	International adoption trends, 1944–2013	128
6.1	Map of Rwanda and neighbouring countries (map data © 2016 Google)	188
6.2	Map of Uganda and neighbouring countries (map data © 2016 Google)	199

Tables

5.1	Children's rights in the Convention on the Rights of the Child	162

Acknowledgements

It all started with a chat over a mug of Redbush tea in a small village of Bubenreuth, where I spent an evening with a cousin of mine discussing our joint research interests in the ethics of oral history, psychosocial and medical research. Thanks, Kerstin! One word led to another and before I knew it, I was beginning to explore issues relating to children fathered by foreign soldiers in recent armed conflicts. This book is the result of the five years of research that followed. Work took me quite literally across the world, to Europe, North America, South East Asia, Africa and Australia; and just as my travel schedule has been extensive, so are my scholarly debts accumulated in the process.

Between 2011 and 2014, an AHRC network grant[1] allowed me to link up with a group of colleagues in order to develop a research strategy. I am grateful to the funders for making this possible; and I am even more indebted to colleagues across many disciplines who contributed to these early conversations and whose insights have pushed a niche subject[2] onto an international research platform in a way that few of us would have believed possible in the early years. My thanks go to the core research group with Susan Bartels, Heide Glaesmer, Jocelyn Kelly, Philipp Kuwert, Ingvill C. Mochmann, Barbara Stelzl-Marx and to many others who participated in one or more of the workshops. The grant also facilitated the development of the participatory aspects of research with children born of war; beyond the direct contributions to the network through workshop participation, numerous children born of war, in particular those conceived during the Second World War and the post-war occupations, have continued to engage in fruitful discussions throughout. My thanks go to Ute Baur-Timmerbrink, Winfried Behlau, Birgrit Michler, Jacqui Maurice and many others who prefer to remain anonymous but who also have never tired of discussing their experiences with us. I am also grateful to Knut Weise for allowing me to reproduce his two paintings *Schattenkinder* and *Distelblüte*, and to Ingvill C. Mochman and Heide Glaesmer for permission to reproduce previously published diagrams that illustrate their methodological contributions to the subject.

Subsequent research was funded by a British Academy Small Research Grant[3] and research allowances of the School of History and Cultures and the College of Arts and Law at the University of Birmingham. A grant from the University's North America Travel Fund facilitated networking activities that greatly benefitted the research, too. Similarly, the University's recently established research assistantship scheme contributed by providing financial support for administrative assistance. Katharina Lee, my summer research assistant and Bethan Strange, our School undergraduate administrative assistant, did an excellent job in finalising the bibliography and references.

A conference supported by the Volkswagen-Stiftung,[4] and jointly organised by Heide Glaesmer, Philipp Kuwert and myself, provided us with the welcome opportunity to discuss the emerging research landscape with experienced colleagues, early-stage researchers and with some of the children fathered by Allied soldiers during the Second World War and the post-war occupations. The meeting occurred at a pivotal point in the writing up, and discussions of this fruitful meeting are revisited in some of the book chapters.

Fieldwork carried out by Eunice Apio and Elizabeth Bramley, which fed directly into one of the case studies, was funded by a Marie Curie Fellowship[5] and a University of Birmingham Undergraduate Research Fellowship respectively. I am indebted to Eunice and Elizabeth, and also to Allen Kiconco, for generously sharing their field notes and research results. They provided invaluable sources for the analysis of Chapter 6.

The University of Birmingham prides itself on its research-led teaching. This book is testimony to the mutually beneficial aspects of such an approach to teaching and learning in Higher Education. While I *hope* that students have benefited from my knowledge, I *know* that I have profited from several year groups of undergraduates and postgraduates who – in more or less heated discussions and conversations – have encouraged me to think and rethink my reasoning and evidence base in the source and data analysis relating to children born of war. More recently, through the generous funding from the European Union, a group of fifteen Ph.D. students[6] have joined the growing research community around children born of war, and they are pushing the boundaries of this research field. Intensive conversations with these young researchers, as well as the many supervisors and partners in the project, have added interesting new perspectives, and I am particularly grateful to Janine Clarke, Marie Kaiser, Bob McKelvey, Maren Roeger, Benedetta Rossi, Jennifer Scott and Elisa van Ee for their probing questioning. Some of them and unnamed others have read parts of the manuscript, and I am extremely grateful for their constructive comments. Librarians and archivists are among the lifelines of historical research. This project is no different, and staff in numerous archives and libraries in the UK, Germany, France, the Netherlands, the US and Canada have helped me exploit the considerable riches of the written material – published and unpublished.

Beyond all, however, it was the tolerance of my family, Han, Katharina

Acknowledgements

and Sebastian, which made this book possible. They had to wave goodbye at airports time after time, as I ventured into new research territories (literally and figuratively), disappeared for conferences and workshops, and came up with ideas of how to add yet another new aspect to the project they had hoped would have been concluded years ago. Thank you so much for the patience and good humour with which you accepted your temporary abandonment. This book will allow you to judge for yourselves whether I have spent that time wisely.

Notes

1. AHRC: AHJ001554//1.
2. Developing among others from the work of the War and Children Identity Project in 2006 in Bergen, Norway, a first research network, the International Network for Interdisciplinary Research on Children Born of War (INIRC), had been engaged in some early work in this field.
3. British Academy: SG110078.
4. Volkswagenstiftung: AZ_89419.
5. FP7-PEOPLE-2011-IIF-911934.
6. H2020-MC-CAITN-2014-642571.

At the time of going to press, the author is aware of some controversy surrounding the article mentioned on p. 184, note 124. No specific conclusion has been reached, and the author would advise the reader to seek further information before drawing upon this source.

Abbreviations

BA	Bundesarchiv
CBOW	children born of war
CRC	Convention on the Rights of the Child
CRSV	conflict-related sexual violence
DCI	Defence for Children International
DRC	Democratic Republic of Congo
ECOMOG	Economic Community of Western African States Monitoring Group
GBV	gender-based violence
HCIA	Hague Convention on Intercountry Adoption
HSM	Holy Spirit Movement
ICA	intercountry adoption
ICRC	International Committee of the Red Cross
ICTR	International Criminal Tribunal for Rwanda
ICTY	International Criminal Tribunal for the former Yugoslavia
IHL	International Humanitarian Law
JRP	Justice and Reconciliation Project
LRA	Lord's Resistance Army
MACV	Military Assistance Command Vietnam
NACP	National Archives at College Park
NGO	non-governmental organisation
NSV	*Nationalisozialistische Volkswohlfahrt*
ONUMOZ	United Nations Operations in Mozambique
POW	prisoner of war
PSEA	prevention of sexual exploitation and abuse
PSO	peace support operations
PTSD	posttraumatic stress disorder
RG	Record Group
SEA	sexual exploitation and abuse
STI	sexually transmitted infection

Abbreviations

TCC	troop-contributing countries
UNAMIC	United Nations Advance Mission in Cambodia
UNHCR	United Nations High Commissioner for Refugees
UNICEF	United Nations Children's Emergency Fund
UNIFEM	United Nations Development Fund for Women
UNLA	Uganda National Liberation Army
UNMIBH	United Nations Missions in Bosnia and Herzegovina
UNOCHA	United Nations Office for the Coordination of Humanitarian Affairs
UNOSOM I/II	United Nations Operation in Somalia I/II
UNTAC	United Nations Transitional Authority in Cambodia
UNTSO	United Nations Truce Supervision Organization
VD	venereal disease

1

Children born of war: an introduction

Few human rights and children's rights topics have been met with a similarly extensive silence as the fate of children born of war (CBOW) – children fathered by foreign soldiers and born to local mothers during and after armed conflicts.[1] Their existence, in their hundreds of thousands, is a widely ignored reality – to the detriment of the individuals and the local societies within which they grow up. Who are they? Where are they? Why are they ignored? And why do they matter? These are some of the fundamental questions serving as a starting point for this study of CBOW in the twentieth century. Beyond the life courses of the children themselves, and beyond giving them a voice to explain their experiences as children of foreign – and often absent – fathers in volatile post-conflict situations, focal points of the analysis will be the responses of others to the children whose mere existence frequently creates personal, familial, societal, cultural and political problems in what are often very unsettled post-conflict communities and states.

In the early twenty-first century, children fathered by foreign soldiers during and after conflicts are often associated directly with gender-based violence (GBV). This is not surprising. Sexualised violence vis-à-vis women during hostilities is not only the oldest war crime, it is also, albeit in a different manifestation, the youngest such crime.[2] Recent conflicts have seen this kind of atrocity used extensively with a level of brutality and disregard for the laws of warfare rarely witnessed in the past. Where there is sexual violence, children are born as a result of it. While the prevalence of conflict-related sexual violence (CRSV) has increasingly made the news headlines in recent years, the children conceived as a result of the atrocities have not found their way onto the front pages of the newspapers or the desks of the Whitehall civil servants or non-governmental organisation (NGO) advisors on humanitarian intervention. Since the 1990s – the time of the mass rapes of the Balkan Wars and the numerous African conflicts, epitomised by the Rwandan genocide with its previously unimaginable acts of sexualised violence – rape as a weapon of war has received the attention of academia, the media, governments, NGOs and international courts. International tribunals such as the International Criminal Tribunal for the former Yugoslavia (ICTY) and the International Criminal Tribunal for Rwanda (ICTR)[3] have pronounced judgements in a way that has changed our thinking about rape as a weapon of war, GBV, crimes against humanity, genocidal and sexualised violence. Recently, the UK Foreign and Commonwealth Office launched a government initiative aimed at the prevention of sexual violence in conflict,[4] and barely two years later, in June 2014, more than 1700 delegates from 123 countries, alongside 73 ministers and representatives of more than one hundred NGOs, met in London for a 'Global Summit to End Sexual Violence in Conflict'.[5] A 'statement of action' addressing CRSV demonstrated the willingness of many countries world-wide to engage with the issue and to start putting in place action plans for the prevention of GBV in conflicts.[6]

The increased attention that the subject has received as a political and humanitarian concern has been matched, if not surpassed, by a wide range of academic literature across several disciplines including history, politics, psychology, psychiatry, law and development studies. Yet, in stark contrast to this extensive interest in CRSV, the fate of the thousands of children born as a result of the often coercive relationships between local civilians and foreign soldiers has hardly been noticed. And if children born to victims of CRSV have received little attention, children conceived in non-violent relationships or encounters, many of whom share a variety of the difficulties experienced by children of CRSV victims, have been ignored almost completely. In other words, where there has been interest in CBOW, it has, almost always, been in the context of CRSV. The most prominent example of academic engagement with this subject is Charli Carpenter's essay collection *Born of War*,[7] which was ground breaking in that it was the first book-length publication dealing exclusively with the children born of wartime sexual violence rather than with their mothers, the direct victims of the assaults. Similarly, Carpenter's subsequent analysis of children born of the Bosnian Wars, which specifically addresses the issue of human rights agenda setting, does so in the context of GBV in war.[8] This focus on children born out of coercive relationships has been evident in what little scholarly and journalistic output has been published since.[9] It is not surprising, therefore, that CBOW are often associated directly with sexualised violence. Given the increasingly prominent role of such violence in contemporary armed conflict, it is no less astonishing that CBOW are perceived to be a relatively recent phenomenon. Yet, neither of these conclusions is accurate. Whenever there is armed conflict, soldiers come into contact with local civilians, and in particular with local women; and almost always a proportion of these military–civilian contacts– no matter how strongly the military leadership and the local communities might object – result in intimate relations, whether friendly and consensual or exploitative, coercive and violent. They frequently lead to children being born. This has always been the case and remains true today.

Research data

Even the most existential question of 'Who are the CBOW?' cannot be answered easily. No reliable data exists about even their numbers, let alone their life courses. Most recently, and in no way atypical, a major project with the aim of mapping sexual violence in armed conflict globally in the last decade of the twentieth century and sexual exploitation and abuse (SEA) by United Nations (UN) peacekeepers since 1999 has been initiated,[10] but children born as a result of this violence are not part of this data gathering. The only collection of numbers currently available is based on very vague estimates from a variety of sources, collated for the one existing survey *The War Children of the World*, a report based on the work of *The War and Children Identity Project*.[11] But the report was issued with a word of caution. When the figures were first published in 2001, it was made clear that while they were the best available, they could not be assumed to be that accurate; the report's author pointed to the fact that the numbers were at best conservative estimates, and – one might add – at worst guesswork. According to Grieg's overview, a minimum of 500,000 children were fathered by foreign soldiers in various twentieth-century conflicts; most academics and practitioners working in the field would readily agree that this is an underestimate, caused by lack of any data for a significant number of conflicts, the incompleteness of evidence where it does exist, a general tendency to under-report, and the familiar problem of making accurate assumptions about hidden populations, which applies to large numbers of CBOW.[12] A *tour d'horizon* indicates the scale and breadth of the phenomenon. Thousands of children are believed to have been fathered by French and British soldiers in Germany during the First World War.[13] An estimated 10,000–12,000 children fathered by German soldiers were born to Norwegian mothers during the Second World War,[14] and the number of German-fathered children of French mothers is estimated to be as high as 120,000–200,000.[15] Almost 30,000 children are believed to have been born of unions between Canadian service men and women in Britain and the rest of Europe between 1940 and 1946 (22,000 in Britain, around 6000 in the Netherlands and around 1000 in other European countries).[16] Estimates of the number of children born of the post-war occupations of Germany and Austria vary widely and are believed to be at least 200,000 and 20,000 respectively;[17] similarly approximations of children born of American GIs and local Vietnamese women during the Vietnam War, generally biracial and many of mixed black/Asian descent, range from 40,000[18] to 200,000.[19] More recently, conflicts in East Timor, Cambodia and Sri Lanka are believed to have led to the birth of thousands of children conceived of liaisons between military personnel and local women.[20] The Balkan Wars of the 1990s, with their Serb 'rape camps' and the use of sexual violence as a means of ethnically motivated warfare, demonstrate a new dimension of the phenomenon of CBOW. It is estimated that during the Bosnian War between 20,000 and 50,000 women experienced sexual violence, that about 4000 women became pregnant and that about half of these pregnancies resulted in children being born.[21] Several thousand miles further south, around the same time, thousands of children were estimated to have been fathered by Hutu fighters and born to Tutsi mothers in the aftermath of the Rwandan genocide; also in the last decades of the twentieth century, thousands of children were born to Lord's Resistance Army (LRA) fathers and female abductees during the Civil War in Northern Uganda, and fathered by Revolutionary United Front soldiers and born to female child soldiers in Sierra Leone.[22]

The above illustrates two basic facts relating to CBOW: firstly, it is clearly a global and significant occurrence with a sizeable group of people directly affected; secondly, as the repeated use of the word 'estimate' demonstrates, it is a phenomenon that lacks reliable data of even the most basic kind, such as the number of people under discussion. This is as much a consequence of methodological challenges of quantitative research in hidden populations as it is a symptom of a general lack of interest in the fate of CBOW. As one commentator put it:

> in the early 1990s organizations such as the international network around children's human rights concluded that stigma and abuse against children born of war were nonissues from the human rights perspective. Therefore, rather than gathering accurate data, establishing programs to address specific needs, and creating rights-based stories to counter misinformed sensationalism about the topic, organizations promoting children's human rights chose silence, a silence that is only very tentatively broken today, nearly twenty years later.[23]

Some notable exceptions to the general disinterest concerning the fate of these children exist. Initiated by Stein Ugelvik Larsen, the above-mentioned *War and Children Identity Project* was formed, with the explicit goals of promoting and securing the human rights of CBOW.[24] While these ambitious objectives have not been achieved, the project has produced an invaluable collection of mostly anecdotal evidence, which has served as a welcome foundation on which to base further research relating to CBOW.

Much of the analysis to follow will be based on estimates, on data which can often not claim accuracy, on material that generally has to be assumed to be an approximation with a significant margin for error or, in some cases, on no available quantitative data at all. This raises some significant methodological issues, as well as questions about the reasons for trying to quantify the problem in the first place. Here it is important to clarify what a quantification does and what it does not aim to achieve. Postulating apparent facts, cloaked in numbers, about GBV or numbers of children conceived of relationships between soldiers and local women, whether or not these were exploitative, is not intended to create a category (or several categories) of victims. Nor does it serve a political purpose in the sense of pointing the finger at certain nationalities or ethnic or religious groups as perpetrators. It does, however,

CBOW: an introduction

intend to document a complex and multi-faceted history and by implication it intends to create a space for academic and non-academic discourse. If the study draws on numbers, however unreliable these might be, it does so in order to illustrate the magnitude of the phenomenon as well as the fact that it is not limited to particular geographical, geopolitical or historical contexts. In emphasising that it is unlikely that historians will ever know exactly how many women and children have been affected and challenged by the circumstances resulting in the conception of CBOW or in a life as a child born of war, the analysis draws attention to the fact that too strong a focus on the accuracy of the figures is not going to enhance our understanding of the core issues of the experiences of CBOW and their mothers, families and local and national receptor communities. Thus, research is important as a basis of the kind of agenda setting that has been referred to above. It is also important for understanding the nature and magnitude of a problem, for appreciating its complexities and its variations across time and space, and for proposing solutions and – eventually – for monitoring and evaluating progress in developments.

Research on CBOW is still in its early stages, and it is often still seen largely as a side aspect of analyses of CRSV. It is in this area, in particular, that significant developments have taken place with regard to academic research, advocacy and public awareness alike. The most extensive systematic research exists on Norwegian children fathered by German soldiers during the Second World War. Based on historical documents, qualitative interviews, register data[25] and quantitative interviews, the life courses of Norwegian CBOW have been analysed thoroughly.[26] Beyond this Norwegian case, studies have largely had an explorative character.[27] One overview of CBOW as a result of sexual violence in more recent conflicts has been provided in the already mentioned *Born of War*,[28] a volume that offers case studies covering as diverse a range of conflict zones as East Timor, Sierra Leone, Northern Uganda and Bosnia. Over and above visualising the wide geographical extent of the problem, the book also tackles issues related to the human rights of these children. Thereby the analysis extends the theme beyond individual cases and raises broader conceptual questions. Several facets, in particular those of human rights of CBOW have found some limited academic interest.[29] The connections between trauma, stigma and identity have begun to interest psychiatrists and psychologists. Here, first studies have focused on CBOW and trans-generational issues that affect their mental health and well-being.[30] Furthermore, recently, inter-disciplinary and inter-sectoral collaborations have been in evidence in networks such as the *International Research Network on Children Born of War*[31] and the Horizon 2020 doctoral Training Network,[32] as well as international conferences such as *Children and War: Past and Present*[33] and the international meeting of the Peace Research Institute Oslo on *The Legacy of War Time Rape: Mapping Key Concepts and Issues*.[34]

Moreover, advocacy and self-help groups have played an increasingly important role in allowing CBOW to express their concerns, needs and wishes, but also – often in search of their own identities – in uncovering important aspects about the history of CBOW more generally. Given the fragmented picture presented by patchy secondary sources, anecdotal evidence from ego-documents, biographies, oral histories and documentaries produced by associations of CBOW provide valuable additional information and, together with quantitative and qualitative surveys they are indispensable for social empirical research.[35] The analysis of their experiences here will, where possible, include those voices of CBOW to complement other quantitative and qualitative data and to fill some of the still considerable gaps in the source base.

In addition, since the mid-1990s, academics and journalists have begun exploring the life courses of some of those fathered by foreign soldiers[36] reinforcing two insights already gained from earlier oral evidence and autobiographical writings: firstly, a very significant number of CBOW were conceived in consensual or non-violent relationships; and secondly, the nature of the parents' relationship has been a poor indicator of the hardships suffered by the children. In others words, children born out of love-relationships did not necessarily have an easier childhood and adolescence than those conceived in exploitative or violent relationships. Early accounts, both from CBOW themselves and from initial research, further suggest that CBOW across time and space, irrespective of the nature of their parents' relationship, the geopolitical and cultural circumstances of their upbringing, face very specific challenges arising out of their biological origins as children of foreign soldiers.[37] These challenges and the individual, familial and societal responses to them are among the themes of this book.

Historical-comparative synthesis: some methodological considerations

This study aims to investigate the situations of CBOW since the Second World War and thereby to provide a historical synthesis that moves beyond individual case studies and to explore circumstances across time and geopolitical location. Its purpose is not only to establish facts and account for the status quo of current research, but to enhance the evidence base through additional case studies, and the comparative analysis of experiences and life courses of CBOW (both as children, in adolescence and in adulthood) in different geopolitical and historical contexts.

While one can argue about the exact numbers of wars, civil wars and armed conflicts, deaths and other brutalities in what the British novelist Margaret Drabble, on account of the increasingly beastly behaviour of humans throughout the twentieth century, called the a 'beastly century',[38] few would take issue with the evaluation that such conflicts were numerous and extremely costly in terms of human lives.[39] For the purpose of this analysis, specific conflict areas were chosen as key case studies on the basis of which to explore several core themes. These conflicts are the Second World War (1939–1945) with the subsequent post-war occupations of Germany and Austria (1945–1955); the Vietnam War (1955–1975); the Bosnian War (1992–1995); some African Conflicts of the 1990s and early 2000s, in particular in Rwanda (1994) and Uganda (1988–2006); and, finally, a number of peace support operations of the early twenty-first century. Given the multitude of other conflicts which are not featuring prominently in this analysis despite the fact that they also formed the setting for the birth of numerous CBOW, this choice requires some explanation.

All these conflicts resulted in large numbers of CBOW, often but by no means exclusively conceived in exploitative relationships. The geographical and chronological spread of the wars is a first indication that children were fathered by foreign soldiers in circumstances which were not determined by time and space *per se*. However, the chosen conflicts demonstrate a clear shift in the nature of warfare which had a significant impact on the development of military–civilian relations in general and the relationship between soldiers and local women in particular. As will be explored in some detail below, sexual violence against women, although widespread throughout the various theatres of war between 1939 and 1945, was by and large not part of war strategy or even war tactics of any of the parties to the conflict.[40] This is not to minimise the scale and impact of such violence on the individuals; nor is it to minimise the severity of the crimes committed. However, whether sexual violence is a by-product of war or whether it is an integral part of war tactics or war strategy, is likely to have an effect on how the victims of such violence and their children are being treated in post-war communities and is thus of significance for our analysis. In sharp contrast to the Second World War and also the Indochina Wars, later conflicts such as the Balkan Wars and the African conflicts of the turn of the century witnessed various manifestations of sexual violence that were not only 'related to' the conflict but were a deliberate and targeted feature of the conflict; they were part of a war strategy. This had different manifestations as, for instance, in the Bosnian rape camps, in the genocidal rapes of Rwanda or in the considered targeting, through abduction, of female child soldiers to serve as sex slaves and bear rebel children in Uganda. Such circumstances provide a very different background to the post-conflict integration of children conceived from liaisons with enemy soldiers, the impact of which will be explored in some detail below.

The geographical expanse of the cases is deliberate also to allow the investigation of racial, national, ethnic and/or religious aspects of significance to the life-courses of CBOW. These played very distinct roles in the different conflicts and post-conflict rebuilding of the affected societies and, as will be demonstrated, in the experiences of CBOW. The exploration of the Second World War and the Bosnian War focuses on European theatres of war. Although the children conceived of relations with foreign soldiers in many cases could be 'hidden' through integration into their maternal families, their identity was often known or speculated about by local communities. This had consequences for the children's relationships within the families and local communities, and in many cases it had significant impact on their mental health. Numerous children born of war and occupation who learnt about their biological origins later in life, often by coincidence and frequently not from their mothers or families directly, suffered identity crises related to their inability to trace their biological roots. But identity issues – though of a rather different nature – were also prevalent in other cultural contexts and among the non-hidden populations. Children fathered by American soldiers in Vietnam were clearly visible and were explicitly associated with the enemy, a situation exacerbated by the fact that this enemy remained a political, cultural and ideological foe in post-war Vietnam which saw the United States as anathema to all that the victorious communist regime had fought for and stood for. Therefore, the children were not only clearly visible, but they were widely perceived (by many non-communist countries elsewhere) to be in danger of being targeted officially and unofficially for stigmatisation and discrimination on the grounds of being a child of a former and current enemy. Vietnam as a chosen case study, therefore, adds to our understanding of racial and political undertones in governmental and non-governmental dealings with CBOW both by their maternal home countries (here Vietnam) and the paternal home countries (here the United States).

In another respect, the Vietnam War is a particularly interesting case, namely in that it is the first example of the paternal home country taking an explicit and widely publicised interest in the children fathered by its soldiers. In two waves, the Babylift of 1975 and the American Homecoming Act of 1986/87, the United States made a specific effort in 'bringing home' its soldiers' children of the Vietnam War. While some nations, most notably France (both during and after the Second World War[41] and during and after the first Indochina War[42]) had claimed children fathered by its soldiers on foreign soil for the French nation, this was done with significantly less fanfare. The Vietnam War, in comparative analysis with the French actions regarding its soldiers' offspring, will facilitate a discussion of the circumstances in which governments chose to allow their soldiers to acknowledge paternity of CBOW and subsequently also to support the children in their claims to their fathers' nationality.

The inclusion of the post-Second World War occupation of Austria and Germany and the experiences of children fathered in this phase of 'non-war' or 'Cold War' adds a further dimension to the discourse. Occupation soldiers were no longer *de iure* enemies of the defeated Germany and Austria; and civilians in the occupied territories, similarly, were no longer officially regarded as citizens of enemy nations. Yet, the dynamics of the military–civilian relations remained complex – quite possibly more complex than in a war situation where the frontiers of permissible and tolerated relationships were more clear cut. It is in this particular context that the blurred boundaries between consensual and non-consensual relations, of violent, exploitative relationships at one end of the spectrum and loving and supportive relationships on the other have been documented most comprehensively; and it is this case which allows some comparative analysis with regard to the question of how the fathers' nationality impacted on the children's experiences bearing in mind that the four occupation powers – the United States, the Soviet Union, Great Britain and France – developed very distinct political relations with the defeated Germany and Austria in the first post-war decade.

The wars of the 1990s and 2000s, both in Bosnia and Africa, are meaningful with regard to the experiences of CBOW in several respects. They were the first of the examined conflicts which took place after the passing of the most significant piece of international legislation regarding children's rights: the Convention on the Rights of the Child.[43] This important yardstick against which the fundamental rights of children have been measured since its adoption in 1989 is the most widely subscribed to instrument of international legislation; yet, it is questionable how fundamentally it affects children's experiences in conflict and post-conflict societies in general and experiences of CBOW in particular. Therefore, the investigation of children born of the Bosnian and African conflicts will explore whether and how children's rights have been affected by human rights legislation, and will consider the specific vulnerabilities of children fathered by foreign soldiers with respect to human and child rights.

Although the book covers a wide range of conflicts, a large number of wars with incidences of CRSV which are known to have resulted in significant numbers of CBOW are not explored in detail. The civil war in Bangladesh, the Armenian genocide, the conflicts in Korea, Kuwait, Sierra Leone or the Democratic Republic of Congo (DRC), the colonial wars of the French in Algeria or the Dutch in Indonesia, the actions of the Italians in Ethiopia, to name but a few, do not feature specifically in this volume. None of these conflicts are less significant as such, nor are the children conceived in these conflicts of greater or lesser research interest *per se*. However, the purpose of this book is not comprehensive historical coverage of the subject of CBOW, but an analysis of their experiences in the light of responses of their mothers, families, local and national communities. Covering several continents and a timespan of almost seventy years, the selected conflicts offer insights into distinct aspects of those experiences of children born as a result of intimate encounters of local women and foreign soldiers during wars and civil wars.

At first sight, juxtaposing the life courses of children born within an extremely diverse range of cultural and political circumstances may appear problematic, in that the experiences of CBOW – in childhood, adolescence and adulthood – are not only individual in their own right, but also clearly affected directly by the circumstances of conception, birth and upbringing in distinct receptor communities. Despite the different environments and conditions across time and space, experiences are comparable and it is exactly this multitude of backgrounds and settings and the variety of outcomes which make a cross-geographical and cross-chronological study enlightening.

This case-study approach requires some additional methodological comments. The above-mentioned data limitations indicate that a systematic comparison based on statistical analysis that might help determine which necessary and sufficient conditions cause particular outcomes in the life courses of CBOW would be an inappropriate approach. Although statistical methodologies and techniques can be powerful in determining such causation, they can only be as potent as the data on which they are based. Therefore, a comparative historical methodology based on a selection of a small number of cases has been chosen to detect and understand patterns of circumstances leading to a range of experiences. In applying this method, the accumulated knowledge of each specific case is utilised to gain an understanding of processes and patterns. In most quantitative and qualitative methodologies, a selection on the basis of the outcomes to be studied is anathema, because such a selection bias can prevent the researcher from encountering the full variation of possible pathways to different outcomes. As the exposition above has made clear, for this study cases have been identified in part with the dependent variables in mind, a prerogative of the historical-comparative methodology which 'sees utility' in such a selection process.[44] The analysis explores consistent connections between circumstances and outcomes and looks for configurations of specific factors across different cases that interact to create certain outcomes. Thus, the aim is to go beyond an illustration of the range of individual experiences and through comparison aims to explore patterns that will give some indication of how common adversities encountered by CBOW irrespective of time and space can be averted and in which circumstances CBOW have been able to develop resilience in the face of these adversities. The diversity of case studies, the different ages of the CBOW (ranging from people in their seventies to children under the age of ten), their different degree of visibility and the range of academic and public interest in aspects of their fate all require different approaches and methodologies: a summary below will explain the structure of the book as well as the methods and sources chosen to research the different cases.

Chapter 2 will explore the state of research on CBOW taking into account, among others, work of historians, social scientists, psychiatrists, lawyers and ethicists. In particular, the currently used definitions and categorisations of CBOW will be presented together with an overview of some key groups of CBOW. This will be done alongside developments that have impacted on our perceptions of war-affected children in general and CBOW in particular, such as concepts of childhood, developments in international humanitarian law (IHL) relating to children, and more child-centred interventions in conflict and post-conflict situations. In a second step, a brief outline of research on CRSV will explore the framework of the discourse. This is necessary because sexualised violence has been and continues to be a significant factor in large numbers of pregnancies conceived in relationships between foreign soldiers and local women during wars and armed conflicts. Therefore, this chapter will be devoted to the discourse on CRSV, not least in response to the changing nature of warfare in the twentieth century, but also in response to important developments in historical and historiographical emphases and increasingly insightful interdisciplinary dialogue on this issue. The section will focus on the theoretical framework of the discourse to date, which will lay the foundation for further exploration of the theme in several of the subsequent case studies. It will include a brief introduction to the gendered discourse on sexuality, deviance, morality, race, ethnicity and criminology as a background to perceptions of the so-called 'sins of the mothers', which are readily transferred onto the children, born out of wedlock as a result of wartime liaisons with foreign soldiers and thus become expression of socially deviant behaviour, often associated also with race, class and gender prejudices.

The Second World War, the case study explored in Chapter 3, is the first conflict for which we have significant data on children fathered by foreign soldiers with local mothers. The nature of hostilities (timescale, geographical expansion, periods of fighting and more or less coercive occupation and collaboration) provides the opportunity to introduce a wide variety of themes of relevance for life experiences of CBOW, including military and governmental policies towards fraternisation between troops and the local population, the actual relationships on the ground, the response of local communities to CBOW, and post-conflict policies relating to 'ownership' of soldiers' children.

Here and in the subsequent case studies, the experiences of the children will be explored against the background of the circumstances of their conception. This requires an analysis of the specifics of the conflict within which they were conceived, a study of diverse situations of the mothers and the circumstances of conceptions, as well as an examination of contemporary perceptions of women who bore children fathered by foreign soldiers. Because of the multitude of countries fighting in the Second World War with widely different attitudes towards military–civilian relations, as well as distinct policies vis-à-vis 'the enemies', this war allows comparative approaches regarding many aspects of the study of the CBOW and their mothers. Moreover, the Second World War is the only conflict for which significant data about the life courses of several subsets of CBOW exist, including quantitative and qualitative survey data for Norway, Denmark, the Netherlands[45] and (through the most recent research) psychosocial analyses for children born of the post-war occupations in Germany and Austria.[46] The first longitudinal studies are now being conducted, and preliminary results have added significantly to our understanding of some of the key experiences of CBOW, including adverse childhood experiences, socio-economic challenges, adverse health outcomes, stigma and discrimination on the one hand, but also significant evidence of resilience with regard to psychosocial challenges on the other.

In recent years, children born of the Second World War and the post-war occupations have been increasingly vocal in 'telling their stories', both in the context of participatory research and in their own public engagements. It is therefore possible to include their own views and evaluations of their experiences in the analysis, too.

Chapter 4 will explore the situation of the so-called *Bui Doi*, children of American soldiers and Vietnamese mothers conceived during the Vietnam War. As indicated above, this particular case study is enlightening for a variety of reasons, which determine the structure of the analysis as well as the methodological choices for the investigation. The children were among a large and diverse range of children left behind by American GIs throughout American military engagement abroad over the centuries. In certain respects, military and governmental policies relating to military–civilian relations on the ground in Vietnam followed in the footsteps of earlier such engagements, for instance during the Second World War. Here the US military – in line with general practice among militaries worldwide – accepted that 'entertainment', including intimate relations with local women, was good for troop morale and therefore was, generally, at best tolerated and at worst encouraged. In other respects, however, American attitudes towards local women, and in particular to the question of long-term or even permanent relations with local Vietnamese women culminating in their support as war brides, differed significantly from earlier conflicts, especially from those in European theatres of war.[47] Given that the level of official support of the military for their soldiers' partners and children and the narrative underlying such provision would have had a significant impact on the options open to the soldiers' girlfriends/partners and their children, this aspect will be explored in some detail in its implications for the experiences of children born of the Vietnam War. In a second step, the actions and reactions to Amerasian children left behind by GIs after the fall of Saigon will be discussed. Almost all the children fathered by American soldiers in Vietnam were biracial, and as such they were clearly visible as children of the enemy in an otherwise broadly monoracial post-conflict Vietnam. This, coupled with the fact that the reconstruction of post-war Vietnam took place in ideological and political contrast to the Americans, who continued to be seen as the enemy, provided the backdrop to a particularly challenging environment for CBOW who embodied this enemy in their mothers' home country. As a result of this, the children were a convenient target for anti-American and anti-capitalist propaganda in communist Vietnam after 1975. The children were not only instrumentalised as political and ideological tools in their maternal home country, but also in their fathers', when in the Babylift and the American Homecoming Act, their immigration into America was facilitated by the American government. The Babylift, which led to the adoption of several thousand Amerasian babies into US, Canadian and European families, opened up the controversy around international and interracial adoption. This aspect will be investigated in some detail in order to assess accurately what the motivations of the controversial Babylift were and how the policy fitted into the emerging regularisation of what some outspoken critics would refer to as the 'Baby Trade'.[48] This will require an exploration of international and interracial adoption practices, which underwent particular scrutiny at this time, but which played a role in the 'management' of CBOW in other conflicts, too.

The second wave of Amerasian immigration followed more than a decade later. The timing and the implementation of Amerasian immigration legislation in the late 1980s raise a number of issues, again relating to the motivation of a policy which was in equal measure humanitarian and political. This adds a potent dimension to the discourse on military and governmental approaches to a group of citizens who represented the 'foreign' and the 'enemy' on the one hand, as well as symbolising a bridge between state animosities of the past and possible more amicable future relations on the other hand.

The final section of this chapter juxtaposes the experiences of Amerasian CBOW who were adopted into the United States as infants or toddlers following the Babylift and those who moved in their late teens or as young adults following the Homecoming Act. This provides the opportunity for a comparative analysis of the different life experiences of both groups of Amerasians with regard to integration into American society. Going beyond historical methodology, this chapter uses sociological, psychological and comparative psychiatric research to examine these different immigration and integration experiences. In addition, because of the existence of a sizeable Vietnamese community in the United States, it is also possible to compare the experience of monoracial Vietnamese immigrants and biracial GI children and the challenges of 'being caught in the middle'.

Chapter 5 investigates the experiences of CBOW in the former Yugoslavia with two particular focuses. The first of these is the specific nature of the civil war, with its ethnic dimension and the widespread use of GBV during the war in Bosnia. This war differed from previous conflicts in that it was the first time GBV was used on a large scale as a weapon of war and, arguably, with genocidal intentions.[49] This had significant influence on the situation of children born of this conflict in a number of ways including mother–child relations and interventions of politicians and religious leaders in attempting to influence the way in which the children were viewed and treated, both by their families and local communities.

The second aspect concerns positive and normative legal issues arising out of the Bosnian War with regard to GBV generally and with regard to CBOW in particular. The widespread and widely reported use of GBV during the conflict, and in particular the practice of rape camps as part of Serbian war strategy, had a profound impact on the redefinition of GBV within the context of IHL, leading to the codification of GBV in conflicts as a war crime and a crime against humanity. What had considerable bearing on the international discourse on the need to protect vulnerable civilians during armed conflicts had surprisingly little impact on the awareness of CBOW as victims of war. This will be analysed in the context of international agenda setting, exploring in particular why, despite the fact that both GBV and children's rights issues more generally have found noteworthy traction in IHL and in the humanitarian advocacy setting in the last twenty years, the same has not been true for this specific group of CBOW. A further legal issue of significance and more directly linked to the situation of CBOW is that the war in former Yugoslavia was the first of the case studies to have taken place after the UN Convention of the Rights of the Child (CRC), a legally binding instrument signed and ratified by all but two countries (the United States and Somalia) worldwide, had come into force. The chapter will examine whether and how this instrument of legal protection affected the situation of CBOW, both legally and practically, and whether and how the rights of children are implemented in cases where they conflict with the (perceived) interests of the mother, families, local communities or wider political interests. These insights relating to different child rights considerations, in particular the complexities of the 'best interest of the child' as the concept underlying all child right provision, will be used to assess the rights of CBOW more generally and to discuss which, if any, of these rights CBOW have been able to enforce in the past and may be able to see enforced in the future.

Chapter 6 examines another set of conflicts that saw widespread GBV with, arguably, genocidal motivation, and similarly raised complex questions of post-conflict integration of large numbers of stigmatised CBOW into extremely volatile post-conflict receptor communities: children born of the Rwandan genocide of 1994 and the civil war between the LRA and Ugandan government troops between 1988 and 2006. Despite the similarities between these conflicts in the late 1990s and early 2000s, the inclusion of the African cases adds several important dimensions to the analysis. Firstly, sub-Saharan Africa is a region where the concept of childhood differs markedly from the ideas underlying individualistic child rights legislation that has been developing since the Second World War and particularly from the last quarter of the twentieth century, most of which has emanated from the legal traditions of the Western or Northern worlds of developed countries. Beyond the notion of childhood, however, another connected feature is of significance: the strong influence of kinship groups, which in many cases eclipse the roles of individuals in a wide range of life choices, needs to be taken into account when considering the situation of CBOW in these societies. If forms of social organisation and the relational understanding of individuals within a given kinship group add an extra dimension to the study of CBOW, then so too does the 'side by side' existence of traditional and modern understandings of all aspects of daily life including family, health, religion and spirituality. Therefore, legal as well as social and spiritual pluralisms which underlie the post-conflict reconstruction processes within which the integration of victims of conflict-related violence and their children takes place have to be explored in detail to come to an understanding of the challenges facing victims of CRSV, perpetrators and their children in the African settings.

The LRA conflict raging in Northern Uganda for the best part of two decades between 1988 and 2006 differs from all other conflicts discussed here in one regard. A particular feature of this civil war was the large number of children fathered by rebel soldiers and born to abducted female child soldiers, an increasingly common phenomenon in sub-Saharan Africa since the 1990s. The war left several thousand former abductee child mothers and their CBOW returning to their local (often displaced) communities after the end of hostilities. The analysis of life courses of these CBOW will have four main strands. Firstly, a significant proportion of CBOW in the conflict were born to underage mothers. On returning from the conflict, either after the end of hostilities, after escape or after release, their status as young and unmarried, linked to enemy rebels who had inflicted unimaginable harm on their communities of origin, as well as the association of the child mothers themselves with brutal atrocities impacted strongly on the upbringing of the CBOW in their mothers' clans. Child protection issues relating to child mothers and their children upon return to their receptor communities will be explored in order to enhance understanding of the mechanisms involved in re-integration processes, both formal and informal. Related to this is the second core question, namely that of kinship. African society in general and Ugandan society in particular, especially in rural areas, is based on a patrilineal and patriarchal concept of social interactions. While patriarchy and patriliny had some bearing on life experiences of CBOW almost anywhere and anytime, late twentieth- and early twenty-first-century Uganda provides a particularly potent example of the significance of kinship within this male-dominated setting in determining the fate of CBOW and their mothers. Being the child of an unmarried mother whose father is not only absent, but also despised as the enemy, has additional consequences. They emanate from the inability of lineage-making in traditional ways in a society where bridewealth[50] and *luk*[51] payments have social and symbolic, as well as economic, significance and where marriage is not only a union between man and woman, but between two families and clans. Here the examination of CBOW, also from an anthropological perspective, will, among others, focus on the commodification of relationships and questions of agency of both CBOW and their mothers within their clan structures.

Thirdly, staying with the question of cultural specificity and returning to the issue of law, many of the IHL provisions have been drawn up within the framework of Western notions of childhood, family and the role of the law; this gives rise to the question of cultural sensitivity of laws, advocacy and programming with regard to implementation of protective mechanisms. These will be analysed with particular emphasis on the effectiveness of disarmament, demobilisation, rehabilitation and reintegration mechanisms for the integration of CBOW into post-conflict societies.

Finally, international protection of vulnerable groups, and in particular the implementation of IHL, is dependent on a state's willingness to enforce such laws. While this has proved problematic in many, if not most, countries, the issue increases in complexity in societies where these legal frameworks are contested at national and local level and where legal pluralism is a significant feature of law enforcement. Here again, Ugandan society, with its tension between traditional and modern conflict resolution mechanisms, provides an excellent case study for an analysis of communities living in mixed legal spaces. Statutory and customary laws regulate matters of justice, demonstrating the connectedness of local communities with their ethnic and religious group, which offer opportunities for civic action and therefore provide the context for post-conflict reintegration mechanisms.

Chapter 7 will consider the relatively recent phenomenon of children fathered by UN peacekeeping personnel as a starting point for a discussion of current developments of the international discourse on CBOW. As a consequence of the allegations against members of the UN peacekeeping forces, the United Nations General Assembly adopted the resolution 'United Nation Comprehensive Strategy on Assistance and Support to Victims of Sexual Exploitation and Abuse by United Nations Staff and Related Personnel'[52] in December 2007 committing the UN, among others, to providing assistance and support to children born as a result of SEA by UN staff or related personnel. This resolution was path-breaking in recognising children fathered by UN personnel as a distinct group and defining responsibilities of the UN towards the child without thereby negating the responsibility of the individual perpetrators of sexual exploitation and violence. The final section of the chapter will analyse the possibilities of implementing such provisions, discussing the potential and limitations of international law in safeguarding the rights of the CBOW.

The epilogue will provide a comparative conclusion drawing on the insights of the different case studies across time and space. It will consider the implications of the findings relating to the experiences of CBOW world-wide in terms of policy making, advocacy and programming on the basis of a nuanced picture of the multitude of experiences of CBOW. At the same time this approach will allow patterns to be foregrounded which assist a better understanding of the challenges faced by these children, their mothers, families and receptor communities.

Notes

1 Kai Grieg, 'The war children of the world', *War and Children Identity Project* (Bergen: War and Children Identity Project, 2001), p. 6.
2 Gill Greer, 'Rape, the oldest and the newest war crime', International Planned Parenthood Federation, 20.6.2008, www.ippf.org/NR/exeres/AD977915-0C90-4BFB-90EE-27D4DEBC704B.htm. (accessed 17.8 2014).
3 United Nations (ed.), 'United Nation Comprehensive Strategy on Assistance and Support to Victims of Sexual Exploitation and Abuse by United Nations Staff and Related Personnel' A/RES/62/214, 21.12.2007 (online), http://dacessdds.

un.org/doc/UNDOC/GEN/N07/476/61/PDF/N0747661.pdf?OpenElement. (accessed 2.7.2015).
4 www.gov.uk/government/topical-events/sexual-violence-in-conflict. (accessed 23.10.2015).
5 www.gov.uk/government/news/global-summit-to-end-sexual-violence-in-confl ict-latest-updates. (accessed 20.10.2015).
6 www.gov.uk/government/publications/statement-of-action-global-summit-to-end-sexual-violence-in-conflict. (accessed 16.10.2015).
7 R. Charli Carpenter (ed.), *Born of War: Protecting Children of Sexual Violence Survivors in Conflict Zones* (Bloomfield, CT: Kumarian Press 2007).
8 R. Charli Carpenter, *Forgetting Children Born of War: Setting the Human Rights Agenda in Bosnia and Beyond* (New York: Columbia University Press, 2010).
9 Donna Seto, *No Place for a War Baby: The Global Politics of Children Born of Wartime Sexual Violence* (Farnham: Ashgate, 2013); Jean-Paul Picaper and Ludwig Norz, *Enfants maudits* (Paris: Edition de Syrtes, 2004); Alison M.S. Watson, 'Children born of wartime rape: Rights and representations', *International Feminist Journal of Politics*, 9 (2007), 20–34; Fabrice Virgili, *Naître ennemi: Les Enfants de couples franco-allemands nés pendant la Seconde Guerre mondiale* (Paris: Payot, 2009); Jonathan Torgovnik, *Intended Consequences: Children Born of Rape* (New York: Aperture, 2009); J.C. McKinley, Jr. 'Legacy of Rwanda violence: The thousands born of rape', *New York Times* (23.9.1996), 1; Bianfer Nowrojee, *Shattered Lives: Sexual Violence During the Rwandan Genocide and its Aftermath* (New York: Human Rights Watch, 1996); See a 'rapid response' by Padmasayee Papineni in the *British Medical Journal* commenting on C. Kiklahan and N. Ewigman, 'Rape as a weapon of war in modern conflicts', *British Medical Journal*, 340 (2010), 3270. Also Elisa van Ee and Rolf E. Kleber, 'Child in the shadowlands', *Lancet* 380:9842 (2012), 642–3.
10 Dara Kay Cohen and Ragnhild Nordås, 'Sexual violence in armed conflict: Introducing the SVAC dataset, 1989–2009', *Journal of Peace Research*, 51 (2014), 418–28. See also Ragnhild Nordås and Dara Kay Cohen, 'Sexual violence in African conflicts', *Centre for the Study of Civil War Policy Brief* 1/201, http://file.prio.no/publication_files/cscw/Nordas-Cohen-Sexual-Violence-Militias-African-Conflicts-CSCW-Policy-Brief-01-2012.pdf. (accessed 12.11.2014).
11 'International war children survey in the making', 9.2.2004, http://humanrights house.org/Articles/5993.html. (accessed 12.11.2014).
12 R. Charli Carpenter, 'Protecting children born of war', in Carpenter (ed.), *Born of War*, pp. 210–24, here p. 214. For some of the research challenges presented by hidden populations see Matthew J. Salganik and Douglas D. Heckathorn, 'Sampling and estimation in hidden populations using respondent-driven sampling', *Sociological Methodology*, 34 (2004), 193–240; Giacomo Tavecchia et al., 'Estimating population size and hidden demographic parameters with state-space modeling', *The American Naturalist*, 173 (2009), 722–33.
13 Magnus Hirschfeld, *The Sexual History of the World War* (New York: Panurge Press, 1934), p. 236.
14 Kåre Olsen, *Krigens barn: De norske krigsbarna og deres mødre* (Oslo: Aschehoug, 1998), p. 48.
15 Fabrice Virgili, 'Enfants de Boches: The war children of France', in Kjersti Ericsson

and Eva Simonssen (eds), *Children of World War II* (Oxford: Berg, 2005), pp. 138–50, here p. 144.
16. Olga Rains, Lloyd Rains, and Melynda Jarratt (eds), *Voices of the Left Behind* (Toronto: Project Roots, 2004), p. 16.
17. Ute Baur-Timmerbrink, *Wir Besatzungskinder: Töchter und Söhne alliierter Soldaten erzählen* (Berlin: Chr.-Links Verlag, 2015), pp. 87, 95; Martin Kugler, '20,000 Kinder von Soldaten: eine vaterlose Generation', *Die Presse*, 29.9.2012, http://die presse.com/home/politik/zeitgeschichte/1295774/20000-Kinder-von-Soldaten_Eine-vaterlose-Generation?from=gl.home_politik. (accessed 12.5.2016). More recently, historians have suggested that the number is as high as at least 400,000 and 30,000 respectively. Silke Satjukow and Barbara Stelzl-Marx, 'Besatzungskinder in Vergangenheit und Gegenwart', in Barbara Stelzl-Marx and Silke Satjukkow (eds), *Besatzungskinder. Die Nachkommen alliierter Soldaten in Österreich und Deutschland* (Wien: Böhlau Verlag, 2015), pp. 11–14, here p. 11.
18. Grieg, *War Children*, p. 8.
19. Michael L. Krenn, Review Thomas A. Bass, *Vietnamerica: The War Comes Home*, H-Pol, H-Net Reviews. May, 1997, https://networks.h-net.org/node/9997/reviews/10372/krenn-bass-vietnamerica-war-comes-home-and-thomas-bass-vietnamerica-war. (accessed 12.1.2015).
20. Grieg, *War Children*, pp. 114f.
21. Joana Daniel-Wrabetz, 'Children born of war rape in Bosnia-Herzegovina and the Convention on the Rights of the Child', in Carpenter (ed.), *Born of War*, pp. 21–39, here p. 23. See also Stuart Hughes, 'Wartime rape survivors losing hope of justice', *BBC News Europe* (1.4.2014), www.bbc.com/news/world-europe-26833510. (accessed 2.2.2015).
22. Susan McKay, 'Girls as "weapons of terror" in Northern Uganda and Sierra Leonean rebel fighting forces', *Studies in Conflict and Terrorism*, 28 (2005), 385–97.
23. Carpenter, *Forgetting*, p. 14.
24. Grieg, *War Children*, p. 6.
25. Lars Borgersrud, *Staten of krigsbarna: En historisk undersøkelse av statsmyndighetenes behandling av krigsbarna i de første etterkrigsårene* (Oslo: University of Oslo, Department of Culture Studies, 2004); Dag Ellingsen, *En registerbasert undersøkelse*, Statistics Norway, Rapport Nr. 2004/19, 2004; Kjersti Ericsson and Eva Simonsen, *Krigsbarn i fredstids* (Oslo: Universitetsforlaget, 2005); Olsen, *Krigens barn*.
26. Ingvill C. Mochmann and Stein Ugelvik Larsen, 'The forgotten consequences of war: The life course of children fathered by German soldiers in Norway and Denmark during WWII – some empirical results', *Historical Social Research*, 33 (2008), 347–63.
27. See for instance Ericsson and Simonssen, *Children of World War II*.
28. Carpenter, *Born of War*.
29. Watson, 'Children born of wartime rape', 20–34; Ya'ir Ronen, 'Redefining the child's right to identity', *International Journal of Law, Policy and the Family*, 18 (2004), 147–77; Thoko Kaime, 'The Convention on the Rights of the Child and the cultural legitimacy of children's rights in Africa: Some reflections', *African Human Rights Journal*, 5 (2005), 221–38; Seto, *No Place for a War Baby*.
30. Heide Glaesmer et al., 'Die Kinder des Zweiten Weltkrieges in Deutschland: Ein

Rahmenmodell für psychosoziale Forschung', *Trauma und Gewalt*, 6 (2012), 318–28; Seyyed Taha Yahyavi, Mehran Zarghami and Urvashi Marwah, 'A review on the evidence of transgenerational transmission of posttraumatic stress disorder vulnerability', *Revista Brasiliera de Psyquiatra*, 36 (2014), 89–94; Rachel Dekel and Hadass Goldblatt, 'Is there intergenerational transmission of trauma? The case of combat veterans' children', *American Journal of Orthopsychiatry*, 78 (2008), 281–329.

31 http://childrenbornofwar.wordpress.com/. (accessed 12.9.2015).
32 www.chibow.org. (accessed 2.6.2016).
33 The triennial conferences (2010, 2013, 2016) attracted a wide range of academic and non-academic participants from a variety of disciplines, and included panels specifically dealing with the question of children born of war.
34 Ingvill C. Mochmann and Ingeborg K. Haarvardsson, 'The legacy of war time rape: Mapping key concepts and issues', *PRIO Paper* (Oslo: Peace Research Institute 2012).
35 Rains et al. (eds), *Voices of the Left Behind*; Pam Winfield, *Melancholy Baby: The Unplanned Consequences of the G.I.s' Arrival in Europe for World War II* (Westport: Bergin & Garvey, 2000); Pam Winfield, *Bye Bye Baby: The Story of the Children the GIs Left Behind* (London: Bloomsbury, 1992); G. Swillen, *Koekoekskind: Door de vijand verwekt 1940–1945* (Antwerpen: De Bezige Bij 2009); Monika Diederichs, *Kinderen van Duitse militairen in Nederland 1941–46: Een verborgen leven* (Soesterberg: Uitjeverij Aspekt, 2012); Ika Hügel-Marschall, *Invisible Women: Growing up Black in Germany* (New York: Peter Lang Publishing, 2008). For research reports based on collaboration between interdisciplinary research groups and self-help and advocacy groups see www.childrenbornofwar.org. Two recent collaborative publications combining autobiographical, biographical and academic contributions are Ute Baur-Timmerbrink, *Wir Besatzungskinder: Töchter und Söhne alliierter Soldaten erzählen* (Berlin: Chr.-Links Verlag, 2015) and Barbara Stelzl-Marx and Silke Satjukkow (eds), *Besatzungskinder: Die Nachkommen alliierter Soldaten in Österreich und Deutschland* (Wien: Böhlau Verlag, 2015).
36 Barbara Stelzl-Marx, 'Die unsichtbare Generation: Kinder sowjetischer Besatzungssoldaten in Österreich und Deutschland', *Historical Social Research*, 34:3 (2009), 352–72; Picaper and Norz, *Enfants maudits*; Sabine Lee, 'A forgotten legacy of the Second World War: GI children in post-war Britain and Germany', *Contemporary European History*, 20 (2011), 157–81; Silke Satjukow, 'Besatzungskinder: Nachkommen deutscher Frauen und alliierter Soldaten seit 1945', *Geschichte und Gesellschaft*, 37 (2011), 559–91.
37 Ericsson and Simonsen, *Krigsbarn i fredstids*; Olsen, *Krigens barn*; Picaper and Norz, *Enfants maudits*; Ebba D. Drolshagen, *Wehrmachtskinder: Auf der Suche nach dem nie gekannten Vater* (Munich: Knaur, 2005); Ingvill C. Mochmann, Sabine Lee and Barbara Stelzl-Marx (eds), 'Special focus. Children born of war: Second World War and beyond', *Historical Social Research*, 34:3 (2009), 263–372; Fabrice Virgili, *The Shorn Women: Gender and Punishment in Liberation France* (Oxford: Berg, 2002).
38 Margaret Drabble, 'A beastly century', *American Scholar*, 70 (2001), 160.
39 For a detailed analysis see Milton Leitenberg, *Deaths in Wars and Conflicts in the 20th Century* (Ithaca, NY: Cornell University, Peace Studies Program, 2006).
40 As the focus of this book is on children born of war, sexual violence in conflict is

discussed almost exclusively in its manifestation as violence against women, i.e. the potential and actual mothers of CBOW. It has now been recognised that CRSV can and is being directed against men and boys, too. This, however, lies outside the scope of this volume.

41 Satjukow, 'Besatzungskinder'.
42 Emmanuelle Saada, *Empire's Children, Race, Filiation, and Citizenship in the French Colonies* (Chicago: University of Chicago Press, 2012).
43 Office of the United Nations High Commissioner for Human Rights, 'Convention on the Rights of the Child', Adopted and opened for signature, ratification and accession by General Assembly resolution 44/25 of 20 November 1989, www2.ohchr.org/english/law/crc.htm. (accessed 22.10.2014).
44 Mikaila Mariel Lemonik Arthur, 'The neglected virtues of comparative-historical methods', in Ieva Zake and Michaal De Cesare (eds), *New Directions in Sociology: Essays on Theory and Methodology in the 21st Century* (Jefferson/NC: McFarland, 2011), 172–92, here p. 172.
45 Ingvill C. Mochmann and Stein Ugelvik Larsen, 'Kriegskinder in Europa', *Aus Politik und Zeitgeschichte*, 18–19 (2005), 34–8.
46 Heide Glaesmer, 'Traumatische Erfahrungen in der älteren deutschen Bevölkerung', *Zeitschrift für Gerontologie und Geriatrie* 47:3 (2014), 194–201.
47 Susan Zeiger, *Entangling Alliances: Foreign War Brides and American Soldiers in the Twentieth Century* (New York: New York University Press, 2010).
48 E.B. Kapstein, 'The baby trade', *Foreign Affairs*, 82:6 (2003), 115–25.
49 R. Charli Carpenter, 'Surfacing children: Limitations of genocidal rape discourse', *Human Rights Quarterly*, 22 (2000), 428–77.
50 Bridewealth is a payment made by the groom or his kin to the kin of the bride in order to ratify the marriage. It is a social, symbolic and economic act.
51 The term *luk* refers to illegitimate sexual intercourse, but it is also used as a term for suit of *luk*, a ritual and payment by the offending man to the girl's kinship group in compensation for the offence and as a way of legitimising their relationship and possible children conceived through the unsanctioned act. See Hayley T.T. Steiger, 'Changes in Lango marriage customs', *Uganda Journal*, 7:4 (1940), 145–63.
52 United Nations, 'United Nation Comprehensive Strategy on Assistance and Support to Victims of Sexual Exploitation and Abuse by United Nations Staff and Related Personnel', A/RES/62/214, 21.12.2007, http://dacessdds.un.org/doc/UNDOC/GEN/N07/476/61/PDF/N0747661.pdf?OpenElement. (accessed 4.3.2016).

2

Children born of war: who are they? Experiences of children, mothers, families and post-conflict communities

A novel phenomenon?

One might be forgiven for thinking that the existence of children born as a result of wartime sexualised violence is a relatively recent phenomenon. Images of Bosnian rape camps,[1] the Human Rights Watch website reporting on mass rape and forced impregnation of black African women by Arab militiamen in Darfur and Chad,[2] journalistic reports about sexual abuse by UN peacekeepers[3] and horrific stories of mass genocide and genocidal rape in Rwanda[4] among others are suggestive of mass sexualised violence and children fathered by foreign soldiers as a phenomenon of the twentieth century. However, intimate contacts between foreign soldiers and local civilians, both coercive and consensual, are likely to have been a feature of almost all wars, from antiquity[5] into modernity; in the middle ages, the Vikings had a reputation for bravery as much as for pillage and rape, as did Genghis Khan and his Mongol soldiers;[6] similarly, during the crusades it was customary for kings to enlist women to provide sexual services for the soldiers, and it was anything but rare for pillage and rape to take place.[7]

No exact statistics relating to children born of pre-twentieth-century conflicts exist, and the little source material that has been uncovered consists largely of anecdotal evidence. Still, we have a considerable understanding of gendered relations, for instance in early modern times. Significant details about the relationship between soldiers and civilians, and soldiers and civilian women in particular have been explored.[8] Various studies of warfare, women's roles within the armies and soldiers' wives and companions give some indication that – then, as now – relations between foreign soldiers and local women could be nuanced. They also confirm that – again, then, as now – as a result of their social positioning women were frequently the more vulnerable part in such relationships. The patriarchal social orders of medieval and early modern times often brought with them dependencies that put women in precarious positions if they did not conform with socially acceptable lifestyle choices. Relationships with soldiers could amount to such unacceptable choices, as they still can today. As a result, women and their children had to deal with prejudice and social exclusion if such relationships did not work out and resulted in what was perceived to be something other than 'normal' family life. In a recent study of religiosity in the military in the sixteenth and seventeenth centuries, the analysis of some letters written to and from soldiers during the Thirty Years' War gives interesting insights.[9] The correspondence demonstrates that many of the features of gendered military–civilian relations of the twentieth century were also prevalent several centuries earlier. The war was one of the longest and most destructive European wars fought mainly between Protest and Catholic states in the fragmenting Holy Roman Empire, and eventually led to a conflict embracing many of the European Great Powers, too. Women were pivotal in the functioning of travelling armies by taking on supporting roles of cleaning, cooking and nursing; they also served as lovers or prostitutes. The general consensus of soldiers' conduct was that they had a rather more lax attitude towards orderly sexual conduct and that they, 'more than other men, employed [violence] in their wooing of women'.[10] But while such violence is documented widely, there are also numerous examples of non-coercive and voluntary liaisons between soldiers and female civilians. Sometimes these relationships were based on promises on the part of the soldier and naïveté on the part of the women, but often they were founded on genuine affection or love.[11] Such relations, as marriage more generally, were not uniformly regulated, not least because soldiers, until well into the seventeenth century, were free to 'marry and court without religious rites and customs'.[12] Consequently women frequently relied on a soldier's promise of later marriage as a basis of what they perceived to be pre-marital intimacy, in the expectation that marriage would follow in due course. This phenomenon is not unusual at times of conflict. It has often been commented on as a spike in extramarital intimacy at times of war and frequently interpreted as a sign of a breakdown of moral values. Yet, in the eyes of the couples, it was understood to be a pre-marital relationship prior to a soldier's departure for combat.[13] Such relationships may not have been 'equal', but the sources suggest that among this particular group of women (unlike those who feature in trial records and whose relationships suggest high levels of coercion), they were often voluntary and consensual. Nevertheless, evidence also suggests that women ended up in difficulties when soldiers did not keep their marriage promises. The situation was particularly precarious for women who bore children from such liaisons, with one young mother describing herself as being 'despised and considered worthless by everyone' and facing a life 'in squalor'.[14]

Implicit in this analysis are three aspects of relevance for our twentieth- and twenty-first-century context. Firstly, given the detailed evidence that has been amassed in recent years about gendered military–civilian relations during and after conflicts – as will be explored in more detail below – it is reasonable to assume that historically as well as contemporarily, many CBOW were conceived in exploitative or coercive relationships. However, it is important to emphasise that evidence also indicates that even in brutal conflicts consensual and love relationships existed and continue to exist. Related to this point is the recognition that these friendly relations as a rule are documentary non-events. Researchers will generally find silence about these consensual liaisons in the sources. Trial records in antiquity, medieval and early modern times, primarily if not exclusively, dealt with those instances where violence was a feature of developments and/or where relationships had gone wrong. Similarly, today loving and caring relationships and successful marriages between soldiers and local women are more likely to remain hidden or unnoticed, whereas conflict-related sexual violence (CRSV) will be more likely to be reported.[15] In the early modern case, it was the exceptional archival find of a body of letters written to soldiers in the summer of 1625 by inhabitants of several towns in the border region of Thuringia and Hesse and some responses written by the soldiers, which gave insights into the predicament of women who had trusted soldiers' marriage promises, and often did not find those promises fulfilled. Most of the cases described in this source testify consensual relationships, but children conceived in such liaisons, which often did not lead to formal marriage, still suffered considerable hardships as a result of the conception 'of the enemy' and out of wedlock. Children born of consensual and love relations between foreign soldiers and local women form part of this study, too. What will become clear in the analysis is that these CBOW also face significant challenges as a result of their biological origins despite – and sometimes because of – the consensual relationship between their parents.

Finally, what has been described for the seventeenth century example points to a significant feature regarding the experiences of CBOW and their mothers. The sixteenth and seventeenth centuries were a period of demarcation of church and state influence over the lives of individuals and families, and therefore also a time of realignment of expectations of family life. In this period, the fate of women whose relationships with soldiers had not worked out (and by implication also the fate of their children) to a large extent depended on communal acceptance. It is in these volatile situations that the vulnerability of the women is particularly noticeable, and irrespective of the agency of the individual women, community perceptions and actions become significant factors in determining life courses.

The excursion into the seventeenth century is a pointer to the fact that although there is no clear continuity of attitudes or practices from early modern into contemporary times, and although the evidence base for research on CBOW prior to the twentieth century is limited, the few sources that do exist indicate that experiences were at least comparable. An analysis of these experiences and life courses of CBOW for the time period that presents us with a more varied and comprehensive body, namely the twentieth century, permits some conceptualisation of the subject with the aim of grasping the phenomenon of CBOW and their experiences across space and time.

Definitions and categories

In the literature, terminology relating to children fathered by foreign soldiers has not been applied consistently, and the categorisation of different groups of CBOW is still under discussion. For the purpose of this study, the expression 'children born of war' will be used (rather than 'war children' or 'war babies'). It includes all children who have one parent who is part of a foreign army, a peacekeeping force or related service personnel and the other parent a local citizen independent of time and geographical context, type of conflict and circumstances of conception.[16]

Within this broad definition, four main categories have been used widely to accommodate the vastly different conflict and post-conflict scenarios that provide the settings for many of the relationships of which the children are born.

Children of enemy soldiers: These children are fathered, often during or immediately after an armed conflict, by foreign soldiers who are perceived as enemies in the mother's home community. Little is known about such children born prior to twentieth-century conflicts, but there is no reason to believe that the twentieth-century picture is anything other than a continuation of an existing phenomenon of children being born as a result of intimate encounters between victor and vanquished in all manner of conflicts through the ages. While great variations exist in the nature, frequency and intensity of such contact between local population and enemy soldiers, none of the more recent conflicts have been without them. For instance, we know of children fathered by British and French soldiers during the First World War,[17] children fathered by members of the German *Wehrmacht*, e.g. in the Netherlands, Norway, France or Eastern Europe during the Second World War,[18] and children of the colonial wars, such as those fathered by French soldiers in Vietnam or Dutch soldiers in Indonesia.[19] Recently, as a result of the increasing number of civil wars rather than international conflicts, children born of such conflicts have added a new dimension to the phenomenon of children fathered by enemy soldiers.

Children of soldiers from occupation forces: These soldiers can be seen as enemies or allies, depending on the conflict and the view of the local population at the time. It is in the nature of occupations that the local population harbours some misgivings about foreign boots on their home ground. However, different conflicts have demonstrated great variation in the level of reservation vis-à-vis occupation forces, with significant implications for military–civilian relations. Furthermore differences exist also within the same conflict, as the attitudes towards occupation forces are frequently based on political, cultural and personal considerations as well as the economic well-being of the occupied. The Second World War demonstrates this clearly. Some French local citizens might have seen the German occupiers in France as friends; many, however, would have regarded them as enemies.[20] At the same time, the American presence in Great Britain during the run-up to the opening of a second front against Nazi Germany between 1942 and 1944,[21] while triggering mixed feelings about the desirability of the prolonged GI presence, was a *de facto* friendly 'occupation'. In contrast, the Allied occupation in post-war Germany, received a mixed reception. Following, as it did, both twelve years of a brutal dictatorship and the experience of a humiliating unconditional surrender, it caused reactions among the Germans which encompassed the entire range, from seeing the occupiers as oppressive enemies at one end of the spectrum to regarding them as most welcome liberators at the other end.[22] The existence of GI children born during the Vietnam and Korean Wars is well known, and, here again, the circumstances resemble a friendly quasi-occupation.

Children of child soldiers: These children are a relatively recent war-related phenomenon. Children have played a role in warfare throughout history, having been included in a variety of military campaigns, perhaps most notoriously in the 1212 Children's Crusade.[23] Conscriptions into armies at times of military crises have been well documented on many other occasions, too, from antiquity into modern times. However, the twentieth century has seen an escalation in the numbers enlisted, as well as a change in the role assigned to children in both combat and non-combat duties. To name but a few examples, during the Second World War, many children fought during insurrections; towards the end of the war, Germans – and other nations – resorted to drafting ever younger boys into the army;[24] the Japanese trained young teens to counter a possible American invasion; during the Indochina Wars, both government forces and insurgent armies used children in combat roles.[25] However, since the late 1980s we have also seen a very different form of child enlistment in the military context. Most notoriously, in Northern Uganda the Lord's Resistance Army (LRA) abducted thousands of children to fight against Ugandan government forces.[26] Similarly, significant numbers of children have been recruited in the civil wars in Sierra Leone, the Democratic Republic of Congo (DRC), Mali, Liberia, Colombia, Nigeria, the Central African Republic, Sudan, South Sudan, as well as Iraq and Syria.[27] In Africa, while the majority of the abducted children remain boys, forcibly recruited to fight the guerrilla bush war, an increasingly large number of girls have been and are being targeted both for combat roles, and – more commonly – to serve as sexual slaves for the rebel outfits, be it the LRA or, as witnessed more recently and publicised widely, in Nigeria's Boko Haram.[28] Many of them conceived in captivity, with the father of the child being a rebel combatant; thousands of these CBOW were born in these circumstances.[29]

Children of peacekeeping forces: Also a twentieth- and twenty-first-century phenomenon – children fathered by members of UN peacekeeping forces and other UN personnel have been an undesired and unintended consequence of the United Nations' engagement in peacekeeping operations. Peacekeepers neither occupy the country in which they serve, nor are they in a state of war with the local population; yet, the relationship between local population and peacekeeping forces resembles that of an occupation force in some respects, that of an enemy army in others. The soldiers, whose main task it is to protect, are generally perceived as in a position of power and control; and they serve in circumstances which are often tense with the threat of fighting imminent. This has a significant effect with regard to the vulnerability of the local population, and in particular of women and children.[30] Internal investigations into the sexual conduct of peacekeeping troops now include reports about sexualised violence of blue helmets against women and children in the Democratic Republic of the Congo, in Haiti, Burundi and Liberia, in former Yugoslavia, Sudan, Somalia and, most recently, the Central African Republic, to name but a few.[31] They all suggest that intimate relations between UN personnel and civilians are far from rare. Children born of such relationships, whether consensual or not, are likely to be facing similar challenges to those of other CBOW.[32]

Any such categorisation is problematic in that it creates the impression of uniformity and patterns, which are likely to camouflage the great variation in the relationship of the parents, plus the experiences of the women and their children. Conflict and post-conflict scenarios vary widely with view to the different relationship patterns evolving between soldiers and civilians. As a result, any investigation of the experiences of the children needs to include an analysis of the relationship between their parents. As indicated above, intimate liaisons between foreign soldiers and local civilians embrace the entire spectrum of relationships, from long-term love affairs to brutal sexualised violence. In order to structure the analysis, five broad patterns of relationships have been identified, in order of increasing level of coercion. It has to be emphasised that the boundaries between these different groupings are fluid, and often relationships cannot be placed unambiguously in one or another category, because they change in nature just as circumstances surrounding the soldiers and local women change.

Love affairs are known to have occurred in almost all conflicts. They are more frequent in less inimical geopolitical circumstances, such as the stationing of American and Canadian soldiers in Britain or the Netherlands during the Second World War;[33] but occasional love affairs have also been recorded in potentially more challenging political situations such as between Soviet occupation soldiers and Austrian and German women after the Second World War.[34]

Friendly 'business arrangements' were often entered into by women without direct coercion on the part of the soldier. Yet, these are not normally entirely voluntary in that circumstances frequently forced young women to offer their services in exchange for security, food or other necessities for themselves or their families. This is well-known, for instance, for relationships between Allied forces and German civilians during the post-war occupation,[35] between American GIs and Vietnamese girls during the Vietnam War[36] or, more recently, between members of peacekeeping forces and local women.[37] Similar relationships between colonial troops and local women, e.g. in Vietnam or Indonesia have also been recorded extensively.[38] Here the boundary between voluntary and involuntary intimacy is particularly difficult to delineate.

Prostitutions, forced or otherwise, are commonplace in times of conflict. The breakdown of 'normal' social structures, increased levels of poverty, disruptions to family and employment patterns or absence of the male wage earner can all contribute towards circumstances which force women into prostitution with varying degrees of coercion. This can be regulated prostitution, such as for instance in the case of Japanese 'comfort women'[39] or prostitution in German military brothels, during the Second World War,[40] but also in less regulated wartime settings, particularly in earlier wars, such as in the Crimean War,[41] the American Civil War[42] or the First World War.[43]

Sexual slavery, more coercive still, is forced on women in various conflicts, depriving them even of residual elements of choice such as, for instance, the sexual slavery in Nazi concentration camps.[44] Although sexual slavery in war has existed for centuries,[45] recent changes in the nature of warfare have led to an explosion of incidences of this phenomenon among child soldiers.[46] This has been evident in particular in numerous African conflicts such as in the large-scale recruitment of child soldiers in Uganda, the DRC, Sierra Leone, Sudan, Nigeria, Syria and elsewhere.[47]

Rape of local women by foreign soldiers, the most coercive forced relationship, has accompanied armed conflict throughout history. This has frequently been understood by the troops and their commanders as a combination of punishment of the defeated enemy and 'just reward' for the victorious soldiers, probably most notoriously in the mass rapes of German women at the hands of the Red Army in the final stages of the Second World War. Recently, however, such systematic *sexualised violence* has been directed at female civilians in the enemy population as part of war strategy, at times linked to forced impregnation and forced maternity. Examples for this are the Bosnian Wars[48] or the Rwandan genocide.[49] At times this CRSV is also linked to the similarly racially motivated policy of forcing women to abort the children conceived through rape, as for instance during the Rwandan genocide.[50]

One of the questions of interest is whether a correlation between the character of a particular conflict in which children are conceived and the nature of the relationship between the parents can be established. One would assume that relationships between friendly troops and local population would – as a rule – be consensual, whereas intimate contacts between enemy troops and local civilians would tend to contain stronger elements of coercion. No such data has been collected, but a superficial assessment of research about such relationships appears to confirm those correlations. For example, many intimate contacts between American soldiers stationed in Britain prior to D-Day were consensual, frequently as part of a lasting relationship which often resulted in marriage;[51] at the other end of the spectrum, intimate relations between advancing Soviet troops were almost exclusively coercive, with rapes in the hundreds of thousands estimated to have occurred in the final stages of the war, well beyond the notorious week of mass rapes between 24 April and 5 May 1945, during which the Red Army secured its hold over the capital.[52]

Yet, anecdotal evidence demonstrates that numerous counterexamples exist. Peacekeepers are known to have raped,[53] relations between Allied occupation soldiers and German and Austrian civilians differed substantially, and the quality of mutual relations was affected much more strongly by factors other than the straightforward questions of whether the occupiers were friends or foes.[54] Even during the most total of wars, the Second World War, numerous examples of love affairs between enemy soldiers and local women existed,[55] just as in the unlikely scenario of the most brutal of civil war situations, such as among LRA abductees taken as sex slaves, cases of love and affection have been recorded.[56]

It has been suggested that, in any investigation of CBOW, it would be useful to distinguish further between children born out of a consensual relationship and those born as a result of coercion of varying degrees. Such proposals are based on the assumption that the children's experiences correlate closely with those of the mothers and are a function of the circumstances of conception. Anecdotal evidence and preliminary quantitative and qualitative survey research[57] suggest that this is not necessarily the case. However, it is difficult to come to clear conclusions about the correlation between the nature of the parental relationship and the experiences of the children, because a differentiation would be fraught with inaccuracies. Many children fathered by foreign soldiers know very little about either their fathers or the nature of the relationship between their biological parents. Secondly, this lack of detailed knowledge is often filled with speculation and fantasies, leading to a tension between 'emotional verisimilitude' and 'historical authenticity'.[58] As a result, a differentiation based on a distinction between different kinds of parental relationships, which would have to be based on the truth content of personal recollections of CBOWs or their mothers, would be problematic. Therefore, while children born out of consensual relationships are explicitly included in this study, an analysis of the impact of the nature of the parental relationship on the experiences of the children will be limited to qualitative studies where the knowledge of CBOW about their conception can be determined with a degree of certainty.

Sexualised violence in war and children born of coercive wartime relationships – the discourse

here is my rifle, here is my gun – one is for the killing and one is for fun.[59]

Although by no means all CBOW are born from coercive relationships, many are. Arguably the changing nature of warfare has changed the impact of hostilities on civilians, to the point where today 'it is perhaps more dangerous to be a woman than a soldier in armed conflict'.[60] The tendency towards less clearly regulated warfare within the confines of the laws of war,[61] together with the increasingly unclear and disputed boundaries between combatants and non-combatants[62] and the growing inclination to use gender-based violence (GBV) as a means of warfare have all contributed to an increase of sexualised war crimes against women and relatively more children born out of such coercive relations. As a recent report puts it: 'Rape in war is by no means a new phenomenon, but its escalation as a deliberate, strategic, and political tactic is now undeniable.'[63] While complexity and scope of wartime rape were largely overlooked until recently, the genocide in Rwanda and attempts at ethnic cleansing by means of sexualised violence in the former Yugoslavia in the 1990s catapulted the issue onto the international agenda; only then did widespread and open debates about the topic commence among academics, the public and in the media, and only then were efforts to react to the problem among the humanitarian agencies intensified.[64]

As will become evident in the analysis of childhood and life course experiences of CBOW, realities and perceptions about military–civilian relations and interactions play a significant role in the children's reintegration into post-conflict societies. Therefore an understanding of the development of CRSV and its potential impact on the experiences of the children of victims of such violence is crucial. Gender-based violence had long been judged an inevitable consequence or by-product of wars, civil wars and other types of armed conflict. In fact, historically, few reports of armed conflicts do not contain accounts of such violence: the Ancient Persian Wars under Alexander the Great and the medieval Crusades are known for rapes, just as are the twentieth-century wars, from the two World Wars[65] to the Vietnam War,[66] the civil war in Bangladesh[67] to Korea, Kuwait, Rwanda, Bosnia, Kosovo, Uganda, Sierra Leone, the DRC or Libya, let alone the conflicts in Iraq and Syria.[68] Yet, rather than being mere by-products of war – inevitable or not – statistics do not support the assessment that rapes are, or ever have been, merely accidental off-shoots of armed conflict. Most scholars now agree that rape is not simply incidental and opportunistic; however, the question remains whether a commonly rehearsed interpretation of rape being functional as a method of warfare captures the complexity of the phenomenon. Recent analysis suggests otherwise.[69]

Considering the Second World War, conservative estimates talk about 2 million rapes on German soil alone, of which 240,000 resulted in the death of the violated women or girls; and the number of rapes committed by German soldiers in the territory of the Soviet Union is estimated to be around 10 million.[70] These figures indicate that rape goes beyond serving the interest of the individual soldiers and is strongly linked also to the collective, be it the military unit, the political or strategic purpose for which the soldier believes to be fighting, or the nation itself. Thus, the 'boys will be boys' mischaracterisation of war rape is inadequate. Reading rape as the male desire to match experiences of killing with experiences of fun, as expressed in the ubiquitous boot camp chant cited in the introductory quote above is equally insufficient as an explanation of the increasingly widespread and vicious occurrence of conflict-related sexualised violence; nor – it is now agreed – is it appropriate or acceptable to explain sexualised violence primarily or exclusively as a result of frustrated sexual urges of military personnel who are deprived of female company during armed conflicts.[71]

It appears that GBV in conflict is 'motivated and perpetuated by a complex mix of individual and collective, premeditated and circumstantial reasons'.[72] Yet, despite extensive research during the last two decades, scholars do not agree about whether sexualised violence is used as a weapon of war and if so how; equally significantly, there is even little consensus over whether sexualised violence is 'a question of sex with violent manifestation, or violence with sexual manifestation'.[73]

Broadly following Jonathan Gottschall's categorisation of explanatory patterns of wartime rape,[74] the United Nations Office for the Coordination of Humanitarian Affairs (OCHA) recently identified four main theories which serve well as a basis of current understanding of the motivation for sexual violence in armed conflict: the gender inequality theory, the psycho-social and economic background theory, the strategic rape theory and the biosocial theory.[75] Some of the thinking underlying these theories gives clues about how rape victims, the violated women and their children conceived of rape, are viewed during and after conflicts. Therefore it is helpful to reflect briefly on attempts at conceptualising CRSV before exploring the situation of CBOW and their mothers more generally.

Gender inequality theory

Susan Brownmiller's ground-breaking and equally controversial study *Against Our Will: Men, Women and Rape*,[76] though not conceived as a history of rape in war, contains the first historical overview of the subject, and her analysis has shaped debates since. Claiming that 'war provide[d] men with the perfect psychological backdrop to give vent to their contempt for women', she argued that all men benefited from the use of rape as a means of perpetuating male dominance by keeping all women in a state of fear. As such, rape was an expression of aggression; it was, as Ruth Seifert elaborated two decades later, 'not the aggressive expression of sexuality, but the sexualised expression of aggression'.[77] The assessment of the centrality of a motivation of expressing power and dominance is echoed in large parts of the feminist literature. Based on the understanding that the relationship between men and women is patriarchal and hierarchical, the argument put forward by historians, psychologists and psychiatrists is that war accentuates pre-existing gender relations and thus reinforces the possessive behaviour displayed by men vis-à-vis women. In other words, aggression and violence, which are part and parcel of any armed conflict, exacerbate the inequalities of gendered power relations and the discriminatory and misogynous behaviour displayed even in peacetime patriarchal societies.

An additional factor beyond the mere expression of dominance over the women is the identification of civilian women with the enemy; thus the violation of women equates to the humiliation and violation of the enemy – the ultimate aim of warfare. In this sense, women are instrumentalised and become part of war itself. Furthermore, women, as spoils of the wars that are characterised by ideas of masculinity and male bonding, assume the role of war trophies, as much as they become, under certain circumstances, focus of revenge.[78] Argued by a feminist scholar elsewhere, war is a ritualised game and violence against women perpetrated by the victorious enemy in the aftermath of battle is part of that game.[79]

As Radhika Coomaraswamy, former UN Special Rapporteur on Violence against Women formulated: 'Rape and other forms of sexual violence are used as instruments of violence and terror – as torture, punishment, intimidation, coercion, humiliation, and degradation. Nonetheless, it is only recently that the international human rights community has begun to recognize rape as violence rather than as an assault on honour or a crime against morality.'[80] Thus, an important corollary of this gender-focused theory is that rape is culturally rooted in a distinct view of female inferiority, or even contempt; this pre-existing cultural paradigm, according to which the aggressive act will be judged, does little to discourage violence against women, as perpetrators will commit their crimes on the assumption of culturally sanctioned impunity.[81]

Psycho-social and economic background theory

The second of the broadly socio-cultural theories focuses on the impact of psychosocial and economic factors on cultivating a climate of excessive violence in general and sexualised violence in particular. It argues that social and economic patterns, particularly in parts of Africa but also elsewhere, have changed in a way that undermines traditional male roles and privileges, which in turn results in men increasingly seeking non-traditional outlets to reassert their social roles. A prominent and frequently cited example of this is the DRC, where young men are no longer in a position to fulfil their traditional role of acquiring sufficient land to create wealth in order to afford a bride and bring up a family. In contrast, women are beginning to acquire status and skills and may no longer be available to men in landless poverty. An alternative to men's traditional wealth creation is presented by the military or a rebel group as a key source of remuneration.[82] The increased level of militarisation, together with the rebalancing of accustomed gender roles and a breaking down of accustomed cultural order, leads to increased aggression directed at women. While these phenomena have been described in detail for the DRC which, because of its excessive use of CRSV, has been one of the focal points of academic study and humanitarian intervention, similar patterns have also been observed in many other recent African conflicts, especially those with high incidence of child soldiering.[83] The spiral of violence can be further exacerbated by traumatisation of the men through military actions and through first-hand experience of armed conflict.[84]

Recent developments that have seen the mass recruitment – across national borders – into extreme Islamist movements globally have raised the question of whether religious factors need to be added to any analysis of GBV in these contemporary conflicts.[85] A recent pilot study among Muslim men in Islamabad, Pakistan, suggests that it is less the religious radicalisation, but the way in which gendered perceptions of the jihad and acceptance of terrorist movements as legitimate ways of living out masculine social roles lead some men to turn to radical Islamism for fulfilment of their own expectations of what it should mean to be a Muslim man, in part independently of socio-economic standing.[86] Attaching a gender perspective to the socio-economic arguments of the frustrated, troubled, discontented and economically oppressed individuals who are taking up weapons in order to defend their threatened masculinities adds an important angle to our understanding not only of recruitment but also the gender-based atrocities.

Another aspect resulting from the military engagement of the individual men is that group conformity 'dilutes individual responsibility'; in wars, groups commit acts which, as individuals in peacetime, men would judge immoral and wrong. In war, the illegal and wrong are no longer perceived as such, in particular if these acts are committed as part of a group, as is often the case in wartime rape.[87] A sense of morality applied by individuals in peacetime may be further undermined if leaders do not set positive examples, if command structures are either not functioning[88] or the military leadership 'controls type and degree of violence wielded by their combatants' by acquiescence or even encouragement.[89] Military leaders may conclude that sexualised violence can serve military strategy both in the narrow sense of weakening the enemy, as will be discussed below, or as aiding the continuing supply of recruits and intelligence. Thus sexualised violence becomes an 'atrocity from above'. How effective military control is – both as encouraging or limiting with regard to such

Strategic rape theory

In Resolution 1820 (2008) the United Nations Security Council noted that 'women and girls are particularly targeted by the use of sexual violence, including as a tactic of war to humiliate, dominate, instil fear in, disperse and/or forcibly relocate civilian members of a community or ethnic group'.[90] As early as 1998 the UN Commission on Human Rights, defined war rape as a 'deliberate and strategic decision on the part of the combatants to intimidate and destroy "the enemy" as a whole by raping and enslaving women who are identified as members of the opposition group'.[91] War rape, as another commentator described, 'attacks women's physical and emotional sense of security while simultaneously launching an assault, through women's bodies, upon the genealogy of security as constructed by the body politic'.[92]

This reflects the currently most widely held theory of war rape, especially for recent conflicts, claiming that these rapes, irrespective of whether they are ordered explicitly by commanders, are strategic; they aim at 'spreading debilitating terror, diminishing the resistance of civilians, and demoralizing, humiliating and emasculating enemy soldiers' who cannot protect their mothers, wives and daughters and thus have failed in their first and foremost duties.[93] Due to the centrality of the role of women in the family, and thus in the local community, women are the backbone of community culture and society as a whole. As such, any attack on the women is perceived to be an attack on the enemy's culture and its entire social fabric, and therefore can potentially serve a military purpose. Moreover, attacks on women create a sense of fear, both among the women and the population as a whole, hence curtailing freedom of movement and thus restricting economic and cultural activity. As a consequence, the population, especially if male soldiers are unable to counter the threat, becomes demoralised and the will to resist any military attack is reduced.[94]

However, in many cases in recent years women have not been targeted exclusively or even primarily because they are women, but according to their ethnicity or religion.[95] Conflicts such as the Bosnian and the Rwandan wars have led to mass rape being understood as genocidal in character.[96] Rape in this context is not merely an attack on the territorial integrity of an enemy, or even the 'male territory' of 'assured female chastity, paternity, and procreative rights' of the enemy.[97] Rape instead becomes a means of ethnic cleansing. Raped women may be forcibly impregnated and may be forced to bear the child. They may suffer severe physical and mental injuries, they may be abandoned by their families and local communities or any combination of the above. Ultimately, this impedes the enemy's ability to 'replenish itself through sexual reproduction',[98] and thus rape is no longer aimed at the individual woman, but it is designed to annihilate a culture and by implication the enemy people.[99] Thus, the 'physical and psychological trauma and disease inflicted by rape renders it a form of "biological warfare" with ripple effects extending to their family and community'.[100]

Biosocial theory

While researchers agree with the assessment that mass wartime rape can and does have the impact described in the explanatory frameworks of socio-cultural theories, some argue that the analysis of effects does not allow any conclusions about motives of mass rape. Instead, they argue that only a biosocial theory can account for the range of sexualised violence witnessed across the centuries. The main argument in favour of this approach is that all other theories do not provide a good fit between theory and observed data. For instance, while widespread rape can have a demoralising impact on the enemy, many counterexamples demonstrate that military planners throughout the centuries have recognised the potentially galvanising effect that the targeting of helpless women can have on the resistance among the enemy's civilian and combatant population. This explains why, in many instances, commanders have attempted to prohibit rapes because of the perceived threat to long-term strategic interests. Examples are numerous and include the thinking behind the establishment of military brothels in order to minimise war rape[101] such as the *Wehrmachtsbordelle* of the German Army during the Second World War[102] or the forced prostitution of the so-called 'comfort women' in Japan.[103] A second criticism of the socio-cultural explanations is that these theories have in common a denial of sexual desire as a significant factor in mass rapes. While, in Brownmiller's words, biology has given men the 'structural capacity' to rape and women the 'structural vulnerability' to be raped,[104] this is where the biological relevance for explaining wartime mass rape ends. In contrast, proponents of biosocial theories argue that while socio-cultural factors cannot be discounted as having an impact on the occurrence and characteristics of war rape, biological factors have to be taken into account too. Wartime rape occurs in societies of all races, ethnicities, religions, and it has occurred across time and space; broad evidence suggests[105] that attractive women of reproductive age are vastly over-represented among the victims. This has led to the conclusion that a significant factor for wartime rape, as peacetime rape, is the sexual desire of individual soldiers.[106]

Despite the unquestionable progress in our understanding of wartime mass rape since the early 1990s, significant gaps remain – gaps which are of great importance in developing a framework for dealing with the causes of sexualised violence during war *and* for dealing with the post-conflict impact of sexualised violence, not least for the children born as a result of rapes. Among the areas that require further study are: explanations of significant variations in incidences of war rapes;[107] the link between socio-cultural factors underlying sexual violence and post-conflict reconciliation; the correlation between sociocultural factors and the integration of children born of rape; the significance of internal dynamics of armed forces (regular or otherwise) for scale and character of sexualised violence; the characteristics of perpetrators; and escalation of sexual violence in some conflicts and not in others.[108]

Childhood and children's rights

As mentioned in the introductory chapter, the UN, in response to allegations of sexual misconduct of members of its peacekeeping missions, developed a 'Comprehensive Strategy' with regard to its support of victims of SEA, including children born of such crimes. The formulation of this UN resolution with its entitlement to support of children born of sexual exploitation was the culmination of significant developments in the UN's internal thinking about the rights and wrongs of soldiers' conduct and the implications of their actions for the standing of the UN as a whole. As importantly, it was also directly linked to the evolving concept of childhood and children's rights, which had seen dramatic conceptual changes in the twentieth century. The concepts of children's rights and even of childhood itself are of relatively recent origin. Ever since Philippe Ariès first highlighted the socially constructed character of childhood in the early 1960s,[109] despite serious reservations about his methodology and his interpretation of historical records,[110] his arguments have been foundational to childhood studies. Ariès argued that awareness of children having a different social experience from adults had only emerged slowly over the centuries, and the realisation that children were different to adults had manifested itself in social, political and eventually also the economic institutionalisation of children's and families' needs. Childhood was no longer seen as simply a biological stage of development but also a social category. As such, childhood became seen to be based on attitudes, beliefs, and values of particular societies at particular points in time.[111]

Notwithstanding this post-Second World War conceptualisation of childhood, on a more practical – and particularly on an educational – level children had been viewed as something distinct from merely being small adults for some time. Inspired by early nineteenth-century educational theorists such as Friedrich Fröbel, a more holistic approach to a child's physical, emotional and intellectual needs gave rise to new child-centred educational initiatives such as those of Maria Montessori or Rudolf Steiner.[112] Alongside this focus on children's needs, and despite the Romantic ideal of childhood as a time of innocence, an increasing politicisation of children and youth could be witnessed. Children entered the body politic as symbols of national identity and patriotism,[113] and at the same time the developing understanding of children as a separate category from adults also led to the conclusion that children deserved or even required special rights and protection. Not unlike the simultaneous and parallel – yet non-uniform – societal and educational child focus, the emerging engagement in children's rights was a product of attitudes and beliefs of individual groups within specific historical contexts. Despite similar developments in different countries at around the same time, initially the formulation of child rights was not a universal or coherent process. Early examples, for instance, were found in the Soviet Union, where communist and proletarian utopias found expression, among others, in a 'Declaration of Children's Rights'. Passed by a local proletkult group in Moscow not long after the Revolution of 1917, this declaration was based on the assumption that family life inhibited the radical potential of children and that youngsters ought to be shielded from parental influence. School and workplace were to become as significant to the children as their own families and the 'Declaration' guaranteed that children could not only choose their own education and religion; they could also leave their parents, if they so desired.[114] This is an early example of the instrumentalisation of children as expedient pawns in political power play; as we will see below, children in general and CBOW more particularly, would continue to be used in similar ways with their rights being championed or denied depending on how they would best serve political purposes.

Prior to the twentieth century, child rights discussions had focused mainly on obtaining a number of protection rights for children, such as regulating child labour (Child Labor Laws in the United Sates from 1832;[115] First Child Labour Law, France 1841;[116] The Mines Act, UK, 1842[117]) and thus protecting children from the worst excesses of the Industrial Revolution. In the early twentieth century, however, in tandem with increasing awareness of children not being mini adults and with the observation of the growing impact of armed conflict on civilians in general and children in particular, a change in the approach to children's rights became apparent. Children were increasingly seen not merely as an object of concern, but as a subject of rights as (equal) citizens of the world.[118] Rights were no longer exclusively regarded as bestowed upon children, but as something they were entitled to. In essence, children's rights were seen as human rights, even before the codification of human rights themselves. In fact the conceptual development of human rights was strongly intertwined with the changing attitudes towards children, both of which can be related to the experiences of the Great War.

In response to the carnage and the international community's apparent inability to solve international conflicts by non-violent means, the League of Nations was founded as an inter-governmental organisation with the principal mission to preserve world peace. It was also tasked with protecting basic human rights standards.[119] While human rights were a concern for politicians and statesmen, furthering the cause of children was often seen as a legitimate enterprise for (upper) middle-class women, for whom 'child saving' was a natural extension of their child-rearing role.[120] This is evident in the fact that engagement in this field was dominated by women, who not only fought for children's rights but also for their own, linking concerns of equality of women with those of the protection of children. It was against this background that the first tentative steps towards a codification of children's rights were taken by the founder of *Save the Children*, the British teacher, Eglantyne Jebb. Her two-pronged approach to children's rights and requirements is at the heart of current debates about the rights of CBOW and as such it is relevant to cite two of the key elements of her engagement. In 1919, on the basis of her experiences of the First World War, she famously remarked: 'All wars, whether just or unjust, disastrous or victorious, are waged against the child.'[121] When she defended herself against the charge of having assisted the enemy when organising food for needy children on both sides of the conflict, she followed this up with the equally widely reported comment: 'My Lord, I have no enemies below the age of 11.'[122] In other words: child protection had to be non-discriminatory. Children deserved and required protection irrespective of race, nationality, ethnicity or religion – in war and in peace.

The second angle of her engagement went beyond the protection of children in wartime and included the formulation of what she believed children were entitled to, namely: the means requisite for their normal development, both materially and spiritually; relief in times of distress; and protection from exploitation and opportunities to earn a livelihood. All these principles eventually found their way into child rights legislation in continuation of Jebb's demands that: 'the child that is hungry must be fed, the child that is sick must be helped, the child that is backward must be helped, the delinquent child must be reclaimed, and the orphan and the waif must be sheltered and succoured' and 'the child must be brought up in the consciousness that its talents must be devoted to the service of its fellow men'.[123]

Though clothed in the language of early twentieth-century England, the demands are as relevant today as they were in 1923, when Jebb initially drafted the Declaration of the Rights of the Child, a set of ideas adopted by the International Save the Children Union in Geneva in 1923 and endorsed by the League of Nations General Assembly in 1924 as the 'World Child Charter'. In some sense, they are even more pressing today, because the 'nature of armed conflict has changed from targeting "men on march"', to 'unpredictable ethnic and religious conflicts in which women and children are the victims, and sometimes even targets of the conflict'.[124]

It would take another 65 years until these rights were first codified when, in 1989, the 'Convention on the Rights of the Child' (CRC) was adopted by the General Assembly of the UN.[125] But the key ideas formulated in the non-binding declaration of 1923/24 can be found in much of the twentieth-century human rights legislation. Based on the notion that 'Mankind owes to the child the best it has to give'[126] the idea of the 'best interest of the child' and special safeguards for children are found in the 1948 'Universal Declaration of Human Rights'[127] and more extensively in the 'UN Declaration on the Rights of the Child of 1959'.[128] The CRC entered into force in 1990 and by December 2008, 193 parties had ratified the Convention. It was the first legally binding instrument to incorporate the civil, cultural, political and social rights of children and is closely connected to the other five human rights conventions.[129] It is based on the recognition, by world leaders, that children, especially children in crisis situations, need protection, and that safeguards are needed to ensure their now universally recognised human rights. It is a promise to children to respect, protect and fulfil their human rights, and it is one of the (if not the) most comprehensive of all human rights treaties containing an expansive list of civil, political, social, cultural and economic rights. No less significantly, it is also the most widely accepted international convention, ratified by all countries except the United States.

Although there are a number of additional human rights instruments of relevance for safeguarding the rights of children, such as the International Covenant on Civil and Political Rights,[130] the Convention on the Prevention and Punishment of the Crime of Genocide,[131] and two optional protocols to the CRC on the sale of children, child prostitution and child pornography[132] and on the involvement of children in armed conflict,[133] it is the CRC that forms the cornerstone of the efforts aimed at protecting and realising children's rights.

The Convention has four guiding principles which inform the implementation of all other children's rights. They are the principles of non-discrimination (Article 2), the best interest of the child (Article 3), the right to life, survival and development (Article 6) and the right to be heard (Article 12).[134] Based on these principles, the Convention contains 42 substantive provisions on a whole range of rights and issues relating to children which are often divided into the 'three Ps' of Provision, Protection and Participation.

Provision rights include rights relevant to the provision of children's basic needs and include among others the right to the highest attainable standard of health and health care (Article 24), the right to a standard of living adequate to ensure the child's development (Article 27), the right to education (Articles 28 and 29), and the right to play, rest and leisure (Article 31).

Protection rights include rights relevant to the protection of children from all forms of harm and exploitation and include the right of children without family care to special protection and the right to alternative care including adoption (Articles 20 and 21), the right of particularly vulnerable children, including refugee children and children with disabilities, to have special protection (Articles 22 and 23), the right to protection from economic exploitation and sexual exploitation (Articles 32 and 34), the right to protection from drugs (Article 33), the right to protection from all forms of harm, neglect and abuse (Article 19) and the rights of victims of such abuse to treatment, counselling and support (Article 39).

Participation rights include the rights of children to participate in decisions made about them and to contribute to society by expressing their views. They include, among others, the child's right to express his or her views and have them given due weight in accordance with the child's age and understanding in all decisions made about them and the child's right to be represented in legal proceedings (Article 12), the child's right to express her or his opinion using a variety of means of expression according to the child's capacity (Article 13), the child's right to freedom of religion and freedom of association (Articles 14 and 15) and the right to access appropriate information conducive to the child's well-being (Article 17), and the right to privacy (Article 16).

The CRC applies to children globally irrespective of the environments in which they grow up. As discussed above, among the driving forces for the formulation of rights of children that secure their protection, also in extreme circumstances, was the experience of war and its impact on children. In recognition of the fact that contemporary warfare has led to children increasingly becoming subjects of targeted attacks and military recruitment, a number of states and non-governmental agencies sought to create a more focused legal framework regarding the association of children with armed forces, which culminated the signing of an Optional Protocol to the CRC laying down guidelines on the involvement of children in armed conflict in May 2000.[135] The obligations of this 'Optional Protocol to the CRC on the involvement of children in armed conflict' (as also of the second 'Optional Protocol to the CRC on the sale of children, child prostitution, and child pornography' of 2000 and the third Optional Protocol to the CRC on a communications procedure of 2011) are additional and not legally binding on states that had already ratified the original CRC treaty before the optional protocols went into force. By March 2012, 130 countries had ratified the Optional Protocol on the involvement of children in armed conflict. The Optional Protocol extends the protection of children during armed conflict afforded by Article 38 of the CRC which stipulates the states' responsibility to ensure that children under the age of 15 do not take direct part in hostilities or be enlisted voluntarily, by raising the lower age limit to 18 years.

The context of the CRC implies that the codification of children's rights reflected an awareness that had grown over decades of the importance of protecting children's rights. Yet, the Convention is a state-centric instrument, based on a state-centric model of enforcements of rights, while the rights of CBOW are often compromised at the horizontal level between individuals and not at the vertical level in the interaction between state and individual.[136] Despite this, the Convention is unequivocal in formulating the obligation on the part of the state to protect the individual and thereby protect against horizontal violations of human rights in general and children's rights in particular.

Children born of war, in the vast majority of cases, are born to mothers in above average volatile situations, exposing them to social, economic, health and political challenges which make them and their mothers vulnerable. In a very significant number of cases the context of their conception involves a degree of coercion. These circumstances are rarely conducive to empowering women and their children to enforce human rights, even if they were aware of those rights. Two of the case studies below, the Second World War and the Vietnam War took place before the codification of children's rights in the CRC.

The detailed analysis of the challenges faced by CBOW and their mothers in volatile post-conflict societies will focus on the case studies relating to conflicts after the ratification of the CRC, particularly the Bosnian War and the African conflicts at the turn of the century as well as the enforcements of rights of children of peacekeepers following the publication of the UN's 'Comprehensive Strategy'.

The next chapters will explore in detail the experiences of CBOW, their upbringing and reintegration into post-conflict societies, policies towards them, responses of families, local and national receptor communities and the impact of such factors on the quality of the life course experiences of the CBOW in the twentieth century.

Notes

1 Beverly Allen, *Rape Warfare: The Hidden Genocide in Bosnia-Herzegovina and Croatia* (Minneapolis: University of Minnesota Press / Amnesty International, 1996).
2 e.g. Human Rights Watch, *Sexual Violence and its Consequences Among Displaced Persons in Darfur and Chad* (New York: Human Rights Watch, 2004).
3 Joseph Guyler Delva, 'UN Haiti peacekeepers face outcry over alleged rape', *Reuters*, US edition, 5.9.2011, www.reuters.com/article/2011/09/05/us-haiti-uruguay-un-idUSTRE7842DY20110905. (accessed 2.11.2015); 'UN troops face child abuse claim', *BBC News Channel*, 30.11.2006. (accessed 2.11.2015); Kate Holt and Sarah Hughes, 'UN staff accused of raping children in Sudan', *The Telegraph*, 2.11.2007. (accessed 2.11.2015); Pagonis Pagonakis and Marcel Kolvenbach, *Gefährliche Helfer*, ARD documentary, January 2013, www.youtube.com/watch?v=NgD0K5vo2YU. (accessed 20.3.2015); Michelle Nicholls, 'U.N. peacekeepers accused of abusing Central African Republic street children', *Reuters*, 23.6.2015, www.reuters.com/article/2015/06/23/us-centralafrica-abuse-un-idUSKBN0P323120150623. (accessed 31.7.2015).
4 Jonathan Torgovnik, *Intended Consequences: Children Born of Rape* (New York: Aperture, 2009).
5 Elisabeth Vikman, 'Ancient origins: Sexual violence in warfare, Part I', *Anthropology & Medicine*, 12 (2005), 21–31.
6 John Man, *Ghengis Khan: Life, Death and Resurrection* (London: Bantam Press, 2004).
7 Guibert von Nogent, *Dei Gesta per Francos*, translated as *The Deeds of God through the Franks* (tr. by Robert Levine, 1997), www.gutenberg.org/ebooks/4370. (accessed 2.10.2014).
8 John A. Lynn II, *Women, Armies and Warfare in Early Modern Europe* (Cambridge: Cambridge University Press, 2008); Karen Hagemann and Ralf Pröve, *Landsknechte, Soldatenfrauen und Nationalkrieger: Militär, Krieg und Geschlechterordnung im historischen Wandel* (Frankfurt / New York: Campus Verlag, 1998); See also Franz Irsigler and Arnold Lassotta, *Bettler und Gaukler, Dirnen und Henker. Außenseiter in einer mittelalterlichen Stadt: Köln 1300–1600* (Munich: Deutscher Taschenbuch Verlag, 1989), pp. 179–227; Ulinka Rublack,

'Metze und Magd: Frauen, Krieg und die Bildfunktion des Weiblichen in deutschen Städten der frühen Neuzeit', *Historische Anthropologie*, 3 (1995), 412–32, translated into English as 'Wench and maiden: Women, war and the pictorial function of the feminine in German cities in the Early Modern Period', *History Workshop Journal*, 44 (1997), 1–21, esp. 11–16; Beate Engelen, 'Warum heiratete man einen Soldaten? Soldatenfrauen in der ländlichen Gesellschaft Brandenburg-Preußens im 18. Jahrhundert', in Stefan Kroll and Kersten Krüger (eds), *Militär und ländliche Gesellschaft in der frühen Neuzeit* (Münster: Lit-Verlag, 2000), pp. 251–73; Karin Jansson, 'Soldaten und Vergewaltigung im Schweden des 17. Jahrhunderts', in Benigna Krusenstjern and Hans Medick (eds), *Zwischen Alltag und Katastrophe: Der Dreißigjährige Krieg aus der Nähe* (Göttingen: Vandenhock & Ruprecht, 1999), pp. 195–225.
9 Nick Funke, 'Religion and the military in the Holy Roman Empire c. 1500–1650' (DPhil thesis, University of Sussex, 2012).
10 Rublack, 'Metze und Magd', 12.
11 Funke, 'Religion', pp. 108–15.
12 Andreas Rennemann, *Privilegia Vnd Freyheiten der Soldatescha*, s.l. 1630, 17, cited in Funke, 'Religion', p. 108.
13 For changing attitudes to illegitimacy, especially in the twentieth century, see 'Illegitimacy', *International Encyclopedia of the Social Sciences*, 1968. Encyclopedia. com www.encyclopedia.com/doc/1G2-3045000554.html. (accessed 9.2.2015).
14 Funke, 'Religion', p. 110.
15 This does not mean that they are 'over reported'. On the contrary, as will be shown below, under-reporting is a problem in the quantitative analysis of CRSV. The point here is that non-violent and unproblematic relations are rarely documented at all.
16 For development of definitions see Sabine Lee and Ingvill C. Mochmann, 'Kinder des Krieges im 20. Jahrhundert', in Barbara Stelzl-Marx and Silke Satjukow (eds), *Besatzungskinder: Die Nachkommen alliierter Soldaten in Österreich und Deutschland* (Wien: Böhlau-Verlag, 2015), pp. 15–38.
17 Magnus Hirschfeld, *The Sexual History of the World War* (New York: The Panurge Press, 1934), p. 236.
18 Ebba D. Drolshagen, *Wehrmachtskinder: Auf der Suche nach dem nie gekannten Vater* (Munich: Droemer Verlag, 2005); Monika Diederichs, *Wie geschoren wordt moet stil zitten: De omgang von Nederlandse meisjes met Duitse militairen* (Den Haag: Boom, 2006); Lars Westerlund (ed.), *Children of German Soldiers: Children of Foreign Soldiers in Finland 1940–1948*, vol. I (Helsinki: Painopaikka Nord Print, 2011); Lars Westerlund (ed.), *The Children of Foreign Soldiers in Finland, Norway, Denmark, Austria, Poland and Occupied Soviet Karelia*, vol. II (Helsinki: Painopaikka Nord Print, 2011); Regina Mühlhäuser, *Eroberungen: Sexuelle Gewalttaten und intime Beziehungen deutscher Soldaten in der Sowjetunion 1941–1945* (Hamburg: Hamburger Edition HIS Verlagsgesellschaft, 2010).
19 No detailed studies of children of colonial wars exist, but support organisations of Eurasians, such as those supporting children of the Indochina Wars and the Dutch-Indonesian War have collected some historical accounts of their situations, www.oorlogsliefdekind.nl/en/; http://foefi.net/actualites2015.html. (accessed 2.2.2015).

20 Fabrice Virgili, *The Shorn Women: Gender and Punishment in Liberation France* (Oxford: Berg, 2002); Jean-Paul Picaper and Ludwig Norz, *Enfants maudits* (Paris: Edition de Syrtes, 2004).

21 David Reynolds, *Rich Relations: The American Occupation of Britain 1942–1945* (London: Harper Collins, 1996).

22 Norbert Frei, 'Kriegsende: Große Gefühle', *Die Zeit* – online, Geschichte, 1/2015, www.zeit.de/zeit-geschichte/2015/01/kriegsende-emotionen-nachkriegszeit-besatzungszonen-1945. (accessed 31.7.2015); Richard L. Merritt, *Democracy Imposed: US Occupation Policy and the German Public 1945–1949* (New Haven: Yale University Press, 1995).

23 P. Raedts, 'The Children's Crusade of 1212', *Journal of Medieval History*, 3 (1977), 279–324.

24 Michael H. Kater, *Hitler Youth* (Cambridge, MA: Harvard University Press, 2004).

25 Susan W. Tiefenbrun, 'Child soldiers, slavery, and the trafficking of children', *Fordham International Law Journal*, 31 (2007), 417–86; Robert M. Tynes, 'Child Soldier Use: The Diffusion of a Tactical Innovation' (Ph.D. thesis, State University of New York at Albany, 2011), http://proquest.umi.com/pqdlink?Ver=1&Exp=02-07-2018&FMT=7&DID=2337132001&RQT=309&attempt=1&cfc=1. (accessed 12.11.2014); David M. Rosen, *Child Soldiers: A Reference Handbook* (Santa Barbara: ABC-Clio, 2012).

26 Donald H. Dunson, *Child, Victim, Soldier: The Loss of Innocence in Uganda* (Michigan: Orbis Books, 2008).

27 https://childrenandarmedconflict.un.org/countries/children-and-armed-conflict-interactive-world-map/. (accessed 9.2.2015).

28 Kevin Sieff, 'From sex slaves to social outcasts: What happens when "Boko Haram wives" are freed?', *Washington Post*, 4.4.16, www.independent.co.uk/news/world/africa/from-sex-slaves-to-social-outcasts-what-happens-when-boko-haram-wives-are-freed-a6967986.html. (accessed 20.5.2016).

29 Eunice Apio, 'Uganda's forgotten children of war', in R. Charli Carpenter (ed.), *Born of War: Protecting Children of Sexual Violence Survivors in Conflict Zones* (Bloomfield, CT: Kumarian Press, 2007), pp. 94–109; Peter Eichstaedt, *First You Kill Your Family: Child Soldiers of Uganda and the Lord's Resistance Army* (London: Lawrence Hill Books, 2009); Priya Joshi, 'Boko Haram in Nigeria: Women describe being "sex machines" for Islamist captors', *International Business Times*, 7.5.2015, www.ibtimes.co.uk/boko-haram-nigeria-women-describe-being-sex-machines-by-islamist-captors-1500247. (accessed 20.5.2016).

30 UN PSEA Taskforce, *To Serve with Pride*, 2009, www.un.org/en/pseataskforce/video_english.shtml. (accessed 10.1.2016).

31 See various documents and reports accessible via the UN PSEA website: www.un.org/en/pseataskforce/focalpoint; also 'Ban Ki-moon says sexual abuse in UN peacekeeping is "a cancer in our system"', *The Guardian*, 14.8.2015, www.theguardian.com/world/2015/aug/14/ban-ki-moon-says-sexual-abuse-is-in-un-peacekeeping-is-a-cancer-in-our-system. (accessed 17.8.2015).

32 Muna Ndulo, 'The United Nations responses to the sexual abuse and exploitation of women and girls by peacekeepers during peacekeeping missions', *Berkeley Journal for International Law*, 27 (2009), 127–61.

33 Olga Rains, Lloyd Rains and Melynda Jarratt (eds), *Voices of the Left Behind*

(Toronto: Project Roots, 2004); Pamela Winfield, *Melancholy Baby: The Unplanned Consequences of the G.I.s' Arrival in Europe for World War II* (Westport: Bergin & Garvey, 2000); Pamela Winfield, *Bye Bye Baby: The Story of the Children the GIs Left Behind* (London: Bloomsbury, 1992).

34 Sabine Lee, 'A forgotten legacy of the Second World War: GI children in post-war Britain and Germany', *Contemporary European History*, 20 (2011), 157–81; Barbara Stelzl-Marx, 'Die unsichtbare Generation: Kinder sowjetischer Besatzungssoldaten in Österreich und Deutschland', *Historical Social Research*, 34 (2009), 352–72, here 353–5; Silke Satjukow, *Besatzer: Die Russen in Deutschland 1945–1994* (Göttingen: Vandenhoek & Ruprecht, 2008), pp. 284–98.

35 Lee, 'A forgotten legacy', 160–1.

36 Robert S. McKelvey, *The Dust of Life: America's Children Abandoned in Vietnam* (Seattle and London: University of Washington Press, 1999).

37 Kathleen M. Jennings and Vesna Nikolić-Ristanović, 'UN peacekeeping economies and local sex industries: Connections and implications', *MICROCON Research*, Working Paper 17, September 2009, University of Sussex. See also J. Doezema, 'Forced to choose: Beyond the voluntary versus forced prostitution dichotomy', in Kamala Kempadoo and Jo Doezema (eds), *Global Sex Workers: Rights, Resistance, and Redefinition* (New York: Routledge, 1998), pp. 34–50.

38 Emmanuelle Saada, *Les Enfants de la Colonie: Les Métis de l'Empire français entre sujétion et citoyenetté* (Paris: Editions La Découverte, 2007); Annegriet Wietsma, *Tuan Papa – Mijnheer de Vader – Suir Daddy: De vergeten kinderen van Nederlandse militairen in Indonesië* (Hellwig Productions, 2010); Philippe Rostan, *Inconnu, Présumé Français* (Jour2Fête & Filmover Production, 2011).

39 Yuki Tanaka, *Japan's Comfort Women: Sexual Slavery and Prostitution During World War II and the US Occupation* (London / New York: Routledge, 2002); Yoshimi Yoshiaki, *Comfort Women: Sexual Slavery in the Japanese Military During World War II* (New York: Columbia University Press, 2000).

40 Christa Paul, *Zwangsprostitution: Staatlich errichtete Bordelle im Nationalsozialismus* (Berlin: Edition Hentrich, 1994); Wendy Jo Gertjejanssen, 'Victims, Heroes, Survivors: Sexual Violence On The Eastern Front During World War II' (Ph.D. thesis, University of Minnesota, 2004); Insa Meinen, *Wehrmacht und Prostitution im besetzten Frankreich* (Bremen: Edition Temmen, 2002).

41 Judith R. Walkowitz, *Prostitution and Victorian Society: Women, Class, and the State* (Cambridge: Cambridge University Press, 1982), pp. 74–5.

42 Catherine Clinton, *Public Women and the Confederacy* (Milwaukee: Marquette University Press, 1999).

43 According to US Army estimates, during the First World War, there were 40 major brothels, 5,000 professionally licensed streetwalkers, and another 70,000 unlicensed prostitutes in Paris alone. Fred D. Baldwin, 'No sex please, we're American', *Warrior Scout*, 24.4.2014, http://warrior.scout.com/story/1387336-no-sex-please-we-re-american. (accessed 9.2.2015).

44 Deborah Cole, 'Exhibition exposes sex slavery at Nazi camps', National Sexual Violence Resource Centre, 26.2.2009, www.nsvrc.org/news/news-field/1253. (accessed 9.2.2015).

45 David M. Rosen, *Armies of the Young: Child Soldiers in War and Terrorism* (Chapel Hill: Rutgers University Press, 2005).

46 Dyan E. Mazurana et al. 'Girls in fighting forces and groups: Their recruitment, participation, demobilization, and reintegration', *Peace and Conflict: Journal of Peace Psychology*, 8 (2002), 97–123.

47 Apio, Eunice, 'Bearing the burden – the children Born of the Lord's Resistance Army, Northern Uganda', 2008, www.google.co.uk/url?sa=t&rct=j&q=&esrc=s&source=web&cd=2&ved=0CCUQFjAB&url=http%3A%2F%2Fmhpss.net%2F%3Fget%3D54%2F1367708997-ChildrenofFormerlyAbductedGirls-Uganda-Opio-2008.pdf&ei=xU5jVPbANOOasQSc9oGYAg&usg=AFQjCNHxO8Dd8_S3V-GB2mbE6gsvTeC5tw&bvm=bv.79189006,d.cWc. (accessed 12.11.2014); Taylor Toeka, 'Grim prospects of DRC's female child soldiers', *International Justice ICC*, 296 (2011), https://iwpr.net/global-voices/grim-prospects-drcs-female-child-soldiers. (accessed 12.11.2014); Jacob Zenn, Elizabeth Pearson, 'Women, gender and the evolving tactics of Boko Haram', *Journal of Terrorism Research*, 5 (2015) (no pagination), http://ojs.st-andrews.ac.uk/index.php/jtr/article/view/828/707. (accessed 31.7.2015); M. Johansson, 'Wartime sexual violence: The case of Islamic State in Iraq and the Levant (ISIL)' (M.Sc. thesis, Lund University, 2015).

48 Allen, *Rape Warfare*; Todd E. Salzman, 'Rape camps as a means of ethnic cleansing', *Human Rights Quarterly*, 20 (1998), 348–78.

49 Christopher W. Mullins, '"He would kill me with his penis": Genocidal rape in Rwanda as a state crime', *Critical Criminology*, 17 (2009), 15–33.

50 Helen M. Hintjens, 'Explaining the 1994 genocide in Rwanda', *The Journal of Modern African Studies*, 37 (1999), 241–86; Bianfer Nowrojee, *Shattered Lives: Sexual Violence During the Rwandan Genocide and its Aftermath* (New York: Human Rights Watch, 1996); Andrea A. Phelps, 'Gender-based war crimes: Incidence and effectiveness of international criminal prosecution', *William & Mary Journal of Women and Law*, 12 (2006), 499–520, here, 510.

51 Melynda Jarratt, *War Brides: The Stories of the Women Who Left Everything Behind to Follow the Men They Loved* (Stroud: The History Press, 2007); Hilary Kaiser, *WWII Voices: American GIs and the French Women Who Married Them* (CreateSpace Independent Publishing Platform, 2012); Miki Ward Crawford, Katie Kaori Hayashi and Shizuko Suenaga, *Japanese War Brides in America: An Oral History* (Santa Barbara: Praeger, 2009); Susan Zeiger, *Entangling Alliances: Foreign War Brides and American Soldiers in the Twentieth Century* (New York: New York University Press, 2010).

52 For discussion see Atina Grossmann, 'A question of silence: The rape of German women by occupation soldiers', *October*, 72 (1995), 42–63; see also Norman M. Naimark, *The Russians in Germany: The History of the Soviet Zone of Occupation, 1945–1949* (Cambridge, MA: Harvard University Press 1995), pp. 69–140; Erich Kuby, *Die Russen in Berlin* (Bern / München: Scherz, 1965); Helke Sander, *Freier und BeFreite: Krieg, Vergwaltigung, Kinder* (Munich: Verlag Antje Kunstmann, 1992).

53 M. Bastick, K. Grimm and R. Kunz, 'Peacekeepers and sexual violence in armed conflict', in M. Bastick, K. Grimm and R. Kunz, *Sexual Violence in Armed Conflict* (Geneva: DCAF, 2007), pp. 169–90.

54 Satjukow, *Besatzer*; R. Lilly, *Taken by Force: Rape and American GIs in Europe During World War II* (London: Palgrave, 2007); 'Central African Republic: Ban

vows decisive action on allegations of sexual abuse by UN peacekeepers', *UN New Centre*, 12.8.2015, www.un.org/apps/news/story.asp?NewsID=51618#.VdHJXJfz57U. (accessed 17.8.2015).

55 e.g. Vladimir Gelfand, *Das Deutschland-Tagebuch 1945–1946* (Berlin: Aufbau-Verlag, 2005).

56 For details about life under the LRA from the perspective of a female ex-combatant and former 'wife' of Joseph Kony see Evelyn Amony, *I am Evelyn Amony: Reclaiming Life from the Lord's Resistance Army*, ed. by Erin Baines (Madison: University of Wisconsin Press, 2016).

57 Heide Glaesmer et al., 'Kinder des Zweiten Weltkrieges in Deutschland: Ein Rahmenmodell für psychosoziale Forschung', *Trauma und Gewalt*, 6 (2012), 318–28.

58 Kerstin Muth, *Die Wehrmacht in Griechenland – und ihre Kinder* (Leipzig: Eudora Verlag, 2008), p. 85.

59 Fred Turner, *Echoes of Combat: The Vietnam War in American Memory* (New York: Anchor Books, 1996), p. 76.

60 Maj. Gen. Patrick Cammmaert at Wilton Park Conference, May 2008, cited in UN Women, *Addressing Conflict-Related Sexual Violence in Conflict: An Analytical Inventory of Peacekeeping Practice*, October 2012, www.unwomen.org/~/media/Headquarters/Media/Publications/en/04DAnAnalyticalinventoryofPeacekeepingPracti.pdf. (accessed 10.2.2015).

61 Edward Newman, 'The "new wars" debate: A historical perspective is needed', *Security Dialogue*, 35:2 (2004), 173–89.

62 See Aimee Kidder, 'A Disappearing Boundary? The Changing Distinction Between Combatant and Civilians from the First World War to the Present Day' (Honors thesis, Colby College, 2010).

63 The PLoS Medicine Editors, 'Rape in war is common, devastating, and too often ignored', *PLoS Med*, 6:1 (2009), np.

64 See for instance R. Lindsey, 'From atrocity to data: Historiographies of rape in the Former Yugoslavia and the gendering of genocide', *Patterns of Prejudice*, 36 (2002), 79–87.

65 J. Burds, 'Sexual violence in Europe in World War II, 1939–1945', *Politics and Society*, 37 (2009), 35–73.

66 Sue San, 'Where the girls are: The management of venereal disease by United States military forces in Vietnam', *Literature and Medicine*, 23 (2004), 66–87.

67 Dara Kay Kohen, 'Explaining rape during civil wars: Cross-national evidence 1980–2009', *American Political Science Review*, 107 (2013), 461–77.

68 Bastick et al., *Sexual Violence in Armed Conflict*.

69 Inger Skjelsbæk, 'The elephant in the room: An overview of how sexual violence came to be seen as a weapon of war' (Oslo: PRIO Report, 2010).

70 'Kriegsvergewaltigungen', Helpline Schleswig-Holstein, www.helpline-sh.de/Kriegsvergewaltigung.html. (accessed 6.3.2016); A detailed academic study of sexualised violence of the German *Wehrmacht* in Eastern Europe can be found in Regina Mühlhäuser, *Eroberungen: Sexuelle Gewalttaten und intime Beziehungen deutscher Soldaten in der Sowjetunion 1941–1945* (Hamburg: Hamburger Edition, 2010).

71 See e.g. T. Gingerich and J. Leaning, *The Use of Rape as a Weapon of War in the Conflict in Darfur, Sudan* (Boston, MA: Harvard School of Public Health and Physicians for Human Rights, 2005); M. Eriksson, P. Wallensteen and M. Sollenberg, 'Armed conflict, 1989–2002', *Journal of Peace Research*, 40 (2003), 593–607; M.B. Olujic, 'Embodiment of terror: Gendered violence in peacetime and wartime in Croatia and Bosnia-Herzegovina', *Medical Anthropology Quarterly*, 12 (1998), 31–50.

72 UNOCHA, 'Sexual violence in armed conflict: Understanding the motivations', Discussion paper of the UN OCHA Research Meeting, 26.6.2008, www.peacewomen.org/assets/file/Resources/UN/ocha_svinarmedconflictmotivations_2009.pdf. (accessed 2.6.2016).

73 Inger Skelsbæk, 'Sexual violence and war: Mapping out a complex relationship', *European Journal of International Affairs*, 7 (2001), 211–37; here 212.

74 Jonathan Gottschall, 'Explaining wartime rape', *The Journal of Sex Research*, 41 (2004), 129–36.

75 UNOCHA, 'Sexual violence in armed conflict'.

76 S. Brownmiller, *Against Our Will: Men, Women, Rape* (New York: Simon and Schuster, 1975).

77 Ruth Seifert, 'Krieg und Vergewaltigung: Ansätze einer Analyse', in A. Stiglmayer (ed.), *Massenvergewaltigungen: Krieg gegen die Frauen* (Freiburg / Br.: Kore Verlag, 1994), pp. 85–108, here p. 88; translated as R. Seifert, 'War and rape: A preliminary analysis', in A. Stiglmayer (ed.), *Mass Rape: The War Against Women in Bosnia-Herzogovina* (Lincoln: University of Nebraska Press, 1994), 54–72.

78 For details see typology of war rape: www.bicc.de/uploads/pdf/publications/other/2011/Dossier-67.pdf (accessed 17.10.2016).

79 Ruth Seifert, *War and Rape: Analytical Approaches* (London: Women's International League for Peace and Freedom, 1992).

80 Cited in Indai Lourdes Sajor, 'Our common grounds', in Indai Lourdes Sajor (ed.), *Common Grounds: Violence Against Women in War and Armed Conflict Situations* 1 (Asian Center for Women's Human Rights, 1998), pp. 24–5.

81 See also Andrea Durbach and Louise Chappell, 'Leaving behind the age of impunity: Victims of gender violence and the promise of reparations', *International Feminist Journal of Politics*, 16 (2014), 543–62.

82 UNOCHA, 'Sexual violence in armed conflict'; see also S. Bartels et al., 'Patterns of sexual violence in Eastern Democratic Republic of Congo: Reports from survivors presenting to Panzi Hospital in 2006', *Conflict and Health*, 4:9 (2010), 48–52.

83 Examples include Sierra Leone, Mali, Liberia, Uganda, the Central African Republic, Sudan, South Sudan, Somalia, but also some recruitment to militant groups in North Africa including Tunisia, Libya, and also the Middle East. See e.g. Pamela Machakanja, 'Reintegration of child soldiers: A case of Southern Sudan', in Sylvester B. Maphonsa, Laura DeLuca and Alphonse Keasley (eds), *Building Peace from Within* (Pretoria: Africa Institute of South Africa, 2014), pp. 88–90; C. Cramer and P. Richards, 'Violence and war in agrarian perspective', *Journal of Agrarian Change*, 11 (2011), 277–97; J. Munin, 'A political economic history of the Liberian State: Forced labour and armed militarization', *Journal of Agrarian Change*, 11 (2011), 357–76; Ches Thurber, 'Militias as sociopolitical

movements: Lessons from Iraq's armed Shia groups', *Small Wars & Insurgencies*, 25 (2014), 900–23; Myriam Denov, *Child Soldiers: Sierra Leone's Revolutionary United Front* (Cambridge: Cambridge University Press, 2010), chapters 1 and 4; Jens Chr. Andvig, 'Child soldiers: Reasons for variation in their rate of recruitment and standards of welfare', NUPI paper 704 (Oslo: Norwegian Institute for International Affairs, 2006).

84 Thomas De Wit, 'Sexual Violence in the Democratic Republic of Congo' (Bachelor thesis, Utrecht University, 2012), http://igitur-archive.library.uu.nl/student-theses/2012-0322-200633/Final%20paper%20DRC.pdf. (accessed 1.2.2015); Marion Pratt and Leah Werchick, 'Sexual terrorism: Rape as a weapon of war in Eastern Democratic Republic of Congo. An assessment of programmatic responses to sexual violence in North Kivu, South Kivu, Maniema, and Orientale Provinces' (USAID, 2004), http://pdf.usaid.gov/pdf_docs/Pnadk346.pdf. (accessed 20.5.2016).

85 Brian Michael Jenkins, *Building an Army of Believers* (Santa Monika: RAND, 2007), www.rand.org/content/dam/rand/pubs/testimonies/2007/RAND_CT 278-1.pdf. (accessed 11.2.2015).

86 Maleeha Aslam, *Gender-Based Explosions: The Nexus Between Muslim Masculinities, Jihadist Islamism and Terrorism* (New York: United Nations University Press, 2012), pp. 145–273.

87 Daniel Muñoz-Rojas and Jean-Jacques Frésard, 'The roots of behaviour in war: Understanding and preventing IHL violations' (ICRC Resource Center, 2005), www.icrc.org/eng/assets/files/other/irrc_853_fd_fresard_eng.pdf. (accessed 12.12.2015).

88 Elisabeth Jean Wood, 'Armed groups and sexual violence: When is wartime rape rare?', *Politics and Society*, 37 (2009), 131–62.

89 Ibid., 136.

90 United Nations Security Council, 'Women, Peace and Security', Resolution 1820 (2008) www.un.org/News/Press/docs/2008/sc9364.doc.htm. (accessed 11.2.2016).

91 UN Sub-Commission on the Promotion and Protection of Human Rights, 'Systematic rape, sexual slavery and slavery-like practices during armed conflict: Final report', submitted by Gay J. McDougall, Special Rapporteur, 22.6.1998, E/CN.4/Sub.2/1998/13, available at: www.unhcr.org/refworld/docid/3b00 f44114.html. (accessed 12.2.2015); Gay J. McDougall, 'Contemporary forms of slavery: systematic rape, sexual slavery and slavery-like practices during armed conflict' (E/CN.4/Sub.2/1998/13). Geneva, Switzerland: UN Subcommission on Prevention of Discrimination and Protection of Minorities, 22.6.1998.

92 Katrina Lee Koo, 'Confronting a disciplinary blindness: Women, war and rape in the international politics of security', *Australian Journal of Political Science*, 37 (2002), 525–36, here 528.

93 Gottschall, 'Explaining wartime rape', 131.

94 Leaning and Gingerich, *The Use of Rape as a Weapon of War*.

95 Ariel Ahram, 'Sexual and ethnic violence and the construction of the Islamic State', *Political Violence @ a Glance*, 18.9.2014, http://politicalviolenceataglance.org/2014/09/18/sexual-and-ethnic-violence-and-the-construction-of-the-islamic-state/. (accessed 11.2.2015).

96   R. Charli Carpenter, 'Surfacing children: Limitations of genocidal rape discourse', *Human Rights Quarterly*, 22 (2000), 428–77.
97   Nancy Farwell, 'War rape: New conceptualizations and responses', *Affilia* 19 (2004), 389–403; here, 395.
98   Gottschall, 'Explaining wartime rape', 131.
99   Allen, *Rape Warfare*; A. Barstow, 'Introduction', in A. Barstow (ed.), *War's Dirty Secret: Rape, Prostitution, and Other Crimes Against Women* (Cleveland, OH: The Pilgrim Press, 2000), pp. 1–12; Chung Hyun Kyung, 'Your comfort versus my death: Korean comfort women', in Barstow (ed.), *War's Dirty Secret*, pp. 13–25, here 20; C.A. MacKinnon, 'Rape, genocide, and human rights', in Stiglmayer (ed.), *Mass Rape*, pp. 183–96; T. Salzman, 'Rape camps, forced impregnation and ethnic cleansing: Religious, cultural and ethical responses to rape victims in the former Yugoslavia', in Barstow (ed.), *War's Dirty Secret*, pp. 63–92.
100 United Nations (ed.), 'Addressing conflict-related sexual violence: An analytical inventory of peacekeeping practice' (New York, 2010), www.unifem.org/attachments/products/Analytical_Inventory_of_Peacekeeping_Practice_online.pdf. (accessed 23.4.2014).
101 Brownmiller, *Against Our Will*, p. 128; Dorothy Q. Thomas and Regan E. Ralph, 'Rape in war: Challenging the tradition of impunity', *SAIS Review*, 14 (1994) 81–99; here 93.
102 Christa Paul, *Zwangsprostitution: Staatlich errichtete Bordelle im Nationalsozialismus* (Berlin: Edition Hentrich, 1994).
103 C.S. Chung, 'Korean women drafted for military sexual slavery by Japan', in H. Keith (ed.), *The Stories of the Korean Comfort Women* (New York: Cassell, 1995), pp. 11–30; here pp. 13–14; Y. Tanaka, 'Introduction', in M.R. Henson (ed.), *Comfort Woman: A Filipina's Story of Prostitution and Slavery under the Japanese Military* (Lanham, MD; Rowman & Littlefield, 1999), pp. vii–xxi. See also the Soviet reasoning that dictated a policy of strictly controlling occupation forces' conduct in occupied Austria in an attempt to present the Soviet power as a civilised and worthy partner to be trusted in the political reorganisation of post-war Europe. Barbara Stelzl-Marx, *Stalins Soldaten in Österreich: Die Innensicht der sowjetischen Besatzung 1945–1955* (Wien / München: Böhlau Verlag, 2012), p. 85.
104 Brownmiller, *Against Our Will*, pp. 13–15.
105 M.P. Ghiglieri, *The Dark Side of Man: Tracing the Origins of Male Violence* (Cambridge, MA: Perseus Books, 2000); O. Jones, 'Sex, culture, and the biology of rape: Toward explanation and prevention', *California Law Review*, 87 (1999), 821–941; R. Thornhill and C. Palmer, *A Natural History of Rape* (Cambridge, MA: MIT Press, 2000); Brownmiller, *Against Our Will*, pp. 45, 52, 55, 58; Chung, 'Korean women', 17; Tanaka, 'Introduction', xvi.
106 R. Littlewood, 'Military rape', *Anthropology Today*, 13 (1997), 7–17; Thornhill and Palmer, *A Natural History of Rape*.
107 For first analyses of these see Wood, 'Armed groups'; Dara Kay Cohen, 'Explaining rape during civil war: Cross-national evidence (1980–2009)', *American Political Science Review*, 107 (2013), 461–77; Laura Albarracin, 'Explaining the Variation of Conflict-Related Sexual Violence: A Comparative Assessment of the Colombian case' (Ph.D. thesis, Rutgers University, 2012), https://rucore.libraries.rutgers.edu/rutgers-lib/37355/. (accessed 2.2.2015).

108 Wood, 'Armed groups'; Inger Skjelsbæk, 'Conceptualizing sexual violence perpetrators', in Morten Bergmo, Alf Butenschø, Skre and Elisabeth J. Wood (eds), *Understanding and Proving International Sex Crimes* (Beijing: Torkel Opsahll Academic Publishers, 2012), pp. 495–509.
109 Ph. Ariès, *Centuries of Childhood* (Bungay: The Chaucer Press, 1962).
110 Richard Evans, *In Defence of History* (London: Granta Books, 1997), p. 63.
111 Colin Heywood, *A History of Childhood: Children and Childhood in the West from Medieval to Modern Times* (Cambridge: Polity, 2001); Lloyd de Mause (ed.), *The History of Childhood* (Ann Arbor: University of Michigan Press, 1974); Hugh Cunningham, *Children and Childhood in Western Society Since 1500* (London: Longman, 1995).
112 William J. Reese, 'The origins of progressive education', *History of Education Quarterly*, 41 (2001), 1–24; see also Dee Joy Coulter, 'Montessori and Steiner: A pattern of reverse symmetries', *Montessori Life*, 15 (2003), 24–5.
113 Edwin D. Lawson, 'Development of patriotism in children: A second look', *The Journal of Psychology*, 55 (1963), 279–86.
114 Lynn Mally, *The Culture of the Future: The Proletkult Movement in Revolutionary Russia* (Berkeley: University of California Press, 1990), p. 180.
115 Child Labor Education Project, University of Iowa, www.continuetolearn.uiowa.edu/laborctr/child_labor/about/us_history.html. (accessed 12.11.2014).
116 Lee S. Weissbach, 'Child labor legislation in nineteenth-century France', *The Journal of Economic History*, 37 (1977), 268–71.
117 *Hansard*, House of Lords, 14.7.1842, vol. 65, cc 101–24; Robert McIntosh, 'The making of modern childhood', in Robert McIntosh, *Boys in the Pits – Child Labour in the Coal Mines* (Montreal: McGill-Queens University Press, 2000), pp. 14–41; Manfred Liebel, 'Working class children as social subjects: The contribution of the working children's organisation to social transformation', *Childhood*, 10 (2003), 265–83.
118 Howard Cohen, *Equal Rights for Children* (Totowa, NJ: Rowman & Littlefield, 1980); in contrast Laura Martha Purdy, *In Their Best Interest? The Case Against Equal Rights for Children* (Ithaca: Cornell University Press, 1992).
119 League of Nations Charter, article 23; *The Avalon Project Documents in Law, History and Diplomacy*, http://avalon.law.yale.edu/20th_century/leagcov.asp. (accessed 15.2.2015).
120 Anthony Platt, *The Child Savers* (Chicago: University of Chicago Press, 1969).
121 Cited in Caroline Moorehead, *Dunant's Dream: War in Switzerland and the History of the Red Cross* (London: Harper Collins, 1998), p. 282.
122 Varindra Tarzie Vittachi, *Between the Guns: Children as a Zone of Peace* (London: Hodder and Stoughton, 1993), p. 9.
123 'Geneva Declaration of the Rights of the Child', www.un-documents.net/gdrc1924.htm. (accessed 2.3.2016).
124 Bo Viktor Nylund, 'International law and the child victim of armed conflict: Is the "first call" for children?' *The International Journal of Children's Rights*, 6 (1998), 23–53, here 23.
125 Office of the United Nations High Commissioner for Human Rights, 'Convention on the Rights of the Child', adopted and opened for signature, ratification and

accession by General Assembly resolution 44/25 of 20 November 1989 (1996), www2.ohchr.org/english/law/crc.htm. (accessed 25.9.2015).
126 'Geneva Declaration of the Rights of the Child'.
127 UN, 'The Universal Declaration of Human Rights', 1948 G.A.res. 217 (III), www.un.org/en/documents/udhr/. (accessed 2.1.2016).
128 UN, 'Declaration of the Rights of the Child', 1959. G.A. res. 1386 (XIV), 14 U.N. GAOR Supp. (no. 16) at 19, U.N. Doc. A/4354, www.humanium.org/en/childrens-rights-history/references-on-child-rights/declaration-rights-child/. (accessed 2.1.2016).
129 These are: the International Convention on the Elimination of All Forms of Racial Discrimination (entered into force 1969); the International Covenant on Civil and Political Rights (1976); the International Covenant on Economic, Social and Cultural Rights (1976); the Convention on the Elimination of All Forms of Discrimination against Women (1981); and the Convention against Torture and other Cruel, Inhuman or Degrading Treatment or Punishment (1987).
130 UN, 'International Covenant on Civil and Political Rights', www.ohchr.org/en/professionalinterest/pages/ccpr.aspx. (accessed 2.1.2016).
131 UN, 'Convention on the Prevention and Punishment of the Crime of Genocide', Article 2, adopted 9 December 1948, 78 U.N.T.S. 277, www.hrweb.org/legal/genocide.html. (accessed 16.3.2016).
132 'Optional Protocol to the CRC on the Sale of Children, Child Prostitution and Child Pornography', www.ohchr.org/EN/ProfessionalInterest/Pages/OPSCCRC.aspx. (accessed 2.1.2016).
133 'Optional Protocol to the CRC on the Involvement of Children in Armed Conflict', www.ohchr.org/EN/ProfessionalInterest/Pages/OPACCRC.aspx. (accessed 12.1.2016).
134 UNICEF, 'Rights under the Convention on the Rights of the Child' (2008), [online, last updated 7.8.2014], www.unicef.org/crc/index_30177.html. (accessed 12.11.2014).
135 'Optional Protocol to the CRC on the Involvement of Children in Armed Conflict'.
136 Harold Hongju Koh, 'How is international human rights law enforced?', Addison C. Harris Lecture, 21.1.1998, www.repository.law.indiana.edu/cgi/viewcontent.cgi?article=2279&context=ilj. (accessed 12.12.2014). See also R. Dhliwayo, 'Understanding the obligations of non-state actors in the realisation of children's rights' (IDASA Occasional Papers, March 2007), www.eldis.org/go/home&id=31310&type=Document#.VGPUg8lFvf0. (accessed 2.1.2016).

3

Children born of war during and after the Second World War

In 2006, the Allied Museum in Berlin, under the title 'It Started with a Kiss', documented a particular feature of the post-war occupation of Germany, that of German–Allied love affairs after 1945.[1] The aim of the exhibition and its trilingual (German/English/French) catalogue was to zoom in on a previously largely untold story of the way in which a multitude of liaisons between American, French and British soldiers and local German women developed despite adverse political circumstances in which occupiers were keen to prevent close contacts with the former enemy that had been defeated unconditionally and – as propaganda made very clear – was not trusted, even when it presented itself in the form of young and seemingly innocent women.

Not long after, in 2008, *Anonyma: Eine Frau in Berlin*,[2] a film based on an anonymously published diary of a Berlin women, dealt with a very different manifestation of intimate contact between occupying soldiers and local women by addressing the mass rapes of German women in the final days of the war. The author had recorded her experiences during eight weeks of the 'liberation' of Berlin, starting from 20 April 1945. After repeatedly being gang-raped she singled out a high-ranking Soviet officer, to whom she made herself available in return for protection and food. When her husband returned from the war in early June 1945, she confessed and let him read parts of the diary. His reaction was one of contempt; he accused her and her friends and acquaintances who had acted similarly of being 'shameless bitches', and he left her.[3] The story of the diary itself and its public perception within Germany and beyond throw light on the ambivalent approach of Germany's coming to terms with those well-known mass rapes in the post-war period. First published in German in 1959,[4] the book 'sank without trace' as it appeared at a time when Germany had chosen to deal with its past in the form of 'collective silence'.[5] If the publication raised any eyebrows then, it was not because of the truthful brutality with which it recounted the fate of numerous Berlin women in the transition from wartime to post-war Germany. Instead, it was the women's choices in trying to negotiate survival,[6] the fact that they attempted to take some control over their circumstances, when the author proclaimed: 'From now on I will decide who gets me', which led to her being accused of 'besmirching the honour of the German women'.[7] As one reviewer rightly explains, the reason for the rejection of the book was less the subject matter itself, but her dealing with it. Her confession of agency, her damning picture of German men in the face of the rape campaigns, her differentiated view of the Red Army and the links with German atrocities on the Eastern Front did not fit into the developing German post-war identity.[8]

When the memoir was finally republished in 2003, two years after the author's death and still anonymously,[9] the reaction could hardly have been more different. The book occupied a place on the German bestseller lists for over four months, and was followed by an English-language edition in 2005 and the above-mentioned widely acclaimed film adaptation in 2008.[10]

The two different examples above, the exhibition and the diary/film, demonstrate several important aspects of the complex military–civilian relations in the twentieth and twenty-first centuries. As already indicated, they confirm that the quality of such relations, even within a single conflict, could differ dramatically. Yet, despite vulnerabilities, women have agency, and – within the confines of the often exploitative and potentially dangerous circumstances, they make choices and suffer the consequences. The two examples also exemplify that, in the case of the Second World War, not only do we have valuable sources that allow insights into the relations between soldiers and local women beyond the anecdotal; what is more, these sources are now shared widely. Where the topic may have been a taboo or where political expediency may have prevented debates in the past, there is now room for discourse, in academia, the media and the public. However, as both film and exhibition also show, while the experiences of the women and occasionally also the soldiers have found their way into the public domain and are being debated, children born out of these intimate relations between foreign soldiers and local women feature at best as an aside or footnote, but have rarely occupied a place centre-stage.

Partly in response to the lack of sources, academic interest in pre-Second World War relations between soldiers and local women has been sporadic and limited to a few very specific questions. Apart from some studies dealing with particular aspects of soldiers' conduct during the First World War[11] and mixed-race children fathered by non-White soldiers,[12] academic works have largely been limited to explorations of the links between soldiers' behaviour and questions of social hygiene, thus in effect mirroring the only point of entry for military engagement with this topic.[13]

While there is continued pre-occupation with the question of venereal disease (VD) control also for conflicts beyond the First World War, the Second World War is the first conflict for which not only a wealth of sources relating to military–civilian relations exists, but also reliable data for groups of children fathered by foreign soldiers. This data will serve as a starting point for an exploration of the life courses of children born of the Second World War and their mothers in post-war societies. This will include an overview of the frequently exploitative and violent military–civilian relations throughout the Second World War in different theatres of war and in various phases of the conflict. The exposition will show that violence was perpetrated by soldiers against the civilian population, but also by irregular forces; furthermore, sexual violence occurred in the form of outright rape, but also forced prostitution in occupied territories, as well as in brothels, mostly notably in the military brothels such as the notorious *Wehrmachtsbordelle*[14] and among the so-called 'Comfort Women' in Japan.[15]

The following discussion will be divided into four parts. The first section will explore relations between soldiers and local women across different, mainly European, theatres of war, the distinct policies of military and political decision makers in attempting to regulate such relations and their attitudes towards potential offspring. The second section will investigate the policies vis-à-vis CBOW and their life courses and experiences in response to both the circumstances of their conception and the geopolitical situation of their post-conflict receptor communities. The third section will address the Allied post-war occupations of Germany and Austria and the experiences of children fathered by Allied soldiers. The final part will explore in more detail – on the basis of recent scholarship, autobiographical accounts and quantitative and qualitative surveys – the assessment of CBOW themselves. Drawing on their own voices, their subjective experiences will complement other data of less personal character and will throw a different light on the post-conflict experiences as children of the enemy or at least as children of foreigners.

The historical-comparative approach of analysing different theatres of war and post-war societies does not allow an exhaustive or fully comprehensive account. Many groups of CBOW are missing from the exposition. The war in the Pacific has largely been excluded, as has the post-war occupation of Japan.[16] Similarly, the significant phenomenon of children of (foreign) forced labourers and Prisoners of War and the specific group of Jewish CBOW have not been analysed separately. Yet, while not comprehensive and complete in all its facets, the comparative synthesis serves as an illustration of the varied phenomenon of gendered military–civilian relations throughout the Second World War, their changing qualities and their use in support of military and political tactics and strategies. This will demonstrate how pervasive an issue that of intimate relations between soldiers and local women was almost everywhere and, as a result, that the consequences arising from the various scenarios for the CBOW deserve closer attention.

Violent conception and brutal policies: CBOW and their fate throughout the war

Conflict-related sexual violence (CRSV) was not the only context of wartime conception of children fathered by enemy or foreign soldiers, but it was a very significant one. The most widely known example of sexual violence during the Second World War was the mass rape by the Red Army in the closing days of the war.[17] As has been pointed out in the literature, this outburst of seemingly unprecedented violence of the Soviet soldiers moving westwards and 'liberating' Germany from the Nazis cannot be understood without acknowledgement of the brutalisation that had occurred throughout the war, and in particular the war at the Eastern Front.[18] It is therefore appropriate to commence the discussion with an analysis of the conduct of the Germans in the process of various occupations throughout the war, before looking at different cases of Allied occupations before, during and after the hostilities they were engaged in. Beginning with – according to Nazi racial pseudo theory – the two diametrically opposed cases of Eastern Europe and Norway, the discourse will then move on to other European countries and here particularly France and the Netherlands, before exploring the cases of some children born of the Second World War beyond Europe.

Eastern Europe

Although intimate relations between soldiers and local women in almost all conflicts will span across the whole spectrum, from consensual love affairs to exploitation and rape, there is little doubt that in many scenarios throughout the Second World War, such relations were based on clear power relations, fear and dire need on the part of the women, and all too frequently on outright coercion. In the immediate aftermath of the war, militaries and war crimes tribunals preferred to portray perpetrators of sexual violence as deviant individuals whose behaviour was out of character for the otherwise honourable armies.[19] This picture has had to be revised substantially after research in the 1990s demonstrated unambiguously that CRSV was widespread across all theatres of war and, while the practice was not always ordered for military strategic purposes, it was often tolerated and sometimes encouraged.[20]

Greater acceptance of violence and a lowering of the threshold of what level of violence is morally acceptable are common in armed conflict, but there is little doubt that the Eastern Front 'differed profoundly'[21] from other war theatres with regard to the conduct of war. This was true also with regard to the treatment of civilians and specifically with regard to violence towards women. In Eastern Europe, German gender-based atrocities were driven by two additional factors compared with those more generally observed in armed conflict. Firstly the distinct racial undertones of the war against the Soviet Union resulted in tacit and explicit acceptance of maltreatment of 'non-Aryans' and made inhumane treatment of enemies who had been degraded in racial terms as *Untermenschen* (subhumans) more justifiable. Secondly the extreme conditions of warfare and the strong Soviet resistance encountered in the initial phase of the conflict led to extreme stress, plummeting morale and subsequently excessively violent actions and reactions on the part of the *Wehrmacht* when encountering the 'civilian face of the hated enemy'.

Alongside most other aspects of life, sexuality was highly regimented in the Third Reich to suit the political and ideological tenets of the Nazi regime. This resulted in the bizarre combination of an unashamedly pronatalist policy aimed at increasing the birth rate of Aryan families in Germany[22] while viciously prosecuting any fraternisation of Aryans with what the Nazis regarded as 'racially inferior stock'. This included the prohibition of illicit liaisons between foreign workers, forced labourers or prisoners of war (POWs) and German women at home, as well as the sexual fraternisation of German soldiers with local non-Aryan women in the East.[23] A clear sign of the inability to limit sexual contact between the German soldiers and Eastern women was the Reich's effort to serve the perceived sexual needs of their soldiers by sending *Einsatzfrauen*, travelling brothels, ideally staffed by 'racially suitable' volunteers who were to provide for the 'sexual needs' of the *Wehrmacht* soldiers. The policy did little to curb sexual violence for two reasons. Firstly, as has been shown convincingly, demand for sexual services far outstripped supply and plenty of evidence suggests a high level of sexualised violence vis-à-vis local Eastern European women wherever the soldiers went.[24] Secondly, although the majority of home-recruited *Einsatzfrauen* were sent to the East, a severe shortage of suitable volunteers meant that voluntary recruitment was soon replaced by forced prostitution of local women.[25] This may have curbed excessive violence against civilians in some locations, but in effect it replaced one kind of gender-based violence (GBV) with another. Random rapes of civilians were substituted with forced and often violent prostitution, especially in cases where local women were given the choice between forced labour and life in a brothel.[26] In addition, it has to be emphasised that the boundaries between voluntary and forced prostitution in Eastern Europe were even more fluid than in other war-affected areas, because of the dire food situation. As one German soldier put it bluntly more than half a century later: 'Where I was stationed, I believe, there were no rapes. Because of the hunger in the population this was not necessary ... If the women wanted to survive, they had to prostitute themselves.'[27]

Violent or not, intimate encounters between soldiers and the local civilian population were frequent, and the military and political leadership were well aware of this fact. What is more, Nazi policies relating to fraternisation during the occupation of Eastern Europe demonstrate a clear recognition in politically influential circles that such fraternisation would have unintended consequences of German-fathered offspring. Given the near obsession of Nazi ideology with racially driven population policies, it is not surprising that the topic of the children of the occupation preoccupied political minds to a much greater extent than was the case in other theatres of war or occupation, except perhaps Norway, which will be discussed below. Without analysing in detail the very complex web of decisions concerning these children between 1942 and 1945 – discussions which were never driven by concern for the individuals involved, least of all the children – it is important to summarise some key features of a policy that seemed at best contradictory.

In the early phases of the war against the Soviet Union, entirely inflated estimates muted among high-ranking SS officials, of hundreds of thousands, if not millions of babies being fathered during the *Wehrmacht's* occupation of Eastern Europe[28] led to a flurry of activity in an attempt to formulate a policy of how to deal with such children.[29] On the one hand they were – by and large – deemed 'unerwünscht' (unwanted) on racial grounds. Eastern Europeans, in accordance with the racial redefinitions of 1942,[30] were classed as 'artverwandt aber stammesfremd' (of a related race but of foreign breed), and thus were deemed undesirable. On the other hand, they presented an opportunity of balancing the population shortfalls that had resulted from the war in general and the war against the Soviet Union in particular.[31] The perceived difficulty of dealing with potentially large numbers of children of German/Slavic origin is evident in the contradictory polices of the Reich, which included, at one extreme, compulsory abortions and forced sterilisation among Eastern European forced labourers[32] and in German-occupied Eastern Europe,[33] and at the other extreme the positive selection, repatriation and 'resocialisation of racially valuable' mixed-race children into German society in an attempt to 'utilise' the paternal German blood that might otherwise 'strengthen the Slavic race'. These conflicting policies, rooted in the inherent contradiction of two mutually exclusive aims of racial purity and maximisation of birth rates, resulted in compromises. Himmler himself verbalised those concessions when he acknowledged that he had to accept compromises between 'notwendiger Quantität und bestmöglicher Qualität' (necessary quantity and best possible quality) of his soldiers' offspring.[34] Interesting in our context are two aspects: firstly, the internal debates themselves about the fate of children, which will be analysed in more detail below; and secondly the fact that the children (and their usefulness to the fatherland) were defined through their racial parentage alone. This, too, happened in an inconsistent manner: depending on the necessity of the political argument to be advocated, *either* the paternal *or* the maternal blood line was taken into account; similarly, depending on which argument was supported more effectively, *either* the German *or* the Slavic heritage was considered. In other words, depending on what was politically and ideologically expedient, one particular side of a child's provenance would be emphasised and the other side overlooked. As will become clear, this approach to CBOW in conflict and post-conflict societies is far from unique. While the National Socialists took such views to an extreme, in that often the mere survival of the children depended on which view was taken about the relative balance of their biological make-up, almost all conflict and post-conflict integration of CBOW is affected by national, regional or local perceptions of the 'merits' or otherwise of their parentage.

Norway

In Eastern Europe, Germanisation with ambitious migration and resettlement programmes, but also with active interest and intervention in the fate of the *Wehrmachtskinder*,[35] was driven by the racial restructuring motto: 'Auslese und Ausmerze' (selection and extermination). In contrast, so-called racial hygiene considerations led to entirely different conclusions in the case of children of *Wehrmacht* soldiers in other occupied countries, most notably Norway, but also the Netherlands, Belgium, France and the British Channel Islands. The fate of the *Wehrmachtskinder* in Norway in particular is inextricably linked with the SS organisation tasked with furthering the birth of Aryan children, the *Lebensborn e.V.*[36] This deserves specific attention.

Lebensborn

Lebensborn e.V. was a racially motivated programme, initiated by Heinrich Himmler, the leader of the SS. It was aimed at reversing the declining birth rates by providing maternity homes and financial assistance for wives of SS members, by running orphanages and by relocating 'racially valuable children'. As such, while not being the breeding programme as which it was portrayed after the end of the Second World War,[37] it was clearly an instrument used to implement racial and population policies of the National Socialists. Beneficiaries were chosen in line with eugenic policies of the Third Reich, and only 'biologically fit' and 'racially pure' parents were selected. The *Lebensborn* had the explicit purpose of promoting the growth of the 'superior Aryian' population of the German Reich. The pronatalist aspects of the programme were complemented by an even more sinister element of Germanisation and population policy in the form of the kidnapping of thousands of North Eastern European children (mainly from Poland) and their forced relocation to Germany with subsequent adoption into German families. Although the Nuremberg Trials found no evidence of the *Lebensborn*'s involvement in the actual kidnapping,[38] the use of *Lebensborn* homes as temporary placement for the younger children prior to adoption demonstrates the significant role of the organisation in the implementation of Nazi racial policies.

Lebensborn was established in December 1935 as an organisation with three main goals: the support of 'rassisch und erbbiologisch wertvolle' (racially genetically valuable) families with many children; the housing of and caring for pregnant mothers-to-be who were expected to bear racially and genetically valuable children; the care for these children and the support of their mothers.[39] Initially *Lebensborn* served as a welfare organisation for families of the SS and provided maternity care and childcare for married and unmarried mothers and their children whose fathers were deemed to be 'racially valuable'. During the war the organisation's geographical focus moved from Germany to some of the occupied countries, most notably Norway and Poland but also Austria, France, Denmark, Belgium, Luxemburg and the Netherlands.[40] The details of the implementation of *Lebensborn* ideas outside Germany have been described in detail elsewhere.[41] Here only some details of significance for the fate of CBOW, mainly children fathered by members of the SS and the *Wehrmacht*, and born to local mothers, will be discussed.

According to National Socialist racial policies, most of the Norwegian population belonged to the so-called Nordic race and was regarded as being genuinely Aryan. As a corollary, relations between Norwegians and Germans were favoured as the offspring was considered particularly 'racially valuable'. A logical consequence was that the activities of the *Lebensborn* would be expanded to include Norway after its invasion. Only weeks after the start of the German occupation of Norway, in March 1941, the Norwegian *Lebensborn* was established, and by the end of the war the *Lebensborn* operated nine homes throughout Norway with more than 6000 registered births in the homes and the overall number of children fathered by German soldiers and born to local mothers estimated at around 12,000.[42] The Norwegian homes, under the auspices of nurses, midwives and army doctors, saw the second highest number of births of all *Lebensborn* homes second only to the Germany Reich.[43] Many of the *Wehrmachtskinder* in general and the *Lebensbornkinder* in particular have spoken out about their experiences in recent years; thus the topic which had been a taboo for them, their families and indeed also the nations in which they eventually settled, has found public and academic recognition.[44]

Occupations of other European countries

Though nowhere as prominent as in Norway, race and population policies were also a significant consideration in the other occupied countries of Northern and Western Europe. Here, too, offspring fathered by German occupiers, the regular forces, the military or civilian administration or the police forces, and born to local mothers, was of some interest to the Nazi leadership. Children were perceived as racially desirable or at least acceptable to fill the gap in the unfavourable population statistics of the Reich.

Therefore, as early as 1941 the Supreme Command of the Armed Forces, the *Oberkommando der Wehrmacht*, suggested that mothers and their children should be given the opportunity to claim alimony and, rather different to other national militaries then and now, it was also considered to have military courts adjudicate possible paternity and alimony disputes.[45] However, Hitler himself ruled that the plans should only be applied to Norway and the Netherlands, which were, in his assessment, of racial, political and eugenic interest to the German Reich, whereas other countries, most notably France, were of lesser value.[46] This evaluation found expression, a year later, in guidelines published about the care of children of *Wehrmacht* soldiers in Norway and the Netherlands.⁴⁷ The 'Verordnung über die Betreuung von Kindern deutscher Wehrmachtssangehöriger in den besetzen Gebieten in Norwegen und den Niederlanden' (Decree about the care of children of members of the German *Wehrmacht* in the occupied territories in Norway and the Netherlands) was aimed at the 'Erhaltung und Förderung rassisch wertvollen germanischen Erbgutes' (preservation and promotion of racially valuable Germanic heritage).⁴⁸ In order to secure the care of such mothers and their children, the *Lebensborn e.V.* and also the *Nationalisozialistische Volkswohlfahrt* (National Socialist People's Welfare organisation, NSV) became active beyond the German borders not only in Norway, as indicated above, but also in the Netherlands. Stigmatisation experienced by Dutch girls who had relations with German soldiers was rife, as – from the very beginning of the occupation – they were branded as socially deviant and unpatriotic.⁴⁹ In March 1941, in response to such stigmatisation, the *Generalkommissar zur besonderen Verwendung*, Schmidt, instructed the NSV to provide childbirth clinics for the expectant unmarried mothers, and in February 1942 the first such clinic was opened in Amsterdam.⁵⁰ *Wehrmacht* policy regarding the relationship of German soldiers with Dutch women, directed by Berlin, was ambivalent throughout. On the one hand, fear of espionage and the ever-present threat of VD resulted in a ban of personal friendship and intimate relations; on the other hand soldiers were permitted, if not encouraged, to procreate.⁵¹ Just as Norway, the Netherlands were covered by the special *Führererlaß* of 28 July 1942, which required the *Reichskommissar* to take 'measures to guarantee special care and attention, at the request of the Norwegian and Netherlandish mothers, for their children parented by members of the *Wehrmacht*'.⁵²

France

In contrast to Norway and the Netherlands, Hitler turned down the proposal by the *Oberkommando der Wehrmacht* to include Belgium, France and the Channel Islands in the special provision for *Wehrmacht* children, stating that from the racial point of view he was simply 'not interested'.⁵³ Yet, throughout the Second World War thousands of children were fathered by German soldiers and born to local mothers, partly as a result of racially motivated policies following the defeat of France⁵⁴ and partly as a result of liaisons between German soldiers and French women outside the politicised sphere of Nazi eugenics.⁵⁵

Leaving aside the deliberate Nazi policy of Germanisation, the realities in the defeated and divided France meant that for many women the situation was dire and survival prostitution was rife. Since the fall of France, 1.6 million French men had been or still were prisoners in Germany, and about half of them were married. Living conditions for their wives left behind were very difficult. As Secretary of State for Health and Family Jacques Chevalier put it in a letter to the Vice President of the *Conseil*, 'the POW's family is condemned ... to looking for non-existent resources. Family allowances are so low that we see a significant development of prostitution on the part of the women and minors in the countryside as well as in the city, in addition to numerous births or expected births in the occupied and even unoccupied zones, of children fathered by Germans'.[56]

Very different principles guided the dealings with the issue of intimate relations between French women and German soldiers in both occupied France and Vichy respectively, largely reflecting the different potential problems associated with such intimacy. While the French, particularly in Vichy France, feared unwanted children, the German military feared VD. As a result, in occupied France, Germany concentrated on preventing the spread of VD by controlling sexual practice; in contrast, the collaborationist Vichy regime never attempted to restrict horizontal collaboration with German soldiers, and the regime's conservative and pro-natalist stances determined policies.

Thus, the German occupiers in the north and west of the country quickly introduced a system of tightly controlled and officially sanctioned prostitution in brothels,[57] while at the same time prosecuting uncontrolled 'free' prostitution.[58] As early as July 1940, the establishment of brothels was ordered, and a large number of existing ones, especially those meeting the hygiene requirements of the German military were requisitioned by the *Wehrmacht*. In addition, numerous new establishments were opened, much to the chagrin of some medical officers, who bemoaned the fact that the running of brothels bound the medical staff needed elsewhere and signalled a relaxed attitude towards prostitution that actually encouraged 'wild prostitution' too.[59]

Control of prostitution lay with the army medical staff; in other words, military personnel operated in an administrative function dealing with the civilian population. They supervised *Wehrmacht* brothels, were involved in the recruitment of prostitutes, and they initiated the prosecution of suspected prostitutes outside the military-controlled system.[60] When the policing duties of the military administration were taken up by the SS in the spring of 1942, the *Reichssicherheitshauptamt* took some interest in the French *Wehrmachtsbordelle*, but overall responsibility rested with the medical staff. The prosecution of *filles soumises*, prostitutes working outside the officially sanctioned system, was increasingly handled by the French police, a particular feature due to the different administrative arrangement of the occupation of France.[61] By late 1941, the *Wehrmacht* had established a total of 143 brothels in the military administration A, about one third of the German-occupied Northern zone, with 1,166 women working in these establishments. A report of one of the medical officers in the administrative area B in September 1940 reinforces the impression of the *Wehrmacht* moving swiftly and comprehensively in the formation of their military brothel system. It details that brothels for soldiers had been established in almost all towns and were being supervised closely. Furthermore, in Biarritz, Bordeaux, La Rochelle, Nantes, Angers, Vannes, La Baule and Lorient *Absteigehotels* (brothels for officers) had been created and the prosecution of free prostitution by French vice squad had successfully been introduced.[62]

Another feature of the French brothel system was the link with internment camps. Women from these camps, often selected on racial grounds, were recruited for the brothel work, formally consensually and upon application of the interned. As this work presented the only reasonable hope of being released from the camp, the voluntary nature of the arrangement, however, has rightly been questioned.[63]

Although the Vichy regime had to follow the German model of regulating prostitution by effectively legalising brothels and limiting prostitutions to these establishments,[64] Vichy France did not attempt to limit contact between German soldiers and French women *per se*. Faithful to their motto: *travail, famille et patrie* the government operated a strictly pronatalist policy, evident in its discouragement of female employment,[65] its attempts to make divorce more difficult and to prosecute abortion more forcefully.[66] However, the regime was concerned about the impact of liaisons between local women and German soldiers. It was recognised that survival prostitution could be perceived as a symptom of failure of Vichy's policy of collaboration. With many of the women wives of POWs, the perceived need of many to engage in prostitution for survival drew attention to the fact that collaboration had failed to bring the soldiers home to France. Not only that, Vichy had failed to provide for the soldiers' wives adequately.[67]

Attempts to limit unregulated intimacy between French women and German soldiers were not as successful as the authorities on both sides had hoped. In Vichy, in particular, the number of children born out of such liaisons was significant. With both contraception and abortion illegal, it was difficult for women to avoid pregnancy. Although no exact figures are known, estimates reasonably speak of tens of thousands of German-fathered babies born during the occupation in France with the upper limit around 200,000.[68]

As indicated above, the Nazis viewed any children born to a German parent in reference to their alleged racial worth. While France did not count among the racially superior Germanic race and as such was not a prime focus of Nazi racially motivated population policies, strategies in occupied France still included significant elements of both racial and population considerations. Although many policies envisaged by the Nazis with regard to the Germanisation of Western Europe were never carried out, it becomes clear from the contemporary sources that their approach vis-à-vis the local population in France was no less utilitarian than in Eastern Europe. In 1942, Hitler in one of his table talks proposed 'syphoning off' the children of the most racially valuable 'Germanic' French population at a young age to help them forget their French heritage and instead assimilate their Germanic qualities.[69] Himmler went as far as calculating the damage that would be done to France if up to one thousand children per annum were moved out of France for this purpose.[70] However, more significant in our context, the fate of the *Wehrmachtskinder* occupied the minds of the Nazi planners, not least because of their potential in the Germanisation process of France and the role these children could play in repopulating Germany after its war-induced population losses. In May 1942 it was estimated that 50,000 children with German soldier fathers had been born to French mothers;[71] by October 1943 the number was estimated to have risen to 85,000.[72] The National Socialist authorities argued that these 'were no less racially valuable' than those of Norwegian mothers. Due to the care they received in France by a widow of a French general, they were 'lost' for Germany and therefore the *Lebensborn* ought to engage 'more energetically' in their care.[73] As a result of these internal considerations, as well as a growing sense of urgency in the face of the worsening military situation, it was decided not only to admit mothers of children of German soldiers to the *Lebensborn* home but also to relocate to Germany children of German soldiers and their mothers.[74] The military administration in Paris had little interest in the Nazi population policies and it left *Lebensborn* to set up its first and only maternity home Westland.[75] However, the home, as the *Lebensborn* activities in France more generally, remained insignificant, as the military developments in late 1944 overtook events.

The Netherlands

On the surface, many similarities existed in the enactment of the Nazi occupation regimes in Norway and the Netherlands – in both countries a civilian administration had been established during the occupation by the German *Wehrmacht*, and in both countries the SS had a foothold under a *Höherer SS- und Polizeiführer*. Yet, the implementation of racial and population policies, and here in particular the engagement of the *Lebensborn*, varied significantly.[76] This was due, not least, to the different views of various high-ranking officials about the relative virtues of the involvement of the *Lebensborn* and the more general Nazi welfare organisation, the NSV.[77] The first and only Dutch *Lebensborn* maternity home, Gelderland, though planned for several years, was never opened, as military developments overtook occupation planning. However, whether or not sanctioned by the occupation regime, the so-called horizontal collaboration was clearly a wide-spread phenomenon. Statistics are not available, and the exact number of Dutch women who had relationships with German soldiers is known no more accurately than the number of children fathered by *Wehrmacht* soldiers. On the basis of NSV figures of children cared for by the NSV, a reasonable estimate is that between 8,000 and 10,000 children were fathered by German soldiers between 1940 and 1945, a figure that accounts for around half of all illegitimate births in the Netherlands during that period.[78]

As discussed above for the Norwegian and French cases, Dutch women who had had relationships with German soldiers were negatively stereotyped; the terms frequently used to describe them, *Moffenhoeren* or *Moffenmeiden*, connected the negative associations of the loathing of the enemy (Moffen – Germans) with the detestation of the socially unacceptable behaviour often associated with the women, namely that of prostitution (hoeren – whores). In addition, explicit and implicit references linked those women to lower socio-economic milieus that implied a willingness to sacrifice national solidarity and honour for personal (financial) gain.[79] As such, *Moffenmeiden*, judged to be displaying socially deviant behaviour, within the then often employed eugenic paradigms, were viewed as intellectually and morally inferior. This assessment, as will be discussed below, had a significant impact on the situation of their children, who were deemed equally culpable by association, if not by inheritance. Thus, *Moffenhoeren*, almost by definition, were seen as a phenomenon confined to prostitutes. This view was further reinforced by post-war academic and popular assessments, most notably an inquiry into youth crime during the occupation which described and characterised 'socially degenerate behaviour' of women who had relations with German soldiers.[80]

Beyond Europe: children of 'comfort women'

The focus of this chapter has been on military–civilian relations in different European theatres of war. However, one of the most abhorrent example of state-sponsored sexual slavery occurred outside Europe: the so-called 'comfort stations' which forcibly recruited 'comfort women' to provide sexual services to the Japanese Imperial Army. Despite the fact that our knowledge relating to children born to these women is limited, if not to say non-existent, no account of GBV during the Second World War should ignore their history; however, due to the inadequate source base, the analysis of the CBOW in this context will be limited to explaining what we do not know rather than what is understood.

After an acrimonious debate about military prostitution and the role played by the wartime Japanese state and military from the late 1980s onwards,[81] in the last two decades the story of the so-called 'comfort women' has been thoroughly researched and published in great detail and will only briefly be summarised here.[82] Despite this significant scholarship, the topic remains controversial, and recent years have seen a marked growth of revisionist voices in Japan who not only question the accuracy of claims about Japanese wartime atrocities, but also claims of international scholarship relating to the 'comfort station' system.[83] The euphemistically named 'comfort women' were women and girls who were forcefully recruited into sexual slavery by the Japanese Imperial Army before and during the Second World War. An estimated 200,000 women[84] were forced to work as prostitutes, with the majority being recruited from Korea and China, but also from the Philippines, Taiwan, Burma, Indonesia, Vietnam, Thailand, Malaysia and East Timor, with a small number of women of Australian and European origin.

Licensed military brothels linked to the Imperial Army had existed from around 1932 onwards. After the Japanese ransacking of the Chinese city of Nanjing, which became known as the 'Rape of Nanjing'[85] because of the extensive and brutal sexual violence committed by Japanese troops, an expansion of these 'comfort stations' was ordered to avoid a repeat of such atrocities.

The rapes had an adverse impact on relations with local populations under Japanese occupation and thus had the potential to stimulate resistance.[86] Furthermore, the limitation of the troops' sexual contact to selected and medically supervised women had the additional advantage of controlling VD more effectively with the obvious economies on medical expenses and the reduction of attendant loss of manpower. Finally, the fact that the majority of women had been taken from foreign countries and frequently could not communicate in Japanese, minimised the danger of espionage.[87]

Extensive accounts of the maltreatment of the young women have provided a comprehensive picture of the horrors experienced by many of them. However, one aspect is missing almost entirely from the extensive documentary material: that of the children born to the 'comfort women'. Although numerous reports talk about 'injections to prevent pregnancies' and although the military prescribed use of condoms as compulsory,[88] few soldiers, and especially few officers,[89] obliged. As a result, pregnancies – though clearly undesirable – were common. Many women reported that they were forced to have abortions; some women, however, recounted that they carried their babies to term or suffered stillbirths. If a woman gave birth, the baby always appears to have been removed from the women immediately afterwards.[90] Although the picture that emerges from the sources is that of consistent disregard for the women's welfare, of no regard for physical or mental health needs of either woman or child, so far we know nothing of the policies vis-à-vis the children. Did they survive? If so, who cared for them?[91] What, if anything, were they told about their background? Did any find out about their biological heritage? This remains an entirely blank part on the canvas of twentieth-century CBOW to 'comfort women'.

Life courses of CBOW: data and their interpretation

Knowledge about CBOW globally is extremely patchy, with considerable variation in the quantity and quality of evidence accessible. Amidst twentieth-century conflicts, sources on the Second World War are the most extensive. Among all the groups of children born to foreign soldiers and local mothers, the sub-group for which the largest amount of reliable data exists is that born to Norwegian mothers, with some reliable sources also available for Danish and to some extent French children fathered by German *Wehrmacht* soldiers during the Second World War.

Analyses of register data of the estimated 10,000–12,000 children fathered by German soldiers clearly point to poorer health (physical and mental), lower levels of education, lower income and higher suicide rates, than other Norwegians from the same age cohort.[92] Furthermore, surveys suggest that children were viewed and treated differently compared with their age-peers by both the government and other public organisations after the war.[93] Often due to their provenance as children of German fathers – and by implication compromised mothers – they were considered enemies who could become a threat to Norway in future. Children were taken away from their mothers, laws were adopted to exclude these children from child benefits; mothers who had married Germans lost their Norwegian citizenship; and the government even offered the children to an Australian delegation looking for labour force. Qualitative interviews indicate that many of the children were exposed to discrimination and stigmatisation both in family and community.[94] Numerous accounts of affected children in their adulthood testify that many grew up in an environment where knowledge of their biological background was withheld from them. Their mothers and other family members constructed a network of lies and half-truths and an environment of secrecy about the child's origin. For many, the topic implicitly or explicitly became a taboo. Often children learned about their background at school or from neighbours, and others learned about their fathers as adults by coincidence.

These patterns are not unusual, as will become evident in the discussions of different cases across time and space. A survey of Norwegian, Danish and Dutch children of *Wehrmacht* fathers allows a glimpse at the impact of their parentage on physical and mental health and life course experiences. With comparatively high incidences of physical and emotional bullying, name-calling and frequent insults based on being the son or daughter of a German, the study points to a very significant impact of parentage on the lives of CBOW.[95] While no similar quantitative and qualitative data exist for CBOW during the Second World War elsewhere, other evidence suggests that experiences may have been similar. For instance, Jean-Paul Picaper and Ludwig Norz, in their book *Enfants maudits*,[96] on the basis of a very different evidence base, opened up the related wide debate about the children of German occupation soldiers in France. Though journalistic rather than primarily academic in their approach, Norz and Picaper shed light on one of the last taboos of the Second World War in France, the *enfants maudits*. Based on interviews with those children of the occupation, the analysis demonstrates how they, too, were treated as pariah by the local communities and often rejected by their own families. The condemnation of their mothers' 'horizontal collaboration with the enemy' was transferred onto the children – an estimated 200,000 according to Norz and Picaper. Apart from the shame they allegedly brought to their family and the resulting discrimination suffered by many, the overriding impression left by many children of the occupation is the identity crisis experienced because they never knew or met their fathers. This is a recurring theme that has been described by many CBOW across the decades and in different geographical contexts. The *enfants maudits* were taken up as an academic research topic by Fabrice Virgili who, after his earlier study of the women who had been punished as horizontal collaborators,[97] went on to produce a detailed academic study of the 'children of the enemy' in France.[98] While there is little evidence of any systematic ostracisation on the part of the French authorities, many of Virgili's findings confirm the general impression already obtained in studies of other CBOW, namely the prevalence of stigmatisation, the rejection by the children's mothers and families, the non-acceptance on the part of the local communities, leaving the children with a feeling that 'their crime was being born'. It was at the level of personal relations – within the neighbourhood, family or local community – rather than at institutional level that the anti-Germanism found expression in stigmatisation and punishment of the 'traitor-mother' and later their children, the 'naître ennemi'.

Little systematic analysis has been done beyond Norway and to some extent France and Denmark, and little is known about the fates and life courses of many of the children born of the Second World War and their families, with research on many geographical areas only recently having started. Preliminary findings, however, indicate many similarities to the cases of Norway, Denmark and France. An initial Dutch case study establishes a clear link between the stigmatisation experienced by Dutch women who had relationships with German soldiers and the discrimination against the 12,000–15,000 children born of these liaisons.[99] The subtitle of a recent study, 'Een verborgen leven'[100] (a hidden life) indicates the core issue for many of the children. In the Netherlands, too, mothers often chose to hide the identity of the fathers of their children from their environment and from the children themselves, and as a result many Dutch *Wehrmachtskinder* only learnt about their biological origins in adulthood. The psychological effects of the identity crises suffered by many of those children are similar to the experiences known from the Norwegian and Danish analyses.[101]

As in the other European countries occupied by the German *Wehrmacht*, Belgium was home to many children fathered by German soldiers during the country's wartime occupation. Conservative estimates put the figure at approximately 20,000 children.[102] Belgium's division into three distinct areas – Flanders, Walloon and the German-speaking territory – resulted in German policies vis-à-vis the local population showing distinct variations. This also affected the way local woman who had relationships with German soldiers were viewed – and by implication also the way their children, fathered by *Wehrmacht* soldiers were received locally. In German-speaking areas, German matrimonial laws were applied. In Flanders women were generally considered Aryan by the German authorities and therefore contact between Germans and Flemish women was encouraged.[103] Furthermore, mothers of children born of *Wehrmacht* soldiers (and subsequently their children, too) were supported, not least through the *Lebensborn e.V.* As described above for other countries, the Nazi approach to children of the *Wehrmacht* soldiers in Belgium was based on strictly racial criteria. The primary purpose of the care system established through the *Lebensborn* in Belgium, as elsewhere, was guided by the wish to 'preserve Germanic stock' for Germany rather than strengthening the Belgium people.[104] As a result, *Lebensborn* operated a maternity home 'Ardennen' there and it was even considered (but not implemented) to grant the children automatic German citizenship.[105] In contrast,

Walloon women (and by implication children born of Walloon mothers) were considered racially inferior and were thus not supported in the same way. If gaps in our knowledge about life courses and experiences of French and Dutch CBOW were described above, even less information about the experiences of the Belgian CBOW has been uncovered.

Another geographical area for which research is only in its early stages is Greece. The number of children born to Greek women and fathered by German soldiers during the occupation of Greece is estimated to be around 100 and is small compared to other occupied countries. Yet, the Greek case study highlights one particular facet of the challenges faced by women who were pregnant with children of *Wehrmacht* soldiers. With abortions readily accessible in Greece at that time, mothers-to-be were confronted with a choice of carrying the child to term. A decision for the child could be read as a conscious decision for something clearly associated with the hated enemy Germany. It is likely that only a small proportion of pregnancies resulted in births.[106] Small as the number of children may be – Greek research to date is based on only six case studies – the experiences of the children of *Wehrmachtssoldaten* confirm what has been noted for other countries. They often grew up with secrecy surrounding their biological origin; they often lived in poverty with stigmatisation of being born out of wedlock in addition to being a 'German bastard', and although the family constellations of the affected CBOW in Greece differed substantially, all seemed to have suffered psychologically as a result of these childhood adversities and the discriminations they had experienced.

In recent years, these preliminary studies of a wide range of children fathered by foreign soldiers have been broadening our understanding. These include children of German soldiers and Polish mothers,[107] of German soldiers and Finnish mothers,[108] of German soldiers and Soviet POWs,[109] to name but a few groups. By and large these investigations confirm that children in almost all circumstances faced stigmatisation and hardship of various kinds – psychological, economic and educational. However, in order to grasp the complexity of their situations and to move towards a comprehensive analysis, one needs to advance beyond the gathering of information on individual case studies and instead engage in a comparative analysis drawing on different disciplinary and interdisciplinary approaches.

A first attempt at conceptualising the different factors impacting on the life courses of CBOW has been made by interpreting children as the centre of what is referred to as four different 'contexts' with a range of factors impacting on the children, as illustrated in figure 3.1.[110]

Figure 3.1 shows the child at the centre of what is referred to as the socioeconomic, the psychological, the medical/biological and the political/judicial dimensions, with factors from all four areas affecting the childhood experiences and development of CBOW. It will be necessary to refine the model, as some of the categories are open to debate and controversy. For example, one

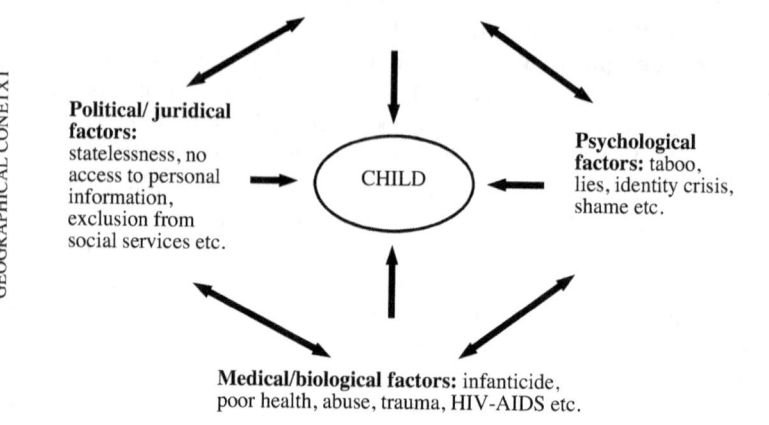

Figure 3.1 Conceptualisation of factors affecting life courses of children born of war

Source: Adapted from I.C. Mochmann, 'Developing a methodology for the research field of "children born of war"', European Survey Research Association Conference, Warsaw, 30.6.2009.

might need to consider whether political and judicial issues are best understood as part of the same 'dimension', whether psychological and medical factors are best understood as different dimensions or whether the links between socio-economic and political factors are best accounted for in the existing model. What is, however, undoubtedly significant is to understand the childhood experiences of CBOW as a complex societal problem. While all the factors included in the model above are of significance for the childhood developments of other children in a variety of situations, CBOW are frequently affected adversely by a large number of factors simultaneously. Thus the conclusion leads to particularly difficult childhood experiences.

A second model has been developed to guide further analysis from a psychological perspective. Based on a study of the historical and political circumstances that surrounded their conception as children of the Second World War and of growing up in post-war Germany as CBOW, the conclusion is that three core factors are of great significance in the assessment of the psychosocial impact of the life-course experiences: identity, stigma/discrimination and childhood adversities.

One's biological origins, and in particular paternity and its perception in a child's immediate environment, are essential for identity development. As will

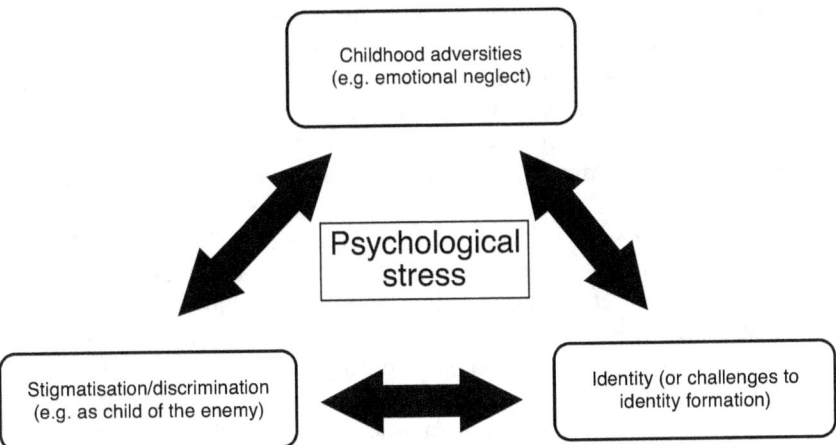

Figure 3.2 Significant factors in the assessment of the psychosocial impact of being a child born of war

Source: Adapted from H. Glaesmer et al., 'Die Kinder des Zweiten Weltkrieges in Deutschland: Ein Rahmenmodell für die psychosoziale Forschung', *Trauma und Gewalt*, 6 (2012), 319–28, here 323.

become apparent in the detailed analysis of CBOW accounts below, the children were often faced with either silence or half truths about their fathers.[111] Frequently they discovered details 'by accident'; often the father remained a taboo subject and the lack of factual knowledge could lead to either idealisation or demonisation of the absent father. Moreover, the missing or obscure part in the parentage affected the child's identity formation.[112] A second factor, childhood adversities and, in extreme cases, traumatic experiences, in many (though by no means all) cases led to difficult developmental circumstances, including physical and emotional neglect and abuse, particularly where children entered the care system. Finally, discrimination as a child born out of wedlock, a child linked to the 'enemy' or the 'foreigner', as a child in extreme poverty or in a malfunctioning step-family frequently accompanied the difficult early childhood experiences of the CBOW.

While this framework has been developed in reference to a specific historical and geopolitical context, it will serve as a general frame for the analysis of CBOW in different historical and geopolitical contexts.

Allied occupations in post-war Germany and Austria and children born of war

As was mentioned in the introductory part of this chapter, by far the most widely reported and subsequently researched instance of sexual violence vis-à-vis women in the Second World War was the mass rape that accompanied the Soviet advance on Germany and the 'liberation' of Germany in the closing stages of the European conflict and the early post-war months. However, as is clear from the above analysis of the conduct of many *Wehrmachtssoldaten,* not only were the Soviet crimes far from unique; as will be demonstrated below, the coercive sexual relations between occupier and occupied, too, were commonplace in wartime and post-war occupations of all different kinds.

Just as German soldiers occupied substantial parts of Europe during the war itself in Germany's quest for territorial domination, Allied forces were stationed in many areas: in preparation of their own deployment (e.g. US and Canadian forces in Britain before D-Day; Canadian forces in the Netherlands after the liberation of the Netherlands); during the war (e.g. Allied forces in formerly Nazi-held territories as part of liberation manoeuvres); and after the war (Allied occupation forces in Germany, Austria and Japan). This was an attempt to safeguard the territorial and geopolitical post-war settlement in Central Europe. In all these cases local women engaged in relationships with foreign soldiers, and as a result tens of thousands of children were born. These relationships ranged from consensual love affairs at one end of the spectrum, via practical 'service arrangements' and survival prostitutions, to sexual violence at the other end of the spectrum. For the purpose of this study, the focus will be on the post-war occupations of Germany and Austria. An interesting comparative case would be the occupation of Japan, but data here is significantly sketchier.[113]

Figures circulated for the number of occupation children in post-war Germany are unreliable. For the Western zones, a survey from the year 1955 speaks of well over 66,000,[114] 37,000 of whom were fathered by American soldiers. However, underreporting, the 'absorption' of illegitimate children into their birth families, either by tacit acknowledgement of paternity by the mother's husband, or the fact that the children's birth families under different circumstances and for a variety of reasons did not publicise the biological parentage of the child, led to the widely held conclusion that the real figure of occupation children was likely to be significantly higher.[115]

For Austria, similarly, numbers are imprecise. According to official statistics, between 1946 and 1953, 8,000 children fathered by foreign soldiers were born, but contemporary estimates speak of at least 20,000 such children up to 1955.[116] How many of these children fathered by occupation soldiers were the result of sexual exploitation and how many were conceived in consensual or love relationships will never be known. For the Federal Republic of Germany and West Berlin, a document of the Finance Ministry gives some indication about the prevalence of sexual violence experienced by German women during the occupation. It reveals that between 1.1.1959 and 31.12.1959, 6,325 applications for financial support were submitted by mothers of children who were conceived as a result of rape by occupation soldiers.[117] As is the case for statistics on CBOW more generally, here too, it is questionable whether the figure is a true reflection of the magnitude of the problem. Be that as it may, as in the case of children of the *Wehrmacht*, it is essential to consider the situations leading to intimate relations between soldiers and local civilians during these occupations in order to understand the experiences of the children born as a result of these liaisons. The historical and social backgrounds to these occupations are distinct, just as the relationships between occupier and occupied, liberator and liberated differed and were undergoing change throughout the wartime and post-war periods, depending on the military and political developments at the time.

The Red Army

The final stages of the war were accompanied by a wave of rapes, and sexual violence occurred all over Central Europe, as the Western Allies and the Soviet Union fought their way into the territory of the Third Reich. The majority of such assaults were committed in the Soviet occupation zones of both Germany and Austria, and estimates of what one historian described as the 'greatest phenomenon of mass rape in history'[118] range from tens of thousands to 2 million, with at least 100,000 women believed to have been raped in Berlin alone.[119] While the exact details of the rapes committed or even the numbers affected may never be known, it has been demonstrated convincingly that rape 'became a part of the social history of the Soviet zone in ways unknown to the Western zones' and that 'women in the Eastern zone ... shared an experience for the most part unknown in the West, the ubiquitous threat as well as the reality of rape over a prolonged period of time'.[120] Rape was indiscriminate, with examples of assaults including young girls and older women, Germans and liberated Nazi victims of other nationalities alike.[121] The diary of a German doctor working in a first-aid station in Berlin, who was critical of the behaviour of German soldiers whom she suspected to have acted no differently to the Soviets, reported 'continuing rapes, VD, unwanted pregnancies and mass abortions' during the early post-war period.[122] It appears that abortion rates varied significantly. In Berlin, facilitated by an almost immediate medicalisation of the rapes and an endeavour to eliminate the consequences (i.e. treatment of VD and termination of unwanted pregnancies) an estimated 90% of pregnancies were terminated.[123] In contrast, in the more rural areas, figures are likely to have been significantly lower, and although no reliable figures of children fathered by Soviet soldiers exist, it is commonly assumed that many women in Germany and Austria decided not to terminate pregnancies, even if the children were fathered by Soviet soldiers.[124] Despite the common perception of the interaction between Soviet soldiers and local civilians being dominated by violence, there were also large numbers of voluntary relationships and love affairs, if not in the initial 'liberation' phase, then during the Soviet post-war occupation.[125]

Contrary to later assumptions, the rape of German women by Soviet soldiers was not silenced in the immediate post-war period, but in fact found its way into diaries, memoirs and novels,[126] as well as being common knowledge among the population more generally.[127] In contrast, love relations would frequently be hidden by the women and their families, because of the stigmatisation feared by those who had fraternised. Such fraternisation was not only illegal, it was viewed with much suspicion by the local population, and even more so, in many cases, by the families.[128] Thus, not surprisingly, children who were born as a result of such relationships appear to have been a taboo for decades after the end of the war and frequently their biological origin was kept a secret, and their Soviet parentage remained hidden.

The majority of the children were part of the 'fatherless generation' – in the words of a recent documentary about the life of children born of the Indochina Wars fathers were 'inconnu – présumé français', only in this case fathers were 'unknown – presumed Russian'.[129] Military authorities either did not know or did not want to know which soldiers had fathered the children; and if they were in possession of such information, more often than not the soldiers were transferred prior to the birth of the children. As a result, children frequently grew up either with grandparents or aunts, in foster families or in care; where they were raised in the mother's household, they often believed their stepfather to be their biological father and, as has been shown in a historical analysis of the offspring of Soviet soldiers in Austria, the children met with a 'wall of silence',[130] and any evidence leading to the father's identity remained hidden from them. Given the deteriorating relationship between the Soviet Union and Western Powers and the subsequent alienation of the Soviet Union and parts of the occupied countries, it is not surprising to see that the stigmatisation of the children of Soviet soldiers was, if anything, more pronounced than that of other children of the occupation. Added to this political distancing between the Soviet Union and Germany/Austria was the racial component; this combination resulted in an environment where discrimination against the mothers and children was rife.[131]

Another significant difference experienced by children of Red Army soldiers was that the search for their fathers was even more difficult than for children of Western Allies. Soviet non-fraternisation policy remained strict and tightly enforced, with marriages between Soviet soldiers and German and Austrian women impossible, with determined efforts on the part of the Soviet authorities to remove the soldiers in question, when marriage intentions or pregnancies of girlfriends became known.[132] Yet, despite (or perhaps because of) the significant obstacles that the Soviet parentage brought with it, many children of Red Army soldiers report of their desire and their efforts to find a trace of the unknown father. As one then 68-year old woman phrased it in response to the question what finding out who her father was would mean for her: 'It would be like a fairy tale if I finally were to know who my father was.'[133]

GI children

The relationship between occupiers and occupied was somewhat more friendly in the case of American and Canadian forces occupying parts of Europe during and after the war, and even more so in the case of these forces being stationed in Britain in preparation for D-Day. Yet, the children born as a result of liaisons between Canadian and American soldiers and local German, British or Dutch women experienced hostility and often grew up knowing little about their biological origins. These children have been the subject of some historical analysis, and rather than merely focusing on the children born of the post-war occupation in Germany and Austria, a more detailed comparison of British and German children fathered by American GIs during and after the Second World War[134] brings to light interesting differences, as well as stark similarities, in the situations of these distinct groups.

By far the largest number of occupation children born in what was to become the Federal Republic of Germany had American fathers. Given the very prominent role of GIs as (absent) fathers globally throughout the twentieth century, it is opportune to throw some light on US policies towards their soldiers' offspring during and after the Second World War, before exploring the children's experiences. American soldiers, prior to their participation in Germany's or Austria's occupation from 1945 had already been stationed on European soil for a significant amount of time. Throughout the Second World War, more than three million US soldiers were stationed in Great Britain temporarily. This 'friendly occupation' provides an interesting comparative counterpart to the analysis of later US military–civilian relations and to their CBOW and occupation. 'Overpaid, over-fed, over-sexed and over here' was a common perception of GIs in Britain.[135] This large number of GIs, coupled with the war-induced demographic changes in Britain, with 30% of the male population conscripted[136] and millions of civilians evacuated,[137] led to qualitative change in the personal experiences of millions of young women on the Home Front. The monotony of the long working days in the factories was broken mainly by cinema, dances or the attention of the locally stationed soldiers. The image of the 'good-time girl', a perception of female promiscuity on the part of disloyal, selfish, pleasure-seeking women, became an increasingly common stereotype. This would later readily be transferred onto the children born out of casual relationships between local girls and GIs.[138]

A significant subsection among the US soldiers stationed in Britain through the last three war years were the approximately 130,000 African-Americans serving within a segregated military. Although there was a widespread acceptance of the presence of non-white GIs, the local civilian population was ambivalent in its attitude towards black soldiers.[139] On the one hand, segregation that would prevent interracial mixing for leisure-time activities such as cinema, dancing, or simply casual contacts on the streets and in public transport was seen as unacceptable by most British. Yet, despite this generally more tolerant attitude, prejudices existed. The main difference between US and British views was that preconceptions in Britain were not purely racial, but linked to class and social status, the more prominent yardsticks used in Britain to demark borders between different sections of society.[140] As a direct consequence, the perception prevailed that women most likely to entertain relations with African-American GIs were less educated, of lower classes and of questionable morality.[141] Therefore, for local women, a relationship with a black GI carried the risk of social ostracism, and many shunned association or regular contacts. Consequently, many African-Americans resorted to payment for sex.[142] This had two significant consequences: first, the prejudices regarding the morality of black GIs were reinforced; and second, the propaganda of the dangers of sexual relations with black GIs and the risk of VDs gained credibility.[143] The disapproving attitude towards intimate relations between white British women and black GIs increased throughout the war and had severe consequences for the children born of these relationships. Judging that an apple would never fall far from the tree, mixed-race children were readily associated with stereotypes about morality, too. Although this phenomenon is amost universal among CBOW across time and space, the visibility of their biological origin amplified the stigma and also, as children grew older, the self-stigmatisation.

It is estimated that at least 22,000 British GI children were born during and after the Second World War, of whom around 1,700 were of African-American descent.[144] The situation of white and mixed-race GI children differed drastically. Thousands of previously unmarried British women, who became mothers of white GI children, could eventually follow the fathers of these children to the United States as 'war brides'[145] – according to statistics of the US Immigration and Naturalization Office, a total of 37,879 British women (and 472 British children) between July 1941 and June 1950.[146] Anecdotal evidence suggests that most white children born of relations between married mothers and GIs were integrated into their mothers' family and many husbands accepted the offspring as their own.[147] The children were adopted by the husband, in many cases did not even know about their biological background and grew up in 'normal' nuclear families. Yet, many report that they still suffered from stigmatisation. Often they did not understand why they were treated differently, because unlike their home and often their neighbourhood environment, they themselves did not know about their biological origins.[148] Although such reported negative stereotyping as children of the 'good-time girls', and for many of the white children of the occupation discrimination, was intermittent and subtle, it still had a significant psychological impact on them.[149]

In contrast, accounts of mixed-race children indicate that their situation was significantly more difficult. The US military did not encourage or support marriages between African-American GIs and British women.[150] In the case of married mothers, integrating a 'brown baby' into the family was much more difficult, as the provenance of the child was clearly visible, and therefore the mothers' husbands were often reluctant to adopt them. As a result, married mothers frequently felt they had no choice but to give up their illegitimate mixed-race children in order to safeguard their existing family. The situation of young single mothers of the so-called 'brown babies' was seldom easier. Single parenting in wartime and early post-war Britain meant financial hardship and social ostracisation. If this marginalisation was exacerbated by a mixed-race child, mothers often saw institutional care or adoption as the best option for their child and for themselves, mothers were 'shunned ... as soon as the news of their pregnancies leaked out' and often had 'no support from their families, the Government or the United States Army'.[151]

Identity has been acknowledged as a significant issue for the majority of adopted children or adults, and it was even more virulent for mixed-race children. In spite of their often good experiences in their immediate family surroundings, among school friends and acquaintances, many 'brown babies' suffered from isolation and identity crises. They continually found themselves reminded of their origins, and the fact that they visually differed from the homogeneous white surroundings for many led to a constant feeling of 'otherness', of being different and of 'not belonging'.[152] This otherness also served as a permanent reminder of the children's illegitimacy, a circumstance which – during the 1950s and 1960s – was still regarded as unacceptable.[153]

Like wartime Britain, post-war Germany was faced with a sizeable presence of US troops and in 1945 around 1.6 million GIs were stationed on German soil. The number quickly decreased, and between mid-1947 and the early 1950s the number of US soldiers levelled at around 135,000, before it increased again in response to the Korean War and growing Cold War tensions, leading to a maximum of around 360,000 soldiers.[154]

In contrast to Great Britain, however, Germany was a defeated country that had surrendered unconditionally. The US promoted a strict non-fraternisation policy trying to prevent all 'friendly, familiar, or intimate contacts with Germans'.[155] Decrees from the top and actions at the grass roots, however, soon started diverging, and it became evident rapidly that the fraternisation prohibition was adhered to reluctantly, and certainly far from consistently, even in the early post-war months. As a result, in October 1945, the non-fraternisation rules were abolished with two important exceptions. GIs were still neither permitted to live with Germans nor to marry a German.[156]

German–American romantic liaisons were observed with suspicion. The women in question were portrayed as a particular 'type', and the image of German *Fräuleins* willing to engage in intimate relationships with GIs soon became a demonised stereotype.[157] In contrast to the allegedly experienced and clever German *Fräuleins*, the GIs were portrayed as the often naïve, young homesick soldiers, who became victims to the seduction of the German girls. In contrast to British 'good-time girls', whose main transgressions were perceived to be selfish disloyalty, the Americans labelled their German equivalents more as dangerous to the point of being parasitic.[158] However, GIs themselves judged differently, thereby confirming that the impression and presentation of the GIs as 'oversexed, over-fed, over-paid and over here' in post-war Germany too, were not merely accidental attributes conjured out of thin air. As one GI put it poignantly, he and his mates judged the fraternisation ban as 'against human nature', and he stressed their own willingness to enjoy their encounters with the German girls.[159]

As in wartime Britain, and in line with most conflict and post-conflict scenarios, the peculiarities of demographics in post-war Germany and the political and economic circumstances of the time had a significant role to play in the development of friendly relations. As a result of the war, in 1946 women between aged 20 and 30 years outnumbered men in that age bracket by 167 to 100. Similarly, for every 100 men aged between 30 and 40 years, there were 151 women.[160] This suggests that young well-mannered men of a particular age were attractive for German women, no matter what their nationality.

As in other theatres of war and occupation, not all sexual encounters were voluntary. Equally, not all of them were forced, and often the boundary between the two was far from clear. Numerous women used their bodies as bargaining chips. Sex that was paid for in goods or money was common, and providing this kind of service was viewed by many women as part of their struggle for survival. It was not forced upon them by the soldiers but by circumstances. However, towards the end of the war, the number of reported rapes also rose dramatically, from 31 cases in February 1945 to 402 in March and 501 in April of that year.[161] While the numbers were significantly below those reported for the same crime committed by the Red Army,[162] they were grounds for concern among the US military command, not least because it was assumed that the quote of reported rapes was only a fraction of the actual offences committed.[163]

The number of children born as a result of relationships between German women and occupation soldiers, consensual or exploitative, was significant. A survey in 1955 reported that 66,730 illegitimate children fathered by occupation soldiers had been born to German women in post-war Germany. Of these, approximately 37,000 had American fathers, and an estimated 4,000 children were of African-American descent.[164] A brief look at the statistics is important to understand why occupation children in West Germany were perceived primarily as an American–German issue, although three occupying powers were stationed in the area that was to become the Federal Republic. Until the mid-1950s, around 55% of children of the occupation had American fathers, 15% French, 13% British, and 5% Russian, with 12% of fathers appearing in the statistics remaining unidentified.[165] While this number can at least in part be accounted for by the statistical density of occupation troops, a second observable fact is less easy to explain. Contrary to expectations, the number of children born to local women and occupation soldiers did not decline after the currency reform and the end of the so-called hunger years – in fact it rose significantly, particularly for American occupation soldiers of any racial background, so that the proportion of children conceived of American fathers in 1953–1954 rose to around 75–80%.[166]

The largely negative images of the women who had had intimate relations with US soldiers were as pronounced within Germany as in the United States, and they were projected onto the children.[167] They were seen as children of the enemy,[168] and their mothers, by choosing a relationship with a GI, were perceived as traitors to their German home, possibly to their German husbands and to the prevailing morality of female obedience that had been preached by the National Socialist regime.[169] In this sense, the reaction to German women forming intimate relations with foreign soldiers – voluntary, exploitative or coercive – was not markedly different to that observed at the end of the war, when German women as for instance the *Woman in Berlin*, were frequently condemned for their choices as they were seen to be letting down their German *Heimat* and nation and thus had failed in their national duty. By implication, the children were tainted. The directives prohibiting marriages between German women and US soldiers were not revoked until December 1946, more than a year after the end of the fraternisation ban. This meant that during the first 19 months of the occupation regime, when the majority of German–American relationships were formed, marriage was impossible. The US military government was unequivocal about responsibilities for children born to local German women, by negating, in principle and practice, any claim for alimony in the case of a soldier fathering a child.[170]

After it had become possible for GIs, under certain circumstances, to marry their German girlfriends from December 1946 onwards, several thousands of couples got married and thousands of women followed their husbands to the United States.[171] Although marriage statistics as such are not available, immigration records show that up to June 1950 14,175 German GI-brides and 750 children of members of the US Armed Forces had emigrated to the United States. In addition, 1,862 German women had travelled to the United States between 1947 and 1949 as fiancées. Many tens of thousands of women, however, did not have this option. The American father of their child may already have been moved elsewhere, he may not have been granted his officer's permission to marry or he could not or did not want to take up his paternal responsibility for other reasons. Military rules and regulations facilitated a decision against mother and child. Moreover, the peculiarities of German laws concerning paternity and social responsibility for children born out of wedlock complicated the situation for the occupation children and their mothers. Illegitimate children were the responsibility of the mother and her family, but the mother was not the legal guardian. Guardianship lay with the state or – in the case of married mothers – with the mother's husband. He became the child's legal father irrespective of biological paternity unless he or the district attorney raised questions of such paternity, as was frequently the case with mixed-race children.[172]

During the post-war years fathers were required to support their children financially until they had reached the age of 16 years, irrespective of whether they were married to the child's mother. Yet, members of the occupation forces, both military and civilian personnel, were excluded from this law.[173] Only after the establishment of the Federal Republic in 1949 was the situation partially revised. The United States passed a law on 11 August 1950 that extended German jurisdiction to members of the Allied forces. But the law contained an important exception: that of cases dealing with the establishment of paternity and alimony claims of children of the occupation! Even after the two German states, for all intents and purposes, had regained sovereignty in 1955 and German women could try to claim alimony for children fathered by occupation soldiers, the deliveries of claims were conditional on either the soldier in question having accepted paternity or a US court having made a ruling to this effect.[174] Even in cases where a father attempted to provide for mother and children, complicated and contradictory laws meant that GIs were frequently prevented from doing so. Ironically, in most cases it was impossible for the soldiers to adopt their own children in order to pave the way for providing for them. US military courts were only permitted to pass judgement in case of a criminal offence: civilian claims had to be dealt with by German courts; these courts, however, did not have jurisdiction over US soldiers, and GIs were not allowed to appear before them. Therefore, the GI-fathers did not have any legal way of legitimising their paternity and to gain sole or shared custody over their children. As a result of this legal jungle, any potential family unification was complicated, and even in cases where both parents intended to build a joint future with and for their children, they were prevented from doing so by bureaucratic idiosyncrasies.

As in Great Britain, public and political debates about the fate of children of the occupation in Germany were initially notable only for their absence. Yet, beyond the confines of academia the constitutional discourse of the late 1940s provided the 'new democratic' Germany with the opportunity to undertake normative debates about the altered political and social circumstances, including the constitutional protection of marriage, family and also illegitimate children. The Social Democrat Friederike Nadig, in the debates on the constitution to be drafted, considered the fate of those members of post-war German society who no longer fitted into the old model of the two-parent nuclear family. Contemplating the 'surplus of women', which effectively was a 'post-war shortage of men', she pleaded for a new form of familial existence, the Mutterfamilie ('mother family'). Commenting on one particular group, illegitimate children, she added that the coloured children of the occupation were hit hardest by the prevailing family laws and social norms.[175]

Children of the occupation in general were mentioned in the debate, amid a general awareness of the social problems associated with illegitimacy in the late 1940s. Yet, it is interesting to note that only piecemeal initiatives were used to deal with the children of the occupation. The impression was given that social and child welfare policies, while having the best interest of the children in mind, also – and perhaps predominantly – served a wider political purpose in Germany, namely the construction of an image of a democratic and racially tolerant and supportive 'new' post-war Germany. In this context, children of African-American descent – who could not hide and could not be hidden – were perceived as facing additional hardship. A symptom of this was that, for better or for worse, they received more attention from the local population and political decision makers. A clear recognition of political responsibility, arising out of the National Socialist legacy, guided sociological and political discussions of the subject. Therefore attempts at a pragmatic solution to the problem of Germany's 'brown babies' had to be formulated as a race-related policy that was distanced from the racist discourse of the Hitler years.[176]

Post-war debates about the integration of mixed-race children took place against the background of the continuing occupation, in which the US occupation power acted with the proclaimed aim of the democratisation of Germany. This was to be based not only on a turning away from National Socialism in general but specifically also on the explicit respect of human rights and a renunciation of antisemitism and racism. Like Germany, the United States was grappling with challenges to entrenched racial ideologies. The US military government in Germany still operated in a segregated way on the basis of racial inequalities, which contradicted the clearly stated aims of democratic re-education of the former German enemy and caused fundamental problems for the credibility of the Americans as pillars of democracy and freedom.[177] Segregation in the United States, and the resulting reluctance on the part of local officers in Germany to grant permission to African-American soldiers to marry their German girlfriends, meant that almost all children of German women and black GIs were born illegitimately. According to German law at the time, children lacking a male guardian became wards of the local or state youth office, and as few white German men would accept responsibility for a mixed-race child, even if they were married to the mother, institutional involvement was a given in the majority of cases. Reports about the dire situation of the Afro-German children[178] coincided with the first discussions about their fate in the emerging Federal Republic, initially at a municipal level. Furthermore, US authorities took first steps to establish the numbers of German GI children, the treatment of different paternity cases, and citizenship issues as well as the living conditions of those children cared for in Germany's children's homes. This led to a memorandum, on 14 September 1948, on 'Paternity of Illegitimate Children'.[179] The dealings with the 'problem' of the mixed-race children took place broadly concurrently at two societal levels: first, the children and their mothers became objects of scientific and particularly sociological studies;[180] and, second, on a political level decisions about their integration into West German society were coupled with an attempt at re-educating the German public. The discourse about the Afro-German children has to be seen in the context of and as a response to the treatment of children born to German mothers and colonial African troops during the French occupation of the Rhineland in the inter-war years. In a race-hate campaign, the so-called 'Black Horror on the Rhine', the children who became known as 'Rhineland Bastards' had been forcibly sterilised under the Nazi regime.[181] The post-war race-related debates, therefore, potentially could be used by German decision makers to demonstrate that such racially motivated injustice was a thing of the past and that the new democratic Germany would 'look after all its citizens' irrespective of race or religion.

It is no coincidence that the first parliamentary debate on illegitimate children of the occupation took place in the *Bundestag* in early 1952, just before the first children entered the school system. As one historian put it, the children moved 'from the inside', i.e. their families or care homes to 'the outside', i.e. society in the form of school.[182] Although it is doubtful that their fate occupied the minds of 'the entire German population' as a 'permanent challenge' the engagement with the topic became more public. However, it was the visibility of the so-called 'Mischlingskinder' which provided the focal point of the debate. Their situation was judged by the *Bundestag* to pose a 'human and racial problem of a special nature'.[183] At the same time, parliamentarians expressed concern that the West German public was not yet capable of assuming a posture 'free of racial prejudice', and that only a 'long-term education process [would] be able to dislodge the traditions that caused a belief in the racial superiority of the white Germans'.[184]

This assessment was in sharp contrast to a 1949 survey that suggested that 'German mothers treated their *"Mischlingskinder"* considerably better than their counterparts in England and Japan', as in Germany 'not only is infanticide unthinkable but even separation is rarely considered'.[185] While this poll commented only on the children's mothers, a more elaborate study of the International Union for Child Welfare in Geneva came to the conclusion that in post-war West Germany 'the cases in which mixed-race children are being rejected by their communities because of their family background should be considered an exception. Generally, the relatives, neighbors, and other children meet them with cordiality and affection.'[186] This appeared to be the case despite the fact that the prevailing view among policy makers in the Federal Republic was that it would be difficult to ensure the children's integration into their birth country. In the political discussions about their future three main possible ways forward had emerged: (1) the children should be integrated as far as possible into German society, whether within the care system, as adopted children or within their own families or extended families; (2) the children should be raised in segregated homes;[187] (3) the children should be adopted by African-American couples.

The idea of segregation was not generally perceived as desirable, and adoption, for a variety of reaons, not least because of the reluctance of the children's mothers to agree to transnational adoptions, did not happen on a large scale. Thus, the majority of mixed-race children of the occupation lived in families, either in the families of their mothers or in adoptive families.[188] After it had become evident throughout the first post-war decade that this pattern would essentially remain the same, state and municipal officials, helped by educators, social workers and at times even journalists, focused on racial re-education within Germany. Concerted actions coincided with integration milestones of what was a relatively age-homogeneous group, for instance school enrolment or the start of post-school vocational training.[189] Considerable educational efforts were made by the welfare officials, care institutions and, equally importantly, by open-minded caring families, who adopted mixed-race children of the occupation, and only 12% of all such children grew up in welfare institutions.[190] Yet, the image prevailed – in political discussions as well as in public debates in West Germany and abroad – that African-German children were unwanted. This impression was reinforced by press coverage within the United States, from where regular 'inspection visits' were initiated to report about the GI children. Between the late 1940s and mid-1950s reports appeared in numerous publications, such as *Newsweek, Chicago Tribune, Pittsburgh Courier, News and World Report* and *Ebony*.[191] It is interesting to note that similar scrutiny was not considered to be necessary in the case of mixed-race children in Great Britain. As a reaction to one such newspaper report, Ethel Butler, an African-American widowed teacher, decided to work towards adopting some of those children and thereby giving them a new home in the United States. After years of bureaucratic wrangling, she succeeded in adopting two children. This had far-reaching consequences for other German mixed-race GI children. The perceived 'fight' against the adoption bureaucracies in both countries, reported elaborately by the African-American press in the United States, led to an increase in public interest of potential adoptive parents. Furthermore, Butler had scored an important bureaucratic and legal victory in that her children were classified as war orphans, allowing them privileged immigration status irrespective of quotas applicable to their birth countries.[192]

Butler's efforts to put the problem of 'brown babies' on the radar of officials in both West Germany and the United States also helped another African-American woman working for a more permanent solution to the insecure situation of many 'brown babies' in German institutions. Mabel A. Grammer, wife of US warrant officer Oscar Grammar, who had been stationed in Mannheim between 1950 and 1954, was herself a journalist for the *African-American*. She instigated the so-called 'Brown Baby Plan', which arranged for the adoption of several hundred children into African-American and African-German families by 1954.[193] Mabel Grammer's initiative had been triggered by her observation of the poverty and stigmatisation experienced by many women who had decided to bring up their mixed-race children in their own families. As Mrs Grammer had observed, negative sentiments towards the mothers, as well as prejudices and social exclusion, were often transferred directly onto the children and led to discrimination. It was this discrimination that she was trying to counteract by working towards transnational adoption.[194] In some respects this was the forerunner of a much more concerted effort of transnational adoption that was to follow in subsequent decades, when GIs increasingly were engaged in Asian theatres of war, leaving behind a trail of almost exclusively mixed-race offspring.

The German response to the privately instigated adoption programmes of Ethel Butler and Mabel Grammar demonstrates the widely held belief that mixed-race occupation children could be better cared for in African-American families rather than in their mothers' families. Adoption plans received an enthusiastic reception from the popular press.[195] Politicians at all levels, municipal, state and federal,[196] argued that emigration to their paternal homeland might be preferable for the children. However, the complexities of inter-country adoptions, and the bureaucratic complications caused by US immigration laws, as well as the severe reservations of the International Social Service against proxy adoption in particular, led to a slow adjustment of views in Germany throughout the 1950s. By the mid-1950s, despite several hundred adoptions, it had become clear that large numbers of mixed-race children would remain in Germany, and the emphasis, as described above, moved away from solving the 'brown baby' problem outside to solving it inside Germany.

In stark contrast to Great Britain where, despite a similarly significant number of mixed-race occupation children no discussions of this kind took place, West Germany continued to address the issue throughout the 1950s at an academic and a political level. A federally funded socio-psychological study carried out by the Hamburg psychologist Klaus Eyferth compared white and mixed-race children of the occupation, investigating in particular the links between race and intelligence and concluded that the study could not determine links between the two.[197] The research, subsequently published in elaborated form as a book on the integration of mixed-race children into German society,[198] became the authoritative source informing policy recommendations in the Federal Republic in the 1960s, at a time when many children, now adolescents, were passing another educational milestone, the move from school into employment.

Post-war reconstruction saw a variety of general debates of how to best serve the interests of European children affected by the war through displacement, expulsion or flight.[199] In contrast, efforts to deal with the situation faced by CBOW were largely nonexistent, especially in the first post-war years. Their number was small in comparison with other displaced and orphaned children. The instrumentalisation of children as 'national property'[200] that has been shown to have played a significant role in the formulation of child welfare policies played less of a role in Britain than on the European continent, where reconstruction went hand in hand with democratisation and nation-building. The only problems that were openly acknowledged at the time were those of mixed-race children whose appearance distinguished them from the surrounding environment. In their case, prevailing familialist values, often lamented to have suffered as a result of wartime social upheavals and systematically revived after the war as a means to 'return to normality'[201] were put aside in favour of a placement of children in the care system. In other words, instead of supporting young mothers of GI children to bring up their children in a nuclear or extended family, a blanket solution of placing the children in care in preparation for adoption into mixed-race or black families at a later stage was favoured.

It has been argued that in the Federal Republic child welfare as evidenced in dealing with mixed-race GI children was treated predominantly as a political tool in order to facilitate the remodelling of West Germany as a tolerant society 'demonstrating good intentions and the willingness for social reform'.[202] This appears unduly critical given that the country – particularly in comparison with Great Britain, the only other West European country with a significant number of Afro-European GI children – allowed public debates and engaged in academic discourse about the sociological and socio-psychological challenges faced by the children, their families and the society that – if belatedly – eventually saw the need to address their integration.

Naître Ennemi – *children of French soldiers*

In most cases attempts at quantifying the numbers of CBOW in any given context are hampered by a lack of accurate statistics. A notable exception to this are the children fathered by French occupation soldiers in Germany, for whom we have relatively concise data. This is partly due to their registration as illegitimate children in Germany, but even more because of the fact that they were also registered separately by French authorities. The latter process is rooted in a fundamentally different approach of the French vis-à-vis their soldiers' offspring, which will be explored further below. Although a better than normal dataset allows researchers to get a sense of the scale of the phenomenon, the literature, even recently, has contained widely different conclusions about the number of French children of the occupation. What is certain is that at least 15,000 files of children fathered by French soldiers between 1945 and 1955 exist.[203] As elsewhere, it is reasonable to assume that this minimum number is significantly lower than the real figure because of under-reporting.[204] The registration which was aimed at the eventual repatriation of French children to France, indicates a distinct French approach to CBOW, which also explains a different attitude to post-war fraternisation. Unlike the British and American military governments the French authorities did not operate a strict anti-fraternisation policy. More significantly in our context, however, is the fact that they had an entirely different approach to race and nationality of its citizens' offspring – legitimate or illegitimate, monoracial or biracial. This has been explored in some detail for the specific case of French children of colonial wars,[205] but the principles also hold for the children of the Second World War. The analysis illustrates how, in the 1928 definition of the status of mixed-race children of the colonies – the 'métis' – the French for the first time allowed race to enter the legal framework of nationality.

This provided the basis for the French understanding that children of French occupation soldiers had a legal right to French citizenship and, in fact, France went some way towards 'claiming' their French children for the nation. The policy is reminiscent of the way in which the Germans had intended to repatriate some selected French-German children during the war. As early as 1945 the French military created offices for the registration, administration and transfer of illegitimate children of their soldiers and German women to France. The advertisements throughout the French occupation zone encouraging mothers to register their children fuelled rumours that mothers could see their children forcibly removed, and the German population spoke of *Kinderraub* (theft of children).[206] Although the term theft may seem extreme, the experiences of the mothers justified a certain degree of suspicion, as the internal communications of the Ministry of the Interior of one region (Baden) demonstrate that some coercion or at least forceful persuasion was used to convince German mothers to give up their children. In August 1946, a decree opened up the possibility for mothers to allow the French authorities to take care of their children. The 'deal' was for mothers to relinquish all their rights in return for the French state resuming responsibilities for the children's welfare.[207] This policy is similar to French actions in Indochina in the late 1940s and early 1950s, when the *Mutuelle de Français*, the *Fédération des ouvres depour des enfants Franco-Indochinois* and *L'Action Sociale*, a section of the military, actively sought out children of French soldiers and Vietnamese mothers, *Enfants de Troupes*, who in French eyes were needed to be reclaimed for France and were sent to French 'orphanages' from 1947 onwards.[208]

In the German case, it is possible that the mothers agreed to surrendering their children in the belief that they would be adopted by their own fathers,[209] as it was only in the small print that it was spelt out that adoption by other families was a possible course of action to be taken by the authorities. Be that as it may, the reality of the fate of children given up by their mothers to be taken care of by the French was, by and large, not a transfer to the father and his family, but in most cases a combination of growing up in care homes and other adoptive families. As a rule, the children would be transferred to French children's homes in Germany such as the former *Lebensborn* home in Nordach but also other care homes in Baden or Rhineland Palatinate.[210] These homes operated until 1949, by which time those who were deemed suitable for adoption were relocated to France or transferred to the responsibility of the *départements et territoires d'outre-mer*.[211] Where adoption was not regarded as a feasible option, the children were passed on to German homes instead. As has rightly been pointed out, this practice was in no way grounded in German legal provisions.[212] German laws put the decision-making powers about fostering and adoption into the hands of youth welfare offices and mothers, a fact which was ignored by French authorities until the end of the occupation in 1955.

The fate of children of French occupation soldiers is another example of CBOW being an object of political decisions which have no regard for the best interest of the children. There is no evidence to suggest that policies were devised with reference to the children's welfare. On the contrary, the fate of the children was decided exclusively on the basis of concurrence with the national policies – in this case the tenet of building the French nation and (re)claiming those citizens deemed valuable in the context of this project.[213] This explains the pre-selection of children who would be part of this project by way of being adopted into French families (thus preserving French blood and stock) – and it similarly explains that some children who failed whatever test had been devised to determine suitability for adoption were dropped from the scheme and instead left under German auspices.

British children of the occupation

If research into the life courses of children of Soviet, American and French occupation soldiers has been demonstrated to have been patchy, similar research for children of British soldiers has been virtually non-existent. Only a small part of one academic study has focused on their situation, and it does not deal with the Federal Republic, but with a part of British-occupied Austria.[214] The reasons for the relative dearth of academic interest are likely to lie in part in the lack of visibility of this group. In the French case children were 'claimed' by the occupation powers; in the American case – through a sizeable minority of mixed-race children – the issue was at least partially visible; and in the Soviet case – as a result of the initially high incidence of sexualised violence and the more extreme negative sentiments vis-à-vis the Soviet occupation power – society and the families affected were more conscious of the phenomenon of children as a result of coercive relationships. In contrast, children of British soldiers largely remained a truly 'hidden population'.[215] It is possible that one of the reasons was that their number was comparatively small. According to a survey in 1961, of the 225 children born of occupation soldiers in the Federal Republic of Germany for whom their mothers received social benefits, only 3.1% had British fathers.[216] The above-mentioned survey of children fathered by the occupation forces in West Germany by 1955 similarly determined that the smallest proportion (about 10%) had British fathers.[217] This impression is further reinforced by the recent study of the psychosocial impact of being a child born of the occupation, in which only around 4% of participants claimed to have had a British father.[218] Also, as is clear from the internal communications between the ministries of the interior, family and youth, finance and justice of the Federal Republic of Germany, about arrangements for children of occupation soldiers, attempts to come to satisfactory solutions for financial burden sharing focused on children of American soldiers, who were clearly numerically by far the most significant problem.[219]

Initially, the situation of German women carrying children of British occupation soldiers was similar to that described above for mothers of children fathered by American soldiers. Non-fraternisation regulations were in place[220] and forbade marriages until August 1946. Therefore marriages were impossible in the early stages of the occupation regime when the largest number of sexual encounters took place,[221] and the vast majority of children of British soldiers were raised in the mothers' families.[222] Often this brought financial hardship, as in Germany until the end of the occupation regime in May 1955, occupation soldiers were not obliged to contribute to the upbringing of their children, and even after the change in regulations following the *Truppenvertrag*,[223] only occupation soldiers who were still resident in Germany could be forced to make financial contributions. Moreover, it may not have been in the mothers' interest to claim any moral or legal rights in terms of alimony for herself or her CBOW on the grounds that at a time of an entire nation, Germany, standing in the 'spotlight accused of a collapse of moral conscience, ... the appearance en masse of a familiar symbol of moral decline, the sexually promiscuous woman', made it easier to avoid thinking about more troubling aspects of the recent past.[224] In other words, coming to terms with the 'sexual past of 1945–1948' was more urgent than coming to terms with the 'violent past of 1933–1945'.[225]

If Germany faced the issue of supposedly 'loose morals' of the early post-war years, in Britain the myth of the war having been a time of unprecedented sexual immorality was prevalent, and the image of the good-time girls was readily employed when judging single mothers after the war, in particular where the assumption was that the father of the child had been a foreign soldier.[226] Similar perceptions prevailed in many other European countries, and they were often mingled with resentment caused by the sacrifices that men had been forced to make at the front. In extreme cases, this resentment culminated in the pronounced stigmatisation of women who did not conform to notions of acceptable behaviour, such as in the case of the so-called *femmes tondues* in France, or *Moffenmeiden* in the Netherlands, *Amischickse* or *Dollarflitscherl*, a stigmatisation which was later readily transferred onto the children born out of relationships between local women and foreign soldiers. The post-war period, thus, was characterised by a strong dichotomy. On the one hand new patterns of family life were emerging in the context of rising rates of female labour participation, improved living standards for many, combined with the safety net of the welfare state, and greater control of family size through better contraception; on the other hand the immediate post-war decades also saw a revival of conventional attitudes towards the family, which stressed the nuclear family with breadwinner husband and homemaker wife as both the norm and the ideal.[227]

The voices of children born of the Second World War: life courses and experiences through the eyes of adult 'children' born of war and occupation

The analysis of intimate relations between local women and foreign soldier fathers – both consensual and exploitative – and of the experiences of the children born of such relations during and after the Second World War has foregrounded interesting patterns of childhood and life course experiences of CBOW and their mothers. Participatory research and an increasingly voluminous body of biographical and autobiographical material published in recent years have allowed researchers to complement earlier historical, anthropological and social science research with new insights into the subjective experiences of larger numbers of CBOW. These sources, by and large, confirm earlier research finding while providing a more nuanced picture of the deep emotional impact that being a child born of war had on many CBOW in childhood, adolescence and adulthood. Giving space to the voices of CBOW should not be understood as oral history in the conventional sense,[228] but as recourse to collected life stories which have been published, sometimes after a period of consolidation of narrative strategies. Such strategies are in part a response to extensive and repeated exposure to research interpretations through participant research and recurrent publication also through the media. Therefore the material has a different quality from qualitative oral history interviews in which researcher and interviewee have greater professional distance.[229]

Much of the recent literature in the form of ego-documents of CBOW has originated from two sources: firstly the support network GI-Trace,[230] the engagement in which has led some CBOW to publish books on the bases of their extensive search experiences; secondly, participatory research in the context of an international interdisciplinary network on CBOW.[231] Particularly significant in this respect has been a recent research project which investigated the long-term psychosocial impact of being a child fathered by Allied forces of the post-war occupations of Germany.[232] Here, many occupation children for the first time in their lives talked about their CBOW background, and – as many would testify – for the first time exchanged thoughts about their experiences with other CBOW. Especially children of Soviet soldiers in the former German Democratic Republic had not been able to talk openly about their circumstances previously; children fathered by Soviet occupation forces had been a taboo during the period of the divided Germany and had largely been forgotten about in the post-unification *neue Bundesländer*.[233] How important the sharing of stories was to this particular group is evident from the fact that not only did they form a support group and now run a website,[234] but they also published a book of personal recollections and accounts of childhood experiences.[235] The website, in conjunction with a social media presence (remarkable for a group of adults whose average age lies well beyond the average age of social media users more generally), facilitates engagement with academic research as well as with other CBOW groups.

The name of the group, *Distelblüten* (thistle blossom) is telling. As one *Russenkind* (Russian child, the term used by the group in referring to their members) explains: the thistle is resilient and able to defend itself, despite being vulnerable at the blossom.[236] Related to this, the image chosen for the cover of the *Distelblüten* book is similarly expressive (see figure 3.3). The steel helmet of

Figure 3.3 Knut Weise, *Distelblüten*

a Red Army Soldier is lying on German soil with a thistle growing out of the helmet, a strong stem which turns into a rose flower at the top.

A second image by the same artist further illustrates how the *Russenkinder* see themselves. The drawing is an adaptation of the *Treptower Ehrendenkmal*, a Soviet War Memorial built in an East Berlin Park to commemorate the soldiers who fell in the Battle of Berlin in April and May 1945. The memorial depicts a Soviet soldier with a sword holding a German child in his arm and standing over a broken swastika. Knut Weise's reworking of the monument in visual form portrays the same protective and supportive soldier on a crumbled monument base from which three children emerge (see figure 3.4). This picture, entitled *Schattenkinder* (children in the shadows) symbolises children left behind by the Red Army who existed in the shadow of society. They were often invisible, not talked about or talked to, living – as one researcher of African CBOW would later phrase it in describing this group – in the shadowlands.[237] The visual images match the written testimonies of the *Russenkinder*, which in turn agree with the accounts of many other CBOW elsewhere and in other historical contexts. Many recount the silence surrounding their biological origin. 'Nobody ever spoke about my father',[238] one CBOW describes her childhood. A study of children of German *Wehrmacht* in Greece during the Second World War found that none of the children interviewed for this research had been told by their mothers 'voluntarily' the truth about their biological fathers. Most had heard about their background through discriminatory remarks of friends and neighbours.[239] Likewise, Anita, a daughter of a German soldier and a French mother, learnt at the age of 18 that the person whom she believed to be her biological father had adopted her. Exasperated she remarks: 'Nobody has ever uttered a word, not for 18 years. I still cannot understand this.'[240] Another CBOW commented about the familial context that what she found most difficult was the silence, 'the not being able to speak about it, the taboo'.[241] This 'Wall of Silence'[242] was only one of the recurring patterns of experiences that many CBOW remember. Other lasting impressions of childhood and youth adversities include rejections by their mothers/families/local communities, a lack of attention, love and warmth, feeling an outsider, but also a feeling of sympathy for the mothers and a longing for the father, frequently linked to an idealisation of the absent parent.

The one characteristic that unites almost all children born of the post-war occupations who have been active in self-help organsations or who have contributed to participatory research,[243] irrespective of the quality of their relations to their mothers, families and local communities, is the desire to find their biological roots: Who am I? Where do I come from? Who is my father?[244] The search is, in the words of one researcher, 'an irrepressible need and a purely subjective and intimate expectation'.[245] This sentiment is echoed by many CBOW who talk about the search for their fathers in terms of 'longing', 'yearning', 'desire', the 'most important aspect of my life', or even 'an obsession'.[246]

The quest to find the absent father may also have been linked to an

Figure 3.4 Knut Weise, *Schattenkinder*

underlying feeling of being unwanted, of being out of place and of not fitting into the home environment – whatever that environment may have been. Being treated as a foreigner, feeling unwanted,[247] and the stigmatising name-calling that many of the children experienced led to a feeling that many expressed in phrases that indicated that they assumed that 'something was wrong with me'.[248] Many CBOW stated explicitly that this feeling only subsided when they discovered, often in the context of participatory research projects, or more haphazardly as part of their own searches for their fathers, that others shared very similar experiences. They learnt that the 'emptiness' in their emotions and the gap in their family tree were a common experience in what the Germans would refer to as a *Schicksalsgemeinschaft* (community of fate) of children of the occupation, or more generally CBOW.[249]

As evident from twelve portraits of occupation children in the recent biographical and autobiographical volume *Wir Besatzungskinder*, the quality of relationships of CBOW with their mothers varies greatly. Some occupation children had good or excellent relations with their birth mothers, perhaps strengthened by the intense bond that can come with single parenthood. Many others, however, refer to their relations as strained; and more generally, CBOW in different contexts describe the family atmosphere as lacking warmth or affection and at times even bordering on the abusive. Not atypical for the experiences of those CBOW is the comment of one study participant explaining: 'We were never mother and child. Our only link was the umbilical cord.'[250] More extreme is another experience: 'I was never given any affection; she (the mother, SL) never hugged me. Absolutely nothing. Only beatings. And she knocked my head against the wall. ... She used me to let off steam.'[251] Or in the words of a French CBOW: 'The sentiment of love, the affection, the small gentle loving touch, the shoulder to put one's head on, I did not have this, a child misses this.'[252] This lack of affection was so painful for some that they asked themselves whether it would not have been better, if their mothers had abandoned them at birth so that they had never learnt about their background.[253] The evidence suggests that a considerable number of CBOW never developed emotional links to their birth mothers; frequently mothers who had been left by soldiers with their offspring did not bond with their children and the raising of those CBOW often rested with the grandparents.[254] While this missing love and the resulting lack of intimacy often affected the CBOW in childhood, many – in later life – became sensitive to the challenges faced by their mothers. Awareness grew that mothers often had been traumatised by their own wartime experiences and further harmed by post-conflict discrimination and stigmatisation. As a result, in many cases the CBOW put their own needs of finding out about their roots second to the perceived greater needs of their mothers to privacy.[255]

If the relations between children and mothers and the immediate family were difficult, the relationship with the (almost always) absent father was equally complex. CBOW in post-war Europe were among the many diverse groups that formed a 'fatherless generation'.[256] However, fathers who were missing or had perished during the war were kept alive in the families' everyday lives in photos or as conversation topics or memories; in contrast, the fathers of CBOW were entirely non-existent. More often than not, they did not even exist as a name.[257] If anything, they only had meaning as a cause for the children's experiences of loneliness, rejection and discrimination, or as a reason for the supposed immoral behaviour of their mothers and the resulting stigmatisation of the post-conflict communities.

Despite these negative projections onto the father by many families and local communities, many CBOW have ambivalent and sometimes outright positive feelings towards their absent fathers. Anger about the difficult circumstances and the adverse childhood experiences are tempered by an idealisation of the father about whom so little is known. For instance, all the children interviewed for the study of Greek children of *Wehrmacht* soldiers portrayed their fathers as good men. They were thought to have supplied their mothers and families with food and to have offered protection. Although almost all *Wehrmacht* fathers were officers and therefore highly unlikely to have been entirely detached from the atrocities of the regime, the CBOW emphasised that their fathers had not been Nazis.[258] This idealisation of the father[259] in part serves the purpose of 'cleansing the father'[260] from the accusations which he is subjected to by family and society. Beyond this, some of the positive attributes associated with the unknown father may have been more fundamentally the wishful thinking of having the perfect father. As one CBOW phrased simply and powerfully: 'I live by the idea that my father was great.'[261]

Many have the desire to find their families, but the reality of the searches was and is that success in locating him or his family is the exception rather than the norm. And even if the paternal family can be located, a smooth and happy family reunion is anything but a foregone conclusion. Where this reunion does happen, in all the biographical narratives available the impact is being described as overwhelming and often life-changing. The language employed, again, is rich in symbolism and emotion. 'Homecoming' is a frequently used word,[262] as is the imagery of being made 'whole', or finding peace and of feeling complete:[263] 'For years it was, as if I was standing on one leg only and attempted to keep my balance and composure, because I did not know who I was. Now I can finally stand on two legs; since I've learnt who my father is.'[264]

The experiences of CBOW in post-conflict Europe are culturally and politically distinct, but as will become evident in the following case studies of CBOW in Asia and Africa in the second half of the twentieth century, similar patterns in the childhood experiences emerge. In many countries it was common for the children to grow up in ignorance of their biological origins, and often they only found out about the identity of their fathers well into adulthood, if at all. Other challenges arise for those CBOW 'who knew', and who as mixed-race children were clearly visible as 'outsiders'. They were subjected to the same kind of discrimination and stigmatisation that affected all CBOW, as illegitimate children of mothers who had had relationships with foreign soldiers. But their situation was made more acute by the fact that they could not hide or be hidden, a fate shared with a growing number of CBOW, as military engagement in the second half of the twentieth century developed in two seemingly divergent directions. On the one hand, wars between neighbours for territorial gains were replaced by more ideologically driven conflicts and proxy wars that resulted in increasingly global engagement which, for instance, saw prolonged American deployment in Asia; on the other hand, especially towards the end of the century, an ever-increasing number of civil wars with ethnic or religious undertones developed. It is the children born of those categories of conflicts who will form the focus of the next chapters.

Notes

1 D. Culbert, '"It started with a kiss": German–Allied love affairs after 1945', *History Today*, 56 (2006), 2–3.
2 The German film: *Anonyma: Eine Frau in Berlin* was released in English as *The Downfall of Berlin: Anonyma*, www.imdb.com/title/tt1035730/. (accessed 12.2.2015).
3 Anon, *Eine Frau in Berlin* (Geneva: Kossodo, 1959), p. 259.
4 The diary had been translated into English and published in the United States in 1954 (*A Woman in Berlin*, New York: Harcourt, Brace, Jovanovich, 1954) and in the UK in 1955 (*A Women in Berlin*, London: Secker and Warburg, 1955).
5 Luke Harding, 'Row over naming of rape author', *The Guardian*, 4.10.2003, www.theguardian.com/world/2003/oct/05/historybooks.germany. (accessed 2.2.2015).
6 J. Bell, 'Anonyma: A Woman in Berlin', *Sight and Sound*, 20 (2010), 54–5.
7 Ibid., 54.
8 Júlia Garraio, 'Verschweigen, feministische Begeisterung, deutscher Opferdiskurs und romantische Trivialisierung: Die vielen Leben des Tagebuches Eine Frau in Berlin', paper presented at Em Trânsito – Übergänge: Grenzen überschreiten in der Germanistik, Faculdade de Letras da Universidade de Coimbra, 28 to 29 October 2011, 2–3, www.ces.uc.pt/myces/UserFiles/livros/1097_485_Microsoft_Word_-_Julia_Garraio.pdf. (accessed 13.2.2015).
9 Shortly after the re-publication, controversially, the identity of the author was revealed as that of Marta Hiller, a German journalist who had lived in Germany until her marriage in the 1950s and then moved to Switzerland, where the first German edition of the diary was published.
10 Holger Pötsch, 'Rearticulating the experience of war in Anonyma: Eine Frau in Berlin', *Nordlit*, 30 (2012), 15–33.
11 Matthias Bjørnlund, '"A fate worse than dying": Sexual violence during the Armenian genocide', in Dagmar Herzog (ed.), *Brutality and Desire: War and Sexuality in Europe's Twentieth Century* (Houndmills: Palgrave Macmillan, 2009), pp. 16–58; Nicoletta F. Gullace, 'Sexual violence and family honor: British

propaganda and international law during the First World War', *The American Historical Review*, 102 (1997) 714–47; John Horne, 'Corps, lieux et nation: La France et l'invasion de 1914', *Annales*, 55 (2000), 73–109; Stéphane Audoin-Rouzeau', *L'Enfant de l'ennemi 1914–1918* (Paris: Aubier 1995).

12   e.g. Keith Jeffery, '"Hut Ab", " Promenade with Kamerade for Schokolade" and the Flying Dutchman: British soldiers in the Rhineland, 1918–1929', *Diplomacy and Statecraft*, 16 (2006), 455–73; R. Harris, 'The "child of the barbarian": Rape, race and nationalism in France during the First World War', *Past and Present*, 141 (1993), 170–206.

13   Michelle K. Rhoades, 'Renegotiating French masculinity: Medicine and venereal disease during the Great War', *French Historical Studies*, 29 (2006), 293–327; Lucy Bland, 'In the name of protection: The policing of women in the First World War', J. Brophy and C. Smart (eds), *Women-in-Law: Explorations in Law, Family, and Sexuality* (London: Routledge, 1985), pp. 23–49; Mark Harrison, 'The British army and the problem of venereal disease in France and Egypt during the First World War', *Medical History*, 39 (1995), 133–58; Michael Imber, 'The First World War, sex education, and the American Social Hygiene Association's campaign against venereal disease', *Journal of Educational Administration and History*, 16 (1984), 47–56; Edward H. Beardsley, 'Allied against sin: American and British responses to venereal disease in World War I', *Medical History*, 20 (1976), 189–202.

14   While *Wehrmachtsbordelle* in some occupied countries, most notably France, have been researched in some detail, far less is known about the military brothels in the occupied territories in the East. See Birthe Kundrus, 'Nur die halbe Geschichte: Frauen im Umfeld der Wehrmacht zwischen 1939 und 1945 – ein Forschungsbericht', in Rolf-Dieter Müller and Hans-Erich Volkmann (eds), *Die Wehrmacht: Mythos und Realität* (Munich: Oldenbourg Verlag, 1999), pp. 719–38; Max Plassmann, 'Wehrmachtsbordelle: Anmerkungen zu einem Quellenfund im Universitätsarchiv Düsseldorf', *Militärgeschichtliche Zeitschrift*, 62 (2003), 157–73; Christa Paul, *Zwangsprostitution: Staatlich errichtete Bordelle im Nationalsozialismus* (Berlin: Hentrich, 1994); Insa Meinen, *Wehrmacht und Prostitution im besetzten Frankreich* (Bremen: Edition Temmen, 2002); Regina Mühlhäuser, *Eroberungen: Sexuelle Gewalttaten und intime Beziehungen deutscher Soldaten in der Sowjetunion, 1941–1945* (Hamburg: Hamburger Edition, 2010), 214–39; Wendy Jo Gertjejanssen, 'Victims, Heroes, Survivors, Sexual Violence on the Eastern Front During World War II' (Ph.D. thesis, University of Minnesota, 2004).

15   Hyunah Yang, 'Re-remembering the Korean military comfort women', in Elaine H. Kim and Chungmoo Choi (eds), *Dangerous Women: Gender and Korean Nationalism* (New York: Routledge 1998), pp. 123–40.

16   For a first study of children of the American occupation of Japan see Walter Hamilton, *Children of the Occupation: Japan's Untold Story* (New Brunswick: Rutgers University Press, 2013).

17   Erich Kuby, *The Russians in Berlin* (London: Heinemann, 1968); Atina Grossmann, 'A question of silence: The rape of German women by occupation soldiers', *October*, 72 (1995), 42–63; Norman M. Naimark, *The Russians in Germany: A History of the Soviet Zone of Occupation, 1945–1949* (Cambridge, MA: Harvard University Press, 1995); Pascale R. Bos, 'Feminists interpreting

the politics of wartime rape: Berlin, 1945; Yugoslavia, 1992–1993', *Journal of Women in Culture and Society*, 31 (2006), 996–1025; Helke Sander and Barbara Johr, *BeFreier und Befreite* (Frankfurt: Fischer, 2005); Anthony Beevor, *The Fall of Berlin 1945* (Harmondsworth: Penguin, 2003).

18 Omer Bartov, *The Eastern Front, 1941–1945: German Troops and the Barbarisation of Warfare* (London: Macmillan, 1985); Omer Bartov, *Hitlers Wehrmacht: Soldaten, Fanatismus und die Brutalisierung des Krieges* (Reinbek: Rohwolt Verlag, 1995); Ben Sheppard, *War in the Wild East: The German Army and Soviet Partisans* (Cambridge, MA: Harvard University Press, 2004).

19 Mühlhäuser, *Eroberungen*, p. 77.

20 Among others a controversial exhibition of the Hamburg Institute for Social Research 'Crimes of the German Wehrmacht – Dimensions of a War of Annihilation 1941–1944' documented the participation of the *Wehrmacht* in crimes committed during the Second World War. www.verbrechen-der-wehrmacht.de/docs/home.htm. (accessed 15.2.2015).

21 J. Burds, 'Sexual violence in Europe in World War II, 1939–1945', *Politics and Society*, 37 (2009), 35–73, here 36.

22 Ibid., 37.

23 Gisela Bock, 'Racism and sexism in Nazi Germany: Motherhood, compulsory sterilization, and the state', *Signs*, 8 (1983), 400–21, here 410–12.

24 Nils Johan Ringdal, *Love for Sale: A World History of Prostitution* (New York: Grove Press, 2004), pp. 325–6.

25 Burds, 'Sexual Violence', 39.

26 Ringdahl, *Love for Sale*, p. 326.

27 'Dort, wo ich war, gab es, glaube ich, nie eine Vergewaltigung. Wegen des Hungers in der Bevölkerung war das auch gar nicht nötig. ... Wenn die Frauen am Leben bleiben wollten, mussten sie sich eigentlich prostituieren.' Cited in Ruth Beckermann, *Jenseits des Krieges: Ehemalige Wehrmachtssoldaten erinnern sich* (Wien: Döcker, 1998), p. 102. tr. SL. NB all translations are by the author unless otherwise indicated.

28 On the basis of a paper of Generaloberst Rudolf Schmidt who had calculated that around 1.5 million German-fathered children ought to be expected as a result of the occupation, Himmler in a speech to SS and police spoke of many hundred thousand such children. RF-SS Himmler, Rede auf der SS- und Polizeiführer-Tagung in der Feldkommandpstelle Hegewald bei Shitomir, 19.9.1942; printed in Hans-Adolf Jacobsen and Werner Jochmann (eds), *Ausgewählte Dokumente zur Geschichte des Nationalsozialismus 1933–1945* (Bielefeld: Verlag Neue Gesellschaft, 1961ff), here vol. 3, pp. 4ff. The figures are not based on reasonable assumptions and will not have been anywhere near as high. See Mühlhäuser, *Eroberungen*, pp. 312–15; Christian Gerlach, *Kalkulierte Morde: Die Deutsche Wirtschafts- und Vernichtungspolitik in Weißrussland 1941 bis 1944* (Hamburg: Hamburger Edition, 1999); Dieter Pohl, *Die Herrschaft der Wehrmacht: Deutsche Militärbesatzung und einheimische Bevölkerung in der Sowjetunion* (Oldenbourg: Wissenschaftsverlag, 2008), p. 133.

29 For details see Mühlhäuser, *Eroberungen*, pp. 309–65.

30 Geheime Anordnung Nr 79/I des RF-SS, gez. Himmler, 23.3.1942; Isabel Heinemann, 'Rasse, Siedlung, deutsches Blut': Das Rasse- und Siedlungshauptamt

der SS und die rassenpolitische Neuordnung Europas (Göttingen: Wallstein Verlag, 2003), p. 476.

31 Oberkommando der Wehrmacht, gez. Keitel, Erlass, betr.: Unerwünschter Verkehr deutscher Soldaten mit Einwohnern in den besetzten Ostgebieten, 15.9.1942, Abschrift, B, Bundesarchiv (BA), NS 19 (Persönlicher Stab des Reichsführers-SS)/1691, p. 1.

32 Bock, 'Racism and sexism', 418; Burd, 'Sexual violence', 41 quotes Bock's figures incorrectly and thus, erroneously, speaks of 2 million women suffering compulsory abortions and forced sterilisation.

33 See Heinemann, 'Rasse, Siedlung, deutsches Blut'.

34 Letter Himmler to SS-Obergruppenführer Eicke, 30.4.1942, printed in Helmut Heiber (ed.), *Reichsführer!... Briefe an und von Himmler* (Stuttgart: Deutsche Verlagsanstalt, 1968), Doc. 107, p. 116.

35 The term *Wehrmachtskinder*, in contrast to previously used terms such as *Kriegskind* or *Besatzungskind*, was popularised by Ebba Drolshagen in her study of children of German fathers and foreign mothers, in particular in the occupied territories in East and West. While the term serves well to emphasise the significant number of children fathered by members of the German *Wehrmacht* during the First World War, it lacks accuracy in that many children of the German occupations during the war were fathered not by soldiers, but by members of the SS, the police or civilian occupiers (Ebba Drolshagen, *Wehrmachtskinder: Auf der Suche nach dem nie gekannten Vater* (Munich: Droemer Verlag, 2005), p. 14). The use of the term can, however, be justified in view of the overwhelming importance of the *Wehrmacht* during the war, with the war across Europe largely being a 'war of the *Wehrmacht*' (Mühlhäuser, *Eroberungen*, p. 62).

36 Georg Lilienthal, *Der 'Lebensborn e.V.': Ein Instrument nationalsozialistischer Rassenpolitik* (Frankfurt: Fischer, 2003); Larry V. Thompson, 'Lebensborn and the eugenics policy of the Reichsführer-SS', *Central European History*, 4 (1971), 54–77; Dieter Wältermann, 'The functions and activities of the Lebensborn Organisation within the SS, the Nazi regime, and Nazi ideology', *The Honors Journal*, 2 (1985), 5–23.

37 See, for instance, as late as 2006 and in a serious newspaper: Mark Landler, 'Result of secret Nazi breeding program: Ordinary folk', *New York Times*, 7.11.2006 www.nytimes.com/2006/11/07/world/europe/07nazi.html?pagewanted=all. (accessed 4.6.2016); also David Crossland, 'Nazi program to breed master race: Lebensborn children break their silence', *SpiegelOnlineInternational*, 7.11.2006, www.spiegel.de/international/0,1518,446978,00.html. (accessed 2.2.2015); For an appreciation of the nature of the organisation see 'Der Lebensborn: Eine Zuchtanstalt?' (Lebensborn – a breeding institution?) in Lilienthal, *Lebensborn*, pp. 146–59.

38 Trial of Ulrich Greifelt and others, *Law Reports of the Trials of War Criminals*. United Nations War Crimes Commission, vol. XIII. London: HMSO, 1949, www.ess.uwe.ac.uk/WCC/greifelt3.htm. (accessed 22.2.2015).

39 Satzung des Lebensborn, 12.12.1935, BA, NS19/329. See also Claudia Sandke, 'Der Lebensborn: Eine Darstellung der Aktivitäten des Lebensborn e.V. im Kontext der nationalsozialistischen Rassenideologie' (Master's thesis, Leipzig University, 2005), pp. 32–4.

40 Lilienthal, *Lebensborn*, pp. 166ff.
41 See in particular Lilienthal, *Lebensborn*. Also Thoman Bryant, *Himmlers Kinder: Zur Geschichte der SS-Organisation 'Lebensborn e.V.' 1935–1945* (Wiesbaden: Marix-Verlag, 2011).
42 Kåre Olsen, 'Under the care of the Lebensborn', in Kjersti Ericsson and Eva Simonsen (eds), *Children of World War II: The Hidden Enemy Legacy* (Oxford: Berg, 2005), pp. 25–34; Eva Simonsen, 'Into the open – or hidden away? The construction of war children as a social category in post-war Norway and Germany', *NORDEUROPAforum*, 2 (2006), 25–49.
43 Lilienthal, *Lebensborn*, p. 177, note 70.
44 See e.g. Dorothee Schmitz-Köster, *Deutsche Mutter bist du bereit: Alltag im Lebensborn* (Berlin: Aufbau-Verlag, 2002); Gisela Heidenreich, *Das endlose Jahr: Die langsame Entdeckung der eigenen Biographie – ein Lebensbornschicksal* (Frankfurt: Fischer-Verlag, 2002); Kåre Olsen, *Vater: Deutscher: Das Schicksal der Norwegischen Lebensbornkinder und ihrer Mütter von 1940 bis heute* (Frankfurt: Campus Verlag, 2002).
45 *Chef des Oberkommando der Wehrmacht*, Schreiben an die Reichskanzlei, 13.1.1941, BA R43 (Reichskanzlei)/II/1520a, p. 160.
46 Note, 27.6.1941, BA, R43/II/1520a, p. 160.
47 RGBl., 1942, §1, p. 488; cited in Raphael Lemkin, *Axis Rule in Occupied Europe: Laws of Occupation, Analysis of Government, Proposals for Redress* (Washington DC: Carnegie Endowment for International Peace, 1944), pp. 79–95; here chapter 9, note 31, www.preventgenocide.org/lemkin/AxisRule1944–2.htm. (accessed 12.2.2015).
48 See Regina Mühlhäuser, '"Diskriminiert als sei es ein Negerbastard": Der nationalsozialistische Blick auf die Kinder deutscher Soldaten und einheimischer Frauen in den besetzten Gebieten der Sowjetuion (1942–1945), *Werkstattgeschichte*, 51 (2009), 43–55, here 45, www.werkstattgeschichte.de/werkstatt_site/archiv/WG51_043-055_MUEHLHAEUSER_NEGERBASTARD.pdf. (accessed 12.2.2015).
49 Monika Diederichs, 'Stigma and silence: Dutch women, German soldiers and their children', in Ericsson and Simonsen (eds), *Children of World War II*, pp. 151–66. See also Monika Diederichs, *Kinderen van Duitse militairen in Nederland 1941–46: Een verborgen leven* (Soesterberg: Uitjeverij Aspekt, 2012).
50 Diederichs, 'Stigma', 154.
51 Nederlands Instituut voor Oorlogsdocumentatie, archief *Wehrmachtsbefehlshaber in den Niederlanden 1940–1945* Tagesbefehl 76/42. For details see Monika Diederichs, '"Moffenkinder": Kinder der Besatzung in den Niederlanden', *Historical Social Research*, 34 (2009), 304–20, here 307.
52 RGBl., 1942, §1, p. 488.
53 Note, 27.6.1941, BA, R43/II/1520a, p. 160.
54 Lilienthal, *Lebensborn*, pp. 160–6.
55 For details see Fabrice Virgili, *Naître ennemi: Les Enfants de couples franco-allemands nés pendant la Seconde Guerre mondiale* (Paris: Payot, 2009).
56 Letter from Jacques Chevalier to François Darlan, 20.7.1941, Archives Nationales Fontainebleau, Secrétariat Général du Gouvernment et Services et Cabinet du Premier Ministre, F60/558, cited in Fabrice Vigili, 'Enfants de Boches: The war

children of France', in Ericsson and Simonsen (eds), *Children of World War II*, pp. 138–64; here p. 138.
57 Patrick Buisson, *1940–1945: Années érotiques: Vichy ou les infortunes de la vertu* (Paris: Albin Michel, 2008); Meinen, *Wehrmacht und Prostitution*, pp. 37–77.
58 Insa Meinen, 'Wehrmacht und Prostitution im besetzten Frankreich', *Einblicke: Forschungsmagazin der Carl von Ossietzly Universität Oldenburg*, 31, www.presse.uni-oldenburg.de/einblicke/30/meinen.htm. (accessed 3.3.2017).
59 Report, Ltd.San.Offz, MVBez A, 20.11.1940, Bundesarchiv-Militärarchiv, RW35 (Militärbefehlshaber Frankreich)/1199.
60 Undated memo (probably June 1940), Bundesarchiv-Militärarchiv, RH20 (Armeeoberkommando) 4/971. See also Meinen, *Wehrmacht und Prostitution*, particularly chapter B II.
61 Meinen, *Wehrmacht und Prostitution*, 85f.
62 Report, 23.9.1940, Archives Nationales Paris, Archives allemandes de la Seconde Guerre mondiale, 40/446, Dr. 1.
63 Meinen's study of *Wehrmacht* and prostitution contains a detailed study of the camps of Jargeau and La Lande, exploring the links between brothels and internment camps. See Meinen, *Wehrmacht und Prostitution*, chapter C.
64 German translation of French memorandum (Ministry of the Interior) on regulation of prostitution, 31.12.1940, Bundesarchiv-Militärarchiv, H20 (Militärmedizin)/143.
65 Francine Muel-Dreyfus and Kathleen A. Johnson, *Vichy and the Eternal Feminine: A Contribution to a Political Sociology of Gender* (Durham, NC: Duke University Press, 2001).
66 H. Eck, 'Die Französinnen unter dem Vichy Regime: Frauen in der Katastrophe?', in Georges Duby and Michelle Perot (eds), *Geschichte der Frauen*, vol. 5 (Frankfurt: Fischer, 1997), pp. 223–55; C. Watson, 'Birth control and abortion in France since 1939', *Population Studies*, 5 (1951/52), 261–86.
67 Sarah Fishman, *We Will Wait: Wives of French Prisoners of War, 1940–1945* (New Haven: Yale University Press, 1992); Virgili, 'Enfants de Boches', 142.
68 Virgili, *Naître ennemi*, p. 154. For problems about accurate data see 'Les Difficultés d'une estimation', ibid., pp. 150–5.
69 Henry Picker, *Hitlers Tischgespräche im Führerhauptquartier* (München: Goldmann, 1979), No. 66, 5.4.1942, p. 195.
70 Vermerk über die Äußerungen des Reichsführers SS, 14.8.1942, BA-NS 19 (Persönlicher Stab des Reichsführer SS)/neu1446.
71 Letter L. Conti to H. Himmler, 29.5.1942, BA-NS 048 (Sonstige zentrale Dienststellen und Einrichtungen der SS)/000030.
72 Note of the immigration office Paris, 15.10.1943, BA-NS 2 (Rasse- und Siedlungshauptamt)/Memo 27.
73 Letter L. Conti to H. Himmler, 29.5.1942, BA-NS 048/000030.
74 Letter *SS-Führer in Rassse- und Siedlungswesen* at the *Höherer SS und Polizeiführer* Zwickler to director of *Rasse und Siedlungshauptamt*, *SS Gruppenführer* Turner, 24.5.1944, BA: NS2/27; letter *SS-Sturmbannführer* Dr Fritz to *SS-Führer in Rasse und Siedlungswesen*, 25.5.1944, BA: NS2/34.
75 See Lilienthal, *Lebensborn*, pp. 192ff. See also Virgili, *Naître ennemi*, pp. 159–62.

76 Konrad Kwiet, *Reichskommissariat Niederlande: Versuch und Scheitern nationalisozialistischer Neuordnung* (Stuttgart: Deutsche Verlagsanstalt, 1968), pp. 57–8 and 86.
77 Gabriele Hoffmann, *NS-Propaganda in den Niederlanden: Organisation und Lenkung der Publizistik unter deutscher Besatzung 1940–1945* (München: Verlag Dokumentation, 1972), p. 35.
78 L. De Jong, *Het Koninkrijk der Nederlanden in de Tweede Wereldoorlog*, vol. 5, part 1 (The Hague: Martinus Nijoff, 1972), p. 246. See also Diederichs, 'Stigma', 153.
79 Diederichs, 'Stigma', 151.
80 J. Koekebakker, *Onze kinderbescherming in oorlog en vrede* (Purmerend: Muusses, 1945), pp. 29–31. See also Diederichs, 'Stigma', 152.
81 Yoshiko Nozaki, 'The "comfort women" controversy: History and testimony', *The Asia-Pacific Journal: Japan Focus* (2005), http://japanfocus.org/-Yoshiko-Nozaki/2063. (accessed 16.2.2015).
82 A substantial body of historical and contemporary research around Japan's forced prostitution now exists, including scholarly works, memoirs, testimonies, legal and political enquiries and American, Korean and Japanese responses. See e.g. Yoshiaki Yoshimi, *Comfort Women: Sexual Slavery in the Japanese Military During World War II* (New York: Columbia University Press, 2000); Toshiyuki Tanaka, *Japan's Comfort Women: Sexual Slavery and Prostitution during World War II and the US Occupation* (London: Routledge, 2002); Sangmie Choi Schellstede and Soon Mi Yu, *Comfort Women Speak: Testimony by Sex Slaves of the Japanese Military* (New York: Holmes & Meier Publishers, 2000); Chungmoo Choi (ed.), 'The comfort women: Colonialism, war, and sex', *Special Issue of East Asia Culture Critique*, 5:1 (1997); Pyong Gap Min, 'Korean "comfort women": The intersection of colonial power, gender, and class', *Gender & Society*, 17 (2003), 938–57; Wallace Edwards, *Comfort Women: A History of Japanese Forced Prostitution During the Second World War* (CreateSpace Independent Publishers, 2013); C. Sarah Soh, *The Comfort Women: Sexual Violence and Postcolonial Memory in Korea and Japan* (Chicago: University of Chicago Press, 2008).
83 Rupert Wingfield-Hayes, 'Japan revisionists deny World War II sex slave atrocities', *BBC News online*, www.bbc.co.uk/news/world-asia-33754932, 3.8.2015. (accessed 13.8.2015).
84 It is impossible to determine accurately how many women served as forced sex slaves, how many survived and how many did not return from the battlefields. No documents with comprehensive data are available and estimates vary, depending on the basic assumption about number of military personnel stationed ratios of soldiers to prostitutes, and rate of the replacement for comfort women. The most widely cited estimate is Yoshiaki Yoshimi's of around 200,000 women in *Jugun Ianfu* (*The Wartime Comfort Women*), Iwanami Shoten, 1995, English translation, *Comfort Women: Sexual Slavery in Japanese Military during World War II* (New York: Columbia University Press, 2000). See also 'Number of comfort stations and comfort women', *Digital Museum: The Comfort Women Issue and the Asian Women's Fund*, www.awf.or.jp/e1/facts-07.html. (accessed 16.2.2015).
85 Iris Chang, *The Rape of Nanking: The Forgotten Holocaust of World War II* (New York: Basic Books, 1996).
86 Yoshimini, *Comfort Women*, pp. 42–75.

87 Carmen M. Argibay, 'Sexual slavery and the comfort women of World War II', *Berkeley Journal of International Law*, 21 (2003), 375–89, here 377.
88 'Testimonies of former "comfort women" from Korea', www.koreaverband.de/wp-content/uploads/2013/04/biographies_KoreanComfortWomen_english.pdf. (accessed 16.2.2015).
89 Tanaka, *Japan's Comfort Women*, p. 53.
90 'Testimonies of former "comfort women"', 6; See e.g. Tanaka, *Japan's Comfort Women*, p. 74.
91 From the sources I am aware of, the identity of only one surviving child fathered by a Japanese soldier and born to a comfort woman, Luo Shan Xue, whose mother fled a comfort station when she was two months pregnant. His mother had been married prior to being abducted, but her husband mistreated the boy and he suffered persistent discrimination from an early age in the local community. Kim Don-wan (director), *63 Years On* (2008), www.imdb.com/title/tt1619828/combined. (accessed 17.2.2015).
92 Dag Ellingsen, *En registerbasert undersøkelse*, Statistics Norway, Rapport Nr. 2004/19, 2004.
93 For further details see Ingvill C. Mochmann and Stein Ugelvik Larsen, 'Kriegskinder in Europa', *Aus Politik und Zeitgeschichte*, Nr. 18–19/2005: 34–8. Mochmann and Larsen, 'The forgotten consequences'. See also Ingvill C. Mochmann and Arne Øland, 'Der lange Schatten des Zweiten Weltkriegs: Kinder deutscher Wehrmachtssoldaten und einheimischer Frauen in Dänemark', *Historical Social Research*, 34 (2009), 282–303.
94 Kåre Olsen, *Krigens barn: De norske krigsbarna og deres mødre* (Oslo: Aschehoug, 1998); Lars Borgersrud, *Staten of krigsbarna: En historisk undersøkelse av statsmyndighetenes behandling av krigsbarna i de første etterkrigsårene* (University of Oslo, Department of Culture Studies, 2004).
95 Mochmann and Larsen, 'The forgotten consequences', 357.
96 Jean-Paul Picaper and Ludwig Norz, *Enfants maudits* (Paris: Edition de Syrtes, 2004).
97 Fabrice Virgili, *La France virile: Des femmes tondues à la Libération* (Paris: Payot, 2000).
98 Virgili, *Naître ennemi*.
99 Diederichs, 'Moffenkinder', 308.
100 Diederichs, *Kinderen*.
101 See also Monika Diederichs, *Wie geschoren wordt moet stil zitten: De omgang van Nederlandse meisjes met Duitse militairen* (Den Haag: Boom Onderwijs, 2006).
102 '"Wehrmacht" children in Belgium', Centre for Historical Research and Documentation on War and Contemporary Society, www.cegesoma.be/cms/rech_encours_en.php?article=734. (accessed 12.1.2015).
103 Lilienthal, *Lebensborn*, pp. 33, 186.
104 For discussion of German *Lebensborn* activities in Belgium see material in BA: R43II/137a.
105 See Lilienthal, *Lebensborn*, pp. 185–6.
106 Kerstin Muth, *Die Wehrmacht in Griechenland – und ihre Kinder* (Leipzig: Eudora Verlag, 2008), p. 81.
107 Maren Roeger, 'Children of German soldiers in Poland', in Lars Westerlund (ed.),

The Children of German Soldiers, vol. 2 (Helsinki: Painopaikka Nord Print, 2011), pp. 261–72.

108 Lars Westerlund, 'Children of German soldiers in Finland', in Lars Westerlund (ed.), *The Children of German Soldiers*, vol. 1 (Helsinki: Painopaikka Nord Print, 2011), pp. 293–303.

109 Paula Uhlenius, 'The hidden children of German soldiers and Soviet prisoners of war', in Westerlund (ed.), *Children of German Soldiers*, vol. 1, pp. 153–9.

110 I.C. Mochmann, 'Developing a methodology for the research field of "Children born of war"', European Survey Research Association Conference, Warsaw, 29.6.2009–3.7.2009.

111 H. Glaesmer et al., 'Die Kinder des Zweiten Weltkrieges in Deutschland: Ein Rahmenmodell für die psychosoziale Forschung', *Trauma und Gewalt*, 6 (2012), 319–28, here 323.

112 Diana Kunitz, '"Kind des Feindes?" Eine Untersuchung zu den Identitätsbildern der deutschen 'Besatzungskinder' des Zweiten Weltkrieges' (Master's thesis, Leipzig University, 2014), pp. 14–15.

113 Walter Hamilton, *Children of the Occupation: Japan's Untold Story* (New Brunswick: Rutgers University Press, 2012); James McGrath Morris, 'Occupation babies: Mixed-race Japanese children', *Wonders and Marvels*, www.wondersandmarvels.com/2015/02/occupation-babies-mixed-race-japanese-children.html. (accessed 12.8.2015); Reiji Yoshida, 'Mixed-race babies in lurch. Facts of occupation life: Abandoned kids from GI–Japanese liaisons', *The Japan Times*, 10.9.2008, www.japantimes.co.jp/news/2008/09/10/national/mixed-race-babies-in-lurch/#.VcsmxPnz57V. (accessed 12.8.2015).

114 See BA:B106/8635.

115 Recently a figure of 'at least 400,000' has been stipulated. See among others Oliver Das Gupta, 'Unerwünschte Kinder des Feindes', *Süddeutsche Zeitung*, 9.2.2015, www.sueddeutsche.de/politik/besatzungskinder-nach-zweitem-weltkrieg-unerwuenschte-kinder-des-feindes-1.2342768. (accessed 12.8.2015).

116 Gertrud Srncik, 'Besatzungskinder: Ein Weltproblem', *Arbeiter-Zeitung*, 3.11.1955, p. 5. For details about the Red Army in Austria see in particular Barbara Stelzl-Marx, *Stalins Soldaten in Österreich: Die Innensicht der sowjetischen Besatzung 1945–1955* (Wien / München: Böhlau Verlag, 2012). More recent works speak of at least 30,000 Austrian children of the occupation. See Bethany Bell, 'Occupation children shunned in post-war German and Austria', *BBC News online*, 6.6.2015, www.bbc.co.uk/news/world-europe-32972893. (accessed 22.5.2016). For details see also Barbara Stelzl-Marx and Silke Satjukow (eds), *Besatzungskinder: Die Nachkommen alliierter Soldaten in Österreich und Deutschland* (Wien: Böhlau Verlag, 2015).

117 'Härteausgleichsregelung', 10.2.1960, BA: B126/28418.

118 Anthony Beevor, cited in Paul Sheehan, 'An orgy of denial in Hitler's bunker', *The Sydney Morning Herald*, 17.5.2003, www.smh.com.au/articles/2003/05/16/1052885399546.html. (accessed 5.7.2012).

119 Barbara Johr, 'Die Ereignisse in Zahlen', in Sander and Johr, *BeFreier und Befreite*, pp. 48, 54–5; Kuby, *Russians in Berlin*, p. 274; Grossmann, 'Question of silence', 46.

120 Naimark, *The Russians in Germany*, pp. 106–7.

121 Daniel Johnson, 'Red Army troops raped even Russian women as they freed then from camps', *The Telegraph*, online edition www.telegraph.co.uk, 24.1.2002, www.telegraph.co.uk/news/worldnews/europe/russia/1382565/Red-Army-troops-raped-even-Russian-women-as-they-freed-them-from-camps.html. (accessed 16.7.2015).
122 Anne-Marie Durand-Wever, *Als die Russen kamen: Tagebuch einer Berliner Ärztin*, unpublished diary, cited in Grossmann, 'Question of silence', 54. See also Hans von Lehndorff, *Ostpreußisches Tagebuch: Aufzeichnungen eines Arztes aus den Jahren 1945–1947* (München: Deutscher Taschenbuch Verlag, 1997) describing similar experiences in East Prussia.
123 Grossmann, 'Question of silence', 61.
124 Barbara Stelzl-Marx, 'Die unsichtbare Generation: Kinder sowjetischer Besatzungssoldaten in Deutschland und Österreich', *Historische Sozialforschung*, 34 (2009), 352–72, here, 362.
125 Silke Satjukow, *Die Russen in Deutschland 1945–1994* (Göttingen: Vandenhock & Ruprecht, 2008), pp. 284–98; Stelzl-Marx, *Stalins Soldaten*, pp. 496–509.
126 Atina Grossmann, 'Eine Frage des Schweigens: Die Vergewaltigung deutscher Frauen durch Besatzungssoldaten. Zum historischen Hintergrund von Helke Sanders Film *BeFreier und Befreite*', *Frauen und Film*, 54/55 (April 1994), 15–28.
127 e.g. Johannes Kaps, *Martyrium und Heldentum ostdeutscher Frauen* (self-published, 1954). Notoriously, James Wakefield Burke instrumentalised the women's suffering in the anti-communist propaganda novel *The Big Rape* (New York: Popular Library, 1953).
128 Soviet rules regarding fraternisation differed in Germany and Austria. Austria, on the basis of the Moscow Declaration of 1943 had been declared a 'friendly' country by the Soviet Union and therefore fraternisation *per se* was not illegal. Intimate contacts between Soviet soldiers and local Austrians, however, were not permitted. Also See Stelzl-Marx, *Stalins Soldaten*, pp. 497, 511–18; Satjukow, *Die Russen in Deutschland*, p. 284.
129 See more generally *Besatzungskinder* as fatherless: Ute Baur-Timmerbrink, *Wir Besatzungskinder: Töchter und Söhne alliierter Soldaten erzählen* (Berlin: Ch. Links-Verlag, 2015), pp. 72–83.
130 Stelzl-Marx, *Stalins Soldaten*, p. 537.
131 See W. Behlau (ed.), *Distelblüten: Russenkinder in Deutschland* (Ganderkesee: Countour, 2015).
132 'Soldatenkinder Tabuthema seit 65 Jahren', *Radio Niederösterreich*, 26.9.2012. http://noe.orf.at/news/stories/2551623/. (accessed 15.3.2013).
133 'Das wäre wie im Märchen, wenn ich jetzt plötzlich wissen würde, wo meine Wurzeln sind.' 'Kinder auf der Suche nach ihrem Vater', *Radio Niederösterreich*, 6.10.2012, http://noe.orf.at/news/stories/2552812/. (accessed 15.8.2015). See also Eleonore Dupuis, *Befreiungskind* (Wien: Edition Liaunigg, 2015).
134 The following section is based on Sabine Lee, 'A forgotten legacy of the Second World War: GI children in post-war Britain and Germany', *Contemporary European History*, 20 (2011), 157–81.
135 This characterisation was popularised by the British comedian Tommy Trinder. The American GIs retaliated by calling their British hosts 'underpaid, undersexed and under Eisenhower'.

136 See Juliet Gardiner, *Over Here: The GIs in Wartime Britain* (London: Collins and Brown, 1992); W.K. Hancock and M.M. Gowing, *British War Economy* (London: HMSO, 1949), pp. 351–2, available at www.ibiblio.org/hyperwar/UN/UK/UK-Civil-WarEcon. (accessed 27.2.2015).
137 Richard Morris Titmuss, *Problems of Social Policy* (London: HMSO, 1950), chapter VII, Appendix II, pp. 543–9.
138 Sonya O. Rose, *Which People's War? National Identify and Citizenship in Wartime Britain 1939–1945* (Oxford: Oxford University Press, 2003), pp. 71–106.
139 Christopher G. Thorne, 'Britain and the Black G.I.s: Racial issues and Anglo-American relations in 1942', in Christopher G. Thorne (ed.), *Border Crossings: Studies in International History* (Oxford: Wiley Blackwell, 1988), pp. 259–74.
140 Anthony Richmond, *Colour Prejudice in Britain: A Study of West Indian Workers in Liverpool 1941–1951* (London: Routledge and K. Paul, 1954), p. 20. See also John Solomos, *Race and Racism in Britain*, 3rd edn (Basingstoke: Palgrave Macmillan, 2003), ch. 3; Kenneth L. Little, 'The psychological background of white-coloured contacts in Britain', *The Sociological Review*, 35 (1943), 12–28, here 14, 18.
141 See Rose, *Which People's War?*, p. 254.
142 Reynolds, *Rich Relations*, pp. 220–37.
143 For details about VD rates among US soldiers see National Archives at College Park (NACP), RG549, box 2207.
144 Credible estimates of the number of GI-children are given in George Padmore to Walter White, 29 April 1947 and enclosed memo of 24 April, in National Association for the Advancement of Coulored People papers, II (General Office File)/A, box 63I: 'US Army – Brown Babies'.
145 Elfrieda Berthiaume Shukert and Barbara Smith Scibetta, *War Brides of World War II* (Novato: Presidio Press, 1988).
146 Immigration and Naturalisation Service: Annual Report 1949, Table 9A and Annual Report 1950, Table 9A, Suitland, MD: Washington National Records Center. See also N.H. Carrier and J.R. Jeffrey (eds), *External Migration: A Study of the Available Statistics, 1815–1950* (London: HMSO, 1953), pp. 40ff.
147 Kate Watson-Smyth, 'GI babies abandoned during Second World War reunite to trace their unknown fathers', *The Independent*, 8.7.2000; Eve-Ann Prentice, 'No peace for GI babies', *The Times*, 24.12.2002, p. 11; Brenda Gayle Plummer, 'Brown babies: Race, gender and policy after World War II', in Brenda Gayle Plummer (ed.), *Window on Freedom: Race, Civil Rights and Foreign Affairs 1945–1988* (Chapel Hill: University of North Carolina Press, 2003), pp. 67–92.
148 Baur-Timmerbrink, *Wir Besatzungskinder*, p. 20; Karin Schmidlechner, 'Kinder und Enkelkinder britischer Besatzungssoldaten in Österreich', in Stelzl-Marx and Satjukow (eds), *Besatzungskinder*, pp. 238–58, here, p. 252.
149 Pamela Winfield, *Bye Bye Baby: The Story of the Children the GIs Left Behind* (London: Bloomsbury 1992), pp. 53–67.
150 Ormus Davenport, 'US race prejudice dooms 1000 British babies', *Reynolds News*, 9.2.1947.
151 Ann Evans in Watson-Smyth, 'GI babies abandoned'.
152 Hazel Carby, in the 2006 Dean's Lecture at the Radcliffe Institute for Advanced Studies, recalls her own childhood experiences as a (non-adopted) mixed-race

person, and powerfully describes the feeling of 'otherness' in what she refers to as British racialised society. Hazel B. Carby, 'Brown babies: The birth of Britain as a racialized state, 1943–1948', 2.1.2006, www.radcliffe.edu/print/events/calendar_2006carby.htm. (accessed 10.5.2015).

153 Kathleen E. Kiernan, Hilary Land and Jane E. Lewis, *Lone Motherhood in Twentieth-Century Britain: From Footnote to Front Page* (Oxford: Oxford University Press, 1998), chapter 4.

154 Memo, Hqs, European Theater of Operations, for Gen Eisenhower, sub: Strength of the US Forces, 30 April 45, in NACP USFET SGS 320.3/2. In 2001 National Archives and Records Administration started reallocating military records from the WWII era to new Record Groups (RGs). Therefore some sources may now have been moved to new RGs. See also Earl F. Ziemke, *The US Army in the Occupation of Germany 1944–1946*, Washington, DC: Center of Military History, United States Army (1990); the American occupation of post-war Germany has been scrutinised beyond the purely military in detail elsewhere. See for instance, Klaus Dietmar Henke, *Die amerikanische Besatzung Deutschlands* (Munich: Oldenbourg, 1995); James McAllister, *No Exit: America and the German Problem, 1943–1954* (Ithaca: Cornell University Press, 2002).

155 Joseph R. Starr, *Fraternisation with the Germans in World War II*, Office of the Chief Historian, US European Command, Planning for the Occupation of Germany, Occupation Forces in Europe Series, 1945–46 (Frankfurt: US European Command, 1947). See in particular 'Policy, relationship between allied occupying troops and inhabitants of Germany', 12.9.1944, Appendix to letter from Eisenhower to Commanding Generals, NACP, SHAEF (Supreme Headquarters Allied Expeditionary Force), RG331, files 091–4.

156 Johannes Kleinschmidt, '"German Fräuleins": Heiraten zwischen amerikanischen Soldaten und Deutschen in der Besatzungszeit 1945–1949', *Frauen in der einen Welt* 4 (1992), 42–58.

157 See for instance: Report by Judy Barden cited in 'The good (looking) Germans', *Newsweek*, 25, 28 May 1945, 64.

158 See chapter 4 below for similar propaganda demonising Vietnamese women as dangerous and potentially lethal companions.

159 See for instance Percy Knauth, 'Fraternisation: The word takes on a brand-new meaning in Germany', *Life*, 2.7.1945, 26. On the GIs' reputation in Europe, see 'You don't know what you want', *Time*, 8 Oct.1945, 30–1; (Serviceman's Name Withheld) to *Time*, 12.11.1945, 6; Toni Howard, 'The idle GI and liberated France are mighty tired of each other', *Newsweek*, 19.11.1945, 56–7.

160 'Zunahme der weiblichen Bevölkerung; Stand 29.10.1946', Länderrat des amerikanischen Besatzungsgebietes: Memorandum über die soziale Lage in der US-Zone, BA, Handakte Preller, 21, 965.170.

161 Starr, *Fraternisation*, 81–2. See also, Ann Elisabeth Pfau, *Miss Your Lovin: GIs, Gender and Domesticity During WWII*, available at www.gutenberg-e.org/pfau/chapter3.html. (accessed 2.6.2016), ch. 3, 22ff.

162 Compare, for example, Naimark, *The Russians in Germany*, pp. 69–140, esp. pp. 113–15; Grossmann, 'Question of silence'.

163 Robert Lilly, *Taken by Force: Rape and American GIs in Europe During World War II* (London: Palgrave Macmillan, 2007). See also John Willoughby, 'The sexual

behavior of American GIs during the early years of the occupation of Germany', *Journal of Military History*, 62 (1998), 155–74. For a recent debate about GI rape in Germany see Miriam Gebhardt, *Als die Soldaten kamen* (Munich: Deutscher Taschenbuch Verlag, 2015) and in response Ellen Kositza, 'Gedanken zu Miriam Gebhardts "Als die Soldaten kamen"', *Sezession in Netz*, 7.4.2015, www.sezession.de/49105/gedanken-zu-miriam-gebhardt-als-die-soldaten-kamen.html. (accessed 12.8.2015).

164 Harold Zink, *The United States in Germany, 1944–1955* (Princeton: D. Van Nostrand Company, 1957), pp. 137–8, using the only survey carried out on behalf of the Federal Government. BA: B106/8635.

165 The *Statistisches Bundesamt* specifies a number of 68,000 children of Allied soldiers who were born in the three Western zones and West Berlin between 1945 and 1955. Statistisches Bundesamt (ed.), *Statistische Berichte*, Wiesbaden, 'Die unehelichen Kinder von Besatzungsangehörigen im Bundesgebiet und Berlin (West)', Arb-Nr. VI/29/6, 1956, Tables 1–19. This is likely to be a conservative figure. See Norbert Schäfers and Roland F. Stiegler, 'Besatzungskinder', *Kriesenjahre und Aufbruchsstimmung: Die Nachkriegszeit in Deutschland 1945–1965*, Internetportal Westfälische Geschichte: Aufwachsen in Westfalen. www.lwl.org/westfaelische-geschichte/portal/Internet/input_felder/langDatensatz_ebene4.php?urlID=896&url_tabelle=tab_websegmente. (accessed 21.3.2015). More recent estimates, based on statistics compiled by Kai Grieg, assume a number closer to 96,000 children of American soldiers alone. Kai Grieg, 'The war children of the world', in *War and Children Identity Project* (Bergen: War and Children Identity Project, 2001), pp. 8–9. For details, see also BA: B153/342, 'Uneheliche Kinder von Besatzungsangehörigen', 5 (no. 323).

166 See also Luise Frankenstein, *Soldatenkinder: Die unehelichen Kinder ausländischer Soldaten mit besonderer Berücksichtigung der Mischlinge* (Munich: Wilhelm Steinbach, 1954); Waldemar Oelrich, 'Die unehelichen Besatzungskinder der Jahrgänge 1945 bis 1954 in Baden-Württemberg', *Statistische Monatshefte Baden-Württemberg*, 2 (1956), 38–9.

167 Anette Brauerhoch, 'Fräuleins und GIs: Besonderheiten einer historischen Situation', *ForschungsForum Paderborn*, http://kw.uni-paderborn.de/fileadmin/mw/Brauerhoch/downloads/FF-Brauerhoch.pdf. (accessed 2.7.2015).

168 This has been investigated specifically for Austria in Ingrid Bauer, 'The GI war bride – place holder for the absent? (De)constructing a stereotype of post-World War II Austrian history, 1945–55', *Homme: Zeitschrift fur Feministische Geschichtswissenschaft*, 7 (1996), 107–21.

169 Claudia Koonz, *Mothers in the Fatherland: Women, Family and Nazi Politics* (London: St. Martin's Press, 1986). See also Brauerhoch, 'Fräuleins und GIs'.

170 Petra Goedde, *GIs and Germans: Culture, Gender and Foreign Relations, 1945–1949* (New Haven: Yale University Press, 2003), p. 95.

171 Exact figures of the number of marriages do not exist. Joachim Kleinschmidt estimates that between 12,000 and 13,000 couples got married and around 20,000 women emigrated as war brides. Johannes Kleinschmidt, 'Amerikaner und Deutsche in der Besatzungszeit: Beziehungen und Probleme', in Haus der Geschichte Baden-Württemberg, Landeszentrale für politische Bildung Baden-Württemberg (eds), *Besatzer – Helfer – Vorbilder: Amerikanische Politik und*

deutscher Alltag in Württemberg-Baden 1945 bis 1949 (Baden-Württemberg: LpB, 1996), 35–54. American immigration statistics confirm this order of magnitude of marriages and emigration.

172 Sybille Buske, *Fräulein Mutter und ihr Bastard: Eine Geschichte der Unehelichkeit in Deutschland 1900–1970* (Göttingen: Wallstein, 2004), pp. 195–210.
173 See relevant remarks in the files of the Ministry of the Interior in Baden-Württemberg, 'Jugendwohlfahrt: Unterhalt für unehelich geborene Kinder von Mitgliegern ausländischer Streitkräfte', Baden-Württembergisches Hauptstaatsarchiv Stuttgart, EA2 (Akten des Innenministeriums Baden-Württemberg)/008. These files refer to children of foreign soldiers, and deal specifically with the American zone of occupation until 1955.
174 Information of Väter-Aktuell. See www.vaeter-aktuell.de/kriegskinder/Deutschland/USA-1945.htm. (accessed 5.6.2016).
175 Friederike Nadig about the legal position of children born out of wedlock, Parlamentarischer Rat, *Stenographischer Bericht* (Bonn, 1949), 18.1.1949, 552.
176 See Heide Fehrenbach, *Race After Hitler* (Princeton: Princeton University Press, 2005), pp. 31–9, 53–61, 80–8.
177 For details, see Peggy Pascoe, 'Miscegenation law, court cases, and ideologies of "race" in 20th-century America', in Martha Hodes (ed.), *Sex, Love, Race: Crossing Boundaries in North American History* (New York: New York University Press, 1999), 464–90; also Samuel Stouffer, *The American Soldier: Studies in Social Psychology in World War II* (Princeton: Princeton University Press, 1949), p. 548; For comparative perspective on Britain, see also Sonya O. Rose, 'Girls and GIs: Race, sex, and diplomacy in Second World War Britain', *International History Review*, 19 (1997), 146–60, here 156–7.
178 Frankenstein, *Soldatenkinder*, 6.
179 Simonsen, 'Into the open', 40.
180 Walter Kirchner, *Eine anthroposiphische Studie an Mulattenkindern in Berlin unter besonderer Berücksichtigung der sozialien Verhältnisse* (Berlin: self-publication, 1952); Rudolf Sieg, *Mischlingskinder in Westdeutschland: Festschrift für Frédéric Falkenburger* (Baden-Baden: Verlag für Kunst und Wissenschaft, 1954).
181 Rainer Pommerin, *Sterilisierung der Rheinlandbastarde: Das Schicksal einer farbigen Minderheit 1918–1937* (Düsseldorf: Droste, 1979).
182 Silke Satjukow, 'Nachkommen amerikanischer und britischer Soldaten in Nachkriegsdeutschland', in Stelzl-Marx and Satjukow (eds), *Besatzungskinder*, pp. 259–93, here p. 276.
183 *Verhandlungen des Deutschen Bundestages*, Stenographische Berichte, 1. Legislaturperiode, 10, 12 March 1952, 8505ff.
184 'What has become of the 94,000 occupation babies?', *Das Parlament*, 19.3.1952, cited in Inez Templeton, 'What's so German About it? Cultural Identity in the Berlin Hip Hop Scene' (D.Phil. thesis, University of Stirling, 2005), p. 78.
185 Survey poll, cited in Peter H. Koepf, 'An unexpected freedom', *The Atlantic Times*, 1.4.2009.
186 Koepf, 'An unexpected freedom'.
187 See details of one such segregated home in BA: B153/342 and in the Archiv des Diakonischen Werkes der Evangelischen Kirche Deutschlands, HGSt1161and 1193.

188 Yara-Colette Lemke Muniz de Faria, *Zwischen Fürsorge und Ausgrenzung: Afrodeutsche 'Besatzungskinder' im Nachkriegsdeutschland* (Berlin: Metropol, 2002).
189 While many policies may have been well intentioned, some biographical accounts suggest that their implementation was not always as devoid of prejudice as one may have hoped. See for instance Ika Hügel-Marschall, *Daheim Unterwegs: Ein deutsches Leben* (Frankfurt: Fischer, 2001).
190 According to surveys of the Public Health Division of the military government in Germany and the *Deutscher Verein für öffentliche und private Fürsorge* 76% of African-German occupation children lived with their mothers or other relatives and only 12% in orphanages or other children's homes. Yara-Colette Lemke Muniz de Faria, 'Germany's "brown babies" must be helped! Will you? U.S. adoption plans for African-German children, 1950–1955', *Callaloo*, 26 (2003), 342–62, here 346.
191 For details, see Fehrenbach, *Race*, pp. 132–7 and 232, note 7.
192 Lemke de Faria, 'Germany's "brown babies"', 343–4.
193 See www.grammerchildren.com. (accessed 14.8.2015).
194 Stephanie Siek, 'The difficult identities of Germany's brown babies', *Spiegel Online International*, 13.10.2009, www.spiegel.de/international/germany/0,1518,651989,00.html. (accessed 13.6.2015).
195 'Mammies für die Negerlein', *Stern*, 27.8.1950, 29; and 'Mammies für die Negerlein', *Stern*, 2.3.1952, 8; see also Correspondence from the editors of *Revue* to the State Youth Welfare Office, Marktredwitz, 22 Feb. 1952, BayHStA, MInn 81096.
196 Fehrenbach, *Race*, 140ff.
197 Klaus Eyferth, 'Eine Untersuchung der Neger-Mischlingskinder in Westdeutschland', *Vita Humana*, 2 (1959), 102–14.
198 Klaus Eyferth, Ursula Brandt and Wolfgang Hawel, *Farbige Kinder in Deutschland: Die Situation der Mischlingskinder und die Aufgabe ihrer Eingliederung* (Munich: Juventa, 1960).
199 Most significantly, Tara Zahra, *The Lost Children* (Cambridge, MA: Harvard University Press, 2011); Tara Zahra, *Kidnapped Souls: National Indifference and the Battle for the Children in the Bohemian Lands* (Ithaca: Cornell University Press, 2008).
200 Eyferth et al., *Farbige Kinder*, pp. 50, 56, 72.
201 Richard Bessel and Dirk Schumann (eds), *Life after Death: Approaches to a Cultural and Social History of Europe during the 1940s and 1950s* (New York: Cambridge University Press, 2003).
202 Simonsen, 'Into the open', 48.
203 Yves Denéchère, 'Des adoptions d'État: Les enfants de l'occupation française en Allemagne, 1945–1952', *Revue d'histoire modern & contemporaine*, 2 (2010), 159–79; here 160.
204 Another source talks of 17,000 files. See Rainer Gries, 'Les Enfants d'État: Französische Besatzungskinder in Deutschland', in Stelzl-Marx and Satjukow (eds), *Besatzungskinder*, pp. 380–407, here p. 383.
205 Emanuelle Saada, *Empire's Children: Race, Filiation, and Citizenship in the French Colonies* (Chicago: University of Chicago Press, 2012).

206 Staatsarchiv Freiburg, D.SO. Generalia 198, Note of the head of the city's social welfare office, 6.7.1947.
207 Staatsarchiv Freiburg, D.SO. Generalia, 198, Decree 9089 'Verlassene Kinder' (Abandoned Children) of the Badisches Ministeriums des Inneren, 27.8.1946.
208 Christina Firpo, 'Crises of whiteness and empire in colonial Indochina: The removal of abandoned Eurasian children from the Vietnamese milieu, 1890–1956', *Journal of Social History*, 43 (2010), 587–613.
209 This is the conclusion in a recent study. Silke Satjukow, 'Besatzungskinder. Nachkommen deutscher Frauen und alliierter Soldaten seit 1945', *Geschichte und Gesellschaft*, 37 (2011), 559–91, here 569. See also, Silke Satjukow and Rainer Gries, *'Bankerte!' Besatzungekinder in Deutschland nach 1945* (Frankfurt: Campus Verlag 2015), pp. 122–62, largely restating arguments from earlier publications. For details of the process see also Gries, 'Les Enfants', pp. 396–8.
210 Michael Martin, 'Französische Besatzungszeit', paper given at the 2012 Franco-German meeting of *Coeurs sans Frontieres*, accessible under www.coeurssansfrontieres.com/index.php?option=com_content&view=article&id=187:lepoque-de-loccupation-francaise&catid=37:rencontre-franco-allemande-2012-a-roissy&Itemid=116&lang=de. (accessed 5.6.2016).
211 See numerous documents in Centre des Archives Diplomatiques, PDR, 5/363/5063.
212 Satjukow, 'Besatzungskinder', 570.
213 See Gries, 'Les Enfants', pp. 400–2.
214 Karin M. Schmidlechner, *Frauenleben in Männerwelten: Kriegsende und Nachkriegszeit in der Steiermark* (Wien: Döcker, 1997), pp. 65–88. See also Ingrid Bauer and Renate Huber, 'Sexual encounters across (former) enemy borderlines', *Contemporary Austrian Studies*, 15 (2007), 65–101, here 89–93.
215 See some initial considerations about children of the occupation as hidden population in Ingvill C. Mochmann, 'Using participatory methods in hidden populations: Experiences from an international research project', European Survey Research Association Conference 2011, Lausanne, 18–22.7.2011.
216 'Erhebung zu Besatzungskindern', 31.1.1961, BA: B126/28419.
217 See note 165.
218 Recent participatory research relying on responses from children of the occupation in both Germany and Austria have confirmed this impression with the children of British fathers being noticeably fewer than those of American, French or Soviet provenance. http://medpsy.uniklinikum-leipzig.de/medpsych.site,postext,forschungsschwerpunkte,a_id,4952.html. (accessed 15.2.2015); see also Marie Kaier et al., 'Psychosoziale Konsequenzen des Aufwachsens als Besatzungskind in Deutschland: Psychologische Hintergründe eines quantitativen Forschungsprojektes', in Stelzl-Marx and Satjukow (eds), *Besatzungskinder*, pp. 39–61, here p. 55.
219 See documents in BA: B126/28418 and 28038.
220 See Manfred Mahlzahn, *Germany 1945–1949: A Sourcebook* (London: Routledge, 1991), p. 71. Montgomery's original non-fraternisation speech is published in *Neue Westfälische Zeitung*, 15.6.1945.
221 After August 1946, marriages were possible in principle, but soldiers on active duty had to wait for 6 months between submitting a marriage application and

the wedding. The exhibition 'It Started with a Kiss. German–Allied Relations after 1945' stipulates that by 1950 around 10,000 such marriages had taken place: Allied Museum (ed.), *It Started with a Kiss: German–Allied Relations after 1945* (Berlin: Jaron Verlag, 2005), pp. 9, 19.
222 For descriptions of patterns of encounters, see Bauer and Huber, 'Sexual encounters', 80–1; the arguments considered for Austria are equally applicable to Germany.
223 BGBl 1955 II, pp. 321ff. See also note Dr Kern (Justizministerium) to Ministry of Foreign Affairs, 3.2.1960, BA: B126/28418.
224 Elisabeth Heinemann, 'The hour of the woman', in Hanna Schissler (ed.), *The Miracle Years: A Cultural History of West Germany 1945–1948* (Princeton: Princeton University Press, 2001), pp. 21–56, here p. 39.
225 Elisabeth Heinemann, in Allied Museum (ed.), *It Started with a Kiss*, p. 49.
226 Sonya O. Rose, 'Sex, citizenship, and the nation in World War II Britain, *The American Historical Review*, 103 (1998), 1147–76; Rose, 'Girls and GIs', 146–60.
227 See Pat Thane and Tanya Evans, *Sinners? Scroungers? Saints? Unmarried Motherhood in Twentieth-Century England* (Oxford: Oxford University Press, 2012).
228 For an analysis of some of the methodological issues arising out of lack of professional distance between interviewer and interviewees in the research of CBOW, as well as the impact of interdependencies between researchers and support networks, see Elke Kleinau, 'Occupation children in German post-war history – of the pitfalls of biographical research and dealing with the networks of those affected', in H. Glaesmer and S. Lee (eds), *Interdisciplinary Perspectives on Children Born of War: From World War II to Current Conflict Settings*, Conference reader, 2015, pp. 103–10, http://medpsy.uniklinikum-leipzig.de/medpsych.site,postext,rueckblick,a_id,1412.html. (accessed 13.11.2015).
229 This disclaimer does not intend to convey a doubt about the authenticity of the reflections of the CBOW cited below, but merely points to some methodological concerns which may be raised with regard to the way in which these sources have been used. See also Wolfgang Voges (ed.), *Methoden der Biographie- und Lebenslaufforschung*, vol. 1 (Heidelberg: Springer-Verlag, 2013). Carl Eduard Scheidt et al., *Narrative Bewältigung von Trauma und Verlust* (Stuttgart: Schattauer Verlag, 2014).
230 www.gitrace.org. (accessed 1.10.2015).
231 https://childrenbornofwar.wordpress.com/. (accessed 1.10.2015).
232 www.zv.uni-leipzig.de/service/presse/nachrichten.html?ifab_modus=detail&ifab_id=5984. (accessed 16.9.2015).
233 *Die neuen Bundesländer* (the new Federal states) was a term used for the five reconstituted East German states that acceded to the Federal Republic of Germany in October 1990.
234 www.russenkinder-distelblueten.de/. (accessed 16.9.2015)
235 Behlau (ed.), *Distelblüten*.
236 Ibid., p. 4.
237 Elisa van Ee and Rolf J. Kleber, 'Child in the shadowlands', *The Lancet*, 380:9842 (2012), 642–3.
238 'Über meinen Vater wurde nie ein Wort verloren', 'Evelyn' in Behlau (ed.), *Distelblüten*, p. 74.

239 Muth, *Die Wehrmacht in Griechenland*, p. 184.
240 'Niemand hat etwas herausgelassen, und das achtzehn Jahre lang. Ich kann das immer noch nicht verstehen.' 'Anita de Provence', in Picaper and Norz, *Enfants maudits*, p. 122.
241 'Das Nicht-Darüber-Sprechen-Können, das Tabu'. Anna-Lena Aßmann et al., 'Stigmatisierungserfahrungen deutscher Besatzungskinder des Zweiten Weltkrieges', *Trauma und Gewalt* 9 (2015), 294–303, here 298
242 'Das Interview: Ute Baur-Timmerbrink – 70 Jahre nach Kriegsende: Besatzungskinder auf der Suche nach ihren Vätern', www.hr-online.de/website/radio/hr-info/index.jsp?rubrik=54163&key=standard_document_55341493. (accessed 18.8.2015).
243 This group is not representative of the CBOW population as a whole. The sample is likely to be biased, as members of GI trace, by construct, are interested in tracing their families; similarly, participants of studies related to CBOW are more likely to be those individuals whose lives have been affected noticeably by their biological origins, and who for that reason may be more inclined to search for their fathers to find some kind of closure.
244 'Renate W', in Behlau (ed.), *Distelblüten*, p. 11.
245 'Un besoin irrépréssible, d'une attente purement subjective et intime'. Picaper and Norz, *Enfants maudits*, p, 28.
246 Ingrid Bauer, '"Ich bin stolz, ein Besatzungskind zu sein". Zeitgeschichtliche Forschungen als Empowerment? Befunde mit Blick auf die einstige US-Zone in Österreich', in Stelzl-Marx and Satjukow (eds), *Besatzungskinder*, pp. 183–206, here p. 185; Picaper and Norz, *Enfants maudits*, pp. 180, 82.
247 For details see Anna-Lena Aßmann, 'Stigmatisierungserfahrungen der deutschen Besatzungskinder des Zweiten Weltkrieges' (Master's thesis, Leipzig, 2014), especially chapters 5 and 6.
248 Baur-Timemrbrink, *Wir Besatzungskinder*, p. 15.
249 Bauer, '"Ich bin stolz"', p. 187.
250 'Wir waren nie Mutter und Kind. Unsere einzige Verbindung war die Nabelschnur' 'Renate W', in Behlau (ed.), *Distelblüten*, p. 13.
251 'Von ihr bekam ich keine Liebe, sie hat mich nie in den Arm genommen. Gar nichts. Nur Schläge. … Und sie schlug mich mit dem Kopf gegen die Wand. … Sie hat sich an mir abreagiert.' 'Anna' in Muth, *Die Wehrmacht*, p. 186.
252 'Le sentiment d'amour, l'affection, la petite caresse, la tête sur l'épaule, je ne l'ai pas reçu, cela manqué à un enfant.' Picaper and Norz, *Enfants maudits*, p. 36.
253 Ibid., 47.
254 Muth, *Die Wehrmacht*, p. 90.
255 Baur-Timmerbrink, *Wir Besatzungskinder*, p. 51, 'Michael', in Behlau (ed.), *Distelblüten*, p. 66.
256 See for instance Lu Seegers, 'Absente Väter der Nachkriegszeit: Vater-Los – Der gefallene Vater in der Erinnerung von Halbwaisen in Deutschland nach 1945', in J. Brunner (ed.), *Mütterliche Macht und väterliche Autorität: Elternbilder im deutschen Diskurs* (Göttingen: Wallstein Verlag 2008), pp. 128–51; H.V. Orlowski et al., 'Psychologie der Vermissung am Beispiel der Kinder von vermissten deutschen Soldaten des Zweiten Weltkriegs', *Zeitschrift für Psychosomatische Medizin und Psychotherapie*, 59:2 (2013), 189–97. Also Barbara Stambolis (ed.),

Vaterlosigkeit in vaterarmen Zeiten: Beiträge zu einem historischen und gesellschaftlichen Schlüsselthema (Landsberg: Beltz Juventa, 2013).
257 Baur-Timmerbrink, Wir Besatzungskinder, p. 73.
258 Muth, Die Wehrmacht, p. 72.
259 See Glaesmer et al., 'Die Kinder des Zweiten Weltkrieges in Deutschland'; also Picaper and Norz, Enfants maudits, p. 58.
260 Picaper and Norz, Enfants maudits, p. 366.
261 'Ich lebe von der Vorstellung, dass mein Vater super war', Helmut Köglberger cited in Bauer, '"Ich bin stolz"', p. 202.
262 See for instance, 'Es war wie ein Heimkommen für mich', Salzburger Nachrichten, 5.1.2012, explored in Bauer, '"Ich bin stolz"', p. 184.
263 See for instance Winfield, Bye Bye Baby; Baur-Timmerbrink, Wir Besatzungskinder, Olga Rains, Lloyd Rains and Melynda Jarratt, Voices of the Left Behind: Project Roots and the Canadian Children of World War II (Toronto: Dundurn Press, 2006).
264 'Die ganzen Jahre war es, wie auf einem Bein zu stehen und zu versuchen, Haltung zu bewahren, wenn man nicht weiss, wer man ist. Jetzt kann ich endlich auf zwei Beinen stehen, seit ich weiss, wer mein Vater ist.' Hans M. in Baur-Timmerbrink, Wir Besatzungskinder, p. 79.

4

Bui Doi: the children of the Vietnam War

If many of the emotional challenges facing children born of the Second World War were a result of them being part of a hidden population,[1] the situation was often the exact opposite for children born of later conflicts. The parentage of children fathered by US soldiers during the Vietnam War, for instance, visibly set them apart from children of Vietnamese parents and thus exposed them to adversities as a result of openly being associated with the enemy. The situation of children born of American GIs in Asia was almost always clear cut: almost all were of mixed racial provenance; almost all stood out in the generally racially homogeneous Vietnam of the 1970s and 1980s; and almost all suffered significant and damaging stigmatisation and discrimination.

There was nothing 'hidden' about their situation. Unlike other groups of CBOW, Vietnamericans were so visible that they were noted even by the wider public outside their birth country – at the latest since the dramatisation of their fate in Claude-Michel Schönberg and Alain Boublil's musical *Miss Saigon*, the 1989 adaptation of Madame Butterfly's tragic tale, set in 1975 Saigon, where an entire song deals with the so-called *Bui Doi* (dust of life).[2] Even away from Broadway and the West End their stories were shared. 'Heartbreaking', a 'riveting family drama' – were the reviewers' comments on *The Daughter from Danang*,[3] a documentary that recounts the story of Heidi Bob, to all appearances an 'all-American girl' in the small town Pulaski, Tennessee. Yet, Heidi is anything but 'all-American'. Born in 1968 as Mai Thi Hiep in Da Nang, one of the major port cities on the South Central Coast of Vietnam, and home to a major air base used by the South Vietnamese and Americans during the Vietnam War, she is the daughter of an American serviceman and a Vietnamese woman. Her mother, fearing for her daughter's safety as the conflict drew to a close in the mid-1970s and when rumours of cruelty towards mixed-race children on the part of the North Vietnamese became commonplace, decided to send Hiep to the US as part of so-called 'Operation Babylift'. The childhood experiences of Mai Thi Hiep and other Amerasian CBOW were complex, varied and often full of emotional challenges, which can only be appreciated against the background of the conflict and its aftermath. Therefore some background to the Vietnam War is presented to facilitate an understanding of the particular situation which the mixed-race children of GIs faced in wartime and post-war Vietnam, as well as in America and Western Europe, when they eventually settled there.

This chapter, after providing the war context and the particular geopolitical circumstances of American engagement in South East Asia, will address the following main themes. US military policies with regard to military–civilian relations in the context of deployment in Indochina and its effect on attitudes towards GI children will be explored. This will be followed by an analysis of two distinct phases of US intervention on behalf of those children (and in the case of the latter also on behalf of their families): the evacuation of babies and young children in so-called Operation Babylift, and – a little over a decade later – the Amerasian Homecoming Act. Finally, the chapter will investigate the experiences of different groups of Vietnamericans, who were 'brought home' at different stages of their lives, as part of these distinct US immigration policies, and compare them with their earlier experiences in Vietnam as well as with the integration of Vietnamese immigrants who had come to the US in large numbers as refugees following the Fall of Saigon.

US military intervention in Vietnam

US post-Second World War engagement in Vietnam started when the Truman Administration provided foreign aid to the French from May 1950 onwards, eventually underwriting more than three quarters of the cost of the Indochina War.[4] This was followed by the establishment of a US Military Assistance Advisory Group later that year. By the end of the Eisenhower Administration in 1961, 600 advisers were operating in Vietnam, and by November 1963 the number had risen to more than 16,000.[5] Although Vietnam was only of tangential interest for the US at the time, John F. Kennedy stated unequivocally in his inaugural address: 'We shall pay any price, bear any burden, meet any hardship, support any friend, oppose any foe to assure the survival and success of liberty.'[6] Vietnam was seen as part of this fight for liberty, with the South being the friend to be supported and the communist North the enemy to be opposed. Kennedy, despite a reluctance to extend US engagement in Vietnam to sending ground troops, underlined the commitment by adding to the number of military advisers which rose to the above-mentioned over 16,000 during his presidency.[7] Also, his rhetoric reinforced the impression of American support for the South, when Kennedy famously told the *New York Times* journalist James Reston, 'Now we have a problem in making our power credible, and Vietnam is the place.'[8]

After the dramatic events in November 1963 which saw the South Vietnamese President Ngo Dinh Diem ousted in an American-approved coup, with Diem and his brother Ngo Dinh Nhu murdered and President Kennedy assassinated, a notable change in US commitment in Vietnam was symbolised by the new President Lyndon B. Johnson. A product of the Cold War who accepted whole-heartedly the domino theory, President Johnson was convinced that if Vietnam fell to communism, so would – eventually – America's more significant allies, namely Germany and Japan. Under Johnson, US involvement in Vietnam escalated; the number of combat troops increased significantly, confirming a change of the rules of engagement from a defensive role of protecting bases to more offensive action. In 1965, the number of US soldiers on Vietnamese soil exceeded 100,000 for the first time, and by 1968 well over half a million American soldiers were deployed.[9] Between 1965 and 1971, the numbers of US soldiers on the ground consistently exceeded 100,000,[10] and their main aim was to secure America's position as a guarantor of liberty and a stalwart against communism. A secondary aim was the protection of South Vietnam. As Assistant Secretary of Defense, John McNaughton tellingly formulated, in a memorandum for Secretary of Defense McNamara in 1965, a quantification of war aims in Vietnam would be that '70% of US aims' would have to be the avoidance of 'a humiliating US defeat (to our reputation as a guarantor)' whereas only '10% involved permitting the people of SVN (South Vietnam) to enjoy a better way of life'.[11]

Having initially convinced the American people that the US were 'winning' the war or, at least, that it would be a short conflict with the return of the troops imminent, the Tet Offensive of 1968 – with its temporary capture by the North Vietnamese of key military installations in the south, and its penetration of Saigon and the US embassy there – awoke the American public and media alike. Coinciding with waves of student anti-war protests, the 'strategic stalemate' following the Tet Offensive when 'neither side faced imminent defeat or victory'[12] had immense impact on public and published opinion. Opposition to the war became more vocal, and anti-war propaganda intermingled with general objections to the draft, moral, legal and pragmatic arguments against US engagement in Vietnam, as well as general anti-government opposition in the form of the free speech movement and the civil rights movement. This general mood of opposition was enhanced by extensive media coverage of the war, including previously unaired violent, explicit images from the battlefields.[13]

The military stalemate after the Tet Offensive led to a rethink of American strategy, and President Johnson, who had already decided not to seek re-election later that year, opted to work towards a negotiated settlement to end the war.[14] His successor, Richard Nixon, while succeeding in reducing combat personnel significantly in a process of 'Vietnamisation', that is, by handing over to the South Vietnamese Army the bulk of the fighting, found it difficult to bring American engagement to an end. Peace negotiations were slow to come to fruition and it took until 1973 until both sides agreed to a series of 'accords' which culminated in the signing of the 'Agreement on Ending the War and

Restoring the Peace in Vietnam' on 27 January.[15] The peace settlement was short-lived. The combination of American troop withdrawal, and the Case–Church Amendment of June 1973, which effectively prevented any further US military action in Southeast Asia,[16] together with the significant reduction in financial assistance given to South Vietnam, clearly signalled that the US would no longer intervene on behalf of the South, even if it were to fall to the communist North. The subsequent North Vietnamese assault on the South led to a swift collapse, and it took less than three months from the secret crossing into South Vietnam of the North Vietnamese Army's military leader General Van Tien Dung on 5 February 1975 until the Fall of Saigon on 30 April that year.

Without going into detail about the Vietnam War and its assessments, some key issues of significance to the fate of the children born of this war need to be emphasised. Firstly, public opinion in the early stages broadly supported American engagement in Vietnam under Truman, Eisenhower, Kennedy and Johnson. The mood changed in response to a difficult to define enemy in a long (by American standards) war, in which a lack of clear strategy, combined with considerable losses and high costs, led to disillusionment among the public, especially after the Tet Offensive.[17] Furthermore, the images of the war, as they entered Americans' homes directly through extensive media coverage for the first time, demonstrated to the public the contradictions of the war in two important respects. They saw a sharp discrepancy between political rhetoric of an easy and swift victory of the democratic South Vietnam against the communist troops of the Viet Cong on the one hand and the apparent realities of the war as it was reported to them in ever greater detail on the other. Similarly significantly, the public were also confronted with imagery that created serious doubts about the moral superiority of American warfare and – ultimately – the ethical justification of fighting the war in the first place.

Secondly, while American engagement in Indochina itself became increasingly controversial, the sudden removal of support from South Vietnam was also regarded as problematic. The rapid withdrawal caused severe hardship among the South Vietnamese. The dire situation of the South Vietnamese, fighting for aims which the Americans broadly supported, namely the defence of Western values such as democracy against communism, resulted in a feeling that the United States was partly responsible for the fate of 'those they left behind'. At the beginning of April 1975, when President Ford was still hoping to persuade Congress to approve an aid package for South Vietnam, he argued that the fact that the South Vietnamese were fleeing from the North Vietnamese in scores was 'a clear indication that they don't want to live under the kind of government that exists in North Vietnam'. His description of the refugee disaster as a 'tragedy unbelievable in its ramifications'[18] set the tone for US governmental publicity and media coverage surrounding the collapse of South Vietnam. It was entirely clear to the Ford Administration that those who had previously been friends of America in the South were the potential victims following the communist victory and takeover. The US felt some sense of obligation towards the South Vietnamese which would eventually result in an evacuation and admissions programme that would rescue around 130,000.[19] Although Congress, during the rapidly unfolding closing down of the Indochina War, rejected the continuation of financial support for several South East Asian countries and thus turned the American back to countries and peoples with whom 'American people had mingled their blood and died', many American officials on the ground shared a sense of guilt and shame for refusing their political friends in Indochina protection and for abandoning them at the most crucial moment. As Prince Sirik Matak said in his letter to the American Ambassador to Cambodia on the eve of his final departure from Phnom Penh, 'I never believed for a moment that you [the American nation] would have this sentiment of abandoning a people which has chosen liberty ... I have only committed this mistake of believing in you, the Americans.'[20]

The ones left behind: Vietnamese 'war brides' and their children

As in previous twentieth-century wars, the Vietnam War placed American GIs in sustained contact with the local population, and in particular with young women. Also as in the past, thousands of young military personnel returned home with foreign-born wives and children. While the Vietnam War in this regard was no different from earlier conflicts with US involvement, the nature of these relationships, the way in which they were perceived by the American military, government, media and, by implication, the public, shifted markedly, even in comparison with conflicts as recent as the Second World War. This would have implications for the way Vietnamese-American marriages would be viewed and military wives and their children would be treated. On the surface, the pattern of attempting to regulate soldiers' sexual behaviour during the Vietnam War followed that of earlier conflicts, as already described in the case of policies during the Second World War. There was a tacit acceptance on the part of the military command that soldiers would (and should) be entertained during their tour of duty, and that this entertainment would include casual sexual encounters. This acceptance was qualified by an explicit discouragement of engagement in any activity which would lead to longer-term commitment, and an even more pronounced and active policy of preventing marriages. As a result, the military, in trying to control the perceived dangers of casual sex, most significantly the spread of STIs among the troops, attempted to regulate sexual encounters.

Despite these similarities and continuities, in many other respects the circumstances under which social and intimate relationships developed in Vietnam differed significantly from earlier periods. Most notably, the conflict saw a continuation of the rise of the camptown as the focal point of social contact between soldiers and local women. These commercial districts for military prostitution at the margins of military bases were not new to military 'occupation'. They had operated in previous conflicts, and had sprung up all over Asia following the trails of American military engagement on that continent after 1945.[21] Recent scholarship has demonstrated convincingly that the Korean War provided a sea change in the utilisation of sexual commerce in the choreographing of relations between Americans and their Asian 'partners'.[22] While it is disputable that the subordination of Korean women to American military personnel was a parallel of Korean subordination to American dominance in exchange for national security, the argument that both America and Korea regarded prostitution in camptowns as a means to 'advance friendly relations of both countries'[23] is persuasive. This policy is clearly visible in the co-operation of the Korean government and the US military in the sponsorship and regulation of the camptown system. This trend continued and intensified in Vietnam, and thus it is hardly surprising to hear Senator Fulbright remark famously in 1966: 'both literally and figuratively, Saigon has become an American brothel'.[24] But it was not only the sheer volume of sanctioned casual sexual encounters which distinguished the Vietnam War from earlier conflicts; it was also the construction of the Vietnamese women as untrustworthy and outright dangerous. Again, the principle was not new. The image of the local woman as potential spy or carrier of debilitating venereal disease (VD) had been a common theme throughout twentieth-century conflicts, but during the Vietnam War, the image of the deceitful local woman had both sexualised and racial undertones that surpassed previous propaganda in intensity of tone and viciousness of the accusations. In a common image in GI folklore, retold by numerous soldiers, the ancient myth of the vagina dentata resurfaced – the idea that the female body has hidden, dangerous secrets and that a man who has sex with a woman may risk castration. This 'toothed vagina' myth circulated among the soldiers and claimed that prostitutes sympathetic to the Viet Cong put razor blades, glass or sand into their vaginas to injure the unsuspecting customers.[25] Whether the stories, alongside similar danger scenarios of Vietnamese girls as carriers of incurable STIs, were circulated deliberately by military leaders to scare their soldiers away from unregulated prostitution, or whether they were part of the rumour mill that permeates military life during combat pauses, is difficult to ascertain conclusively.[26] Soldiers interviewed about the myth reported different memories about the origins of the warnings,[27] but the effect would have been similar, namely a deepening of suspicion of the Vietnamese women, feeding the insecurities of the young American soldiers. Although the very wide-spread use of prostitutes appears to indicate that the warnings by and large fell on deaf ears among the soldiers on the ground, this interpretation might be misleading. Two books, written in 1966 and 1968 respectively, by Ken Melvin, a pseudonym of two American soldiers,[28] mirrored the impressions of the troops that 'surviving in Vietnam meant fighting off gold-digging bar girls'. The stories and images used in Melvin's books portrayed troops as fragile and Vietnamese women as 'calculating'.[29] At the heart of the myths lay the anxieties of Americans about the danger and deceitfulness of the Vietnamese people, which were rooted in a lack of understanding of Vietnam as a country and Vietnamese culture. This was coupled with an inability to communicate in a meaningful way which could have dispelled some of the myths. Thus knowledge and understanding were substituted by stereotypes, both racial and gendered. The reading of the Vietnamese woman as the sexual saboteur containing elements of the 'dragon lady' – the core component of the Asian stereotype expressed widely in American popular culture – was mixed with admiration of the graceful exotic beauty, displaying a 'deep cultural ambivalence'.[30]

The effect of this complex web of admiration and fear, of desire and distrust was that far less of the customary socialising between military and civilian population took place on an *ad hoc* and informal basis. Instead, encounters occurred almost exclusively in officially sanctioned economic and labour exchanges that went hand in hand with the gigantic American military effort. These included Vietnamese women working in the barracks and in the soldiers' living quarters, as cleaners, waitresses, cooks, laundry workers or stockers in the shops, as well as less formal arrangements between individual soldiers and local women, with the 'hooch maid' cleaning, cooking, and doing the laundry or, in some cases, providing additional services at the soldiers' request.[31] The most common place for encounters between GIs and local women leading to intimate relations, however, remained the entertainment sector: the bars, brothels and night clubs. Le Ly Hayslip, in a memoir of her childhood and youth as a Vietnamese maid, black market vendor, waitress and hospital worker as well as – eventually – a prostitute, describes the complicated social hierarchies.[32] Arrangements included slave traffic of a thoroughly exploitative nature at one end of the spectrum to mutually beneficial service arrangements on the other, where 'live-in' contract girlfriends frequently formed longer-term and often exclusive relationships with a particular GI.[33]

While these arrangements were by and large tacitly tolerated by the military, the 'establishment' also played a more active part in other forms of 'entertainment', most notably the Military Assistance Command Vietnam (MACV)'s elaborate, ambitious and costly Rest and Recuperation (R&R) programme.[34] This involved a seven-day leave to a tourist destination in or outside Vietnam, designed to boost morale and motivation of the GI's during their long tour of duty. Favourite locales were Bangkok and Sydney for single men and Hawai for those uniting with their wives.[35] Veterans' and journalists' accounts are numerous, and almost all of them emphasise the centrality of the sexual element in the expedition. The main message conveyed to the soldiers was that women in the chosen locations were 'open for business', and that the utilisation of the services on offer would come with no strings attached, no responsibilities or consequences, as long as the men frequented the 'checked' and 'clean' services.[36]

As in almost all similar circumstances, the liaisons were unequal but by no means one-sided. Similar to the wide variety of different relationships between soldiers and local women in the Second World War, consensual or not, exploitative or not, the Vietnam War associations between GIs and locals presented a myriad different scenarios. Sex slavery and rape were present as much as love affairs and consensual business arrangements and anything in between. Wants and needs on either side met wants and needs on the other – yet the outcome was almost always an unequal arrangement: a relationship that for a young GI may have been a question of fulfilling hormonal and emotional needs would often be a matter of survival for the local woman and her family. Whereas for the GI the meeting would generally be inconsequential, for the woman 'selling her body' in a country with a conservative moral code carried the risk of ostracisation, abandonment by family and friends, and of course the ever present risk of pregnancy and in this case of carrying a mixed-race child fathered by a foreigner.

While the vast majority of relations between GIs and local Vietnamese women remained casual, despite the military's best efforts of discouraging long-term and more committed relationships, around 8000 American GI's eventually married local women from Vietnam.[37] As one GI recalled, long-term relationships between soldiers who extended tours of duty and, staying for years and civilian and government employees who were also in Vietnam for many years were not uncommon. In these cases, couples behaved as though they were married – cohabiting – irrespective of whether or not they had officially tied the knot,[38] an arrangement described vividly in Graham Greene's *The Quiet American*, though here based on the earlier Indochina Wars of the 1950s.[39]

Recent research has highlighted the lengths to which the American military establishment went in order to discourage such long-term liaisons, and it has been argued convincingly that the Korean and Vietnam Wars were a watershed marking the 'demise of the war bride'. While the military had traditionally been cagey in providing any reasoning for their restrictive marriage policies, the US Press at the time identified security concerns as one reason, combined with the paternalistic rationale of protecting young and 'vulnerable' soldiers from making rash decisions arising from a combination of loneliness and a sense of 'freedom' away from home.[40] While one may rightly be critical of the US military policies towards prostitution and 'no-strings-attached' casual relationships in the camptowns and beyond, the cautious policies towards marriage may indeed have had some justification other than the institutional racism that the establishment has often been accused of. There may have been a genuine concern for the well-being of the troops in Vietnam, who were the youngest US fighting force in the twentieth century. Although the average age circulated widely in literature and media of combat forces as 19 years[41] is disputed, even the more conservative military statistics put the age at around 22 and therefore make this a very young military cohort.[42] Given the relative youth of the forces, a cautious attitude on the part of the military chaplains and commanding officers would not be surprising. What is more, if one accepts army statistics on soldiers' age as accurate, a recent analysis of a random data sample of seventy couples which the MACV had approved for marriage, does not back the argument that the Army maintained 'an unspoken policy of disapproving marriage for younger GIs'. Although only one of the approved applicants (i.e. less than 2%) was under 20 at the time of application, this represents far less of a disparity than might appear at first sight.[43] With the typical age of male marriage applicants being 22, they were close to the average age of soldiers; the demographic patterns of marriages in the Vietnam War 'are most remarkable for how unpatterned they are' and 'soldier-husbands represent a cross-section of the fighting force in Vietnam'.[44] While the numbers of American-Vietnamese marriages were significant and, relative to the numbers of soldiers and lengths of their stays, were comparable with the First World War,[45] this was very much despite MACV policies rather than because of them.

Before the Second World War, the War Department had taken full financial responsibility and supervisory oversight of the safe passage of soldiers' brides and children back to the United States. This was a significant undertaking, with estimates of over 100,000 marriages between American soldiers and women from over fifty countries during the Second World War alone.[46] In contrast, during the Vietnam War soldiers were responsible for their spouses' transport, and this proved to be the biggest obstacle to American-Vietnamese marriages, as the cost of passage was well beyond the means of ordinary soldiers. As soldiers were required to supply an affidavit to the MACV confirming that they were in possession of sufficient funds to secure transport for their future wives to the destination of their discharge,[47] most marriage applications had already ground to a halt by this point. As Hayslip reported in her memoirs of her own departure from Vietnam in 1970, the expenses were not limited to the airfare and processing fees, but also included costs for a marriage broker, as well as other bribes, which added to the already prohibitively expensive undertaking. Given these obstacles, it is surprising that as many as 8000 marriages were concluded; this is partly explained by the fact that a significant number of American soldiers, who found it impossible to marry under the purview of the military, either returned to Vietnam as civilian workers after completing their tour of duty to marry their girlfriends or deserted from the army rather than deserting their wives-to-be.[48]

In the absence of conclusive documentary evidence about attitudes held in the military towards marriages of GIs throughout the twentieth century, an exploration of the change in policies towards war brides in the post-war period is best attempted in the form of an analysis of war brides legislation. In the immediate post-war years, the US Congress took legislative steps to clarify the status of foreign spouses of American soldiers and their children, most importantly in the War Brides Act of December 1945.[49] Among the most controversial aspects of this Act was the question of so-called admissible and inadmissible aliens. Despite animated debates in the House Committee on

Immigration and Naturalisation, which showed some support for a relaxation of the ban of Asian immigration in the form of an Asian inclusion amendment of the War Brides Act, the Act in practice continued the long tradition of exclusion of Asians from immigration into the US,[50] and has to be seen as a sign of continued deep-seated racial prejudice among the political elites. From 1947 onwards, largely in response to the US occupation of Japan, in which almost 1 million US soldiers passed through this Asian country, Congress provided a series of time-limited waivers to racial immigration restrictions to the previous exclusions of Asian war brides,[51] very much against the wishes of the military.[52] It was not until 1952 that the Immigration and Nationality Act (McCarran Walter Act) finally established the right of naturalisation for Asian immigrants. This paved the way for GI spouses from inadmissible countries to immigrate into the US; however, by that time, the benefits that the War Brides Act had accorded to GIs and their spouse and children had been discontinued. It is clear that for the military, Asian wives met in camptowns represented an unwelcome mingling of two parts of military life that were to be separated: prostitution and marriage. While prostitution was seen as a constructive influence on troop morale and as such could and should be accepted, soldier marriage was quite a separate issue. As a result the support of war brides whose provenance was pointing towards camptowns and prostitution was not deemed the responsibility of the military,[53] and thus the privileged position of the war brides, already undermined during the Korean War, was entirely eroded in the Vietnam War.

The reason for elaborating on the political and cultural background of the war, as well as on the circumstances of intimate contacts between GIs and local women during the conflict, is that the children were the visible and recognisable outcome of those relationships – born into a complex web of loyalties, allegiances, emotions, hardships, and political, ideological and cultural preconceptions in both Vietnam and the United States. As the prevalent reminder of the conflict which had affected the countries of both parents, they became a symbol of the military and ideological conflict during the final stages of the war and the post-war period.

Drawing on Mochmann's conceptualisation of the historical, military, geographical and cultural contexts that form the background to the childhood adversities of CBOW, the above context provides the backdrop against which the socio-economic, psychological, medical, political and cultural factors can be investigated to understand both the actions and reactions of political players vis-à-vis the phenomenon of Vietnamericans as well as the impact of their parentage on the children themselves. With respect to the CBOW, the Vietnam War differed significantly from many earlier conflicts in that the children were not only visible to the outside world, but they were instrumentalised by politicians and policy makers both in their mothers' and their fathers' home countries in a more consistent manner than had hitherto been the case. This led to the unusual situation that – more than a decade after the end of hostilities in Vietnam – the United States started engaging in a policy that would pave the way for American citizenship for children of US soldiers fathered during the Vietnam War. Such policies stood in marked contrast to common military and governmental policy, not just in the United States but globally, where militaries have traditionally refused to take any responsibility for the children fathered by their soldiers to the point of facilitating the soldiers' evading their own personal responsibilities by assisting them to 'escape' by arranging for swift transfers away from the children and their mothers.

Operation Babylift

Despite the fact that racism was still rife in American culture generally and in American military culture more specifically, the fate of those who had become particularly vulnerable due to the US withdrawal following the Fall of Saigon, struck a chord with the American public, as well as with the political establishment. It is these sentiments of guilt and shame, communicated openly to the American public by American officials and parts of the American establishment, which provide the background to the US response to one particularly vulnerable 'high risk' group, namely the children of American soldiers and Vietnamese women, the so-called *Con Lai* (bastards) or, even more derogatorily, *My Lai* (American half-breeds).

The US had been caught unprepared for the speed of the final collapse of South Vietnam in the spring of 1975. On 30 March Da Nang was taken, and by mid-April Saigon was under sustained attack from three sides. With South Vietnam's reluctant agreement, President Gerald Ford – who had replaced President Nixon after the latter's resignation in the wake of the Watergate scandal on 8 August 1974 – announced on 3 April 1975 that Operation Babylift would fly orphans out of Vietnam.

In the spring of 1975, as South Vietnam moved closer to complete military collapse, foreign aid agencies, which cared for well over 800,000 Vietnamese 'orphans' often saw international adoption as the only way out of misery for large numbers of children, many of whom were orphans not in the literal sense of their parents having deceased but orphans in the sense that they did not have a parent willing or able to look after them.[54] The US-government-backed Operation Babylift, thus, was only one of several moves to deal with the humanitarian crisis of neglected children of the Vietnam War. This particular initiative, targeting, among others, children of American servicemen, was funded by $2 million from a special foreign aid children's fund, and thirty flights were planned to evacuate babies and young children. A combination of private and military transport planes was used for the evacuation: more than 2,000 children were flown to the United States, and approximately 1,300 to Canada, Europe and Australia.[55] Organisations coordinating flights included Holt, Friends of Children of Viet Nam, Friends For All Children, Catholic Relief

Service, International Social Services, International Orphans, and the Pearl S. Buck Foundation. Despite the evident hardship suffered by the young children, even as the evacuation was unfolding, debates around the wisdom of the operation, soul-searching about the motives and concern about the impact of its implementation on the children were taking place.[56]

Initially the main criticism focused on the insufficiently planned and badly executed disastrous first flight. A C-5A cargo plane, at the time the largest airplane in the world, yet ill-equipped to carry passengers, had been loaded with 330 children and accompanying adults. Shortly after take-off a mid-air explosion blew off the rear doors of the aircraft and the plane crashed, killing 154 of the passengers.[57] Ultimately, however, the controversies moved from this specific tragedy on to debates around the fact that many of the so-called orphans did in fact have families, and that the documentation on which the process was based was at best sketchy and inaccurate, at worst fraudulent. A second question raised persistently over the years was whether the adoptions had, in fact, been initiated with the best interest of the children in mind or were, in contrast, motivated by the desire to satisfy the needs and wants of prospective adoptive parents.[58] It is this debate in its wider historical context that requires some closer scrutiny in order to evaluate the situation of Vietnamese GI children and their situations both in Vietnam and – whether evacuated or adopted as part of US immigration programmes – in the United States.

International and interracial adoption: the controversies

After the Second World War and during the early Cold War, adoption as a phenomenon globalised. This was the result of a convergence of social and political factors in receptor and sender countries. Wars, refugee migrations and natural disasters, poverty, lack of social welfare and social upheaval led to growing numbers of orphans. In an increasingly information-driven society, the fate of these children became more widely visible and more readily acknowledged globally. In the US and Western Europe in particular, pictures and stories about the struggles of those children found their way into newspapers, radio and later television, and public awareness of these orphans increased. In addition, some of the receptor countries, in particular the United States itself, became part of the growing problem; with US service personnel stationed in countries and continents across the world, their presence as occupiers in Germany, Austria and Japan, and as soldiers and sailors eventually stationed in Korea, Vietnam and in other Asian countries, left behind large numbers of GI children, often of biracial provenance. More often than not these half-American children suffered severe stigmatisation and discrimination and it was their growing number and often very difficult living conditions, among other factors, which prompted significant developments with regard to international and, in particular, interracial adoption. To name but one prominent example, thousands of war-orphaned Korean children and biracial children whose mothers were Korean and fathers were American military personnel were adopted shortly after the Korean War, and it is estimated that between 1955 and 2001 more than 110,000 children were adopted from South Korea to the United States alone.[59]

The analysis above of children fathered by Afro-American GIs in Britain and Germany during and after the Second World War and adopted into Afro-American families in the United States discussed two comparatively small-scale examples of international adoption as a strategy of dealing with mixed-race CBOW. It was not until the American engagement in Korea and Indochina led to much larger number of GI children in Asia that this approach was explored more extensively. In 1958, Pearl Buck, Nobel laureate in literature and an international adoption advocate, alerted the American public to the destiny of half-American children in Korea. Commenting on the situation after the American abrogation of essential provisions of the Armistice between North and South Korea she remarked: 'Many children will be born, many more than even now are being born, belonging to no country and to every country. Most of them will be half-American. ... They are children who are born displaced, children not wanted in the lands of their birth, and not recognized in the land of their fathers. Nevertheless they live. ... What is to become of these children?'[60]

At that stage, proxy adoption, in which American couples could adopt in absentia in a foreign court, was already the most widely used form of international adoption in the United States, especially after Bertha and Harry Holt had adopted eight Korean war orphans in 1955,[61] and had, in the process, achieved the passing of the so-called Holt Bill, which paved the way for international adoption[62] and thus instigated the first large-scale intercountry adoption initiative. In the wake of their own adoptions, the Holts founded Holt International Children's Services and initiated what has become the longest running intercountry adoption program between the United States and South Korea. Thus, for decades before Operation Babylift, there had been Asian-US adoptions in significant numbers, and those two decades between the Holt Bill and President Ford's baby rescue operation had seen further regulation of what, in the mid-1950s had been an unregulated phenomenon.

It has to be remembered that adoption, even domestic, is a relatively recent phenomenon. Traditionally, in many cultures children have been exchanged within fostering arrangements, which, in many developing nations, are still operating today. In these, children are looked after, temporarily or longer term, in other family members' or other families' homes either to work, to be educated or, in case of need, for charitable support. In such fostering arrangements the children remain tied to their birth families, both legally and often also emotionally. Important in the context of the debates of the legal status of orphans rescued in Operation Babylift is also the fact that traditionally children have also temporarily been left in so-called orphanages for childcare, food and education while the birth parents tried to improve their economic circumstances in order to be in a better position to provide for their children in the long term.[63]

It was not until the mid-nineteenth century that the first law authorising the permanent replacement of kinship bonds by legal bonds based on non-kinship considerations was passed, in the *Act to Provide for the Adoption of Children* in Massachusetts.[64] Not long after, the so-called Orphan Train Movement took up the idea of providing for underprivileged children by placing them in the care of well-meaning parents elsewhere.[65] Born out of the desperate situation of an estimated 34,000 homeless children in New York, the theologian and social reformer Charles Loring Brace had formed the Children's Aid Society in 1853[66] and a year later set in motion what he conceived of as a Christian rescue mission for poor New York youngsters. Brace removed children (aged 6–18) from badly run orphanages, the city streets, and from those he judged to be unfit parents and placed them in homes across the United States, often in the Midwestern and Western states of the United States.[67] His deep-rooted sense of Christian duty and responsibility to improve the welfare of the needy children was mixed with the missionary ideas that Christian upbringing, education and hard work were the prerequisites of a purposeful and fulfilled life.[68] Thus he argued that the complementary needs of food, shelter and family protections of the children on the one hand ought to be matched up with the need for hard-working additions to the family on the part of the many settlers in the West and Midwest of the United States.[69] This feature of complementarity of children's needs and the potential adoptive parents' needs would be one to determine debates a century on, when adoptions had moved from domestic arrangements to international ones, with poor donor countries 'supplying' children to rich recipient countries, again trying to match complementary requirements in no less controversial a fashion.

The Orphan Train Movement came to an end in 1929 and with it its attempts at salvaging the potential of poor and neglected children – whether or not orphans in the strict sense of the word – by placing them with socially, economically, culturally or religiously 'worthy' families. Between 1853 and 1929 more than 200,000 children had been placed in this ambitious, unusual and controversial social experiment which is now widely held as the beginning of the foster care concept in the United States.[70] While Brace's driving force was a desire to alleviate the suffering of impoverished children, at the heart of his actions was a Christian missionary and evangelical humanitarianism that was echoed in the first large-scale international adoption efforts of the Holts in Korea and Rosemary Taylor, the formidable lady behind much of the in-country groundwork putting in place Operation Babylift in Vietnam.

In another respect, the Orphan Trains set a precedent for later international and transracial adoptions from Indochina into the United States and other Western countries. The study of the Children's Aid Society's records have demonstrated that the majority of the children placed as part of the initiative had only been placed in institutional care temporarily; they had been 'shared and had certainly not been given up' permanently.[71] What may have been possible to be reasoned as appropriate in the context of the virtually unregulated nature of fostering and adoption in the mid-nineteenth century[72] could no longer be evaluated in those terms in the mid-twentieth century. Adoption laws had been spread and were by then accepted throughout the Western world, thus allowing for the legal and permanent severance of children's biological ties to their birth families, replacing them with socially constructed new ties. But the conditions under which this severance was acceptable were still very much under negotiation.

The intensification of cross-national contacts, the globalisation of international travel and – above all – the globalisation of international conflict with the legacy of increasing numbers of often biracial CBOW fuelled further development in adoption practice, theory and law, and since the Second World War international adoptions have become a more widespread phenomenon. But beyond that, some have argued that in the half century following the Holt Bill, adoption transformed from a primarily humanitarian and charitable endeavour to a private industry, displaying an ever increasing discrepancy between the undisputed humanitarian need for child welfare on the one hand and questionable methods of at times almost aggressive international adoption agencies on the other.[73]

A short review of the salient points of this debate, which since the Hague Convention on Intercountry Adoption (HCIA) in 1993[74] has been rekindled and fought with renewed fervour, will throw light on some significant issues of relevance for the situation of CBOW more generally, most notably with regard to the commodification of children as part of a political process both during Operation Babylift and thereafter.

The starting point for the analysis will be the HCIA, a piece of legislation deemed necessary for three main reasons. First, since the Second World War, and more specifically since the 1960s, intercountry adoption had become a much more widespread phenomenon, involving not only rapidly increasing numbers of children and families, but also migration of children over long geographical distances away from their birth families, societies and cultures.[75] Second, the international community recognised that the numerical and geographical expansion of international adoption had led to 'serious and complex human problems, ... among other things manifold complex legal issues'; and third, it had become evident that the absence of domestic and international legal instruments required urgent attention on the basis of a multilateral approach.[76] The HCIA follows other child rights legislation of the post-war period in declaring the best interest of the child paramount (preamble, Article 1). Its principal goals are to prevent the abduction, exploitation, sale and trafficking of children. Under this premise, the HCIA enshrines the code of subsidiarity, i.e. it is based on the principle that all states should keep children living within the birth family system (extended family or kinship group). Should this prove impossible, then domestic adoption that preserves language and culture should be aimed for (Article 4). Once these options have been exhausted, children may be approved for inter-country adoption through the country's central authority. Furthermore, states are obliged to preserve information about the child and his or her birth family (Article 30), to evaluate thoroughly prospective adoptive parents (Article 5), to match the child with a suitable family (Article 16) and to impose additional safeguards as the situation might require.

From its inception, the provisions of the HCIA have been hotly debated, with the discussions developing around three core concerns. The first of these is the best interest of the child in need of a home, for whom an in-country adoptive home cannot be found and who could be placed into an adoptive home in another country. The second issue concerns the right of the sending country, including the rights of birth parents and those children for whom no international adoptive placements can be found; thirdly, there is the issue of abuses of the international adoption processes in the form of baby trade, extortion, coercion and other violations of adoption laws.

Commentators roughly fall into three camps: abolitionist, proponent and pragmatist.[77] Critics of international adoption range from outright opponents to adoption on the grounds that it inherently present a violation of human rights[78] – the argument being that many intercountry adoptions serve merely as a cover for illegal child trafficking,[79] – to a large body of human rights activists who have argued strongly and critically against international adoption, stressing that it presents substantial dangers to the best interest of the child. UNICEF's assessment, for instance, leading to a critical position vis-à-vis such adoptions, is that:

> Over the past 30 years, the number of families from wealthy countries wanting to adopt children from other countries has grown substantially. At the same time, lack of regulation and oversight, particularly in the countries of origin, coupled with the potential for financial gain, has spurred the growth of an industry around adoption, where profit, rather than the best interests of children, takes centre stage. Abuses include the sale and abduction of children, coercion of parents, and bribery.[80]

In contrast, advocates of intercountry adoption (ICA) argue that the positive developmental outcomes of children who are adopted internationally more than outweigh the potential risks involved in the process[81] and that abuses of ICA represent only a very small minority of adoption cases.[82] They point out that international policies which have led to a significant drop in number of ICAs since 2004 (see below Figure 4.1)[83] represent a breach of human rights of the children, who are deprived of being adopted internationally as a result of governmental and non-governmnental policies.[84] In other words, advocates argue strongly that adoption is an act of welfare that ought to be promoted in the best interest of unparented children.[85]

The middle ground in the debate is occupied by those who on the one hand see ICA as a legitimate way of family building which has become a reality in

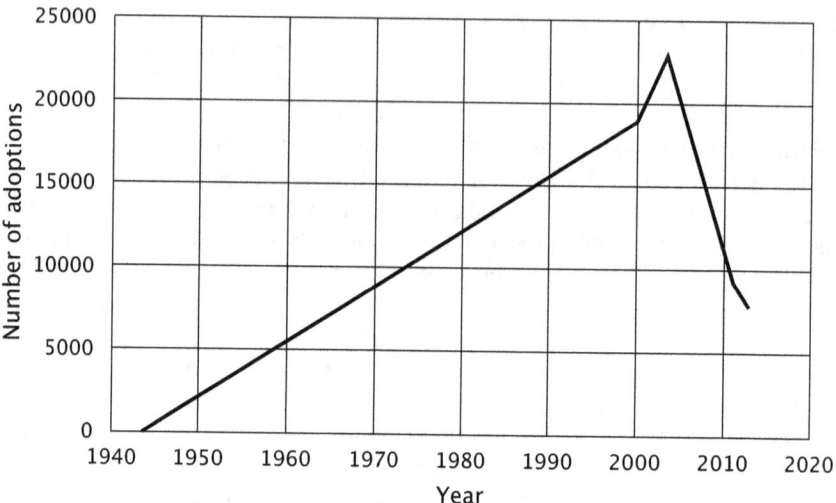

Figure 4.1 International adoption trends, 1944–2013

Source: Adapted from Bartholet, 'The international adoption cliff: Do child human rights matter?', 29.5.2013, www.law.harvard.edu/faculty/bartholet/IA%20Adoption%20Cliff%20 5-30-13.pdf; data taken from http:adoption_state.gov/about_us/statistics.php (2004) and http://travel.state.gov/content/adoptionsabroad/en/about-us/statistics.html (all accessed 27.2.2015).

the second half of the twentieth century, but who acknowledge the need to improve current ICA practice. They propose the development of better and more effective adoption mechanisms while at the same time addressing the lack of support and welfare systems within the sending countries, with which to improve prospects of children in their birth countries.[86]

Although the HCIA came into being two decades after Operation Babylift, it can help zoom in on the arguments that had already been raised in the mid-1970s in relation to the adoption of children in the closing stages of the Vietnam War.

Abolitionists focus on birth families' rights, and in particular on unfairness in the 'exchange' as a result of the economic disparity of sending and receiving countries. They view the adoption process as a 'trade', with children being a commodity[87] and point to the fact that often children declared as orphans have living parents or extensive family networks. It has been argued that the fundamental distinction between legitimate adoption and illicit sale of children remains unclear, both in legal theory and in adoption practice. This reasoning is based on the fact that in the absence of clear and binding rules based on unambiguous definitions, it is impossible to determine conclusively the nature of a transaction between birth parents, adoptive parents and various intermediaries, often involving significant amounts of money changing hands in exchange for consent to relinquishing parental rights and for providing services on the part of intermediaries. While neither gifts to birth parents nor fees for adoption services are unethical *per se*, 'the context in which the law permits these activities renders them questionable and allows children to be commercialised and commodified',[88] an argument that had already been put forward by Ethan Kapstein in the provocatively entitled paper 'The baby trade'.[89] It highlights malpractices in international adoption amid a situation where 'demand for infants from poor families in developing countries is rising among adults who live in wealthy ones' and as a result 'corruption has distorted the baby trade' because 'unscrupulous go-betweens buy or abduct infants from needy biological parents and sell them to eager adoptive families'.[90]

Thus international adoption, under certain circumstances, is tantamount to child trafficking 'not because adoptive families in rich countries obtain poor children from developing and transition economy nations', but 'because the law and current systems of intercountry adoption permit it to operate as such'.[91] Thus the core of the problem lies in the inability of the current ICA process to prevent it from degenerating into illicit child trafficking. This comprehensive array of arguments raising serious doubts about the desirability of ICA in the early twenty-first century mirrors many of the concerns raised around Operation Babylift. As indicated above, adoption documentation of the children transported out of Vietnam in Operation Babylift was sketchy, which – given the chaos surrounding the rapid progress of the North Vietnamese Army into and across the South of the country and the equally hasty withdrawal of US troops – is hardly surprising. It became clear that many of the supposed orphans did, in fact, have families in Vietnam. But it was equally apparent that many of those families, especially families of mixed-race GI children, actively encouraged the participation of the children in the adoption process. It is also beyond doubt that the situation for orphans or other unparented children in post-conflict Vietnam was difficult, and it was even more challenging for mixed-race children. The welfare of children orphaned by the war was far from a priority, and although no comprehensive statistical data exist, and any detailed analysis of the children born of the Vietnam War is riddled with issues concerning the completeness and reliability of data, the impression is that GI children and their families more often than not suffered greatly in the aftermath of the war. This conclusion is strongly supported by the information that became available in the 1980s, when the Amerasian Immigration and Homecoming Acts allowed GI children's emigration to the United States.[92]

Adoption experiences of children of Operation Babylift

The discussion above points to the core question of the relative value of different goods that form part of child welfare: cultural heritage, birth kinship, educational opportunity, economic wealth, ethnic and religious belonging, right to health and safety, but also conflicting interests and rights of the birth parents and families. The relative merits of these different goods are at the heart of the many of the arguments proposed in favour of ICA now and in the debates surrounding Operation Babylift. Proponents emphasise the positive developmental outcomes for the majority of children adopted internationally compared with peers in their birth country (gains in cognitive, emotional and physical development[93]). This was also an argument put forward with a slightly different twist in the 1970s. Given the physical state in which many of the orphans rescued in Operation Babylift arrived in the United States, it is hard to dispute that such developmental outcomes in the adoptive United States would almost certainly have been better than in their native Vietnam. When doctors boarded the Babylift planes on arrival in the United States, they found children suffering from dehydration, pneumonia, diarrhoea, chicken pox and assorted viral diseases.[94] Many children had already been gravely ill when they embarked on their journey across the Atlantic. One of the children, Kristin Topham, reportedly was so small that she could be held in the palm of an attendant's hand,[95] and conditions in the orphanages were reliably described as dire. Betty Tisdale, one of the attendants at the An Lac orphanage, whose children were airlifted out of Vietnam recalled: 'The rusted cribs were chipped enamel and no sheets, hammocks made of rugs strung between two cribs, two or three babies crammed into one crib – everything reeked of desperation.'[96] Not surprisingly then, the vast majority of adoptees remained profoundly grateful for the opportunities that Operation Babylift provided for them and are unequivocal in their respect for the effort. Kinh, one of the children rescued from An Lac orphanage, plainly stated: 'If Betty[97] hadn't rescued me, I would have been dead.'[98] Slightly less draconian, but still explicit about the benefits of adoption despite all the difficulties of acculturation and assimilation, another adopted orphan stated about her fate: 'The politics have never interested me, but the fact is that not one of the 30 people I've managed to contact so far (who shared her fate as a Vietnam War adoptee) has the slightest regret about what happened to them. ... We all feel that our lives have been better here than they could ever have been after the war.'[99]

Others, however, despite acknowledging the benefits of being brought up in the United States, were more sceptical about the virtues of the operation, recognised the political character of the enterprise and criticised what they perceived to be the neo-colonial and neo-imperialistic features of the rescue and adoption operation. In the words of one adoptee:

> Ultimately, the Holts and Operation Babylift justified the act of taking small babies from their countries of origin and raising them in a Western image by reducing the child's circumstances to one of two alternatives: left to rot in an inhumane orphanage or raised up in a loving family where, with time and material excess, everyone would forget and be the better for it. With a mixture of good old paternalism and a pinch of racial superiority, and under cover of civil wars, social upheavals, and economic instability, they extracted us without any sense of irony that Western countries had a big hand in triggering these crises. Praising us as Asian angels borne from cargo holds and cardboard boxes, we were never expected to

look back and think about our lives before adoption, much less about our countries of birth. The American flags we were given upon assuming citizenship were supposed to blind us with starspangled magnificence. It is only within the past decade that many of us have become wise to the racial self-hatred that had been instilled in us and have questioned the multiple loyalty tests we have been forced to take in order to prove our legitimacy in the eyes of our fellow Americans.[100]

Leaving aside the cynicism of the commentary, the criticism levelled here, namely a lack of sensitivity vis-à-vis the needs of children, the expectation that the youngsters would assimilate and never desire to establish or re-establish links with their birth country, its culture, religion – in retrospect – addresses a significant problem for many adoptees. Evidence, though anecdotal rather than empirical, suggests strongly that many Amerasians who came to the United States as part of the post-war rescue operations grew up with Caucasian parents and had little contact with their native culture, ethnicity and religion. Most of them are 'totally and by and large happily' Americanised.[101] Nicholas Leduc, one of the survivors of the ill-fated Galaxy C-5A flight, is proud to be speaking 'with more of a Boston accent than his parents who are Massachusetts natives';[102] the colour-blind adoption practices of the past tacitly encouraged the reproduction of the 'as-if'[103] genealogical myth of normative adoption kinship[104] which led to what psychologist Richard Lee refers to as the transracial adoption paradox.[105] Adoptees, visibly racially different from their Caucasian family and other social environment, are perceived and treated by others, and sometimes by themselves, as though they are members of the majority culture into which they have been adopted.

At the time of Operation Babylift, little was understood about the psychosocial impact such experiences would have on the individual child, and many adoptive parents envisaged adoption across cultures and/or ethnic or racial boundaries to cause few additional complications once the children had arrived in the United States. Only since the 1990s have the identity experiences of adopted individuals been taken up as a phenomenon that requires deeper understanding, especially with regard to the complex relationship of race, ethnicity and culture. Children typically become aware of racial distinctiveness at the age of around four or five years, and this is the time when transracial adoptees are likely to notice that their own racial features do not match their parents'.[106] It is also the time when many of them are confronted with unsettling comments from peers at school. As one adoptee who was raised in a Caucasian family remarked, as a child she did not think she was Asian, but that did not stop other children from mocking her features.[107] In other words, society treats transracial adoptees as a racial minority, and to some adoptees this comes as a shock, as they are not themselves aware of their minority status in early childhood.

Despite this, many of the adoptees continued, in adolescence and even adulthood, to associate with being White,[108] with research confirming that the majority of transracially adopted children do not identify with their own race.[109] Yet, in later adolescence, many adoptees start questioning their cultural identity. As one Korean college student and transracial adoptee phrased it:

> The older I get, the more I realize I can't avoid being Korean. Every time I look into the mirror, I am Korean. When I look at family pictures, I feel that I stand out. I guess it shouldn't bother me, but sometimes it does. Even though I may seem very American ... I want to be distinctly Korean. I know I'm not in terms of having all the Korean traditions, but I don't want people to see me and say, 'Because she grew up in a Caucasian family, and because she is very Americanized, she's white.' That's not what I want anymore.[110]

Little research has been done on the life courses of the children rescued during Operation Babylift and transplanted into US, Canadian or European society, but since the mid-1980s the long-term effects of transracial adoptions more generally have been investigated. A study based on a national survey of 372 adoptive families in America concluded that transracially adopted children of Columbian, Korean and Afro-American background adjusted no more poorly than their in-racially adopted counterparts.[111] Recently, a meta-analysis of one specific adoption-related issue, namely that of secure attachments,[112] concluded that adopted children can overcome early adversity and form secure attachments as often as their non-adoptive counterparts.[113] However, children who were adopted after their first birthday were shown to be less capable of overcoming childhood adversities and of developing secure attachments. A second outcome of the study, of some relevance for the ICA debates, is the study's finding that adopted children were considerably less frequently disorganised in their attachments than institutionalised children. This leads to the conclusion that adoption may actually have to be seen as an effective intervention in the best interest of the child. Similarly, a meta-analysis investigating self-esteem of adoptees ranging from childhood to adulthood found no difference in self-esteem between adoptees and non-adopted peers. International adoptees did not present lower self-esteem compared with domestic adoptees, and transracial and same-race adoptees showed no significant difference in self-esteem.[114] In a separate meta-analysis (based on a small sample of only three studies), higher levels of self-esteem in adoptees compared with non-adopted institutionalised children were found, again confirming that adoption may be an intervention genuinely in the best interest of the child. Research offers a range of explanatory factors for the finding of normative self-esteem development in adoptees, ranging from protective factors within the adopted family context which may help overcome childhood adversities and even trauma,[115] to the genetic predisposition to resilience as some children had already survived extreme adversities and deprivation in early childhood as to suggest higher than average resilience.[116] An additional supporting protective factor may be that adoptive parents frequently invest significantly in their children's upbringing by focusing strongly on providing emotional support as well as cognitive enrichment.[117]

While much of more recent research, at least partially, draws on international and transracial adoption experiences in more race-sensitive settings than Operation Babylift, the findings are supported by anecdotal evidence from adoptees of the Vietnam War and also those of mixed-race GI children evacuated in Operation Babylift. Well assimilated, a young adoptee, student of business and criminal justice, who had suffered from trauma-induced illnesses that confined him to hospital for months after arriving in the United States, reflected that the Babylift had given him a second chance and contemplated that 'it was hard, especially for the older ones, to be uprooted, ... but if we had stayed in Vietnam, most of us would not have made it'.[118] When a Boston newspaper, at the time of the twentieth anniversary of Operation Babylift traced around half of the 50 children who were raised in New England, the reporter found not only that none of them spoke any Vietnamese, but that most admitted not knowing much about Vietnamese culture and that few had Asian friends. It was the GI children among the evacuees who appeared to have struggled most with finding their place in American society, saying that they inhabited 'an uncomfortable limbo'. As a 27-year-old adoptee observed: 'I feel slightly out of place. I'm American, but not really; Vietnamese, but not really. I feel left out.'[119]

Rosemary Taylor, in her 1988 account of Operation Babylift, reported on the progress of the children 13 years on, and concluded that the vast majority of adoptees had expressed 'a sense of total belonging with no trace of anxiety about their origins. The children know that they come from Vietnam but for the most part they do not identify themselves as Vietnamese but as American, French, or Australian and so on.'[120] While this may well have been true in 1988 when the adoptees were in their early teens, many of them later sought to reclaim their neglected heritage.[121] As adults, thousands of adoptees who had migrated from Asia in the 1970s and 1980s have since returned in search of their birth parents, to learn the language or to recoup the heritage that they lost in early childhood. The complexity of this racial/ethnic identity is borne out by recent research. A study of Korean transracial adoptees found that 78% of them reported thinking they were white or wanting to be white as children, but the majority of them later felt compelled to heighten their racial awareness and shifted their identification to match their Asian birth heritage.[122] This may be rooted in the dissonance which those adoptees' experience of discrepancy between their physical appearance on the one hand, which leads to an 'expected' cultural belonging, and their lived familial and cultural practice and affiliation on the other hand, which leads them to attempt to reclaim their birth culture. This has been shown to take different forms involving different intensity of immersion (education in ethnic studies, language courses, homeland tours, study abroad visits), a process which has recently been termed 'reculturation', defined as a process of identity development and navigation through which adoptees develop their relationship with their birth and adoptive cultures.[123]

The Amerasian Homecoming Act

Operation Babylift was one small episode in the long and convoluted story of Vietnamese emigration in the wake of the Vietnam War. It was discussed in some detail here, because it involved CBOW who were fathered by foreign, American, fathers and born to local Vietnamese mothers. These GI-fathered evacuees, in almost all cases, were not orphans: they had mothers, and in many cases, they also had fathers; yet almost none of the children transported out of Vietnam know much about their birth parents, and, conversely, their birth parents knew and know little or nothing about them.

A second American initiative, another attempt to 'bring home' the children of American GIs born in Vietnam to local mothers, was the so-called American (or Amerasian) Homecoming Act, passed well over a decade later. No less controversial, this was the second act of what many perceived as the drama, the humanitarian challenge of children of American military and civilian personnel who had been left behind in Vietnam. Since US authorities, as detailed above, discouraged marriages between soldiers and local women, only a small proportion of GI Americans married their Vietnamese girlfriends, who were, in many cases, the mothers of their children. Only the most committed and single-minded soldiers managed to bring their Vietnamese wives and their children back to the United States before the withdrawal of US troops,[124] and only a fraction of the remaining children were evacuated in Operation Babylift or thereafter.

That the phenomenon of a sizeable minority of children of South East Asian-American children of GIs was not a new one, is clear from the above analysis of American Second World War and post-war deployment in Asia; but in fact this was not the beginning of Asian-American offspring born of war either. As early as the late 1800s American troops in the Philippines had fathered children by local women and then abandoned the children along with their mothers.[125] And this phenomenon accompanied the American soldiers wherever they were deployed in Asia (as elsewhere) in the twentieth century. As elsewhere, not only the girlfriends of GIs were of little concern for the military and political establishment, but also their children. Except during Operation Babylift, at a politically highly charged time when it appeared politically expedient – though still controversial – to focus on the fate of Amerasian children left behind, the *Bui Doi*, just like their counterparts of earlier American deployments in Asia, became another forgotten legacy of twentieth-century foreign military engagement. Several factors contributed to the development which led from the United States' early lack of action concerning the care for their soldiers' children in the late 1970s to the later activism which culminated in the Homecoming Act. The sheer number of mixed-race children left behind after the Fall of Saigon may have been one factor, the specific political situation in Vietnam may have been another. In Vietnam, the former military and continuing ideological enemy, the United States, was widely despised and anybody linked to that enemy – as visibly the half-American GI children were – potentially could become a target of Anti-Americanism. This created a mood in the United States that was more supportive of the welfare of the children of US soldiers. Further, the above-mentioned sentiment that the south of the country had been abandoned in the face of the threat of the Viet Cong ultimately led to a change of heart and law in America which allowed Amerasians to emigrate to the United States. It was initially the initiative on the part of a journalist and the activism of a group of high school students who were touched by the fate of an individual *Bui Doi* which triggered a remarkable process that eventually led to the passing of the American Homecoming Act. The story is well known and well rehearsed. In October 1985, *Newsday* photographer Audrey Tiernan, on assignment in Vietnam, on the streets of Ho Chi Minh City, took a photo of Minh, a young Amerasian who, with long lashes, hazel eyes, a few freckles and a handsome Caucasian face was visibly out of place in a racially homogeneous country like Vietnam.[126] He had been abandoned by his mother at the age of 10, possibly because he was physically disabled as a result of polio. Since then he had slept rough, surviving by begging. The photo taken by Tiernan was published around the world, and four high school students from Long Island translated their emotional response to the photo into action. They collected 27,000 signatures on a petition to bring Minh to the United States for medical attention. With the help of Tiernan and their Congressman Robert Mrazek, they eventually succeeded. More significantly in the long run however was the fact that Minh's fate and a visit to Vietnam sensitised the Congressman to the thousands of Amerasians in Vietnam, and he pushed on the legislative process which led to federal legislation designed to ease immigration of Vietnamese Amerasian children and their close relatives into the United States. This resulted in the Amerasian Homecoming Act of 22 December 1987, which came into effect in March 1988

Even before the Act it had been possible for Amerasians to enter the United States. In 1982, the US Congress passed the Amerasian Immigration Act,[127] which allowed, in principle, the immigration of Vietnamese Amerasians. Largely due to the lack of co-operation from the Vietnamese government, only about 6,000 Amerasians and 11,000 of their relatives reached the United States under this law as part of the Orderly Departure Program that had begun in 1979.[128] And even this limited avenue for Amerasian immigration came to an end in 1987, as Vietnam objected to the program's classification of Amerasians as refugees.[129] In response, the US Congress passed a bill sponsored, among others, by Robert Mrazek: the Homecoming Act. It became the basis of the first large-scale repatriation of CBOW to their American fathers' home country. Under the law, Amerasians (who had to be children of American citizens and had to have been born between 1 January 1962 and 1 January 1976) and their relatives could apply for immigration to the United States. Although they did not have refugee status, they were given full refugee assistance. By 2009, approximately 25,000 Amerasians and between 60,000 and 70,000 of their relatives had immigrated to America under the Homecoming Act.

The legislation was the culmination of almost twenty years of changing moral, philosophical and, above all, political and legal positions taken by various policy makers and politicians in both America and Vietnam. The length of the process demonstrates that the question of who felt obligated to take responsibility for Vietnamese Amerasians was a function of domestic and international politics as much as of moral judgement. In 1970, after several years of US engagement in Vietnam, a Department of Defense Paper argued that 'care and welfare of those unfortunate children ... has never been and is not now considered an area of [US] Government responsibility'.[130] In contrast, a decade after the withdrawal of US troops from Vietnam, the emphasis had shifted, with kinship being regarded as rather more significant a consideration than before when, in the context of changing policies in the Orderly Departure Program (the main vehicle that had allowed Vietnamese refugees to emigrate to the United States legally and relatively safely since 1979) the then Secretary of State Schultz declared that Vietnamese Amerasians were of special concern to the United States 'because of their *undisputed* ties to our country'.[131]

Although much of the evidence about the treatment of Amerasians is anecdotal, and as such the picture remains impressionistic, it is evident that many had suffered discrimination and stigmatisation. Most were abandoned by their fathers, and some were also abandoned by their mothers.[132] As described above, this was already the case before the American withdrawal around the time of the Fall of Saigon, and the number of lost and abandoned Amerasians multiplied when the victory of the Viet Cong was imminent. The description of one Vietnamese woman is representative of many similar accounts: 'People were panicking. There were so many rumors going around, including that the communists would kill anyone ever involved with Americans. Of course that included anyone with an Amerasian in the family, and the Amerasians themselves.'[133]

The massacres which had been dreaded, and the fear of which may well have been fuelled by American anti-Viet Cong propaganda, never took place. However, what did take place was discrimination on a large scale. When the head of the Department of Social Welfare in Ho Chi Minh City said about Amerasians in 1980, that 'our society does not need these bad elements', he summed up an attitude that could explain policies of previous years. 'Many orphanages were closed, and Amerasians and other youngsters were sent off to rural work farms and re-education camps. The communists confiscated wealth and property and razed many of the homes of those who had supported the American-backed government of South Vietnam.'[134] Discrimination was partially politically motivated, but other factors played an important part, too. Almost everyone in Vietnam had lost a loved one in the conflict, and in postwar Vietnam the Americans were seen as the culprits who had caused this suffering. Similarly, what was perceived to be continuing economic warfare on the part of the Americans, who continued the 1975 trade embargo that had been imposed on Hanoi until 1994,[135] reinforced the image of the United States as the enemy, as the American policy had severe adverse consequences for the country's reconstruction efforts after the long and very destructive war.[136] Beyond that, the Amerasians were evidently the result of relationships between Vietnamese and foreigners, and traditionally, any liaison with foreigners met with disapproval, especially, if these foreigners were racially different. A Vietnamese proverb 'It is better to marry a village dog than a rich man elsewhere',[137] neatly summarises the sentiments of this homogeneous society in the 1960s and 1970s. The shame of the 'inappropriate' liaison was first and foremost projected onto the women, but was also transferred to the children and the extended families. Added to the disgrace of miscegenation was the equally despised and scorned fact that almost all children had been conceived and born outside marriage. More important than being born out of wedlock was the social stigma attached to the fact that 'most Vietnamese believed all Amerasians were children of prostitutes'[138] who in turn were equated with lower classes inviting additional prejudice.

For the children, as is reported almost unanimously by Vietnamese Amerasians, this prejudice frequently translated into name-calling, teasing and degrading treatment at school. As one Amerasian summarised: 'In Vietnam, kids beat us and call us names – American halfbreeds with twelve assholes. They hit us and stop us from going to school.'[139] While almost all Amerasians met with some form of discrimination and prejudice, 'black' Amerasians appear to have experienced more severe disadvantages.[140] One Vietnamese American who had been raised in an orphanage described her experiences immediately after the Fall of Saigon and the subsequent closure of her orphanage: 'The local officials allowed each nun to keep two orphans, one Vietnamese and one Amerasian. When people came to pick orphans, they would choose first the good-looking strong Vietnamese kids, then the good-looking healthy white Amerasians; and so on, until only the ugly weak Vietnamese and last of all, the black Amerasians would be left.'[141] In the case of Afro-Amerasians, the stigma of illegitimacy and by implication immorality was exacerbated by class prejudice, as the presumed social and economic status of not just the mother but also the father affected the children's status. As one observer commented: 'Vietnamese, like other Asian groups, look down on those with dark skin which they equate with lower peasant class or *ethnic* minorities.'[142]

The degree to which discrimination really was institutionally and politically promoted in a systematic manner has been disputed. Anecdotes about interrupted schooling as a result of long-term stigmatisation and discrimination, readily accepted by teachers, are just as common as reports of families with

Amerasians ties being economically disadvantaged, being sent for political re-education and being singled out for resettlement in the 'New Economic Zones' where they were supposed to help overcome the country's food shortages by farming desolate, remote and sparsely populated virtually empty lands.[143] However, the majority of such accounts were given by Amerasians who had chosen to leave the country of their birth, and as such may not be a representative sample, as this migration indicates the existence of a significant push factor out of Vietnam. In a 1994 survey, 71% of Amerasians interviewed in the United States reported experiences of discrimination in Vietnam, including difficulty in accessing schooling, negative attitudes of teachers, grade discrimination and persistence and offensive teasing by peers;[144] according to the same survey, children often reacted to the discrimination by withdrawing, dropping out of school or by fighting (which in turn led to expulsion from school), thus leading to wide-spread educational underachievement by Vietnamese Amerasians.[145] This was confirmed by studies of premigratory experiences of Vietnamese Amerasians who later settled in the United States.[146]

Discrimination – real or feared – led to mothers of Amerasian children eradicating or hiding evidence of their links to the declared enemy, the United States. Photographs, letters and official papers that offered confirmation of their American connections were destroyed. 'My mother burned everything', says William Tran, now a 38-year-old computer engineer in Illinois. 'She said, "I can't have a son named William with the Viet Cong around." It was as though your whole identity was swept away.'[147] While this created significant crises of identity for the young GI children who would find it near impossible to trace their fathers once they were allowed to emigrate to the United States in the wake of the Homecoming Act, many Amerasians in this difficult situation saw themselves as the lucky ones in the face of the even more drastic reaction of some other mothers of Amerasians – the above-described abandonment of their children in an attempt to sever the links to the United States. A study of the impact of maternal loss on Vietnamericans demonstrated a clear link between maternal and (single or multiple) surrogate caregiving on the psychological and educational outcomes among Vietnamese Amerasians. Those who had lived continuously with their biological mothers had fewer symptoms of psychological distress than did either group raised by surrogate caregivers. Moreover, those living continuously with either their mothers or a single surrogate had better educational outcomes than did those raised by multiple surrogates.[148] Striking is also the fact that immigrants' expectations had a significant impact on their mental health prior to resettlement, but also on the success of integration, adaptation and acculturation. High expectations and hopes were associated with few mental health symptoms and mental health problems prior to migration. Yet, exaggerated expectations later translated into higher levels of depression in cases where integrative support from the Vietnamese community in the United States was not forthcoming.[149] Therefore, it is not surprising that those Amerasians who came to the United States with their mothers did best in assimilating into American society.

Vietnamericans in America

The story of Vietnamericans' integration into the United States is inherently linked with the role ascribed to them by American policy makers and the media, and has to be understood in the context of the construction of Vietnamericans as biological Americans rather than immigrants. Yet by 'mapping a discourse of national redemption onto Vietnamese Amerasians', policies and media images 'reinscribed hierarchies of race and sexuality grounded in the history of Asian exclusion'.[150] The above-described political processes, the congressional and other political debates surrounding first the Amerasian Amendment of 1982 and later the Homecoming Act, resulted in Amerasians entering the United States as a category very explicitly set apart from other refugees or immigrants. In contrast to other 'illegal aliens' or foreigners, they entered – or so the political discourse claimed – as Americans. The rationale was often provided by emphasising the visible American racial characteristics of the children, pointing to 'round eyes' 'curly hair', 'blond hair and freckles' and thus this logic racialised Amerasians in a way that stood in stark contrast to long-standing anti-Asian stereotypes that had underscored Asian exclusion policies in the past. This construction of Vietnamerican identity is particularly significant in that the influx of Vietnamese Amerasians in the 1980s coincided with the immigration of hundreds of thousands of Vietnamese refugees. Hence, deliberately setting the GI children apart from other Asian and Asian-American population groups had an impact on the way Vietnamericans interacted with other Vietnamese immigrants, how they perceived themselves and were perceived by others.

The question remains as to the rationale for singling out Vietnamese Americans, a significant yet comparatively small groups of Asian-Americans, in such a way. The argument that this was another act of 'calculated kindness' of American refugee policy of a 'half-open door' is convincing. As one commentator argues persuasively, Amerasians were redefined as '*Americans* and potential vessels of reconciliation' and, as one might add, vessels of redemption.[151] Moreover, the decision of the Reagan Administration to separate provision for Amerasians from that for other Vietnamese refugees served the President well at a time when he was looking to improve his own image, which had been dominated by views of him being 'uncaring'. Personal support of the Amerasian Amendment provided him with a welcome opportunity to give a 'humanitarian gesture' that could counter such a negative perception effectively. By referring to the legislation pushed through under his watch as a 'humane law' that would 'welcome home' Amerasians in a move that was portrayed to be a heartfelt desire on the part of the American people, the US

President again reinforced both the idea of humanitarian intervention and the distinguishing features of Amerasians as compared with other refugees, for whom America was not naturally the 'home'.[152]

An essential point here is that, again, as in the case of children born of the Second World War and the post-war occupations, children born of the Vietnam War were treated as a commodity in the political process rather than as individuals for whom the circumstances surrounding conception, birth, family and social integration presented significant childhood and lifetime adversities. As such they were forgotten where no political capital could be gained, but instrumentalised when it seemed expedient to do so.

Another issue of significance in evaluating US policies vis-à-vis GI children born of the Vietnam War is the approach to Asian familial ties of those children and in particular the way in which the legislation dealt with the children's mothers. The 1982 Amendment initially failed to include mothers in the legislation and thus forced Amerasian children to choose between their Vietnamese mothers, families and heritage on the one hand and their American dream, an (almost always elusive) American GI father on the other. Thus, family in the context of the Amendment was defined, perhaps unsurprisingly, patrilineally as well as along (Caucasian) racial markers. It was not until 1988, that Vietnamese women, on the basis of their maternal relationship to the GI child, were allowed to emigrate to the United States and to accompany their children. The fact that Amerasian applications for emigration to the United States rose dramatically[153] is an indicator that many GI children had not been prepared to choose the United States over and above their Vietnamese mothers, but were keen to emigrate as soon as they were able to preserve those maternal ties.

There is little doubt that GI children in Vietnam were faced with myriad adversities and in some cases extreme hardships. However, as has been reported extensively both in the psychological, psychiatric and sociological literature, and also in biographical and autobiographical writing, integration into the United States was far from easy either.[154] Significantly, most had to abandon the dream of a family life that included both parents, as only 3% of Amerasian immigrants managed to contact their American fathers after arriving in the United States.[155]

By 1992, more than 70,000 Amerasians and their families had resettled in the United States, 21,000 of whom were Amerasians and 49,000 accompanying relatives. Research supports what common sense suggested, namely that Amerasians with limited schooling, limited English and few transferable skills, as well as those who had Afro-American fathers, found adaptation particularly challenging.[156] Most of them came as so-called free cases without relatives in the United States who would support the settlement, and as such they found themselves in one of the forty cluster sites that the US government's Office for Refugee Resettlement had set up to administer the adaptation and integration process. Vietnamerican settlements showed similarities as well as differences to other refugee resettlements. As others, they often had to opt for run-down inner-city neighbourhoods where rent was affordable, but the social fabric detrimental to integration. Yet, unlike other Asian immigrant communities, including the Vietnamese community in the United States, they had no strong family ties in the United States and as a corollary they had few community or other social support structures to rely on.[157] Also, unlike other Asian immigrants, who had been under little misapprehension about their 'otherness' upon entering the United States as refugees, Vietnamericans – after years of having been identified among the homogeneous Vietnamese society as the 'American' element – were more likely to identify with America. On arrival, however, they were faced with the reality of linguistic limitations, lack of familiarity with American culture, and little opportunity to develop a sense of belonging. Consequently, many found themselves in the ironic predicament of 'having left Vietnam to escape life on the fringe of Vietnamese society, only to find themselves in the same situation in one of the various little Saigons around the United States'.[158] Moreover, at those fringes they encountered very similar attitudes that had marred their social experiences in their birth countries: they were perceived as the outcome of immoral relationships of cheap bar girls and as such were seen as the result of dishonourable conduct for reasons of personal profiteering.[159]

Research about the life courses of Amerasians has been patchy, with clusters of research around psychosocial factors and mental health pathologies on the one hand and explanatory work of the living conditions, often based on anecdotal evidence collected in oral history projects, on the other. As such, it is not surprising that the picture remains inconsistent. While the literature is in agreement about childhood and life-time adversities for the GI children (and their mothers), many commentators are at pains to stress that the collection of experiences is also full of success stories – despite the formidable challenges faced by the individuals. In order to gain a full understanding of adaptation, integration and assimilation – whether successful or not – it is necessary to go beyond the anecdotal case study research and engage in systematic quantitative and qualitative studies that evaluate the effect of integrative mechanisms, support structures, and social and economic conditions that underlie the long-term outcomes for CBOW who chose to settle in their paternal home country.

Notes

1 The term 'hidden population' does not refer to the visibility of the population *per se* but to the fact that these populations are hard to reach, because the trait which sets them aside from their peers is in some way 'threatening'. This is normally due to the fact that such traits are either illegal (e.g. prohibited drug use) or socially unacceptable (e.g. rape victim, sufferers of STIs). See e.g. Marinus Spreen, 'Rare populations, hidden populations, and link-tracing designs: What and why?' *Bulletin de Methodologie Sociologique*, 36 (1992), 34–58. Also Matthew J. Salganik,

'Commentary: Respondent-driven sampling in the real world', *Epidemiology*, 23 (2012), 148–50.
2. *Bui Doi* (dust of life) refers to all those who exist on the periphery of life: homeless, street people, etc. who are blown about 'like dust of life'. It was only after 1975 that the term was associated specifically with Amerasians born during the war. In Vietnam, Amerasians are also referred to as *My Lai* (mixed American and Vietnamese) or *Con Lai* (mixed-race child), a disparaging term best translated as 'bastard'.
3. www.daughterfromdanang.com. (accessed 9.10.2015).
4. Anthony O. Edmonds, *The War in Vietnam* (London: Greenwood, 1998), p. 11.
5. Richard Polenberg, *One Nation Divisible: Race, Class and Ethnicity in the United States Since 1938* (New York: Penguin, 1980); David E. Kaiser, *American Tragedy: Kennedy, Johnson, and the Origins of the Vietnam War* (Cambridge: Belknap Press, 2000), chapters 3–7.
6. Inaugural Address John F. Kennedy, 20 January 1961, www.bartleby.com/124/pres56.html. (accessed 1.2.2015).
7. James H. Willbanks, *Vietnam War Almanac* (New York: Checkmarck Books, 2010), p. 526.
8. Quoted in Stanley Karnow, *Vietnam: A History* (New York: Viking Press, 1983), p. 247. A slight variation on his quotation is: 'now we have a problem in making our power credible and Vietnam looks like the place'. John Hellmann, *American Myth and the Legacy of Vietnam* (New York: Columbia University Press, 1986), pp. 50–1.
9. Mark Leepson and Helen Hannaford, *Webster's New World Dictionary of the Vietnam War* (New York: Macmillan, 1999), p. 484.
10. Department of Defense Manpower Data Center, table on Vietnam War Allied Troop Levels 1960–1973, www.americanwarlibrary.com/vietnam/vwatl.htm. (accessed 1.2.2015).
11. John T. McNaughton, Memo to John McNamara, 24.3.1965, in George Donelson Moss (ed.), *A Vietnam Reader: Courses and Essays* (Englewood Cliffs, N.J.: Prentice Hall, 1991), pp. 80–1.
12. Vincent H. Demma, 'Strategy and tactics', in Stanley Kutler (ed.), *Encyclopedia of the Vietnam War* (New York: Scribner Book Company, 1996), p. 520.
13. Daniel C. Hallin, *The Uncensored War: The Media and Vietnam* (Berkeley: University of California Press, 1989).
14. Henry Kissinger, *Ending the Vietnam War: A History of America's Involvement in and Extrication from the Vietnam War* (London: Simon and Schuster, 2003), pp. 51ff.
15. 'The Paris Agreement on Vietnam: Twenty-Five Years Later', Conference Transcript, The Nixon Center, Washington, DC, April 1998. Reproduced on www.mtholyoke.edu/acad/intrel/paris.htm. (accessed 5.2.2015).
16. 'The Church–Case Amendment', in Spencer C. Tucker (ed.), *The Encyclopedia of the Vietnam War: A Political, Social and Military History*, 2nd edn (Santa Barbara: ABC-Clio, 2011), p. 174.
17. William L. Lunch and Peter W. Sperlich, 'American public opinion and the war in Vietnam', *The Western Political Quarterly*, 32 (1979), 21–44, here 30–2.
18. The President's News Conference of 3 April 1975, *Weekly Compilation of Presidential Documents*, vol. 11, no. 14, 328.

19 Gil Loscher and John A. Scanlan, *Calculated Kindness: Refugees and America's Half-Open Door, 1945 to the Present* (London: Collier Macmillan Publishers, 1986), p. 102.
20 Sirik Matak to John Dean, cited in William Shawcross, *Sideshow: Kissinger, Nixon and the Destruction of Cambodia* (New York: Simon and Schuster, 1979), p. 362.
21 See e.g. Saundra Pollock Sturdevant and Brenda Stoltzfus, *Let the Good Times Roll: Prostitution and the US Military in Asia* (New York: New Press, 1993); Katharina H.S. Moon, *Sex Among Allies: Military Prostitution in U.S.–Korean Relations* (New York: University of Columbia Press, 1997); Ji-Yeon Yuh, *Beyond the Shadow of Camptown: Korean Military Brides in America* (New York: New York University Press, 2004).
22 Na Young Lee, 'The Construction of US Camptown Prostitution in South Korea: Transformation and Resistance' (Ph.D. dissertation, University of Maryland, 2006).
23 Moon, *Sex Among Allies*, p. 2.
24 J.W. Fulbright, address to the School of Advanced Studies at Johns Hopkins University, 5 May 1966. The remark was widely reported in the press, also reprinted in *US News and World Report* 60 (23.5.1966), 113–19.
25 Heather Marie Stur, *Beyond Combat: Women and Gender in the Vietnam War Era* (Cambridge: Cambridge University Press, 2011), pp. 38–63.
26 See also Erik Fischer, *Die USA im Vietnamkrieg: Kriegsverbrechen amerikanischer Soldaten* (Hamburg: Diplomica Verlag, 2009), pp. 120–7, here pp. 122–3.
27 Monte Gulzow and Carol Mitchell, '"Vagina dentata" and "incurable venereal disease" legends from the Viet Nam War', *Western Folklore*, 39 (1980), 306–16, here 307ff.
28 Ken Mclvin, *Sorry 'Bout That: Cartoons, Limericks and other Diversions of GI Vietnam* (Tokyo: The Wayward Press, 1966); Ken Melvin, *Be Nice: More Cartoons and Capers of GI Vietnam* (Tokyo: The Wayward Press, 1968).
29 Stur, *Beyond Combat*, p. 41.
30 Susan Zeiger, *Entangling Alliances: Foreign War Brides and American Soldiers in the Twentieth Century* (New York: New York University Press, 2010), p. 217.
31 Gloria Emerson, *Winners and Losers: Battles, Retreats, Gains, Losses, and Ruins from the Vietnam War* (New York: W.W. Norton & Company 1985), p. 16.
32 Le Ly Hayslip, *When Heaven and Earth Changed Places* (London: Penguin, 2003).
33 Steven De Bonis, *Children of the Enemy: Oral Histories of Vietnamese Amerasians and their Mothers* (Jefferson: McFarland & Co, 1994), p. 18.
34 Sue Sun, 'Where the girls are: The management of venereal disease by United States military forces in Vietnam', *Literature and Medicine*, 23 (2004), 66–87, here 72–3.
35 Communication from former marine, 17.12.2013, in author's possession.
36 e.g. John Ketwig, *... and a Hard Rain Fell: A GI's True Story of the War in Vietnam* (New York: Macmillan, 2008), pp. 98–9; Tracy Kidder, *My Detachment: A Memoir* (London: Random House Digital, Inc., 2006), pp. 114–15. See also Emily Nyen Chang, 'Engagement abroad: Enlisted men, US military policy and the sex industry', *Notre Dame Journal of Law, Ethics & Public Policy*, 15 (2001), 621. Also, Zeiger, *Entangling Alliances*, p. 221.

37 See e.g. Suzan Ruth Travis-Robyns, '"What is winning anyway?" Redefining veteran: A Vietnamese American woman's experience', in Linda Trinh Võ and Mariam Sciachitano (eds), *Asian-American Women: The Frontiers Reader* (Lincoln: University of Nebraska Press, 2004), pp. 125–49.
38 Communication from former marine, 17.12.2013, in author's possession.
39 Graham Greene, *The Quiet American* (London: Vintage, 1955).
40 Judy Klemesrud, 'Vietnamese war brides', *New York Times*, 13.9.1971, 42.
41 See e.g. Christian G. Appy, *Working-Class War: American Combat Soldiers and the Vietnam War* (Chapel Hill: University of North Carolina Press, 1993), p. 27.
42 In comparison, the average age of US soldiers during the Second World War was around 26. See e.g. www.uswings.com/about-us-wings/vietnam-war-facts/. (accessed 6.6.2016).
43 Zeiger, *Entangling Alliances*, p. 224.
44 Ibid., p. 225.
45 John Chambers, *The Oxford Companion to American Military History* (Oxford: Oxford University Press, 2000).
46 Robyn Arrowsmith, *All the Way to the USA: Australian WWII War Brides* (self-published, 2013). Also in ibid., 'Travelling for love: Journeys of WWII War Brides', www.slq.qld.gov.au/__data/assets/pdf_file/0010/97795/SLQ_-_Travelling_for_Love_-_War_Brides_talk_-_Robyn_Arrowsmith.pdf. (accessed 7.2.2015).
47 MACV Directive 608-1, 22.6.1966, 'Procedures to Marry', NACP, RG472, Box 43.
48 *Chicago Tribune*, 10.11.1975, 11; 22.7.1976, 6.
49 The 1945 War Brides Act, H.R. 4857; Pub.L. 79–271; 59 stat 659.79th Congress; 28 December 1945, http://library.uwb.edu/guides/usimmigration/59%20stat%20659.pdf. (accessed 7.2.2015).
50 The 1870 Naturalization Act, the 1882 Chinese Exclusion Act and the Immigration Acts of 1917 and 1924 all discriminated against Asians by excluding them from immigration. US Immigration (ed.), *Asian American History Timeline*, www.us-immigration.com/asian-american-history-timeline/. (accessed 2.2.2015).
51 Cable Act, chapter 411, §§3,5,42, Stat. 1022, Immigration Act of 1917, chapter 29, §§3, 39, Stat 874, 876. See Mary Yu Danico (ed.), *Asian American Society: An Encyclopedia* (Los Angeles / London / New Dehli: Sage, 2014), pp. 1316–18.
52 Elfrieda Berthiaume Shukert and Barbara Smith Scibetta, *War Brides of World War II* (California: Presidio Press, 1988), chapters 12–14.
53 NACP, RG200, ARC papers, group 4, 1947–1964; See also papers in RG472, Adjutant General's Office.
54 Rosemary Taylor, *Orphans of War: Work with Abandoned children of Vietnam 1967–1975* (London: Collins, 1988), pp. 217ff.
55 Exact figures are difficult to ascertain as sources vary. Operation Babylift, PBS, *Precious Cargo* documentary talks about at least 2,700 children being flown to the United States and approximately 1,300 children to Canada, Europe and Australia. United States Agency for International Development, *Operation Babylift Report (Emergency Movement of Vietnamese and Cambodian Orphans for Intercountry Adoption, April–June 1975)*, Washington, DC, pp. 1–2, 5, 6, 9–10, 11–12, 13–14, talks of a total of 2,547 orphans processed under Operation Babylift, with 1945 remaining in the US and around 600 leaving to other countries.

56 See for instance: 'Refugees: Clouds over the airlift', *Time Magazine*, 28.4.1975, which is symptomatic of extensive debates.
57 For details about the tragedy see Taylor, *Orphans of War*, chapter 14, pp. 158–83.
58 See e.g. E.B. Kapstein, 'The baby trade', *Foreign Affairs*, 82:6 (2003), 115–25.
59 Madelyn Freundlich and Joy Kim Lieberthal, 'The gathering of the first generation of adult Korean adoptees', *Perceptions of International Adoption*, Evan B. Donaldson Adoption Institute, 2002, www.holtintl.org/pdfs/Survey2.pdf. (accessed 4.2.2015).
60 Pearl Buck, 'The waiting children', box 23, folder 34, International Social Service American Branch records, Social Welfare History Archives, University of Minnesota. Draft to appear in revised form in *Ebony*, June 1958, 28–31, under the title: 'Should white parents adopt brown babies?'
61 The first formal international adoptions had in fact been those of four Korean children in 1953 (K. Lovelock, 'Intercountry adoption as a military practice: A comparative analysis of intercountry adoption and immigration policy and practice in the United States, Canada, and New Zealand in the post W.W.II period', *International Migration Review*, 34 (2000), 907–23) and it is likely that before this, informal arrangements may have been made outside any official or legal framework.
62 Barbara A. Moe, *Adoption: A Reference Handbook* (Santa Barbara: ABC-Clio, 2007), p. 157.
63 Dana Sachs, *The Life We Were Given: Operation Babylift, International Adoption and the Children of War in Vietnam* (Boston: Beacon Press, 2010), pp. 99, 103.
64 'An Act to Provide for the Adoption of Children', *Acts and Resolves passed by the General Court of Massachusetts*, Chap. 324 (1851). www.houseofrussell.com/legalhistory/alh/docs/adoptionact.html (accessed 27.4.2017).
65 The 'placing out' of children has been fictionalised and brought to a wider audience in books and films, but has found relatively little academic interest. See Marylin Irvin Holt, *The Orphan Trains: Placing Out in America* (Lincoln and London: University of Nebraska Press, 1992), pp. 2–3. James Magnusen and Dorothea G. Petrie, *Orphan Train* (New York: Dial Press, 1978), later adapted as CBS television movie; also Joan Lowery Nixon, *A Family Apart* (New York: Bantam Books, 1987).
66 Children's Aid Society, *The Children's Aid Society of New York: Its History, Plan and Results / Compiled from the Writings and Reports of Charles Loring Brace, and from the Records of the Secretary's Office* (New York: Children's Aid Society, 1893).
67 The information in this section is based largely on material of the National Orphan Train Complex, a museum and research centre dedicated to the preservation of the stories and artefacts of those who were part of the Orphan Train Movement from 1854–1929, www.orphantraindepot.com/index.html. (accessed 27.2.2015).
68 See Brace's thoughts in 'Individual influences and home life as better than institutional life', 'Lessons of industry and self-help as better than alms', The implanting of moral and religious truths in union in supply with the bodily wants', in The Children's Aid Society of New York, p. 3.
69 Angelique Brown, *Orphan Trains (1854–1929)*, The Social Welfare History Project, www.socialwelfarehistory.com/programs/orphan-trains. (accessed 27.2.2015).

70 www.childrensaidsociety.org/about/history/orphan-trains. (accessed 27.2.2015).
71 'Orphan Trains', The Adoption History Project, http://darkwing.uoregon.edu/~adoption/topics/orphan.html. (accessed 27.2.2015).
72 See also Clausdieter Schott's summary of legal history of adoption *Kindesannahme – Adoption – Wahlkindschaft, Rechtsgeschichte und Rechtsgeschichten* (Frankfurt: Wolfgang Metzner Verlag, 2009).
73 See e.g. D.M. Smolin, 'Child laundering: How the adoption system legitimizes and incentivizes the practices of buying, trafficking, kidnapping and stealing children', *Wayne Law Review*, 52 (2006), 113–200.
74 'Convention on Protection of Children and Co-operation in Respect of Intercountry Adoption', 29 May 1993, reproduced on www.hcch.net/upload/conventions/txt33en.pdf. (accessed 17.6.2013).
75 G. Parra-Aranguren, 'Explanatory report to the Hague Convention of 29 May 1993 on protection of children and co-operation in respect of intercountry adoption', www.hcch.net/upload/expl33e.pdf. (accessed 2.2.2015).
76 Ibid.
77 J. Masson, 'Intercountry adoption: A global problem or a global solution?' *Journal of International Affairs*, 55:1 (2001), 141–66.
78 See e.g. Baroness Emma Nicholson, 'Red light on human traffic', *Society Guardian*, 1 July 2004, www.theguardian.com/society/2004/jul/01/adoptionandfostering.europeanunion. (accessed 27.2.2015). For details about Baroness Nicholson's position see 'European parliamentarians break the Nicholson monopoly on international adoptions', *Bucharest Daily News*, 8.3.2006, accessible on www.charlestannock.com/pressarticle.asp?ID=1190. (accessed 17.6.2014).
79 Chaitali B. Roy, 'Child trafficking new form of slavery. Interview with Emma Nicholson', *Arab Times*, www.arabtimesonline.com/NewsDetails/tabid/96/smid/414/ArticleID/160266/t/Child-trafficking-new-form-of-slavery/Default.aspx. (accessed 27.2.2015).
80 UNICEF's position on inter-country adoption, www.unicef.org/media/media_41118.html. (accessed 17.6.2013).
81 Elizabeth Bartholet, 'International adoption: The human rights position', *Global Policy*, 1, 2010. http://ssrn.com/abstract=1446811. (accessed 2.1.2015).
82 J. Oreskovic and T. Maskew, 'Red thread of slender reed: Deconstructing Prof. Bartholet's mythology of international adoption', *Buffalo Human Rights Law Review*, 14 (2008), 71–128.
83 Peter Selman, 'The rise and fall of intercountry adoption in the 21st century', *International Social Work*, 52 (2009), 575–94.
84 Elizabeth Bartholet, 'The international adoption cliff: Do child human rights matter?', 29.5.2013, www.law.harvard.edu/faculty/bartholet/IA%20Adoption%20Cliff%205-30-13.pdf. (accessed 11.11.2016).
85 For a debate of these two views see Elizabeth Bartholet and David Smolin, 'The debate', in Judith L. Gibbons and Karen Smith Robati, *Intercountry Adoption: Policies, Practices, and Outcomes* (London: Ashgate, 2012), pp. 370–96.
86 K.S. Rotabi and K.M. Bunkers, 'Intercountry adoption reform based on the Hague Convention on intercountry adoption: An update on Guatemala in 2008', *Social Work and Society News Magazine*, 11/2008, www.socmag.net/?p=435. (accessed 7.9.2014).

87 Kapstein, 'The baby trade', 116–20.
88 David M. Smolin, 'Intercountry adoption as child trafficking', *Valparaiso Law Review* 39 (2005), 281–325. Available at: http://works.bepress.com/david_smolin/3. (accessed 21.1.2015), 322.
89 See e.g. Kapstein, 'The baby trade'.
90 Ibid., p. 115.
91 Smolin, 'Intercountry adoption as child trafficking', pp. 323–4.
92 See below pp. 137–8.
93 F. Juffer and M.H. Van IJzendoorn, 'A longitudinal study of Korean adoptees in the Netherlands: Infancy to middle childhood', in K.J.S. Bergquist et al. (eds), *International Korean Adoption: A Fifty-Year History of Policy and Practice* (Binghampton, NY: Haworth Press, 2007), pp. 263–76; N. Jaffari-Bimmel et al., 'Social development from infancy to adolescence: Longitudinal and concurrent factors in an adoption sample', *Developmental Psychology*, 42 (2006), 1143–53.
94 Judith Gaines, 'Orphans ... survivors ... successes', *The Boston Globe*, 19.2.1995.
95 Ibid.
96 Deepa Bharath, 'Reunited with their rescuer; in April 1975 Betty Tisdale helped evacuate 2,919 children at Saigon orphanage', *The Orange County Register*, 23.5.2010.
97 For information about Betty Tisdale see: www.bettytisdale.com/halo/founder.html. (accessed 27.2.2015).
98 Bharath, 'Reunited with their rescuer'.
99 Dennis Ellam, 'Our escape from Saigon', *The Sunday Mirror*, 28.3.2010, 36–7.
100 Kevin Minh Allen, 'Operation Babylift: An adoptee's perspective', *Humanist*, 69 (2009), 21.
101 Judith Gaines, '2 decades after the U.S. carried out "Babylift" in South Vietnam, you should see them now', *St. Louis Post Dispatch*, 26.2.1995.
102 Ibid.
103 Eleana J. Kim, *Adopted Territory: Transnational Korean Adoptees and the Politics of Belonging* (Durham, NC: Duke University Press, 2010), p. 92.
104 Judith Modell, *Kinship with Strangers: Adoption and Interpretations of Kinship in American Culture* (San Francisco: Berkeley: University of California Press, 1994), pp. 129–39, 225–38.
105 Richard M. Lee, 'The transracial adoption paradox: History, research, and counseling implications of cultural socialization', *The Counseling Psychologist*, 31 (2003), 711–44.
106 R.M. Lee et al., 'Cultural socialization in families with internationally adopted children', *Journal of Family Psychology*, 20 (2006), 571–80, here 571–2.
107 Adriana Barton, 'Unearthing the roots of adoption', *The Globe and Mail*, Vancouver, 31.7.2007. www.theglobeandmail.com/life/parenting/unearthing-the-roots-of-adoption/article4266097/. (accessed 14.3.2017).
108 Here we only discuss by far the most common case of the adoptive parents being Caucasian, and the adoptees being of a different race or being biracial with features that clearly identify them as being of different ethnicity.
109 W. Feigelman and A.R. Silverman, 'The long-term effects of transracial adoption', *Social Services Review*, 8 (1984), 588–602.
110 J. Bishop, 'Adopted', in E.H. Kim and E.-Y. Yu (eds), *East to America: Korean*

American Life Stories (New York: The New Press, 1996), pp. 306–13; here p. 309.
111 Feigelman and Silverman, 'The long-term effects', 590, citing Dong Soo Kim, 'Intercountry Adoptions: A Study of Self-Concept of Adolescent Korean Children Who Were Adopted by American Families' (Ph.D. thesis, University of Chicago, 1976).
112 L. Van den Dries et al., 'Fostering security? A meta-analysis of attachment in adopted children', Children and Youth Services Review, 31 (2009), 410–21.
113 J. Bowlby, Maternal Care and Mental Health (Geneva: WHO, 1952); J. Bowlby, A Secure Base: Clinical Applications of Attachment Theory (London: Routledge, 1988).
114 F. Juffer and M.H. Van IJzendoorn, 'Adoptees do not lack self-esteem: A meta analysis of studies of self esteem of transracial, international and domestic adoptees', Psychological Bulletin, 133 (2007), 1067–83, esp. 1078–9.
115 E. Werner, 'Protective factors and individual resilience', in J.P. Shonkoff and S.J. Meisels (eds), Handbook of Early Childhood Intervention (Cambridge: Cambridge University Press, 2000), pp. 97–116, here pp. 97–8.
116 Marten W. DeVries, 'Temperament and infant mortality among the Masai of East Africa', The American Journal of Psychiatry, 141 (1984), 1189–94.
117 Jesús Palacios et al., 'Family context for emotional recovery in internationally adopted children', International Social Work, 52 (2009), 609–20, here 610.
118 Gaines, '2 decades'.
119 Gaines, 'Orphans ... victims ... survivors'.
120 Taylor, Orphans of War.
121 Barton, 'Unearthing the roots of adoption'.
122 Hollee McGinnis et al., Beyond Culture Camp: Promoting Healthy Identity Formation in Adoption (New York: Evan B. Donaldson Adoption Institute, 2009), p. 36.
123 Amanda L. Baden et al., 'Reclaiming culture: Reculturation of transracial and international adoptees', Journal for Counselling and Development, 90 (2012), 387–99.
124 Zeiger, Entangling Alliances, 222.
125 Katrina Chludzinski illustrates the attitudes vis-à-vis these liaisons on the part of both Europeans and Americans in 'The fear of colonial miscegenation on the British colonies of South East Asia', The Forum, Cal Poly's Journal of History, 1 (2009), 54–64, here 57ff.
126 David Lamb, 'Children of the Vietnam War', Smithsonian Magazine, June 2009, www.smithsonianmag.com/people-places/Children-of-the-Dust.html?c=y&story=fullstory. (accessed 12.12.2014).
127 1982 Amerasian Immigration Act (An act to amend the Immigration and Nationality Act to provide preferential treatment in the admission of certain children of United States citizens) S. 1698; Pub.L. 97–359; 96 Stat. 1716. 97th Congress; 22 October, 1982, http://library.uwb.edu/guides/usimmigration/1982_amerasian_immigration_act.html. (accessed 30.12.2014).
128 Judith Kumin, 'Orderly departure from Vietnam: Cold War anomaly or humanitarian intervention?', Refugee Survey Quarterly, 27 (2008), 104–17; GAO, The Orderly Departure Program from Vietnam, Washington DC, 1990, http://archive.gao.gov/t2pbat10/141353.pdf. (accessed 30.12.2015); Min Zhou and

Carl L. Bankston, *Growing up American: How Vietnamese Children Adapt to Life in the United States* (New York: Russell Sage Foundation, 1998), p. 34.
129 Thomas A. Bass, *Vietnamerica: The War Comes Home* (New York: Soho Press Inc., 1997), p. 41.
130 Stephen D. Goose and Kyle Horst, 'Amerasians in Viet Nam: Still waiting', *Indochina Issues*, 83 (1988); cited in J. Kirk Felsman et al., 'Vietnamese Amerasians: Practical implications of current research', *ERIC* (1989), 11.
131 George Gedda, 'US to seek release of thousands of Viet Cong prisoners to resettle here', *Schenectady Gazette*, 12.9.1984, 10, http://news.google.com/newspapers?nid=1917&dat=19840912&id=IREhAAAAIBAJ&sjid=H3QFAAAAIBAJ&pg=2434,2521908. (accessed 12.12.2014). Emphasis in original.
132 Robert S. McKelvey, *The Dust of Life: America's Children Abandoned in Vietnam* (Seattle: University of Washington Press, 1999), p. 21.
133 Trin Yarborough, *Surviving Twice: Amerasian Children in Vietnam* (Washington: Potomac Books, 2006), p. 40.
134 Lamb, 'Children of the Vietnam War'.
135 Patrick Cockburn, 'US finally ends trade embargo', *The Independent*, 4.2.1994, www.independent.co.uk/news/world/us-finally-ends-vietnam-embargo-1391770.html. (accessed 27.2.2015).
136 Myron Allukian jr and Paul L. Atwood, 'Public health and the Vietnam War', in Barry S. Levy and Victor W. Sidel (eds), *War and Public Health* (Washington: American Public Health Association, 2000) pp. 215–37, here p. 226.
137 US General Accounting Office, *Vietnamese Amerasian Resettlement: Education, Employment, and Family Outcomes in the United States* (Washington, DC, US General Accounting Office, 1994), p. 2.
138 Yarbrough, *Surviving Twice*, p. 46.
139 Patrick Du Phuoc Long, *The Dream Shattered: Vietnamese Gangs in America* (Richmond: Northeastern University Press, 1997), p. 102. See also Yen Le Espiritu, 'Possibilities of a multiracial Asian America', in Teresa Williams-León and Cynthia L. Nakashima (eds), *The Sum of Our Parts: Mixed-Heritage Asian Americans* (Philadelphia: Temple University Press, 2001), pp. 25–33, here p. 28.
140 Robert S. McKelvey, John A. Webb and Alice R. Mao, 'Premigratory risk factors in Vietnamese Amerasians', *American Journal of Psychiatry*, 150 (1993), 470–3.
141 Yarbrough, *Surviving Twice*, p. 46.
142 Kieu-Linh Caroline Valverde, 'From dust to gold: The Vietnamese Amerasian experience', in Maria P.P. Root (ed.), *Racially Mixed People in America* (London: Sage Publishers, 1992), pp. 144–61, here p. 147. Emphasis in original.
143 See e.g. Yarborough, *Surviving Twice*; McKelvey, *Dust of Life*.
144 US General Accounting Office, *Vietnamese Amerasian Resettlement*, p. 71.
145 Ibid.
146 McKelvey, Webb and Mao, 'Premigratory risk factors', 470–3.
147 Lamb, 'Children of the Vietnam War'.
148 Robert S. McKelvey, and John A. Webb. 'Long-term effects of maternal loss on Vietnamese Amerasians', *Journal of the American Academy of Child & Adolescent Psychiatry*, 32 (1993), 1013–18.
149 Robert S. McKelvey and John A. Webb, 'Premigratory expectations and post-

migratory mental health', *Journal of the American Academy of Child & Adolescent Psychiatry*, 35 (1996), 240–5.
150 Jana K. Lipman, 'The face is the road map: Vietnamese Amerasians in U.S. political and popular culture, 1980–1988', *Journal of Asian American Studies*, 14 (2011), 33–68.
151 Ibid., 37. Emphasis in original.
152 Ronald Reagan, Remarks on Signing S. 1698 into Law, 12.10.1982, www.presidency.ucsb.edu/ws/index.php?pid=41904. (accessed 27.2.2015).
153 Mary Kim DeMonaco, 'Disorderly departure: An analysis of the United States policy toward Amerasian immigration', *Brooklyn Journal of International Law*, 15 (1989), 641–710, here 681–2, note 205.
154 Bass, *Vietnamerica*; De Bonis, *Children of the Enemy*; McKelvey, *Dust of Life*; Yarborough, *Surviving Twice*; Valverde. 'From dust to gold'.
155 Lamb, 'Children of the Vietnam War'.
156 Donald E. Ranard and Douglas F. Gilzow, 'The Amerasians', *In America* (June 1989), especially 1–3, http://files.eric.ed.gov/fulltext/ED323751.pdf (accessed 16.3.2017).
157 De Bonis, *Children of the Enemy*, p. 14.
158 Ibid.
159 See also Valverde, 'From dust to gold', 157ff.

5

Bosnia: a new dimension of genocidal rape and its children

The analysis of conflicts considered in previous chapters was characterised by the challenge of limited and patchy documentation of the relationship between military and civilian populations in general, and violent or exploitative relationships in particular. This changed significantly in the 1990s with the emergence of a number of ethnic conflicts involving the targeting of civilians in order to eliminate certain ethnic groups or displace them for political or resource-related reasons. These included Bosnia and Herzegovina (1992–1995), Rwanda (1994) and Kosovo (1998–1999). It was in these partially or wholly ethnically motivated conflicts that sexual violence began to play an increasingly prominent role which in turn resulted in a significant effort at documenting atrocities of this kind, culminating in a recent project aimed at the creation of a comprehensive cross-national dataset on wartime gender-based violence (GBV).[1] This more elaborate and more sophisticated documentation of GBV contributed significantly to a revaluation of the nature of sexual violence in war. In the words of one observer, the case of Bosnia 'was a turning point in international recognition of protection for women in conflict and in attempts by governments and aid workers to solve the problems of women and girls'.[2] This may be a slight overstatement of the facts, as war-related rape was already starting to be taken more seriously in the 1980s in the Americas, as well as also Asia and Africa,[3] but 'what these acts of violence have come to mean for the larger conflict patterns, and how they affect international peace and stability were largely unacknowledged questions. The Bosnian war change[d] this conceptualization.'[4]

This chapter will begin by outlining some of the key facts around GBV in the Yugoslav wars before exploring who the children born of those wars were and what we know about their post-conflict experiences. The second half of the chapter will explore a specific aspect of the CBOW discourse, namely that of children's rights within the context of the wider human rights issues affecting the children's immediate environment.

Of the case studies discussed in this volume, the Balkan Wars were the first conflict that took place after the signing of the Convention on the Rights of the Child (CRC). In order to ascertain whether, and if so how, this law impacted on the lived experiences of children fathered by foreign soldiers, the CRC will be explored in some detail and some of the key rights of particular interest to CBOW will be investigated in more detail against the background of conflicting rights of family and local community.

Gender-based violence in Bosnia

In late 1992, reports of sexual abuses committed during the armed conflict in the former Yugoslavia first alerted the world to rape and other sexual atrocities as part of a deliberate and systematic campaign for victory in the war. *Newsday* journalist Roy Gutman reported mass rapes, seemingly carried out under orders in a systematic campaign of ethnic cleansing,[5] an account implicitly confirmed when the UN, in its Security Council resolution 820, condemned the 'massive, organized and systematic detention and rape of women'.[6] Although the exact figures of these acts of sexual violence will never be known, and estimates vary widely,[7] some key factors can be asserted with some degree of confidence: The systematic rape had at least several thousand victims. Many of the victims were under age. Often the assaults were committed in the presence of others, including the victim's parents or children, and frequently, victims were violated by multiple assailants.[8] These facts are consistent with a wide range of oral testimony which has found its way into a now significant body of documentary literature.[9]

The vast majority of commentators agree on several other key points. All sides of the war committed atrocities and all warring factions used GBV.[10] However, most atrocities were committed by Serb forces, regular but more frequently irregular units, against Muslim women.[11] In most cases, rape was not spontaneous, but was used in order to humiliate the victim herself and her ethnic community and to destroy the victim's identity. It was this systematic and directed use of rape in the context of war which was instrumental in the rethinking of sexual violence in the international legal context. After having been regarded as a by-product of war rather than a criminal act *per se*, the atrocities committed in Bosnia (and also concurrently in Rwanda) led to a reconsideration of how rape was viewed in legal terms.[12] The 1977 Additional Protocol II of the Geneva Convention had already included rape as one of the atrocities or, as the protocol phrased it, 'outrages upon human dignity' that were explicitly prohibited by the Convention.[13] But it was the International Criminal Tribunal for Rwanda (ICTR) and the International Criminal Tribunal for the former Yugoslavia (ICTY) which started the process of formalising the recognition of rape as a war crime in their prosecutions for crimes against humanity which included acts of sexual violence.[14] Moreover, under the Rome Statute of the International Criminal Court, rape and sexual slavery, alongside forced prostitution, forced pregnancy, enforced sterilisation and similarly grave acts of sexual violence have now been recognised as both crimes against humanity and war crimes.[15]

In addition, since then these issues have featured in a variety of UN resolutions, detailing the member states' obligations relating to gender-related adversities in and around conflicts.[16] UN Security Council Resolution 1325 (2000), entitled *Women, Peace and Security*, which addressed the impact of war on women during and after conflicts called on 'all parties to conflict to take special measures to protect women and girls from GBV, particularly rape and other forms of sexual abuse'.[17] This was followed by UN Security Council Resolution 1820 (2008) which was devoted in its entirety to sexual violence in armed conflict and explicitly treated it as a security issue with specific and explicit recognition of the fact that it had been used as a weapon of war against civilians, and as such was a threat against peace and security.[18] A year later, UN Security Council Resolution 1888 emphasised the need to bring perpetrators to justice and to include provisions for the protection of women and children from rape and other forms of sexual violence in the mandates of UN peacekeeping operations and UN-supported peace negotiations, while also demanding monitoring and reporting of sexual violence in conflict and post-conflict situations, as well as the appointment of a special representative for sexual violence.[19] Most recently, UN Security Resolution 1960 not only expressed concern about the slow progress on resolving the issues of sexual violence in armed conflict, but it reminded states to comply with international law and leaders to demonstrate commitment to prevent sexual violence, combat impunity and uphold accountability. It further demanded that perpetrators be prosecuted and impunity not be tolerated to enable post-conflict societies to recover.[20]

Despite the myriad resolutions and despite greater awareness of conflict-related GBV and a much more proactive approach towards addressing such violence among the international community, there is remarkable silence with regard to advocacy on behalf of the children born as a result of sexual violence, forced impregnation and forced maternity. This is surprising given that forced impregnation, a wide-spread violation committed during the Bosnian War, was 'inextricably linked to the genocide and because forced impregnation implies birth of children'. Although not all rapes in Bosnia amounted to genocidal war strategy, many did, and therefore the children born of rapes are not just 'a party within the genocidal equation', but a very central part. Yet their particular status as 'rights-bearer, victims of genocide or refugees of war' has only been addressed at a superficial level.[21]

Children born of the Bosnian Wars: who are they?

In Bosnia, as elsewhere, no precise figures exist about rape-related pregnancies. Forced impregnation and the above-described practice of detaining raped women until the resulting pregnancies were too far advanced for an abortion to be possible may well have resulted, in certain situations, in a higher rate of pregnancies and maternity among raped women. However, this has been countered by the fact that the vast majority of the women who had the opportunity, sought abortions in the early stages of pregnancy and as a rule could access them. For instance, among 29 impregnated women who took part in a study of psychosocial consequences of war rape, 17 had had abortions.[22] The Mazowiecki Report, a report by the Special Rapporteur of the Commission on Human Rights on the situation in former Yugoslavia, indicates that the number of abortions performed in hospitals in Sarajevo and Zagreb in 1992, at the time of the highest number of reported rapes, increased noticeably.[23] Although rape-related pregnancy estimates vary, at least several hundred children were brought to term. On the basis of the European Community's estimate of 20,000 rape victims and a rape-related pregnancy rate of around 9%,[24] as well as extrapolations about how many pregnancies resulted in births, Carpenter arrives at a figure of around 1,800 pregnancies and 504 births nationwide, which lies within the range of the estimate of between 400 and 600 CBOW given by doctors.[25]

While forced pregnancy was not, as some have claimed, invented by the Bosnian Serb Army and its North Yugoslav National Army supporters, the practice involving systematically abducting and detaining women and girls of child-bearing age, subjecting them to rape until pregnant and releasing them only after it was too late for an abortion was codified as a war crime by the Rome Statute International Criminal Court in response to exactly these practices during the Bosnian conflict.[26]

Yet, forced pregnancy was not new; neither were the overt ethnic connotations. Mass rape during Bangladesh's war of secession from Pakistan had been as explicitly ethnically motivated,[27] as had the intention, in Darfur, to create 'lighter-skinned babies' among the country's Arab population.[28] In such cases, rape and forced pregnancy were part of the arsenal of weapons employed in psychological warfare against entire communities and the nation; and the profound impact on those communities as well as the individuals lives on, personified in the CBOW. Despite raised awareness of the gendered nature of conflict and the necessity of addressing violence against women, as well as the increasing awareness of the ethnic motivation of conflict-related rape, 'evaluating responses to CBOW is measuring a non-event'.[29]

Before turning to the specific situation of the CBOW rape in Bosnia, it will be useful to consider the impact that the existence of a sizeable group of children born as a result of forced pregnancy had on the legal discourse around the construction of rape as a war crime. As discussed above, the Geneva Conventions of 1949 and the 1977 Protocols had already explicitly prohibited enforced prostitution, rape and indecent assault. But in these provisions the offences were not treated as a war crime but as a crime against honour or an outrage upon personal dignity. The widespread condemnation of rape in Bosnia led to a reconsideration of this position and war rape came to be seen as a 'grave breach' of humanitarian law, primarily based on an assessment of the psychological damage that the pregnancies caused irrespective of whether these were coincidental or intentional consequences of rape.[30] As one commentator put it: 'the fact of pregnancy, whether aborted or not, continues the initial torture in a most invasive form; and bearing a child of rape, whether placed for adoption or not, has a potentially life-long impact on the woman and her place in the community'.[31] Eventually, this altered perception found its way into the statute books in the Rome Statute of the International Criminal Court, as described above.[32]

Being a child born of rape

While the impact on the mother of carrying a child born of rape is now widely acknowledged, the impact of being born of rape for the children themselves is far less well understood. Among the themes that need further exploration are both the familial stresses and societal adverse reactions.

There is no doubt that trauma has impact on interpersonal relations generally, and on relations within the family more specifically. A recent study of intergenerational transmission of trauma explored mother–infant prenatal attachment and found that trauma history in general does not impact negatively on prenatal attachment and post-partum bonding. In contrast, interpersonal trauma (e.g. rape, sexual abuse, criminal assault) does have a significant impact.[33] Posttraumatic Stress Disorder (PTSD) symptomatology had previously been identified as a specific risk factor for negative psychological and physical outcomes among expectant mothers,[34] but little trauma research with pregnant women themselves has been conducted.[35] In terms of the impact of maternal trauma on CBOW, the two core issues to be considered are those of transgenerational trauma transmission and the link between trauma and parental attachment. Transgenerational transmission of trauma is well documented.[36] It can be understood in terms of traumatic experiences resulting in reduced parental ability to provide physical and emotional care. Moreover, as a consequence of frightening or frightened maternal behaviour the child may display similar behavioural patterns, which in turn may be perceived by the mother as threatening.[37] A far less well-researched aspect of transgenerational effects of trauma lies in the pre-natal formation of the 'self', which is not related to social interaction but has a genetic basis. Both factors contribute to neural maturation. Early social and, to a lesser degree, biological environments determine the formation and stabilisation of the self, an issue now explored in epigenetic research which indicates that the social environment may have a direct impact on the exprimation of genes and therefore modulates 'the self' or character of an individual considerably.[38] This research is controversial, not least because of it race and class implications,[39] but also because it is reminiscent of some discredited theories of nineteenth-century scientists such as Lamarck, who proposed that organisms pass down acquired traits to future generations.[40] Yet, if intergenerational transmission through these mechanisms cannot be ruled out, it is worth exploring in the case of CBOW.[41] Given the severity of interpersonal trauma experienced by multiple rape victims in war, it is reasonable to assume that this effect, if confirmed by further research, affects children born of wartime GBV and thus calls for specific intervention aimed at the children themselves.

A second, related question is that of parental attachment, because the infant–caregiver relationship is essential as a foundation of any child's mental health.[42] Recent research concerned with the intergenerational effect of trauma exposure and PTSD specifically suggests that there may be a link between maternal trauma exposure and a mother's experience of the relationship with her infant and – by implication – on her interactions with and attachments to her child.[43] Specifically, expectant mothers with a history of interpersonal trauma reported significantly lower prenatal attachment development with their unborn child pointing to such history being a unique factor in future attachment relationships.[44] These findings are mirrored in anecdotal evidence based on individuals' accounts of their personal experiences after war-related rape in Bosnia as well as in African countries. One young mother from the Central African Republic, the first conflict where the number of alleged assaults reportedly surpassed the number of casualties of the conflict, described her son as 'a shadow of a past that will haunt me forever', explaining how she is continually comparing her son's face to the features of what she remembered of the five assailants who had raped her.[45] She further describes her complex feelings towards her son as fluctuating between love (because he was her own flesh and blood) and hate (because he resembled the rapists). In response to this, her actions towards her son similarly oscillated between tenderness and harshness.[46] Numerous reports from Bosnian rape victims and their children demonstrate that this pattern of a love/hate relationship between mothers and their children born of rape was common in Bosnia, too.[47]

Leaving aside the psychological impact of being conceived of GBV, other health risks accompanying pregnancies, if a mother's reproductive health is compromised or if a mother experiences physical and emotional trauma during pregnancy, need to be considered. It has been observed that a disproportionately large number of CBOW in Bosnia were born with disabilities.[48] This has raised the question of a possible link between the physical and mental trauma of the act of conception and foetal development. Given the high incidences of attempted abortions in Bosnia, many of which were carried out in unsafe circumstances, one possible explanation for the compromised health of many children born of rape in Bosnia is the impact of botched abortions on children brought to term. Again, little is known about this,[49] but the combination of little or no assistance during birth, because pregnancies were hidden or mothers were in captivity, combined with a general lack of antenatal and maternal care is likely to have had an adverse impact on health outcomes for the children conceived of rape in Bosnia.

Moreover, not all women who carry their children to term, voluntarily or involuntarily, are able to cope with the experience of motherhood following the traumatic conception of their child, and anecdotal evidence suggests a disproportionally high incidence of infanticide in the aftermath of the mass rapes in Bosnia.[50] The fact that the theme of infanticide has infiltrated the literary and societal discourse on children born of war-related sexual violence[51] is an indication that it was part of the popular lived experiences. Of the case studies collected as part of a UNICEF study of GBV in Bosnia, two cases ended in real or attempted infanticide and in three other cases mothers 'reportedly considered infanticide as a solution'.[52] This confirms the assessment of the World Health Organisation, which reported infanticide as one of the dangers to which CBOW are exposed.[53] Furthermore, although no explicit link has been established between war rape and raised infanticide rates in post-conflict Bosnia, the figures, even taking into account the small sample sizes and some concerns about the representativeness of the material, are stark. A study of the infanticide rates for Croatia in 1989–2002 found neonaticide rates to be approx. 0.008 %, compared with infanticide attempts affecting 8% children born of war-time rape in Bosnia.[54]

As seen in the cases of both the Second World War and the Vietnam War, another solution sought by mothers who found bringing up a child born of rape impossible could be their institutionalisation. In Bosnia, too, a significant number of children carried to term ended up in the care system, either after being abandoned by their mothers and families or consciously and deliberately being placed in care by families who saw this as the least bad option for the child, family or both. Often it was the reality (or threat) of economic hardship that forced mothers to leave their children, because they lacked the financial resources to care for them and were refused support from families or welfare agencies.[55]

The evidence collected by UNICEF also confirms for Bosnia what is known from the studies of children born of the Second World War and the Indochina Wars and has been described above, namely that CBOW have significantly less good economic outcomes than their peers. In Bosnia, too, CBOW were disadvantaged as a result of the economic marginalisation of their mothers. Again, the cycle seems similar: women who suffered rape are stigmatised and as a result suffer disproportionally more economic hardships than others; this moral stigma of rape is exacerbated by the supposedly morally controversial decision to bear and raise the child, who is permanent evidence of the assault.[56]

For those children who cannot be cared for by their mothers, adoption could be an alternative. But here, too, the stigma attached to having been conceived of rape, appears to have impacted negatively on adoption prospects in Bosnia itself.[57] In addition, the Bosnian authorities actively prohibited adoption in the hope that the children's birth mothers would learn to accept them. In any case, whether institutionalised or growing up in families, many insisted that children had to be brought up as citizens of Bosnia. The government contracted an Egyptian agency to look after the CBOW who had been abandoned in Zagreb hospitals.[58] At the time, the main concern was to preserve the optionality of mothers accepting their children at a later stage. This policy was controversial at the time, because it was already assumed then that very few mothers would take up this option, and it was recognised by doctors and psychologists that if adoption were to be in the best interest of the child, then an early adoption would be favourable to a lengthy period of institutional care. Yet, as the prevailing policies demonstrate, concerns other than the best interest of the children or even their mothers, namely questions of nationality, ethnicity and religion, featured more prominently in the decision-making processes of policies vis-à-vis CBOW than the children's needs themselves.

While being a CBOW impeded early inner-Bosnian adoption, outside Bosnia the fate of being a child born of rape may actually have worked to a child's advantage in terms of adoption prospects. Not dissimilar to the drive to facilitate international adoption following the Fall of Saigon, the year 1993 saw a development of 'calculated kindness' in the UK. This took the form of facilitation of international adoption with the specific purpose of allowing children born of war rape in Bosnia easier access to the UK. This move was reminiscent of the US Babylift of 1975 in that it seemingly served two purposes: firstly, it provided absolution for what Brendan Simms called Britain's 'Unfinest Hour', an episode of what he termed the 'hypocrisy and incompetence' of a 'weak and jaded British government, ... sometimes inspired by the best of intentions' leading to 'disaster' for Bosnia;[59] secondly, it offered a possibility, under the mantra of humanitarianism, to solve an adoption crisis, namely the lack of babies available for adoption in Britain itself.[60]

Leaving aside British adoption policies, national and international actors showed relatively little interest in placing CBOW high on the agenda of humanitarian intervention. Given this apparent absence of any concerted action on the part of humanitarian actors in term of policies vis-à-vis CBOW in general and in Bosnia in particular, one might assume that the issue was not actually tabled at a time when many other war-induced crises demanded urgent attention in the early 1990s. However, aid organisations had developed an awareness, and some resources were deployed into understanding the difficulties facing children born of rape.[61] A European Commission study in late 1992 and early 1993 raised the issue,[62] as did a UNHCR analysis[63] and a joint study of UNICEF, UNHCR and Defence for Children International (DCI).[64] All three considered children born of rape, albeit briefly, in particular the dangers of stigmatisation; yet, all three as well as an ICRC report published in 1995,[65] while acknowledging the volatile situation into which these children were born, concluded that women 'were dealing with the matter themselves' and that engagement of outside agencies would be 'intrusive and unhelpful'.[66] Moreover, agencies, by the mid-

1990s, agreed that the scale of the problem had been exaggerated and that the best way forward would be to 'assist local support systems as required and requested'.[67]

Where international humanitarian agencies failed in their recognition that rape babies may not be best served as being treated as 'unaccompanied children', 'orphans', or 'displaced children', indigenous NGOs were more prepared to consider the particular needs of children born as a result of rape. As will be discussed in more detail below, Islamic NGOs enacted policies targeting specifically children born of rape and their mothers.[68] Their actions were based on Ali D'adulhakk's 'Fatwa on Children Born by Raped Women in Bosnia-Herzegovina'. The sheikh of Al-Azhar in Egypt was explicit in giving guidance both on religious and moral judgments, as well as on sharing responsibilities for the consequences of war rape, with regard to both the women's situation and their children's. The fatwa ruled unequivocally that raped women were not at fault, therefore they were not sinners and were not to be treated as such, because the rape had been beyond their control. This was in stark contrast to an almost universal tendency to condemn raped women as adulterous which had dominated public opinion for centuries, if not millennia.[69]

What was more, rather than cloaking their description in terms of victimhood, as had often been the case in Western discourse, the fatwa encouraged a view that utilised language of war heroism. Raped women were conceptualised not as victims, but as martyrs of Islam who had been fighters in their own right and who had made a sacrifice through the 'loss of the most precious thing that they possess, which is their virginity'.[70] All Muslims were asked to respect and support these women and their children during the healing process. Furthermore, the fatwa ruled that abortion, although as a rule regarded a sin, was permissible in certain circumstances.[71] Further, it determined clearly the line of responsibility for the children conceived through rape, placing it into the hands of the mothers in the first instance and – where they could not cope and abandoned the children – into the hands of the community. In particular, it was seen as the duty of the community to protect these (Muslim) children against external threats including adoption into third countries, because 'Islam obliges society and individual to protect children, even illegitimate ones, in order to make them useful (to mankind); their identity should be emphasized in order to secure social adaptation and in order not to remind them ever of their origins'.[72]

The policy of treating war rape victims as war heroes was not new. Following the Bangladesh Liberation War in the early 1970s, which reportedly saw hundreds of thousands of rapes, resulted in rape survivors being referred to as *biranganas* or war heroines. Yet, despite the fact that rehabilitation centres were set up and men were offered rewards for marrying rape victims, the stigma remained and many Bengalis refused to marry the women or reintegrate them into their natal families.[73]

The fatwa had consequences at different levels for the violated women, their children and the local communities. Evidence suggests that the conceptualisation of raped women as war heroes had some impact on family and community reaction to them in that there were cases of women receiving support and protection from their family rather than being ostracised.[74] This would suggest that the commonly held view of all rape victims having suffered stigmatisation as a result of being held responsible for bringing shame on their families or local communities[75] requires some qualification.

Islamic NGOs provided a multitude of services for women and their children, such as safe houses, anti-stigma campaigns, and intervention on a case-by-case basis, which encouraged families and local communities to support the women and their children conceived of rape, including giving financial support.[76] The underlying assumption of intervention of the religious leadership and Islamic organisations was that the children born of rape of Muslim women were to be claimed for Islam, not unlike children of French soldiers born to German women during the Second World War, or Vietnamese women during the Indochina Wars, had been reclaimed for the French Nation. In other words, while children were instrumentalised in the discourse surrounding the French nation, children in Bosnia were instrumentalised as part of the discourse of the religious interpretation of the Bosnian conflict. This is nowhere more evident than in the fact that Islamic assistance was not indiscriminate and was targeted at Muslim women, and specifically at women whose children would be raised as members of Muslim families and communities. As such, as will be explained in more detail below, the needs and rights of the children were of secondary concern, especially where they conflicted with the stated purpose of the support programme, namely a 'reconfirmation of a sense of Muslim victim identity'.[77]

The rights of children born of war under the Convention on the Rights of the Child[78]

While some investigations have explored the moral status of children[79] and tackled the complex philosophical problems of the interplay of children's human rights and the conceptualisation of CBOW as victims,[80] the question of safeguarding children's rights as enshrined in the CRC in the difficult situations of CBOW remains a largely unchartered territory.[81]

The yardsticks against which the children's situations are measured are the provisions of the CRC. This Convention was the outcome of a lengthy process of social, cultural and legal repositioning of views on children's rights, closely related to the changing concept of childhood.[82] This repositioning had begun in the interwar years, and gathered momentum in the aftermath of the Second World War, parallel with developments in both the altering understanding of childhood and family, and concurrent developments in international law and particularly international humanitarian law.

The Convention on the Rights of the Child

The concept of children's rights is of relatively recent origin, and different conceptions of the nature of childhood at different periods in history clearly demonstrate that childhood is a 'social construct'.[83] Only after the First World War, when children were beginning to be recognised as an autonomous group, did the formulation of their rights find its first expression in the form of the 'Declaration of Geneva of 1924', adopted later that year by the League of Nations. Based on the notion that 'Mankind owes to the child the best it has to give'[84] the idea of the 'best interest of the child' and special safeguards for children are found in the Universal Declaration of Human Rights of 1948[85] and more extensively in the UN Declaration on the Rights of the Child of 1959.[86]

Thirty years after the Declaration on the Rights of the Child, in 1989, the CRC was adopted by the General Assembly of the United Nations.[87] It entered into force in 1990 and by December 2008, 193 parties had ratified the Convention. It was the first legally binding instrument to incorporate the civil, cultural, political and social rights of children and is closely connected to the other five human rights conventions.[88] The CRC is based on the recognition, by world leaders, that children, especially children in crisis situations, need protection and that safeguards are needed to ensure their by now universally recognised human rights.

The CRC is conceived on the idea of universality – both with regard to the states subscribing to its principles and rights formulated within it and with regard to the applicability to all children. Given the almost universal adoption of the law by national governments, it is indeed the most widely subscribed to convention of all. But as will be demonstrated below, the implementation of the idea of impartiality, i.e. the universal applicability of the provisions to all children, irrespective of their gender, nationality, religion or social status, is often not realised for CBOW, who are frequently prevented from exercising these universal rights.

The Convention has four guiding principles which inform the formulation of all other children's rights: the principles of non-discrimination (Article 2); the best interest of the child (Article 3); the right to life, survival and development (Article 6); and the right to be heard (Article 12). Based on these guiding principles, the Convention contains 42 substantive provisions covering a wide range of rights and issues relating to children. They are understood as belonging to one of three groups, the 'three Ps' of Provision, Protection and Participation.

The Bosnian conflict was the first conflict with widespread use of GBV and forced impregnation alerting the world to rape as a weapon of war; it was also the first such conflict after the adoption of the CRC and, as such, was an appropriate litmus test for the way in which the CRC contributes to the protection of children in general, war-affected children more particularly and CBOW most specifically. Before this question is explored, it is important to consider two

Table 5.1 Children's rights in the Convention on the Rights of the Child

Provision rights (*relevant to the provision of children's basic needs*)	
Right to the highest attainable standard of health and health care	Art. 24
Right to a standard of living adequate to ensure the child's development	Art. 27
Right to education	Art. 28, 29
Right to play, rest and leisure	Art. 31
Protection rights (*relevant to the protection of children from all forms of harm and exploitation*)	
Right to protection from discrimination	Art. 2
Right to protection from all forms of harm, neglect and abuse	Art. 19
Right of children without family care to special protection and the right to alternative care including adoption	Art. 20, 21
Right of particularly vulnerable children, including refugee children and children with disabilities, to have special protection	Art. 22, 23
Right to protection from economic exploitation and sexual exploitation	Art. 32, 34
Right to protection from drugs	Art. 33
Right of victims of such abuse to treatment, counselling and support	Art. 39
Participation rights (*the rights of children to participate in decisions made about them and to contribute to society by expressing their views*)	
Child's right to express his/her views and have them given due weight in accordance with the child's age and understanding in all decisions made a-bout them and the child's right to be represented in legal proceedings	Art. 12
Child's right to express his/her opinion using a variety of means of expression according to the child's capacity	Art. 13
Child's right to freedom of religion and freedom of association	Art. 14, 15
Right to privacy	Art. 16
Right to access appropriate information conducive to the child's well-being	Art. 17

specific points of relevance for the question of implementing humanitarian law:

Firstly, beyond the CRC, several other legal instruments are of significance for the legal protection of children during and after conflicts. The Fourth Geneva Convention and its Additional Protocols provide detailed provisions for the treatment of war-affected children and lay down the obligations of the state actors to provide for basic needs of children, including the facilitation of family reunification, basic education, and protection of children from ill-treatment,[89] while the Genocide Convention protects children's identity and family rights.[90] As such, an examination of the CRC alone will result in only a partial picture; however, this partial picture will not be altered substantially by inclusion of all other relevant provisions, as the issues arising out of the inadequacy of the implementation of laws are similar in all cases.

Secondly, it is important to consider briefly how humanitarian law operates and, more specifically, how it is enforced. International humanitarian law is state-centric; it is based on laws adopted by states as actors and, as such, laws bind states rather than individuals as actors. However, atrocities during conflicts are often committed not by states or even on behalf of states;[91] moreover, the most common violations, while often committed as part of war tactics or strategy, are directed at individuals and these individuals have to take on perpetrators through a legal system that presupposes the existence of functioning states and governments within which to approach the legal processes. This is not a foregone conclusion during and immediately after conflicts. Even a cursory glance at this system of law enforcement and retribution through the courts reveals that the odds are stacked heavily against successful implementation and enforcement of international humanitarian laws, in particular in cases where the victims are children.[92] Furthermore, and of great significance in the case of GBV and war-affected children, if there is no support among the populace to live up to the standards or norms the state has agreed to uphold, the state's efforts to implement those norms against the people's will will be severely compromised. In the case of children's rights, their implementation depends to a large extent on the cultural legitimacy accorded to such rights in any given society, which varies enormously across the globe. It is these considerations which have to be borne in mind when investigating the rights of children born of rape during the Bosnian War, as in all other conflicts.

Right to life

The most fundamental human right is the right to life. This right is codified, among others, in Article 6 of the CRC, and beyond the 'inherent right to life' accorded to all children in this provision, the state has responsibility to 'ensure to the maximum extent possible the survival and development of the child' (Article 6(2)). Considering what has been elaborated on above about the occurrence of infanticide in Bosnia, it is evident that the most fundamental human right, the right to life, is compromised for CBOW. It is impossible to ascertain, on the basis of the patchy evidence across all conflicts, how widespread this phenomenon of killing unwanted children is. Yet, as the cases of *Lebensborn* and Bosnian children, as well as field studies from recent conflicts in sub-Saharan Africa suggest, while incidents of infanticide appear to be isolated cases, they present a genuine threat to the life of CBOW under certain circumstances.

However, while few would disagree that post-natal children are alive and as such are bearers of some human rights, it is immediately evident that new-borns depend on adults, most notably their parents and in particular their mothers to enforce these rights. Twenty-first-century Western scholars may be inclined to see a child's right to life post-natally as a universal and indisputable right, but historically and traditionally the right to life has been rather more strongly culturally determined. A recent study of infanticide and population growth in Japan since the mid-seventeenth century, for instance, has shown that Japanese parents regarded their new-borns as liminal beings, whose 'worth' and 'value' for the familial or ancestral order had to be identified in order to ascertain a child's 'right' to live.[93] This discourse lives on as the moral status of early human life remains contested. Recently, it has been argued that it may be morally permissible to kill a new-born even if it is healthy, on the basis that the moral status of a human life does not change by moving from the inside of the womb to the outside, and thus replacing the term infanticide with 'after-birth abortion'.[94] This is not the place to take a position about the morality or otherwise of abortion or infanticide, but it is important to make clear that both pre-natally and after birth, rights of the mother (or parents) can conflict with the rights of the born and unborn child. While these conflicting rights are widely debated in abortion controversies, less room is given to them in the case of neo-natal infants.[95] But even taking the view that an infant's right to life is indisputable, in the case of the killing of CBOW, such infanticides do not necessarily imply legal culpability. While the killing in these tragic cases is a violation of the child's right, the mothers are often driven to the act by the circumstances in which they conceived and had to raise their children, and indirectly by the failure of their environment – familial, local and national – to support them when coming to terms with the trauma of war rape and enforced pregnancy. Retroactive prosecutions for infanticide are unlikely and would be unjust in almost all cases, because in most, if not all, cases mothers kill for reasons that are rooted in their victimhood in war itself, mostly in the traumatisation as a result of war rape, exacerbated by the stigmatisation and marginalisation following rape, pregnancy and motherhood of a child born of war rape. In other words, while the act of infanticide is wrong, the question of responsibility – both legal and moral – is a complex one. Interestingly, in much of the literature the rights of the children who are victims of infanticide are not part of the narrative; as such, their right to life is implicitly denied through debates about the violation of their mother's right which indirectly led to the children's death. It has been suggested that one solution to the absence of discussion of the rights of children born of war under these circumstances would be to treat them and their mothers not only as victims of war but as war veterans;[96] however, the above-mentioned inconclusive evidence of the success of this practice in particular with regard to the position of the children born of rape suggests, at least for this specific case, that veteran status of the mothers has only limited impact on the well-being of both mothers and children. This tension between the rights of the mothers and children is a common thread woven through almost all aspects of the CBOW rights discourse.

Non-discrimination

The right to non-discrimination (Article 2) is one of the key rights[97] enshrined in the CRC, which rules that children should not be subjected to discrimination on the basis of their parents' or legal guardians' 'race, colour, sex, language, religion, political or other opinion, national, ethnic or social origin, property, disability, birth or other status'.[98] What is more, in the second half of the Article, states are tasked with taking affirmative action to ensure the child's protection from all such forms of discrimination.

Yet, as has been demonstrated for all conflicts under consideration including the Bosnian conflict, CBOW have experienced systematic as well as *ad hoc* discrimination exactly because of the identity of their parents, both their mothers and their fathers. Most societies remain firmly patriarchal and as a result patriarchal norms have enforced traditions that led to the child – in the perception of those in its immediate environment – taking on the characteristics or identity of the father. In other words, in post-conflict societies, the children are directly associated with the perpetrator father and thus are associated directly with the atrocities committed by 'the enemy'.[99] This is reinforced in conflicts where rapes had genocidal character from the outset, such as in Bosnia, where the proclaimed aim of the rape camps had been the creation of 'Chetnik Babies'.[100] The negative association of children born of rape with the father's violent acts is amplified by prejudices against the mothers. As described in detail in the cases of CBOW during the Second World War and the Vietnam War, rape victims often encounter partialities relating to their own morals, and raising a child born out of wedlock as a single mother further strengthens preconceived stereotypes of illegitimacy and loose moral standards.

The ensuing discrimination against the child operates at different levels: at its most fundamental level lies the above-described rejection of the children on the part of the mothers, due to the child's association with the perpetrators. An important aspect of the children's segregation and discrimination is the name-giving and name-calling. At societal level, this has been noted for almost all children fathered by enemy soldiers from the *Bui Doi* in Vietnam to the *tserkunge* (child of a German) in post-war Norway; from *krigsbarn* (war child) to *enfants maudits* (cursed children) and *enfants non-desirés* (unwanted children). Even more pronounced is the negative impact, if the names of the children are directly associated with the suffering of the mothers, such as *enfants de mauvais souvenir* (children of bad memories) or 'children of hate'. Finally, in some cases, individual children were given names directly associated with the plight of the mothers, such as in Uganda, where children fathered by LRA rebels frequently were given such names including *Odokorac* (things have gone bad), *Momakech* (I am unfortunate) or *Anenocan* (I have suffered), thus reinforcing the fact that the child is a living reminder of the mother's suffering.[101] Hence, even at this fundamental level of name-calling and name-giving, CBOW experience discrimination, not to mention subtle exclusion experienced by children fathered by enemy soldiers in all the post-conflict societies discussed earlier.

Right to nationality and birth registration: the question of identity

Discrimination does not only happen at a personal, familial, neighbourhood or regional level; it also occurs at national level, most notably in the form of assigning (or not assigning) children a nationality. In accordance with the CRC, children must be 'registered immediately after birth and shall have the right from birth to a name, the right to a nationality' (Art. 7). Birth registration is an essential prerequisite of a child's further development; it establishes the child's legal identity, documents parentage and serves as the basis for claiming further civil rights and services, including the ability to access psychosocial, financial and other support as well as – eventually – education. Many children born to war-rape victims are not registered at birth for a variety of reasons. Circumstances in conflict and post-conflict situations are not conducive to smooth registration generally, and as victims of GBV frequently are on the move, be it as refugees or more generally displaced persons, registration formalities are even more difficult to complete. Furthermore, the shame of having to reveal the identity of the father is an obstacle for some women. In the case of Bosnia, war-rape children were not always registered. Women were either too ashamed to reveal the identity of the father or they were unable to because they did not know the rapist.[102]

An additional significant issue arises from current rules and practices of conferring nationality, which have resulted in some CBOW remaining stateless. Different states operate different modi for determining the nationality of a new-born,[103] either depending on where the child was born (*ius soli*), the nationality of the child's parents (*ius sanguinis*) or a combination of both. For example, in the Balkans, Bosnia and Croatia employed a policy of conferring nationality according to *ius sanguinis*. A child's nationality depended on the nationality of the parents and was independent of the place of birth, which meant that children born to Bosnian women in Croatia did not have the right to Croatian citizenship. Thus, until the amendment of the regulation in 1996,[104] which allowed the conferral of citizenship of Bosnia and Herzegovina to children born abroad to a citizen of a former Republic of Yugoslavia, those children could not claim any nationality and remained stateless.

It is implicit in much of what has been said about CBOW during and after the Second World War and the Vietnam War that a key issue for many children fathered by foreign soldiers is the question of identity. Who am I? Who is my father? Where are my roots? Do I have family I am unaware of? Who are they? Where are they? It is this right of children, enshrined in the CRC, to know their biological parents, which causes the most significant tension between the legitimate interests and concerns of mothers and the frequently conflicting interests of the children.[105] A child's right to know her or his origins has been recognised in principle for some time,[106] but recently this has become a more pressing issue which has attracted attention of scholars and practitioners alike, because of the expansion of children whose biological and social parentage no longer coincides. As a result of a rise in national and international adoptions, and progress in biogenetics leading to a greater variety of means of conception, but also non-conventional family settings leading to larger numbers of children not being raised by their biological parents, the phenomenon has been given significantly more consideration than previously.[107]

The CRC was the first legal instrument not only to guarantee one's right to know one's origin, but also the *child's* right to such knowledge. This right to know one's origin is not a vague concept to be claimed at some point in the distant future, but a right that can – in principle – be claimed by a child. While the key provisions of the above-mentioned Article 7, safeguarding birth registration, nationality and care, repeat existing legislation,[108] the CRC goes further by stating the 'right to know and be cared for by one's parents', which not only refers to a child's social or legal parents, but also birth parents.[109] This provision of the right to parental care is linked to the child's identity, as is evident when considering the subsequent Article 8, which explicitly determines the states' responsibilities to 'respect the right of the child to preserve his or her identity, including nationality, name and family relations'. While the Article is innovative in granting identity rights and granting them specifically to children,[110] it does not define identity, but merely provides a non-exhaustive list of three elements: nationality, name and family. However, other elements are understood to be protected by this provision including the child's personal history, race, culture, religion and language.[111]

Enforcing the child's right to know his or her origins can – and for CBOW often does – conflict with others' rights, including the human rights of the biological mother, the mother's husband or the biological father. In the case of war-rape victims, the mother may have a fundamental interest in keeping her identity, the identity of the child's father or both secret; the mother's husband may have recognised the child legally as his own and therefore may have an interest in keeping the child's biological father secret, either for reasons of social acceptance, or in order to prevent any negative impact of such knowledge for the ties between himself and the child. Leaving aside the conflicting rights of the child relative to others, there may also be a genuine conflict of interest regarding the child's own interests, when a child is judged to be better protected by her or his identity remaining unknown. The question of which right should take precedence in case of such conflicts has attracted some scholarly discussion. Some have argued that the overriding principle has to be the best interest of the child (Article 3 CRC) which has become the underlying consideration of all child rights legislation; other argue that Article 7 with its more concise provisions should take precedence over the rather vague and ill-defined 'best interest' concept.[112] Others have concluded that it is essential to read both provisions in conjunction, arguing that Article 3 should be understood as a limiting provision, being employed only in cases where the right to know clearly counteracts the child's best interest in a concrete situation.[113] Although virtually all countries are bound by the CRC, the enforcement of the child's right to know varies significantly. This difference is largely explicable by different historical, social and cultural backgrounds leading to a different weighting of conflicting interests in the interpretation of international human rights laws.[114] This has been made possible by qualifiers in the legislation, such as in Article 7 of the CRC which states that the state has to enforce the child's 'right to know' 'as far as possible', thus leaving some room for discretion and interpretation of what is deemed possible. To name two examples at either end of the spectrum, French national law does not guarantee the child's right to know his or her origins, granting the mothers not only the right to give birth anonymously, but also the right to withhold consent to the release of identifying data in the future.[115] In contrast, in Switzerland the child's right to know her or his origin is seen as an absolute right.[116] Both extremes are now seen to contravene both the spirit and the letter of human rights legislation, and it has rightly been argued that the weighting of the different rights of children and their parents has to be a balancing act, and that national legislators have to engage in a discussion of the balancing criteria based on principles of legality, proportionality and the existence of rights and interests of all parties without *a priori* assumptions of the relative significance of conflicting human rights claims.[117] However, it is widely accepted now that an absolute prohibition of the child's right to know his or her biological parents is contrary to the CRC.[118] In the case of the children of war-rape victims in Bosnia, their right to know their identity was compromised severely by the governmental policy of encouraging secrecy to the point of destroying evidence that allowed children to trace their origins. Here, the child's right to know her or his biological father (or in the case of abandoned children their biological mothers, too) could be refused to the war-rape orphans, because it was regarded not be in the best interest of the child.[119]

Although circumstantial evidence informs us about the setting in which the Bosnian children were born, little is known about the children themselves and how they experienced childhood, upbringing and the question of identity. A first step towards approaching this sensitive topic was Jasmila Zbanic's film *Grbavica*.[120] Based on true events, it tells the story of a single mother, Esma, and her 12-year-old daughter, Sara, in the Grbavica district of Sarajevo, exploring far-reaching trauma sustained in the war in Bosnia which remain unhealed. Growing up in an environment where status among the children hinged on whether they were offspring of long-dead fathers who were Bosnian loyalists or the unspeakable alternative, being the product of their mother's rape by a despised Chetnik Serb, Sara believes that she is the daughter of a deceased war hero. She continually asks her mother about her father, about his characteristics and personality, his appearance and possible similarities with herself. Eventually her mother is forced to tell the truth about her being the 'product of rape'. How widespread the problems portrayed in *Grbavica* are is not known. The children of rape victims are currently in their early twenties, an age, as we know from other studies of CBOW, when those children typically have started thinking about their identity, and an age when other CBOW have started to search for their biological origin.

Grbavica was not the first film about a Bosnian child born of war. Two years earlier, a short documentary, *A Boy from a War Movie*, had depicted the story of then 10-year old Alen Muhić, the child of a Bosnian rape victim who had been abandoned by his mother and adopted by the caretaker family of the hospital in which he was born.[121] The documentary project, seen by director Semsudin Gegić as a humanitarian intervention of empowerment on behalf of a CBOW was highly controversial. Gegić was criticised for exposing Alen and thus potentially endangering him; there were concerns about his psychological health and questions of media ethics were raised vociferously – genuinely questioning the motives of the director.[122] Leaving aside the rights and wrongs of the film, it undoubtedly raised the profile of the issue of children born of wartime rape in Bosnia. Yet, research into the medium- and long-term effects of their biological origin on these Bosnian CBOW is only in its infancy, and results preliminary.[123] One limited study has thrown some light on the feelings of the children born of war rape. On the basis of life-course interviews with eleven Bosniak girls aged between 14 and 16 at the time, some key themes emerged in their self-perception as well as their assessment of their life circumstances.[124]

Firstly, the girls attested a continued sense of hostility well beyond the end of the war, because they – due to their 'Serbian blood' – were legitimate and socially acceptable victims of hate attack, serving as a valve for their peers to relieve frustrations over unrelated issues. Terms used by the CBOW were 'scapegoat', 'new war victim', 'being hated'. In other words, the adolescents felt victimised on the grounds of ethnicity, because reconciliation between the ethnic groups had not happened, and their victimhood presented itself in stigma, social exclusion and physical abuse. While they generally agreed that they could cope with this exclusion, as well as socio-economic disadvantage on the basis of their mothers' poverty, many described learning about their biological origins and the circumstances of their conception as traumatic, often expressed in terms that had a connotation of death ('a day from hell'; 'the day when my old "me" died').[125]

The second theme identified in the interviews pointed to a strong internalisation of guilt, with the children regarding themselves as destructive forces that bore the responsibility of the ill that had befallen their families: poverty, family breakup and in particular the complex relationships with their mothers. The children were aware of the suffering that had been endured by their mothers, and they regarded themselves as constant reminders of their violent and demeaning conception, as bringing continual pain and suffering by their mere presence, and in one case as being responsible for the mother's suicide.

This matches very closely the impression recounted recently in a collection of biographies of children 'with a difference' which, among others, gives room to children born of rape. Here, the author demonstrates the debilitating experience of a child 'feeling complicit in his/her mother's vulnerability through their very existence'.[126] As one of the Bosnian girls put it: 'my mother is all about pain and suffering, and my hugs bring her even more pain'.[127]

A third theme identified in the research was that of role reversals between mothers and daughters, with the daughters taking on responsibilities of their mothers, because the latter were ill or could not cope with the demands of everyday life.

One girl, whose socio-economic background differed from that of the other interviewees, had been brought up in a stable middle-class family. Her mother (a teacher) had married and the girl herself had been adopted by her stepfather. The narrative emerging from her life story was diametrically opposed to the other girls' self-perception. She saw herself in a reconciliatory role, and she expressed that her mixed blood and mixed heritage enabled her to connect the former enemies. Unlike the other girls, she had a positive self-image, but she also used positive language to describe her environment, talking about 'community', 'meaning of life', 'sense of purpose', and she had a clear desire to become a force for the good in her native Bosnia.[128] This raises interesting questions about self-stigmatisation, but even more so about both positive and negative potential of CBOW in post-conflict societies and how the positive potential of CBOW in such societies could be incorporated constructively in the development of programming and intervention. The case studies suggest that socio-economic circumstances, education or a combination of both not only affect the individual's self-image, but also have a significant bearing on how individuals perceive their role within a post-conflict society and the social reconstruction process.

While this study is not representative, not only in view of the small sample size, but also in view of the fact that is only includes Bosniaks and that only girls volunteered for the research, it gives a clear indication of how complex, unsettling and potentially destructive the experiences of children born of war rape are. It also demonstrates that despite official efforts to encourage family, social and community inclusion of victims of war rape and their children by civil and religious authorities, discrimination and stigmatisation were prominent features in the daily lives of the interviewees. Thus, although the existence of the fatwa itself is often cited by the Bosnian government as proof that the integration of children born of rape has succeeded, this evaluation is not borne out entirely by more detailed research and, in fact, has been questioned by other observers. Sabiha Husić, Islamic theologian and therapist, who has worked with some of the rape victims, has warned that in the absence of psychosocial support many children suffer from identity crises and remain stigmatised as children of the enemy.[129] The few examples of seemingly unproblematic integration into Bosnian society are outweighed by numerous examples of children who are rejected by their mothers and are ostracised and traumatised by their families' rejections.[130] What was a problem in the immediate aftermath of the conflict remains a serious challenge more than twenty years later, with the UN reporting a lack of comprehensive services for survivors, with 'non-governmental organisations ... offering mainly psychosocial support with limited geographical coverage', and plans for a referral system for comprehensive services still 'at an early stage'. What is more, the same UN report also remarks that 'the paucity of data on the number of children born as a result of rape requires urgent attention by service providers and researchers in order for the needs of these young people to be addressed.'[131]

Best interest of the child

As mentioned above, one key principle underlying all children's human rights legislation has been the concept of the 'best interest of the child'. In the CRC it is formulated most explicitly in Article 3(1), but it is written into numerous other provisions[132] such as guidance relating to the separation of a child from the family setting (Article 9), parental responsibility for the upbringing and the development of the child (Article 8) including in the adoption context (Articles 20 and 21) and in relation to children in the justice system (Articles 37 and 40). It is also important to emphasise that more than most child rights concepts the 'best interest principle' is a reflection of the development of the legal processes in the twentieth century as it has found its way into a whole array of human rights laws and guidelines from the Geneva Declaration of 1924 and the Declaration of the Rights of the Child of 1959[133] to the 1979 Convention on the Elimination of all Forms of Discrimination Against Women (Articles 5b and 16(1)(d)), the Declaration on Social and Legal Principles relating to the Welfare of Children[134] to the African Charter on the Rights and Welfare of the Child (Article IV).[135]

Notwithstanding the abundance of references to the best interest of the child, the starting point and cornerstone of any discussion of the notion remains the CRC. It is significant because despite the lack of precision in defining the best interest, the CRC makes clear the scope of the concept by determining that the principle applies beyond the narrow legal context 'in relation to *all* actions concerning children',[136] whether undertaken by public or private social welfare institutions, courts of law, administrative authorities or legislative bodies. Article 4 further elaborates that it is the duty of the state to undertake all appropriate legislative, administrative and other measures for the implementation of the rights recognised in the CRC. In Bosnia, the Muslim community had a clear view of what would be in the best interest of the child, and rules were implemented which sought to protect the children. However, what was perceived to be in the children's best interest was in conflict with the rights of the children to learn about their biological origins and thereby their identity. Article 5 lays down the state's obligation to respect the responsibility of parents, family or extended community to provide direction and guidance to the child. In Bosnia this was attempted in a most general way through the fatwa, though the lack of necessary support structures to secure a success of this guideline in part jeopardised the outcome. As we will see below, it is the tension between best interest of the child and his or her human rights on the one hand, and rights and interests of people in the child's immediate surroundings on the other, which provide the greatest challenges in implementing the provisions of the CRC. Some of these tensions arise from children's right to know their identity; another significant issue is children's right to be with their parents.

The right to be with one's parents

The CRC goes well beyond merely assigning a right to know about one's origins; a range of Articles gives guidance on the children's rights to be with (both) their biological parents. Article 7 emphasises that children have the right 'as far as possible' to be cared for by their parents and Article 9 states that children have the right to live with their parent(s), provided that this is in their best interest. This Article also rules that children whose parents do not live together have the right to stay in contact with both parents, unless this is not in their best interest. Furthermore, Article 18 determines the states' obligation to facilitate arrangements that allow both parents to participate in the upbringing of their children and the underlying concern of the best interest of the child is reiterated. Beyond this, Article 10 specifically guides on family reunification and lays down the states' responsibility to facilitate inter-country travel of different family members so that parents and children can stay in contact or get back together as a family. This issue is of particular relevance for those CBOW whose parents had a consensual relationship and want to (re-)establish family relations across national borders. But as is clear from survey data, anecdotal evidence and qualitative interviews, even where CBOW do not know about the nature of the relationship of their biological parents or where they know that the relationship had been exploitative, they are often keen to learn about their fathers and family roots. The CRC is clear about the states' obligation to facilitate arrangements that allow a child to be cared for by biological parents and tasks them with designing domestic laws and inter-state procedures that respect the interest of the child above all to be cared for by the parents, and as such the state 'bears a positive obligation to develop such forms of alternative care that allows for the development of children and respect of their rights'.[137]

Rights of children born of war: a retrospective

Although the CRC only came into force in 1989, it is fruitful to examine the situation of children born of earlier twentieth-century conflicts and post-conflict occupations with these provisions in mind. As a rule, armed forces, regular or irregular, have shown little interest in the offspring of their soldiers or civilian staff, with the exception of the cases where GBV took on a distinctly ethnically motivated, genocidal character. As explored in detail above, the military leadership in most countries involved in the Second World War tried to avoid the complications of dealing with the consequences of their soldiers' liaisons or intimate relationships of any kind, predominantly by moving soldiers on as soon as commanding officers became aware of such relationships, and even more so when there was a prospect (or reality) of children having been fathered. Neither the women's nor the children's interest played any part in the deliberations of any of the decisions taken by the military leaders under consideration. The key concern in most cases was the safeguarding of military preparedness and the units' fighting strength at a time when treatment of venereal disease (VD) was a non-trivial challenge and STIs were among the most important causes of military ineffectiveness.[138] Similarly, sexual conduct of troops in colonial wars or in the Korean and Vietnam Wars was scrutinised primarily from the point of view of potential impact on military effectiveness. As such, within the parameters set by the military, ensuring that the perceived sexual needs of the troops were catered for was common, provided necessary precautions to prevent the ever-present threat of STIs were taken. This was judged to be beneficial for morale, for the *esprit de corps* and by implication for the soldiers' motivation. In contrast, consideration for the well-being of women who provided the sexual services or intimate partnerships of a more or less exploitative nature, let alone concern for the children who were the result of such contacts was largely non-existent.

Where women and children became the focal point of governmental or military policy, the overriding policy objectives, again, were not the best interest of women or children, or indeed any reflexion on their rights. Frequently such policies were triggered by the often racially motivated ideologies and resulting social and political programming. The Nazi strategies aimed at the Aryanisation of Europe were one example, evident in the practices propagated through *Lebensborn*, but also in the policies vis-à-vis children fathered by *Wehrmacht* soldiers during the occupation of Eastern Europe. Without any consideration for the children themselves or their mothers, their fate was determined exclusively by whether or not the German soldiers' offspring was deemed 'racially desirable' or not. Although the principle of the best interest of a child had been formulated during the inter-war years, clearly it had no place in political or military decision making generally, and certainly not in wartime Nazi Germany. But the arguably extreme case of the Third Reich, which generally did not have any respect for human rights of any kind wherever they conflicted with ideological tenets, was not the only regime that disregarded the interests of CBOW. France's policies of claiming children fathered by French soldiers for the French nation were driven by considerations that left no room for the rights and interests of either the children or their mothers. Both during and after the Second World War, as well as in the aftermath of the Indochina

Wars, it was the value of the CBOW for the French nation that determined policies towards them.

The disregard for the needs of CBOW was equally prevalent in their birth countries. Many of the children who participated in the earlier-explored Norwegian survey elaborated on their childhood dreams of finding and making contact with their biological fathers. However, the Norwegian government did nothing to facilitate or support any form of family communication, re-unification or even contact with Germany during the first post-war decades. On the contrary, contact with the German fathers was actively discouraged by the Norwegian authorities, and mothers who sought such contacts were discriminated against.[139] Similarly, CBOW in France or Germany often felt disadvantaged.[140] Even today, at a time when the UK government is playing a leading role in initiatives focusing on the prevention of GBV in conflict, it is still not possible for children fathered by British soldiers during the Second World War and beyond to receive support in identifying their fathers and making contact with them.

An interesting case is that of children fathered by American GIs throughout the twentieth century. At first sight, both Operation Babylift of 1975 and the American Homecoming Act of 1986/87, which allowed the immigration of Vietnamese-American GI children conceived during the Vietnam War to the United States from 1987, appear to have been motivated primarily by humanitarian considerations for the welfare of the children. It is tempting to read a genuine concern for the rights and needs of the children and their mothers into American policies in a way that could almost be seen to be foreshadowing some of the later CRC provisions on the right of a child to be cared for by her or his parents or the right to nationality, education and others. However, as the analysis above demonstrated, the well-being of the children was only one of many triggers to the policy of taking responsibility for at least some GI children. First and foremost, the 'calculated kindness' was a politically opportune measure which happened to coincide with what many would have judged to be a policy in the interest of these children. It is telling, however, that American willingness to take care of children fathered by troops on active duty remained targeted in line with political objectives, with citizenship rights afforded only to a small number of selected children and their mothers in specific political circumstances.

As in Bosnia, children born of war and occupation during and after the Second World War also experienced tension between what was supposed to be in their best interest, namely not being told about their biological origin on the one hand, and the right to name, nationality and – by implication – an identity on the other hand. Here, the conflict was enhanced by the fact that often family, friends and neighbours knew about the child's background, but failed to disclose it.[141] As many such cases have shown, if the child's social environment – family, friends, neighbours, local communities – had knowledge about the child's biological origins, this was likely, eventually, to become known to the child him- or herself, and it was not unusual for a child born of war to be confronted with such facts by fellow pupils, friends or children in the neighbourhood. Evidence suggests that many of the children had long suspected that 'something' was odd, or had felt that something in their sense of belonging was missing, and only when learning in adulthood about their origin, did they understand what this 'something' had been.[142] Judging from research of CBOW of the Second World War, many of those deprived of contact with their biological fathers suffered psychologically, and the blanket policies of disallowing such contacts to develop (both on the part of the soldier fathers' military authorities and their birth countries' civil authorities) were not in the children's best interest.[143] Similarly, children born of the post-war occupations of Germany and Austria, the vast majority of whom were not given the opportunity to learn about their biological origins, later articulated unequivocally that they would have wanted to have had the choice of learning about their biological fathers, and that not being able to do so had significant negative psychological impact.[144]

International human rights law in general, and children's rights law in particular, are dependent on the will of the member states of the international community for their effective implementation. The CRC is one of the examples of international law having made the individual a legitimate subject matter of international law. However, the implementation still depends on the states' willingness and ability to interpret and enforce the law for the benefit of the individual.

If – even in the face of partial and sketchy data on CBOW[145] – it is accepted that the continued deprivation of human rights decades after the acceptance of the CRC persists, this raises the question why the Convention has not diminished the human rights compromises for CBOW, although it is the most universally accepted Convention with all but one country (the United States) having signed up to it. Carpenter, in her investigation of the use of current legislation, comes to the conclusion that 'prevailing international law was not constructed to deal with the rights or needs of children'.[146] Indeed, what she showed about the inadequacy of the existing legal and theoretical approaches for addressing children's rights in genocidal conflicts similarly holds true for the position of CBOW across time and space.

There is little doubt that many CBOW have suffered systematic and non-systematic discrimination at all times and that many of the rights now enshrined in the CRC have been compromised. The core question remains of whether and how human rights violations of this kind can be addressed adequately by existing legislation. The implementation of survival and development rights, rights of education, and citizen's rights all pre-suppose – as a bare minimum – a functioning state and government, ideally matched by a willingness to address human rights issues at a time when other pressing, potentially competing, issues of seemingly greater urgency will distract from prioritising human rights concerns. Under those circumstances, children's rights, just as other human and civil rights, may not be enforced or may not be enforceable.

Moreover, even presupposing the existence of a functioning structure allowing the implementation of rights in theory, there remains another fundamental challenge. While it is the state that has to safeguard the implementation of children's rights, in this case for the benefit of CBOW, it is often not the state who is the primary abuser of those rights, but, as a secondary actor, is held responsible for a failure to prevent appropriate behaviour of its citizens. If there is 'no support among the populace – the now primary abusers – for the standards or norms the state has agreed to uphold, the state's efforts to implement those norms against the people's will is fraught with difficulties and most likely doomed to failure'.[147] Specifically, the implementation of children's rights depends to a large extent on the cultural legitimacy accorded to such rights in any given society. This was true before the codification of these laws as much as is has been since. All principles of the CRC can come into conflict with the local and regional cultural practices, and some such practices 'command even more legitimacy than the universal standards for the protection of children'.[148] This tension between culture and rights is in evidence in all the cases described above. Whether based on national stereotypes, or ethnic prejudice, or a combination of these, in the cases of CBOW, where a combination of these factors come to play it appears that the rights accorded to children universally will not be implemented as long as the cultural barriers persist.

Looking specifically at the child's right to identity, despite the fragmentary nature of the evidence, there is little doubt that this has been a major factor affecting the development and mental health of CBOW in all the cases discussed. The legal body appears inadequate to protect the child's right to identity, especially if it conflicts with cultural notions of what is perceived to be in the best interest of the child.

Although assimilation of children's rights norms into mainstream democratic culture[149] has resulted in a broader recognition of a child's individual identity,[150] exclusion, stigmatisation and even victimisation of CBOW have been allowed to continue, and societies across the globe continue to withhold eligibility to rights from children in general and children affiliated to minorities, especially CBOW. As will be discussed further in the next chapter, concrete steps from the mid-1990s onwards beyond the normative, the CRC and associated legislation, have led to some significant and real progress in the implementation of children's rights in armed conflict more generally – but these have all but bypassed the specific challenges facing CBOW. The final case study, conflicts in sub-Saharan Africa, will allow zooming in on some of these core issues of the importance of local culture for the implementation of rights and cultural sensitivities visible in legal pluralism.

Notes

1 The project is led by Dara Cohen (Harvard) and Ragnhild Nordhas (PRIO). See www.sexualviolencedata.org/people/principal-investigators/. (accessed 13.3.2015).

2 Julie Mertus and Judy A. Benjamin, *War's Offensive on Women: The Humanitarian Challenge in Bosnia, Kosovo, and Afghanistan* (Bloomfield, CT: Kumarian Press, 2000), p. 20.
3 Joni Seager, *The State of Women in the World Atlas* (London: Penguin, 1997), pp. 56ff; Ximena Bunster-Burotto, 'Surviving beyond fear: Women and torture in Latin America', in June Nash and Helen Safe (eds), *Women and Change in Latin America* (South Hardley: Bergin & Garvey, 1986), pp. 297–325; Michele L. Leiby, 'Wartime sexual violence in Guatemala and Peru', *International Studies Quarterly*, 53 (2007), 445–68; Megan Bastick, Karin Grimm and Rahel Kunz, *Sexual Violence in Armed Conflict: Global Overview and Implications for the Security Sector* (Geneva: DCAF, 2007); *Asia Watch* and *Africa Watch* (Divisions of Human Rights Watch), e.g. 1993, 1994.
4 Inger Skjelsbæck, *The Political Psychology of War Rape* (Abingdon: Routledge, 2012), p. 59.
5 Roy Gutman, *A Witness to Genocide* (New York: Macmillan, 1993), pp. 64–76.
6 UN Security Council Resolution 820, 17 April 1993, Article 6, www.nato.int/ifor/un/u930417a.htm. (accessed 29.1.2014).
7 For a list of different estimates by a variety of organisations, as well as examples of estimations used and misused for political purposes, see Inger Skjelsbaeck, 'Victim and survivor: Narrated social identities of women who experienced rape during the war in Bosnia-Herzegovina', *Feminism and Psychology*, 16 (2006), 373–403, here 398, note 1.
8 Adapted from Silva Meznaric, 'Gender as an ethno-marker: Rape, war and identity in the Former Yugoslavia', in Valentine Moghadan (ed.), *Identity Politics and Women: Cultural Reassertion and Feminism in International Perspective* (Boulder, CO: Westview, 1994), pp. 76–97, here p. 92.
9 See, in particular, report by Helsinki Watch, *War Crimes in Bosnia-Herzegovina*, 2 vols (New York, 1993) and Center for Investigation and Documentation of the Association of Former Prison Camp Inmates of Bosnia-Herzegovina, *I Begged them To Kill Me: Crimes Against the Women of Bosnia Herzegovina* (Sarajevo: CID, 2002).
10 Helsinki Watch; See also United Nations Economic and Social Council, *Situation of Human Rights in the Territory of the Former Yugoslavia*. Report submitted by the Special Rapporteur of the Commission on Human Rights, 10 February 1993 E/CN.4/1993/50 and 21 February 1994 E/CN.4/1994/110, www.unhchr.ch/huridocda/huridoca.nsf/70ef163b25b2333fc1256991004de370/c0a6cfd5274508fd802567900036da9a?OpenDocument. (accessed 29.1.2014) and http://daccess-dds-ny.un.org/doc/UNDOC/GEN/G94/111/86/IMG/G9411186.pdf?OpenElement. (accessed 29.1.2014). See also E. Wood, 'Multiple perpetrator rape during war', in M.A.H. Horvath and J. Woodhams (eds), *Handbook of the Study of Multiple Perpetrator Rape: A Multidisciplinary Response to an International Problem* (New York: Routledge, 2013), pp. 132–59.
11 Final Report of the Commission of Experts Established Pursuant to Security Council Resolution 780 (1992), p. 60, www.icty.org/x/file/About/OTP/un_commission_of_experts_report1994_en.pdf. (accessed 29.1.2014).
12 Doris Buss, 'Knowing women: Translating patriarchy in international criminal law', *Social and Legal Studies*, 23 (2014), 73–92. See also Rana Jaleel, 'Weapons

of sex, weapons of war: Feminism, ethnic conflict and sexual violence in public international law during the 1990s', *Cultural Studies*, 27 (2013), 115–35.
13 Additional Protocol to the Geneva Conventions of 12 August 1949, and relating to the Protection of Victims of Non-International Armed Conflicts (Protocol II), 8 June 1977, Article 4.2 (e), www.icrc.org/applic/ihl/ihl.nsf/Article.xsp?action=openDocument&documentId=F9CBD575D47CA6C8C12563CD0051E783. (accessed 29.1.2014).
14 ICTY Trial Chamber Judgment Prosecutor v. Anto Furunžija (Case number IT-95-17/I-T). For a definition of sexual violence see World Health Organization, *World Report on Violence and Health* (Geneva: World Health Organization, 2002), p. 149. For interesting perspectives on the trials see Dubravka Zarkov and Marlies Glasius (eds), *Narratives of Justice in and out of the Courtroom: Former Yugoslavia and Beyond* (Heidelberg: Springer 2014).
15 Rome Statute of the International Criminal Court, A/CONF.183/9 of 17 July 1998, Article 7 (g), www.icc-cpi.int/nr/rdonlyres/ea9aeff7-5752-4f84-be94-0a655eb30e16/0/rome_statute_english.pdf. (accessed 20.1.2014).
16 For an insightful analysis see: Karen Engle, 'The grip of sexual violence: Reading UN Security Council Resolution on Human Security', in Gina Heathcote and Dianne Otto (eds), *Rethinking Peacekeeping, Gender Equality and Collective Security* (Basingstoke: Palgrave, 2014), pp. 23–47. Also S. Qureshi, 'Progressive development of women's human rights in international humanitarian law and within the UN System', *Journal of Political Studies*, 19 (2012), 111–24.
17 UN Security Council, Resolution 1325, 31 October 2014, Article 10, www.un.org/en/ga/search/view_doc.asp?symbol=S/RES/1325%282000%29. (accessed 24.1.2014).
18 UN Security Council, Resolution 1820, 19 June 2008, www.un.org/en/ga/search/view_doc.asp?symbol=S/RES/1820%282008%29. (accessed 24.1.2014).
19 UN Security Council, Resolution 1828, 30 September 2009, www.un.org/en/ga/search/view_doc.asp?symbol=S/RES/1888%282009%29. (accessed 22.1.2014).
20 UN Security Council, Resolution 1960, 16 December 2010, www.un.org/en/ga/search/view_doc.asp?symbol=S/RES/1960%282010%29. (accessed 22.1.2014).
21 R. Charli Carpenter, 'Surfacing children: Limitations of genocidal rape discourse', *Human Rights Quarterly*, 22 (2000), 428–77, here 429.
22 Mladen Lončar et al., 'Psychological consequences of rape on women in 1991–1995 war in Croatia and Bosnia and Herzegovina', *Croatian Medical Journal*, 47 (2006), 67–75.
23 Situation of Human Rights, 1992; A year later, his report states that of 119 verifiable rape-related pregnancies, all but 34 were terminated; another report stated that of the 38 rape-related pregnancies of refugee women, all early pregnancies and 2 advanced pregnancies were terminated.
24 Anthony Lathrop, 'Pregnancy resulting from rape', *Journal of Obstetric, Gynecological, & Neonatal Nursing*, 27 (1998), 25–31, here 25.
25 R. Charli Carpenter, *Forgetting Children Born of War: Setting the Human Rights Agenda in Bosnia and Beyond* (New York: Columbia University Press, 2010), p. 23.
26 Beverly Allen, *Rape Warfare: The Hidden Genocide in Bosnia-Herzegovina and Croatia*

(Minneapolis: University of Minnesota Press / Amnesty International, 1996), theme 4.
27 Susan Brownmiller, *Against Our Will: Men, Women and Rape* (New York: Simon and Schuster, 1975), p. 84.
28 Eric Reeves, 'Rape as a continuing weapon of war in Darfur: Reports, bibliography of studies, compendium of incidents', *Sudan, Research Analysis and Advocacy*, http://sudanreeves.org/2012/03/04/rape-as-a-continuing-weapon-of-war-in-darfur-reports-bibliography-of-studies-a-compendium-of-incidents/. (accessed 14.2.2014)
29 Carpenter, *Forgetting*, p. 11.
30 Anne Tierney Goldstein, *Recognizing Forced Impregnation as a War Crime Under International Law* (New York: Center for Reproductive Law and Policy, 1993).
31 Rhonda Copelon, 'Surfacing gender: Reconceptualizing crimes against women in time of war', in Alexandra Stiglmayer (ed.), *Mass Rape: The Way against Women in Bosnia-Herzegovina* (Lincoln: University of Nebraska Press, 1994), pp. 197–218, here p. 203.
32 Additional Protocol to the Geneva Conventions of 12 August 1949, and relating to the Protection of Victims of Non-International Armed Conflicts (Protocol II), 8 June 1977, Article 4.2 (e), www.icrc.org/applic/ihl/ihl.nsf/Article.xsp?actio n=openDocument&documentId=F9CBD575D47CA6C8C12563CD0051E783. (accessed 29.1.2014).
33 Kami L. Schwerdtfeger and Briana S. Nelson Goff, 'Intergenerational transmission of trauma: Exploring mother–infant prenatal attachment', *Journal of Traumatic Stress*, 20 (2007), 39–51.
34 E. Robertson et al. 'Antenatal risk factors for postpartum depression: A synthesis of recent literature', *General Hospital Psychiatry*, 26 (2004), 289–95.
35 For details about ethical issues relating to trauma research with pregnant mothers see K.L. Schwerdtfeger, 'Intergenerational Transmission of Trauma: Exploring Mother–Infant Prenatal Attachment' (Master's thesis, Kansas State University, Manhattan, KS, 2004).
36 S. Fraiberg, E. Adelson and V. Shapiro, 'Ghosts in the nursery: A psychoanalytic approach to the problems of impaired infant–mother relationships', *Journal of the American Academy of Child & Adolescent Psychiatry*, 14 (1975), 387–421.
37 D.S. Schechter et al., 'Psychobiological dysregulation in violence-exposed mothers: Salivary cortisol of mothers with very young children pre- and post-separation stress', *Bulletin of the Menninger Clinic*, 68 (2004), 319–36; Karlen Lyons-Ruth and Deborah Block, 'The disturbed caregiving system: Relations among childhood trauma, maternal caregiving, and infant affect and attachment', *Infant Mental Health Journal*, 17 (1996), 257–75; Mary Main and Erik Hesse, 'Parents' unresolved traumatic experiences are related to infant disorganized attachment status: Is frightened and/or frightening parental behavior the linking mechanism?', in M.T. Greenberg et al. (eds), *Attachment in the Preschool Years: Theory, Research, and Intervention* (Chicago: University of Chicago Press, 1990), pp. 161–82; Daniel S. Schechter et al., 'Mother–daughter relationships and child sexual abuse: A pilot study of 35 days', *Bulletin of the Menninger Clinic*, 66 (2002), 39–60.
38 Research so far has mainly explored cortisol traits in Holocaust survivors. See

e.g. R. Yehuda et al., 'Parental posttraumatic stress disorder as a vulnerability factor for low cortisol trait in offspring of holocaust survivors', *Archives of General Psychiatry*, 64 (2007), 1040–8.

39 Janell Ross, 'Epigenetics: The controversial science behind racial and ethnic health disparities', *National Journal*, 20.3.2014, www.nationaljournal.com/next-america/health/epigenetics-the-controversial-science-behind-racial-and-ethnic-health-disparities-20140320. (accessed 13.3.2015).

40 See for instance David Crews and Andrea C. Gore, 'Transgenerational epigenetics: Current controversies and debates' (2014), www.utexas.edu/research/crewslab/pdfs/Crews_Gore_Chapter_Final.pdf; also www.rationaloptimist.com/blog/epigenetic-inheritance-is-a-wild-goose-chase.aspx. (accessed 12.3.2015).

41 See Kenneth J. O'Brien, 'The uncounted casualties of war: Epigenetics and the intergenerational transference of PTSD symptoms among children and grandchildren of Vietnam veterans in Australia' (eprint, 2007), http://eprints.qut.edu.au/13794/1/13794.pdf. (accessed 14.3.2015). Laura Spinney, 'Born scared: How your parents' trauma marks your genes', *New Scientist*, 2 December 2010, 46–9.

42 J. Bowlby, *Attachment and Loss: Vol 1. Attachment* (New York: Basic Books, 1969).

43 See e.g. A.C. Huth-Bocks, A.A. Levendosky and G.A. Bogat, 'The effects of domestic violence during pregnancy on maternal and infant health', *Violence and Victims*, 17 (2002), 169–85; A.C. Huth-Bocks et al., 'The impact of maternal characteristics and contextual variables on infant–mother attachment', *Child Development*, 75 (2004), 480–96.

44 Schwerdtfeger and Goff, 'Intergenerational transmission of trauma', 47–8.

45 Elisa Van Ee and R.J. Kleber, 'Child in the shadowlands', *The Lancet*, 380 (2012), 642–3.

46 Ibid., 642.

47 Belma Bećirbašić and Dzenana Secic, 'Invisible casualties of war', *Institute for War and Peace Reporting*, 2005, http://iwpr.net/report-news/invisible-casualties-war. (accessed 25.4.2014).

48 Carpenter, *Forgetting*, p. 30, notes 113 and 114.

49 See Ludwig Janus, *The Enduring Effects of Prenatal Experience* (London: Jason Aronson Inc. Publishers 1977), reproduced online: www.mattes.de/buecher/praenatale_psychologie/978-3-930978-52-6.pdf. (accessed 8.5.2014).

50 R. Charli Carpenter, 'Children born of wartime rape in Bosnia Herzegovina: A preliminary study', UNICEF report 2005.

51 Slavenka S. Drakulić, 'Women hide behind a wall of silence', *The Nation*, 13 (1993), 268–72; Catherine Bonnet, 'Le Viol des femmes survivantes de genocide au Rwanda', in R. Verider, E. Decaux and J.-P. Chretien (eds), *Rwanda: Un genocide du XXieme siècle* (Paris: L'Harmatten, 1995), pp. 17–29; Rachid Benhadj, *Mirka* (Paris: DD Production, 2000).

52 Carpenter, *Forgetting*, p. 205, note 86.

53 Van Ee and Kleber, 'Child in the shadowlands', 642.

54 Carpenter, *Forgetting*, p. 25.

55 Ibid., p. 29.

56 Maja Šoštarić, 'War victims and gender-sensitive truth, justice, reparations and non-recurrence in Bosnia and Herzegovina', *Perspectives Series. Impunity Watch*

(2012), www.nuhanovicfoundation.org/user/file/bosnia_final.pdf. (accessed 13.3.2015).
57 Stacy Sullivan, 'Born under a bad sign', *Newsweek*, 23 September 1996.
58 Carol J. Williams, 'Bosnia's orphans of rape: Innocent legacy of hatred', *The Times*, 24.7.1993, posted on http://bosniagenocide.wordpress.com/2011/03/31/what-do-to-with-bosniak-children-born-to-rape-victims-in-bosnia/. (accessed 9.5.2014).
59 Brendon Simms, *Unfinest Hour: Britain and the Destruction of Bosnia* (London: Penguin, 2001), pp. ix–xiv.
60 For debates surrounding this issue see: Alan Travis, 'Britain will ease way for adoption', *The Guardian*, 4.1.1993; leading article, 'The babies of Bosnia', *The Guardian*, 8.1.1993; Linda Grant, 'Anyone here been raped and speak English?', *The Guardian*, 8.8.1993, p. 10; Stanley Penny, 'Reporting of mass rape in the Balkans: Plus ça change, plus c'est la même chose? From Bosnia to Kosovo, *Civil Wars* 2 (1999), 74–110, here 87–92.
61 See e.g. Carpenter, *Forgetting*, p. 89.
62 Anna Warburton, 'EC investigative mission into the treatment of Muslim women in the former Yugoslavia: Report to Foreign Ministers', www.womenaid.org/press/info/humanrights/warburtonfull.htm. (accessed 16.4.2014).
63 UNHCR, Report on Situation of Women and Children in Bosnia Herzegovina and Croatia (Geneva, 1993).
64 DCI, UNICEF and UNHCR, Report on the Joint Mission of UNICEF, UNHCR and DCI in Collaboration with The Hague Conference on Private International Law for the Protection of the Rights of Unaccompanied Children, www.hcch.net/upload/unaccompanied.pdf. (accessed 16.4.2014).
65 ICRC, *Protection of the Civilian Population in Periods of Armed Conflict* (Geneva, 1995).
66 DCI, UNICEF and UNHCR, Report on the Joint Mission.
67 Ibid.
68 Muharem Omerdić, 'The position of the Islamic community on the care for children of raped mothers', in Mirsad Tokaca (ed.), *The Plucked Buds* (Sarajevo: Commission for Gathering Facts on War Crimes in Bosnia and Herzegovina, 2002), pp. 428–32.
69 See Stephanie K. Wood, 'Woman scorned for the "least condemned" war crime: Precedent and problems with prosecuting rape as a serious war crime in the International Criminal Tribunal for Rwanda', *Columbia Journal of Gender and the Law*, 13 (2004), 274–327.
70 Cited on *Onislam*, www.onislam.net/english/ask-the-scholar/crimes-and-penalties/mischief/175151-aborting-a-fetus-resulting-from-rape.html. (accessed 5.5.2014).
71 Vardit Rispler-Chaim, 'The right not to be born: Abortion of the disadvantaged fetus in contemporary fatwas', in Jonathan E. Brockopp (ed.), *Islamic Ethics of Life: Abortion, War, and Euthanasia* (Columbia, SC: University of South Carolina Press 2003), pp. 87–8.
72 Omerdić, 'The position of the Islamic community', p. 430.
73 Lisa Scharlach, 'Rape as genocide: Bangladesh, the Former Yugoslavia, and Rwanda', *New Political Science*, 22 (2000), 89–102; here 95; Bina D'Costa,

Nationbuilding, Gender and War Crimes in South Asia (London: Routledge, 2010), pp. 121–2.
74 Skjelsbæk, The Political Psychology, p. 99.
75 Allen, Rape Warfare; Ruth Seifert, 'War and rape: A preliminary analysis', in Stiglmayer (ed.), Mass Rape, pp. 54–72; Catharina A. McKinnon, 'Rape, genocide, and women's human rights', in Stiglmayer (ed.), Mass Rape, pp. 183–96.
76 Carpenter, Forgetting, p. 94.
77 Ibid., p. 98.
78 Some of the aspects discussed in this section are explored preliminarily in Ingvill C. Mochman, and Sabine Lee, 'The human rights of children born of war: Case analyses of past and present conflicts', Historical Social Research/Historische Sozialforschung, 35 (2010), 268–98.
79 Michael D.A. Freeman, The Moral Status of Children: Essays on the Rights of the Child (The Hague: Martinus Nijhoff Publishers, 1997).
80 Michael Goodhart, 'Children born of war and human rights: Philosophical reflections', in Carpenter (ed.), Born of War, pp. 188–209; Michael Goodhart, 'Sins of the fathers: War rape, wrongful procreation, and children's human rights', Journal of Human Rights, 6 (2007), 307–24.
81 Notable exceptions are Watson's work on the rights and representations of children born of wartime rape (Alison M.S. Watson, 'Children born of wartime rape: Rights and representations', International Feminist Journal of Politics, 9 (2007), 20–34) and specifically with reference to Bosnia Joana Daniel-Wrabetz, 'Children born of war rape in Bosnia-Herzegovina and the Convention on the Rights of the Child', in Carpenter (ed.), Born of War, pp. 21–39. For further exploration of the subject see for instance, Carpenter, Forgetting; Mochmann and Lee, 'Human rights' and more recently though rather less convincingly, Donna Seto, No Place for a War Baby: The Global Politics of Children Born of Wartime Sexual Violence (Farnham: Ashgate, 2013), pp. 127–45.
82 Joseph L. Zornado, Inventing the Child: Culture, Ideology, and the Story of Childhood (New York: Garland, 2001).
83 Michael Freeman, The Rights and Wrongs of Children (London: F. Pinter, 1983), p. 7.
84 League of Nations, 'Geneva Declaration on the Rights of the Child', 26 September 1924, www.un-documents.net/gdrc1924.htm. (accessed 25.4.2014).
85 UN, 'The Universal Declaration of Human Rights', 1948, www.un.org/en/documents/udhr/. (accessed 25.4.2014).
86 UN, 'Declaration of the Rights of the Child', 1959, www.unicef.org/malaysia/1959-Declaration-of-the-Rights-of-the-Child.pdf (accessed 25.4.2014).
87 UN, 'Convention on the Rights of the Child', 1989, www.ohchr.org/EN/ProfessionalInterest/Pages/CRC.aspx. (accessed 25.4.2014).
88 These are: the International Convention on the Elimination of All Forms of Racial Discrimination (entered into force 1969); the International Covenant on Civil and Political Rights (1976); the International Covenant on Economic, Social and Cultural Rights (1976); the Convention on the Elimination of All Forms of Discrimination against Women (1981); and the Convention against Torture and other Cruel, Inhuman or Degrading Treatment or Punishment (1987).
89 Denise Plattner, 'Protection of children in international humanitarian law',

International Committee of the Red Cross-ICRC, 1984, www.icrc.org/eng/resources/documents/article/other/57jmat.htm. (accessed 1.5.2014).

90 United Nations, 'Convention on the Prevention and Punishment of the Crime of Genocide', Article 2 (e), www.hrweb.org/legal/genocide.html. (accessed 30.5.2014).
91 Kenneth W. Abbott, 'International relations theory, international law, and the regime governing atrocities in internal conflicts', *American Journal of International Law*, 93 (1999), 361–79.
92 International Bureau for Children's Rights (ed.), *Children and Armed Conflict: A Guide to International Humanitarian and Human Rights Law* (Quebec: IBCR, 2010).
93 Fabian Drixler, *Mabiki: Infanticide and Population Growth in Eastern Japan, 1660–1950* (Berkeley: University of California Press, 2013), particularly pp. 47–60.
94 Alberto Guibilini and Francesca Minerva, 'After-birth abortion: Why should the baby live?' *Journal of Medical Ethics* (2012), http://jme.bmj.com/content/early/2012/03/01/medethics-2011-100411.full. (accessed 23.3.2015).
95 Catherine Damme, 'Infanticide: The worth of an infant under the law', *Medical History*, 22 (1978), 1–24; Michelle Oberman, 'A brief history of infanticide and the law', in Margaret G. Spinelli (ed.), *Infanticide: Psychosocial and Legal Perspectives on Mothers Who Kill* (Arlington: American Psychiatric Press Inc., 2002), pp. 3–18.
96 Susan Harris Rimmer, '"Orphans" or veterans? Justice for children born of war in East Timor', *Texas International Law Journal*, 42 (2007), 323–44, here 343.
97 Samantha Besson, 'The principle of non-discrimination in the Convention on the Rights of the Child', *International Journal of Children's Rights*, 13 (2005), 433–61.
98 CRC, Article 2 (1).
99 S. Fischer, 'Occupation of the womb: Forced impregnation as genocide', *Duke Law Journal*, 46 (1996), 91–134.
100 Todd A. Salzmann, 'Rape camps as a means of ethnic cleansing: Religious, cultural and ethical responses to rape victims in the Former Yugoslavia', *Human Rights Quarterly*, 20 (1998), 348–78.
101 Eunice Apio, 'Uganda's forgotten children of war', in Carpenter (ed.), *Born of War*, pp. 94–109, here p. 101.
102 Daniel-Wrabetz, 'Children born of war rape', p. 32.
103 Lawrence LeBlanc, *The Convention on the Rights of the Child: UN Lawmaking on Human Rights* (Lincoln: University of Nebraska Press, 1995).
104 The High Representative, *Introduction to National Citizenship Laws*, 1997, http://eudo-citizenship.eu/databases/national-citizenship-laws/?search=1&year=&country=Bosnia%20and%20Herzegovina&name=&page=2. (accessed 1.5.2014).
105 Samantha Besson, 'Enforcing the child's right to know her origins: Contrasting approaches under the Convention on the Rights of the Child and the European Convention on Human Rights', *International Journal of Law, Policy and the Family*, 21:2 (2007), 137–59.
106 See e.g. J. Fortin, *Children's Rights and Developing Law* (London: Butterworth, 2003); Samantha Besson, 'Das Grundrecht auf Kenntnis der eigenen Abstammung', *Zeitschrift für Schweizerisches Recht*, 1 (2005), 39–71.
107 See, for instance, Dorett Funcke's work about the psycho-historical dimension of identity search in semen donor children. D. Funcke, 'Der unsichtbare Dritte: Ein

Beitrag zur psychohistorischen Dimension der Identitätsfindung am Beispiel der Spendersamenkinder', *Zeitschrift Psychotherapie & Sozialwissenschaft*, 11 (2009), 61–98.

108 e.g. International Convention on Civil and Political Rights of 1966, Article 24; European Convention on Human Rights of 1950, Article 8. See D. Hodgson, 'The international legal protection to the child's right to a legal identity and statelessness', *International Journal of Law Policy and the Family*, 7 (1993), 255–70, here, 256.

109 R. Hodgkin. and P. Newell, *The Implementation Handbook for the Convention on the Rights of the Child* (New York: UNICEF, 2002), pp. 116–17.

110 Besson, 'The child's right to know', 143.

111 Hodgkin and Newell, *Implementation Handbook*, p. 125.

112 For conflicting views see Katherine O'Donovan, 'A right to know one's parentage?', *International Journal of Law, Policy and the Family*, 2 (1988), 27–45, here 37; Ya'ir Ronen, 'Redefining the child's right to identity', *International Journal of Law, Policy and the Family*, 18:2 (2004), 147–77.

113 Hogkin and Newell, *Implementation Handbook*, chapter 7.

114 O'Donovan, 'Right to know', 2002.

115 Besson, 'The child's right to know', 139.

116 Besson, 'Principle of non-discrimination'.

117 Besson, 'Enforcing the child's right', 156–7.

118 See ECtHR, *Odievre v. France*, 15 January 2003, Judgments and Decisions 2003-111, paras. 44, 47. See also joint dissenting opinion by Judges Mr Wildhaber, Sir Nicolas Bratza, Mr Bonello, Mr Loucaides, Mr Cabral Barreto, Mrs Tulkens and Mr Pellonpää. http://hudoc.echr.coe.int/sites/eng/pages/search.aspx?i=001-60935#{%22languageisocode%22:[%22ENG%22],%22appno%22:[%2242326/98%22],%22documentcollectionid2%22:[%22GRANDCHAMBER%22],%22itemid%22:[%22001-60935%22]}. (accessed 27.2.2015).

119 Daniel-Wrabetz, 'Children born of war rape', p. 33.

120 *Grbavica*, 2006, www.imdb.com/title/tt0464029/. (accessed 12.11.2014).

121 Boban Karovic, 'One Bosnian man's search for his father, the rapist', *Newsweek*, 16.3.2015, www.newsweek.com/2015/03/20/one-bosnian-mans-search-his-father-rapist-313985.html. (accessed 22.10.2015).

122 www.theguardian.com/world/2015/jul/12/alen-muhic-bosnia-war-baby. (accessed 21.10.2015).

123 For an initial study on the long-term impact of Bosnian war rape on the victims see Amra Delić, 'Kvalitet Života i Dugoročne Psihičke Posljedice u Žena sa Iskustvom Ratnog Silovanja' (Master's thesis, Tuzla University, 2015) with an English summary of the core results in Amra Delic and E. Avdibegovic, 'War-rape context, posttraumatic stress disorder and silence related to war rape in Bosnia and Herzegovina: Experiences and reflections 1992–2015', in H. Glaesmer and S. Lee (eds), *Interdisciplinary Perspectives on Children Born of War: From World War II to Current Conflict Settings* (2015), http://medpsy.uniklinikum-leipzig.de/medpsych.site,postext,rueckblick,a_id,1412.html. (accessed 13.11.2015).

124 K. Erjavec and Z. Volčić, 'Living with the sins of their fathers: An analysis of self-representation of adolescents born of war rape', *Journal of Adolescent Sudies*, 25 (2010), 359–86.

125 Ibid., 368.
126 Andrew Solomon, *Far From the Tree: Parents, Children and the Search for Identity* (London: Random House, 2013), p. 477.
127 Ibid., 372–3.
128 Ibid., 377–80.
129 Sabiha Husić, 'The legacy of wartime rape in Bosnia', *Infosud: Human Rights Tribune*, 25.2.2008, www.infosud.org/The-legacy-of-wartime-rape-in,2781. (accessed 5.6.2014).
130 Bećirbašić, and Secic, 'Invisible casualties of war'; Eljavec and Volčič, 'Living with the sins'.
131 United Nations, Secretary General, *Conflict-Related Violence*. Report of the Secretary General, 13.3.2014, S/2014/181 http://reliefweb.int/report/world/conflict-related-sexual-violence-report-secretary-general-s2014181. (accessed 9.6.2014).
132 Philipp Alston, 'The best interest principle: Towards a reconciliation of culture and human rights', *International Journal of Law and the Family*, 8 (1994), 1–25.
133 United Nations, Convention on the Elimination of All Forms of Discrimination against Women, Resolution adopted by the General Assembly 34/180 (1979), www.un-documents.net/a34r180.htm. (accessed 29.5.2014).
134 United Nations, Declaration on Social and Legal Principles relating to the Protection and Welfare of Children, with Special Reference to Foster Placement and Adoption Nationally and Internationally (1986), www.un.org/documents/ga/res/41/a41r085.htm. (accessed 29.5.2014).
135 'African Charter on the Rights and Welfare of the Child', OAU Doc. CAB/LEG/24.9/49 (1990), www1.umn.edu/humanrts/africa/afchild.htm. (accessed 29.5.2014).
136 Sharon Detrick, *A Commentary on the United Nations Convention on the Rights of the Child* (The Hague: Martinus Nijhoff Publishers, 1999), pp. 90–3. Emphasis added.
137 Ineta Ziemele, *Commentary on the United Nations Convention on the Rights of the Child, Article 7: The Right to Birth Registration, Name and Nationality, and the Right to Know and Be Cared for by Parents* (The Hague: Martinus Nijhoff Publishers, 2007), p. 27.
138 Thomas H. Sternberg et al., 'Communicable diseases', in US Army Medical Department (ed.), *History of the Office of Medical History. Preventive Medicine in WWII, Volume V*, http://history.amedd.army.mil/booksdocs/wwii/communicablediseasesV5/chapter10.htm. (accessed 6.6.2014). See also Mark Harrison, 'Sex and citizen soldier: Health, morals and discipline in the British Army during the Second World War', *Clio Medica/The Wellcome Series in the History of Medicine*, 55 (1999), 225–49.
139 I.C. Mochmann and Stein Ugelvik Larsen, 'Kriegskinder in Europa', *Aus Politik und Zeitgeschichte*, 18–19 (2005), 34–8.
140 Jean-Paul Picaper and Ludwig Norz, *Enfants maudits* (Paris: Edition des Syrtes, 2004); Fabrice Virgili, *Naître ennemi* (Paris: Payot, 2009).
141 See Ute Baur-Timmerbrink, *Wir Besatzungskinder: Söhne und Töchter alliierter Soldaten erzählen* (Berlin: Chr.-Links Verlag, 2015), pp. 16–17, 20.
142 Pamela Winfield, *Bye Bye Baby: The Story of the Children the GIs Left Behind*

(London: Bloomsbury, 1992); Ebba D. Drolshagen, *Wehrmachtskinder: Auf der Suche nach dem nie gekannten Vater* (Munich: Droemer, 2005).

143 M. Kaiser et al. 'Depression, somatization and posttraumatic stress in children born of occupation after World War II in comparison with a general population sample', *The Journal of Nervous and Mental Disease*, 203:10 (2015), 1–7.

144 Heide Glaesmer et al., 'Die Kinder des Zweiten Weltkrieges in Deutschland: Ein Rahmenmodell für die psychosoziale Forschung', *Trauma & Gewalt*, 4 (2012), 319–28; Stefan Strauß, 'Wo bist du? Besatzungskinder: Die Suche nach dem Vater', *Berliner Zeitung*, 27.10.2013, www.berliner-zeitung.de/berlin/besatzungskinder--die-suche-nach-dem-vater-wo-bist-du--3640012. (accessed 28.2.2017).

145 UN Secretary General, *Conflict-Related Sexual Violence*, para. 8.

146 Carpenter, 'Surfacing children', 477.

147 Sonia Harris-Short, 'International human rights law: Imperialist, inept, and ineffective? Cultural relativism and the UN Convention on the Rights of the Child', *Human Rights Quarterly*, 25 (2003), 130–81, here 179–80.

148 Thoko Kaime, 'The Convention on the Rights of the Child and the culture of legitimacy of children's rights in Africa: Some reflections', *African Human Rights Journal*, 5 (2005), 221–38, here 228.

149 Alston, 'The best interest principle'.

150 Y. Ronen, 'Redefining the child's right to identity', *International Journal of Law, Policy and the Family* (2004), 147–77, here 151–2.

At the time of going to press, the author is aware of some controversy surrounding the article mentioned on p. 184, note 124. No specific conclusion has been reached, and the author would advise the reader to seek further information before drawing upon this source.

6

African conflicts

Around the same time as the Balkan Wars shook Europe, a wave of genocidal conflicts rippled through the African continent. They displayed patterns previously not characteristic of warfare in general and tribal warfare in particular. While violence, civil unrest, insurgencies and civil wars had been a recurring feature in many countries of the African continent, since the late 1980s, a number of large-scale and long-running conflicts of immense brutality, increasingly involving the civilian population, both women (as most numerous victims of gender-based violence (GBV)) and children (e.g. as child soldiers) have been seen. Many of these wars are ongoing, with conflicts raging, among others, in the Central African Republic, the Democratic Republic of Congo (DRC), Sudan and South Sudan, Somalia, Nigeria, Mali or Jemen to name just some of the most persistent pressure points on the continent.[1]

Several features distinguish the wars of the last three decades from earlier ones. Many had distinctly genocidal character. Alarmingly, in many conflicts, both regular and even more so irregular forces resorted to the recruitment of child soldiers, and the practice – often forceful and through abduction – became widespread. All conflicts were accompanied by extensive and in some cases systematic GBV, and as a corollary most resulted in significant numbers of children born of war. These included children born as a result of rape of local women by members of armed forces or militia men during and after hostilities, many as a result of sexual slavery and 'forced marriage' of abducted female child soldiers, integrated into rebel forces.[2]

This chapter will focus on two conflicts in sub-Saharan Africa: the Rwandan genocide of 1994 and the Lord's Resistance Army (LRA) conflict in Northern Uganda between 1987 and 2006. Investigating these will help understand some of the challenges faced by African societies during and after conflicts and in particular the difficulties experienced by CBOW in the processes of post-conflict reconstruction. What will become clear is that although the conflicts under consideration have very distinct characteristics, and although both also differed profoundly from the armed conflicts and occupations discussed

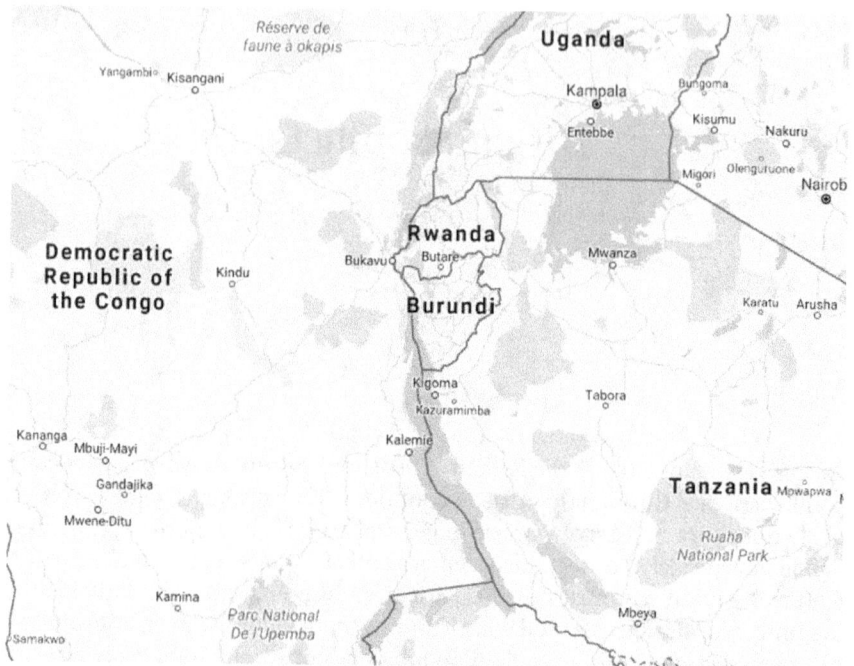

Figure 6.1 Map of Rwanda and neighbouring countries

in earlier chapters, the situation of the CBOW shows similarities, in particular with regard to the politics and policies of identity and their impact on the life courses and experiences of the children.

The Rwandan genocide

The Rwandan genocide of 1994 was one of the most brutal acts of premeditated and state-sponsored murder ever committed. The country, the landlocked 'land of thousands hills' bordered by Uganda in the north, Tanzania in the East, Burundi in the South and the DRC in the West covers an area of around 26,338 square kilometres, which makes it one of the smallest in Africa.

In 1994, Rwanda's population of seven million was composed of a Hutu majority (85%), and the Tutsi (14%) and Twa (1%) minorities.[3] Without going into detail about the pre-colonial, colonial and post-colonial developments, some core facts about Rwandan society prior to 1994 need to be presented in order to place the developments of the genocide into context. Traditionally, Tutsi, who entered Rwanda from southern Ethiopia between the eleventh and fifteenth centuries, had been pastoral people. They quickly established themselves as an important force in the country, dominating the Hutu majority (traditionally horticulturalists) militarily, economically and socially.[4] With regard to physical features, the three population groups differed markedly, with Tutsis generally taller, slimmer and slightly lighter skinned; Hutus with a more stocky build; and Twa, a tribe of pygmies notably shorter still. Yet, the physical distinctions, particularly between Hutu and Tutsi, that may have been very pronounced centuries ago, have been blurred by interactions between people divided by a somewhat permeable demarcation between two essentially Bantu people. Under German and Belgian colonial rule, pre-existing divisions between the Hutu majority and the Tutsi and Twa minorities were reinforced, with European powers generally favouring the Tutsis by way of positioning them in important government and administrative positions, which in the words of one commentator resulted into 'crushing Hutu feelings until they coalesced into an aggressively resentful inferiority complex'.[5] The Belgians, in the 1930s, legally mandated ethnic affiliation by enforcing an identity card system that indicated ethnicity. Yet, ironically, the colonial powers mixed questions of ethnic background with that of economic wealth by using ownership of cattle as the key criterion for determining which group an individual belonged to. In other words, it was not the biological distinctions that determined the formulation of formal criteria of ethnic identities, but rather the opposite: economic criteria were superimposed on biological distinctions which had become rather ambiguous over time.

While the colonists and other European powers in post-colonial times, over the decades, changed their policies with view to which population groups they would favour, the mutual distrust between population groups, and the tendency to think along ethnic lines in terms of accounting for economic well- or ill-being, remained with all ethnic groups in Rwanda. In the years immediately preceding the genocide, Hutu extremists within Rwanda's political elite had blamed the Tutsi minority population for the country's increasing social, economic and political challenges; conversely Hutus accused Tutsi civilians of supporting a Tutsi-dominated rebel group, the Rwandan Patriotic Front. Within this climate of radicalised political propaganda, mutual mistrust and fear, on 6 April 1994 a plane carrying President Habyarimana, a Hutu, was shot down. This provided the pretext for extremist Hutus to embark on a campaign of terror and murder aimed at the destruction of the entire Tutsi civilian population alongside more moderate forces among the Hutus who might have endangered this drastic project. The civil war and genocide only ended when the Tutsi-dominated rebel group, the Rwandan Patriotic Front, defeated the Hutu perpetrator regime and President Paul Kagame took control.

The 100 days: genocidal murder and rape

In the infamous 100 days between 6 April and 16 July 1994, hundreds of thousands of Tutsis and some moderate Hutus were killed. It is not possible to establish exact figures of the losses; estimates refer to 800,000 deaths,[6] more recently a report has cited a figure of close to two million.[7] Even according to the most conservative estimates, around 70% of the Tutsi minority population were exterminated during the Hutu-orchestrated campaign, with the majority of those killed at the time being male. The conflict was an ethnic conflict, but it was also a gendered conflict in which 250,000–500,000 women were raped[8] and an estimated 10,000 children conceived and brought to term as a result of these rapes.[9]

The large number of rapes was not coincidental but rather the result of an ethnic conflict, some of which had been framed in gendered terms. Much of the pre-genocide propaganda was directed specifically at Tutsi women in that the media portrayal of the women created the image of a highly promiscuous group who acted as proxies of their male relatives – fathers, brothers and sons. According to prevailing propaganda, the women were agents of the ethnically motivated injustices supposedly committed by the Tutsis. They were caricatured as 'devious seductresses who would use their beauty to undermine the Hutu'.[10] Among the so-called Hutu 'Ten Commandments' published by the editor of *Kangura*, a bimonthly publication which became well known for its 'hysterical hatred of Tutsi and any Hutu who expressed a desire for change, freedom and democratic openness',[11] were four 'commandments' which dealt specifically with women.

> 1. Every Hutu should know that a Tutsi woman, wherever she is, works for the interest of her Tutsi ethnic group. As a result, we shall consider a traitor any Hutu who: marries a Tutsi woman; befriends a Tutsi woman; employs a Tutsi woman as a secretary or a concubine.
> 2. Every Hutu should know that our Hutu daughters are more suitable and conscientious in their role as woman, wife and mother of the family. Are they not beautiful, good secretaries and more honest?
> 3. Hutu women, be vigilant and try to bring your husbands, brothers and sons back to reason.
> 7. The Rwandese Armed Forces should be exclusively Hutu. The experience of the October [1990] war has taught us a lesson. No member of the military shall marry a Tutsi.[12]

These ideas were reinforced by relentless propaganda efforts on the part of the extremist media. In the Media Trial of the International Criminal Tribunal for Rwanda (ICTR) this led the Chamber to note that Tutsi women, in particular, were targeted for persecution. In the words of the trial judge:

> The portrayal of the Tutsi woman as a femme fatale, and the message that Tutsi women were seductive agents of the enemy was conveyed repeatedly by RTLM[13] and *Kangura*. *The Ten Commandments*, broadcast on RTLM and published in *Kangura*, vilified and endangered Tutsi women. By defining the Tutsi woman as an enemy in this way, RTLM and *Kangura* articulated a framework that made the

sexual attack of Tutsi women a foreseeable consequence of the role attributed to them.[14]

This above-described portrayal may indeed explain the level of sexual violence, which formed a critical part of the Rwandan genocide, as well as the ferocious brutalities which were directed at the women. As many as 90% of Tutsi women are estimated to have been violated in some way during the genocide,[15] mostly systematically by the Hutu militias, the *Interahamwe*. One example is particularly striking – Butuare province, where 30,000 women are thought to be rape survivors. This province has become a focal point of international attention as the area in which Pauline Nyiramasuhuku, the first woman to be convicted of genocide by the ICTR and the first woman ever to be convicted of genocidal rape, committed the majority of her war crimes. Yet, the number of rape victims is much higher than that of rape survivors, because rape was often the precursor of murder – with Nyiramasuhuko's orders reportedly having been: 'Before you kill the women, rape them'.[16] The rapes themselves, often committed in front of whole communities to add to the degradation and humiliation, were carried out with intense brutality. Often, women were penetrated with gun barrels, spears, stamens of banana trees, machetes,[17] and many suffered mutilation. The gendered and ethic dimensions of the atrocities are visible in this maiming, as symbols of Tutsi ethnicity such as long fingers and noses were targeted alongside symbols and vehicles of female sexuality, with vaginas and breasts mutilated with machetes, boiling water and acid.[18]

International responses

It was the wide-spread and systematic nature of the acts committed, as well as the callousness and ruthlessness of the offences which resulted in a drastic re-evaluation of GBV in conflict – in line with similar rethinking in connection with the events in the Balkan Wars. As in former Yugoslavia, it was an International Criminal Tribunal, the ICTR which played the crucial role, not only in the prosecution of the crimes but also – through its case law – in the redefinition of criminal acts. The ICTR handed down the first conviction for the use of rape as a weapon of war during a civil conflict, and it was the first time that mass rape during wartime was found to be an act of genocide since the intent of the mass violence against women was to destroy, in whole or in part, a particular ethnic group.

It might appear marginal to the issue of CBOW to consider the impact of the Rwandan genocide and the post-genocide tribunals on the development of international law, but as will become clear, these legal developments were based on a clear conviction that post-conflict reconstruction and transitional justice had to address the underlying (gendered) circumstances. Those circumstances had not only allowed the genocidal nature of the conflicts to develop, but would also – if unaddressed – be likely to perpetuate the ethnic division. These divisions, in turn, would trap the children born of GBV in Rwanda and similar genocidal conflicts who lived at the intersection of former enemies and who would therefore be in danger of remaining a focal point of future aggression.

Thus, spurred on by the atrocities directed at civilian women, as with the International Criminal Tribunal for the former Yugoslavia, the ICTR also attempted to reconceptualise sexual and gender-based violence as a weapon of war and therefore as a threat to international peace and security in international law. The two tribunals, by their very nature, were in a position to contemplate larger political and military contexts, and as such were better placed than national legislators to reconsider the references to conflict-related sexual violence (CRSV) as previously addressed in the Hague Regulations and the Geneva Conventions and Additional Protocols. In these earlier provisions,[19] the concept of sexual crimes was limited to the prohibition of rape, with no express definition of what constituted rape.[20] Moreover, at the time of the Hague Regulations and Geneva Convention, the kinds of atrocities witnessed in Yugoslavia and Rwanda would have been beyond the imagination of the legislators. By the 1990s, as one commentator put it, 'the opportunistic rape and pillage of previous centuries ha[d] been replaced in modern conflict by rape used as an orchestrated combat tool'[21] which was far more complex than the male-defined understanding of warfare and its strategies and tactics could account for. Similar to the use of conventional weapons of war, in Yugoslavia and Rwanda, rape was used as 'part of a systematic political campaign which has strategic military purposes'.[22] Rape – as described in the Bosnian case above – in Rwanda too, turned women's bodies into battlegrounds over which opposing forces struggled, with men often being forced to watch the assaults, turning them into humiliation for both women and men.[23] This impacted strongly on the experiences of CBOW, both with regard to transgenerational trauma transmission and societal attitudes vis-à-vis children linked to the Hutu enemy.[24]

Another dimension was added to the use of rape as a weapon of war, which persisted long after the occurrence of the actual physical assaults. The Rwandan conflict was the first in which the spread of HIV/AIDS played a significant role in the post-conflict lives of the victims.[25] As detailed in a UNIFEM report, many of the victims were infected with HIV by perpetrators during the genocide, causing an ongoing crisis for Rwandans.[26] According to Rwanda's first post-conflict President, Paul Kagame, it became known in post-genocide Rwanda that 'the government [had been] bringing AIDS patients out of the hospitals specifically to form battalions of rapists'.[27] This implies the murderous intentions of the rape campaign beyond the humiliation of the victims, because in the mid-1990s HIV/AIDS infection was a long-term death sentence. A high transmission rate is indeed supported by evidence. One study, based on interviews with 30 HIV-positive rape survivors, not only refers to victim statements which indicate deliberation in the rapists' actions with regard to HIV transmission, but also points to several key factors suggesting strongly the intentional, if not systematic nature of the rape campaign with the aim of infecting the women.[28] The most persuasive piece of evidence is the abnormally high incidence of HIV/AIDS infection among women raped during the genocide (66.7%–80% compared with the national average of 13% at the time). Furthermore, the timeline of first diagnoses is highly suggestive of a purposeful infection strategy: the first cases of HIV/AIDS among rape victims became known in 1998, which corresponds to the incubation period of between three and ten years. Beyond that, the multitude of rape-related health complications which had not been experienced by the women prior to the genocide is similarly indicative of ill health caused by the rapes. An additional factor to be taken into account is the fact that while children born to the raped women prior to 1994 had been healthy, many of the rape victims had been confirmed to have been ill or have died prior to giving testimony to the ICTR. These facts, together with the knowledge that the vast majority of men did not use condoms at a time when AIDS awareness in Rwanda was comparatively high, support the assertion that infection was not coincidental, but premeditated.[29] Thus, while the details above are not proof, they indicate with a high degree of probability that systematic sexual violence during the Rwandan conflict has to be supposed to have served a purpose beyond the often assumed psychological scarring of the victims and their local communities; it had the genocidal aim of destroying the entire Tutsi population.

When the tribunals addressed the war crimes committed in Yugoslavia and Rwanda, they did so by basing 'their case laws on their respective Statutes as well as on customary international law', thus giving them much greater traction in local communities, as 'customary international law inevitably affects all states'. This allowed the tribunals to draw upon a frame of reference that facilitated viewing rape and sexual violence as part of a wider framework including torture, grave breaches to the Geneva Conventions, violations to the laws or customs of war, crimes against humanity, and genocide.[30]

The international tribunals of the mid-1990s onwards also differed from earlier legislation in unambiguously linking the atrocities (including sexual offences) with post-conflict justice mechanisms. The ICTR explicitly put sexual violence on the agenda for post-genocide reconstruction by likening rape to torture and thus reinterpreting the rape offence as something going well beyond the above-mentioned Fourth Geneva Convention's understanding of rape as an offense against the honour of the victim. This broadened perception of CRSV came about in direct response to the concerns of non-governmental organisations, which '[the Chamber] consider[ed] as indicative of public concern over the historical exclusion of rape and other forms of sexual violence from the investigation and prosecution of war crimes', something, the Chamber added was required in the 'interest of justice'.[31]

The International Criminal Tribunal for the former Yugoslavia had considered GBV as part of international humanitarian law because it could be argued that despite the civil war character of the Balkans Conflict this was actually an international conflict between the fragmented regions of the former Yugoslavia. Similarly, the ICTR judgments made clear the analogous links between the prevalence of GBV and the political agenda of military and genocidal objectives of the internal conflict in Rwanda. As one commentator pointed out, the *Prosecutor v. Akayesu* case, which brought about the first conviction of an individual for the charges of genocide and international crimes of sexual violence, was groundbreaking in three aspects. Firstly, it recognised sexual violence as an integral part of genocide in Rwanda, and found the accused guilty of genocide for crimes that included sexual violence. Secondly, it recognised rape and other forms of violence as independent crimes constituting crimes against humanity. And thirdly, it enunciated a broad, progressive international definition of both rape and sexual violence.[32]

Thus, GBV, especially if committed as such extreme manifestation as in the Rwandan genocide – causing long-term physical and psychological pain, resulting in forced impregnation and unwanted children, and in many cases leading to a long-term death sentence by AIDS through deliberate infection with HIV – formed the backdrop to post-conflict reconstruction, a fact recognised in the trials. Hence, it acknowledged that if such violence remained unaddressed, it would make hate, mistrust and scepticism all but inevitable, and reconciliation all but impossible.

Children born of war in the Rwandan genocide

It is this situation of genocidal brutality into which children, conceived through rape, were born in their thousands. Given what has been said above about the nature of the conflict and the magnitude of atrocities committed during the genocide, it is impossible to give an exact figure of the number of children born of rape following the 100 days. The National Population Office of Rwanda estimated that between 2000 and 5000 children were born as a result of rape or forced impregnation, but there is general agreement that this figure is an underestimate.[33] In post-conflict Rwanda, these children conceived of rape are often referred to as *enfants indésirés* (unwanted children) or *enfants mauvais souvenir* (children of bad memories),[34] or even as 'children of the devil'[35] and 'little killers'.[36] Jonathan Torgovnik's short documentary *Intended Consequences* strikingly portrays not only the suffering of raped women, but also the torment of pregnancy and motherhood following such sexual violence. One young mother refers to herself as 'leftover of the militia's sexual appetite', adding that she hates herself whenever she thinks about her violation. Another mother clearly articulates that she loves her older daughter, because she was born of a love relationship with her husband, but hates her younger child who was the 'result of unwanted circumstances'. Yet another mother remembers that she did not know she was pregnant until late, but when she realised she wished she would die, and she contemplated suicide; then she waited for the day of the birth intending to kill her child.[37] As described in the case of the Bosnian rape victims, in Rwanda the traumatic circumstances of conception led to well-documented ambivalent relationships between mothers and children.

Moreover, Rwanda – like many countries in Africa – is a patrilineal society; children are identified with the lineage of their fathers and, as such, as belonging to the enemy – a fact most clearly evident in that locals started referring to the children as 'little Interahamwe'. They live in the complex web of their mothers' and the local communities' preconceptions of who they are – based on the fact that they are their fathers' children. It is this fact, the link to their (generally unknown) fathers, which results in negative memories and stereotypes associated with the brutal genocidal enemy being superimposed onto the children. For the local communities these associations may be abstract: that is, a child is connected with the enemy by association and by being a 'blood link' to this ethnic enemy. But for the mothers, this association is a lot more concrete: the child embodies the perpetrator (or group of perpetrators) who personally violated her, who may have killed her relatives – husbands, parents, siblings, children; in some cases the child may resemble the father, either in reality or in the mother's imagination. The accounts of mothers, willing but unable to love these children are numerous.[38] The account below is representative of many:

> Some days, when she looks at her round-faced baby boy, L.M. feels that she no longer wants to live. It is not the child's fault. ... But the baby reminds her of all her family members who died in the massacres ... He also reminds her of the three soldiers of the majority Hutu group who gang-raped her.[39]

Abortion in Rwanda was illegal at the time of the genocide, but numerous women still requested terminations following rape. In one study conducted after the war across two cities 716 cases of rape were reported; 472 of these resulted in pregnancies, of which 282 were terminated.[40] Some pregnant women committed suicide rather than give birth to a child of a Hutu[41] and reportedly some women committed infanticide, because they could not cope with the reality of bringing up a child born of rape.[42] As discussed above these were desperate acts by desperate women which reflect the huge psychological impact of the multiple traumas of their rape experiences. According to some reports of those women who carried their babies to term, it is estimated that 80% abandoned them.[43] But even children who grew up with their biological mothers faced immense hardships as a result of the difficult circumstances and the mothers' vulnerabilities. The vast majority suffered both physical ill health and economic hardship coupled with psychological long-term effects of the genocide. Clark calls rape a 'crime of identity'[44] and argues that it can attack women's identities threefold. The horrific bodily injuries 'impair her physical sense of what it means to be a woman'. Moreover, by destroying the physical procreative abilities, through infection with STIs and through the stigma which may prevent the woman from engaging in future relationships or marriages, they are depriving the victim of the opportunity of finding a husband or having a family. Finally, in the case of the rape of a virgin by 'creating a false rite of passage' the rape leaves the young women feeling socially disorientated and uncertain of her status within the community.[45]

There is ample evidence to demonstrate that all three phenomena were common and prominent experiences of rape survivors in Rwanda. The physical impairment was often due to the effects of the multiple rapes, as well as ill treatment at the hands of the *Interahamwe*, and – in the overwhelming majority of cases – HIV/AIDS. The two other factors identified by Clark are connected with the powerful societal stigma attached to rape. These are very closely linked to cultural factors. As has been pointed out in various contexts of CRSV, stigma attached to survivors of rape and sexual slavery derives from the 'unwarranted or misunderstood association with prostitution, which is deeply stigmatized'. This in turn leads not just to societal shame but to self-stigmatisation, because being the victim of rape is being 'connected with certain cultural traditions in which family honor is stained by *any* violation of sexual property norms'.[46] For Rwandan rape victims this stigma was further accentuated by the high infection rate.[47]

All these factors have led researchers to consider the question of whether the children born of these violations themselves can justifiably be regarded as victims of the rape offences, and a strong case has been made to regard them as secondary victims first and foremost on the grounds of trauma, stigma and less so, the resulting socio-economic discrimination they face. While the children certainly do not experience the trauma of rape directly in the way their mothers do, the transgenerational transmission of trauma, discussed in the case of Bosnian children born of rape,[48] was clearly also a significant factor in the life-courses of children born of rape in Rwanda. Evidence suggests that many mothers had attachment difficulties and struggled to bond. Two testimonies of Torgovnik's documentary[49] may serve as examples: 'Maybe with time I will love this daughter of mine ... But for now ... no!' regrets one rape survivor. Another one confesses: 'I could not imagine how I would nurse this child. I wanted to kill this child. I looked at him and I wanted to kill him. I beat him even when I was nursing him. I beat him even now'.[50] Another mother goes further and admits, even years after the rape, to have murderous thoughts when her son reminds her of his father's crimes: 'I never loved this child. Whenever I remember what his father did to me, I used to feel that the only revenge would be to kill him. But I never did that.'[51] As many mothers are unable to disassociate the child from the crime which provided the circumstances of conception, the recurrent maternal trauma of rape can deprive the child of one of the most crucial elements of early childhood development – maternal love.

The stigmatisation experienced by the mothers and their children, in the Rwandan case furthered by the high rates of HIV infection among both mothers and children, creates a mixture of adverse conditions which condemns many of the victims of the genocidal rape to poverty, hardship and economic marginalisation. A collection of testimonies collected 14 years after the mass rapes bears witness to exactly these conditions. Sixteen women and one man describe the violence and the long-term impact it had on their lives.[52] But the children are affected also by the fact that they are labelled not because of their actions, by anything they have done, but by virtue of their fathers' actions. One woman described the situation she feared for her rape child:

> I knew that I was going to have an unwanted child and that I was not able to look after a baby. But I didn't want to behave like an Interahamwe and abandon my baby. ... Almost all my family members have refused to accept the baby – it is a child of an Interahamwe. They have told me that they do not want a child of wicked people. They always tell me that when my baby grows up that they will not give him a parcel of land. I don't know what is going to happen to him.[53]

What the child's mother relates is an example of what in patrilineal societies is the norm – the creation of an inextricable tie between the father and the child, which in the case of children born of rape creates an inseparable link between the child and the enemy out-group; what has been described as a community's fixation on the children's 'otherness due to an inability to disentangle them from the circumstances of their conception'.[54] In this way, their identity becomes constructed in a way that is inextricably linked to their rapist fathers, even though it is others who raise them'.[55] These children born of rape carry the burden of their traumatic conception and their mothers' pain. As outlined above for Bosnian CBOW, this circumstance often manifests itself in guilt, as the children view themselves as a source of misery, as tainted.

As in many twentieth-century conflicts, the legacy of being of mixed ethnicity was an additional burden to be carried by the vast majority of children born of rape in Rwanda. They had to negotiate their personal and social identities. They were 'out of place' in many different respects – as children born out of wedlock, in economic hardship, often with educational deficits and being of mixed ethnicity. Although Rwanda, due to the fluidity of ethical definitions/divisions, as well as a significant number of mixed marriages, pre-genocide already had many families with different ethnicities, 'mixed' ethnicity did not exist *per se*, because ethnic registration, 'irrespective of ethnicity' was done on patrilineal descent lines and children took on their father's 'formal' ethnicity. After the genocide, mixed ethnicity also did not feature, because in post-genocide Rwanda, all references to ethnicity were officially banned.[56] Yet, children born of rape were still out of place – as one commentator described it, they found it difficult to reconcile their multiple identities: 'they are Hutu offspring yet they are raised by Tutsi mothers and they are children of genocide perpetrators who are raised by genocide victims. They who grew up thinking of themselves as 'genocide orphans' have to integrate the dissonant reality that they are also "children of rape"'.[57] In order to fit into the post-genocide Rwanda, more often than not, they have to suppress part of their identity, emphasising one side of their ethnicity while subduing or hiding the other. Which form this act of choice took, depended to a large extent on where the children grew up. If they were part of the sizeable group of refugees who fled Rwanda in the final stages of the genocide, growing up in refugee camps in Zaire or Burundi, where a Hutsi-dominated ideology ruled, youngsters would be likely to emphasise their Hutu identity at the expense of their Tutsi roots; if in contrast, as the case for most children born of rape in Rwanda, they were raised in Rwanda itself, they would try to navigate between the newly established social categories that had replaced the ethnic demarcation of *rescapé* (Tutsi genocide survivor) and *génocidaire* (Hutu genocide perpetrator), trying to emphasise Tutsi roots and downplaying Hutu identity. If it was difficult for children to find their place in post-1994 society, it became even more complex for adolescents, because as in most African societies, relationships and marriages were not a private affair between two individuals, but, as will be explored in more detail in the next section when discussing the challenges caused by the LRA conflict, it was a matter for families and clans to negotiate. Thus families could 'influence dating patterns, ... approve or refuse to approve relationships and ... support or hinder marriage prospects'.[58]

The Lord's Resistance Army conflict

Like the Rwandan genocide, the civil war between government troops and the LRA in Northern Uganda which forms the background to the second case study of CBOW in sub-Saharan Africa, was the result of a potent mixture of ethnic and political conflicts sewn by colonial policies and exacerbated by post-colonial developments of a violent nature. In order to understand the LRA conflict, the nature of the civil war and the role of female forced conscripts, as well as the impact of those factors on CBOW there, it is important to consider the historical, geopolitical and cultural background.

Uganda is a landlocked East African country, bordered to the east by Kenya, to the north by South Sudan, to the west by the DRC, to the southwest by Rwanda and to the south by Tanzania.

Alongside many of its neighbouring countries the 'state' Uganda was created by colonial powers without much consideration for ethnic divides and tribal needs and wants.[59] This indifference to the pre-existing structures, geographical distribution of various population groups, levels of political organisation, and their local and regional identities would become one of the key problems of fitting heterogeneous groups of people and their organisational structures into a unitary system that did not match these groups' needs.

Ugandans can be divided into broad linguistic groups: the Bantu-speaking majority occupy the central, southern and western parts of the country. The non-Bantu-speakers occupy the eastern, northern and north eastern parts of the country. Nilotic language speakers include the Iteso and Karamojong

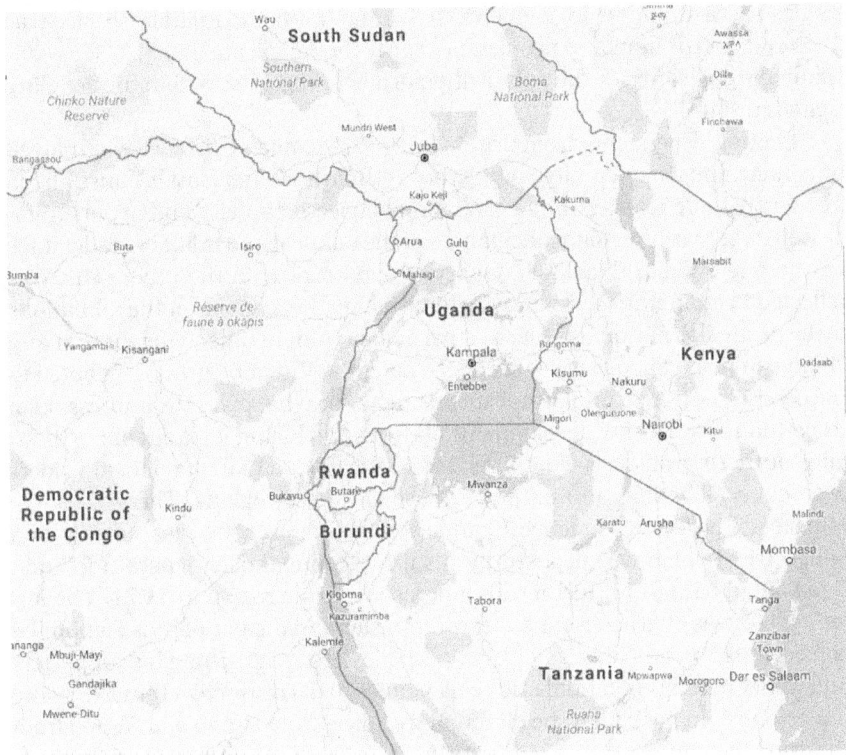

Figure 6.2 Map of Uganda and neighbouring countries

ethnic groups, who speak Eastern Nilotic languages, and the Acholi, Langi and Alur, who speak Western Nilotic languages. As will be explained below, the LRA conflict primarily affected the geographical area inhabited by Western Nilotic speakers, the Luo-speakers of Lango and Acholiland.

The colonial period was characterised by a combination of inter-tribal conflict and a period of pacification in which local chiefs – as a corollary of colonial rule – took on roles less explicitly linked to military activities and thereby partially shifted their loyalty from their kinship groups to their colonial rulers. The post-Second World War period, however, saw a move away from colonial subordination towards Ugandan self-rule. This was characterised by a largely united front mainly of political activists from both peasantry and old tribal monarchical backgrounds who engaged in dialogue for self-rule as one nation.[60] But the need to act in a united way during the struggle for independence only covered the tribal divides, some of which had been amplified by Britain's colonial rule.[61] Not unlike Rwanda, in Uganda, too, one of the key characteristics of this rule had been the stratification of opportunities along ethnic lines. This was most noticeable in the fact that agriculture and civil service opportunities were concentrated in the south and military service was 'reserved' for the northern peoples, primarily the Acholi and Langi.[62] This contributed significantly to the polarisation of different groups within the fledgling Ugandan state.

After its independence from Britain in 1962, Uganda's existence was marred by conflict and violence, often along those ethnic lines, not least because all too frequently there was a strong correlation between ethnicity and opportunity, as well as between regional allegiances of the political and military leaderships on the one hand and lack of equality of opportunity on the other. This was reflected in changing fortunes of regional groups dependent on the affiliations of the particular national leader at a particular point in time. It meant that any change in political power was seen as a potential threat by groups affiliated to the deposed power. Thus it is not surprising to see what gives the impression of something of a see-saw development of rising and falling fortunes of northern and southern groupings closely related to the rise and fall of political leaders with close affiliations to and power bases in these regions. The first Prime Minister of post-independence Uganda, Milton Obote, who was the son of a Lango tribal chief, was deposed by his army commander, General Idi Amin Dada, a Lugbara from Northern Uganda's West Nile region in 1971. The latter's reign was characterised by terror, murder and torture of those whom he considered to stand in his way,[63] and his policy of strengthening his supporters and weakening his potential and real enemies had a distinctly ethnic/regional undertone.[64] In particular, he eliminated soldiers from Lango and Acholi from the army in an attempt to remove any support for Obote within the military. It is estimated that between 300,000 and 500,000 Ugandans were killed during Idi Amin's reign.[65] Amin himself was overthrown by an amalgam of Tanzanian government soldiers and Ugandan exiles in 1979.[66] The period following this coup is of particular significance for an understanding of CRSV in Uganda and of children born of such violence during the subsequent LRA conflict because the violent deposition of Idi Amin through Tanzanian-supported insurgents created a precedence of wide-spread GBV which was later to become one of the defining features of the LRA atrocities. At least 40,000 Tanzanian soldiers are estimated to have spent more than two years in Uganda from 1979; they committed rape, murders and other crimes in the country they had helped liberate.[67] Beyond the sexual violence, Tanzanian soldiers also entered into consensual sexual relationships with Ugandan women and these liaisons resulted in many CBOW. When the soldiers returned to Tanzania the women and their children generally remained in Uganda. As has been observed in the context of post-Second World War occupations in Europe, most of the children grew up as children of single mothers in their maternal domestic contexts. In Uganda, too, they did not know the identity of their biological fathers, and this group of CBOW appears to have been integrated into their maternal communities.

Soon after Amin's defeat, Obote returned to power, now retaliating against those who were suspected of having supported his predecessor, similarly resorting to torture, rape, looting and destruction of property, and again leaving hundreds of thousands dead, this time primarily those from the south of the country.[68] This second Obote rule was characterised by civil unrest and armed conflict, and after years of guerrilla war waged by former exiles around Yoweri Museveni, who had been disenfranchised by Obote, in 1985 a military coup by a section of the government army, the Uganda National Liberation Army (UNLA), overthrew Obote for the second and final time. The subsequent period of consolidation of power was again dominated by lootings and vengeful killings, this time targeting primarily Obote's regional support base, the Langi.[69] This regime, however, was soon deposed by rebels of the National Resistance Army led by Yoweri Museveni. Among his most immediate concerns was the cleansing of the country of fleeing UNLA soldiers and other insurgent groups, again mostly ethnically motivated actions targeting the Acholi.[70]

The LRA conflict, abduction and captivity

The prolonged period of civil armed conflict was economically and politically disastrous for the young East African country. Moreover, it had a deeply unsettling impact on civil society, traditional belief and justice systems, local and regional cohesion and the prevailing clan and ethnic system with its traditional organisational structures and spiritual and religious foundations which were tightly linked to clan and tribal rituals. It is before this background of decades of armed civil conflict, disorientation of large groups of militarised youngsters and civil war returnees, unable to fit into their impoverished home communities and having been alienated from them through the war experiences that, in 1986, Alice Auma Lakwena, a 27-year-old 'spirit medium'[71] from the outskirts of Gulu (Acholi) mobilised followers to join in a military struggle for a re-birth of the Acholi people. Her calls were received keenly by many former UNLA soldiers, not primarily because of the mysticism around Lakwena's so-called 'Holy Spirit Movement' (HSM), but because they expected and feared a repeat of ethnic cleansing of the 1970s.[72] Although the HSM itself was defeated in 1987, it set the scene for similar rebel outfits, most of which were made up of remnants of the HSM and rebels of the Uganda People's Defence Army.[73] Most notable among these was the group around Joseph Kony, a 'spirit medium'[74] related to Alice Lakwena, whose LRA was quickly developing into the leading rebel group in the region and relying on abduction as a major strategy of negotiating recruitment from among the Acholi and parts of neighbouring Lango.[75] Unlike other rebel groups, however, the violence perpetrated by the LRA went far beyond what had been experienced in Uganda's previous armed conflicts, with the 'blind terror' seemingly without political or military agenda,[76] eventually being branded as terrorism by both the African Union and globally.[77] The LRA terror, spanning from 1987 to 2006 affected the entire Acholi region, large parts of neighbouring Lango and later some parts of the Teso region. Lacking popularity among the Acholi,[78] the

LRA had to resort to forceful recruitment and abducted tens of thousands of adults and children to serve in their fighting forces. Moreover, rebel commanders forced girls, some as young as 12, to serve as sexual and domestic servants. These girls and young women were referred to as 'wives', a phenomenon that will be discussed in more detail below.[79]

New recruits, including girls, were forced to inflict horrific injuries on defenceless civilians, including families and neighbours, such as cutting off the ears, noses, lips, and limbs; sometimes they were ordered to murder members of their own families.[80] These acts had a dual purpose. They served as a ritualisation of LRA indoctrination, while at the same time cutting recruits off from the pre-existing moral and social restraints both mentally and physically.[81] The fact that these forced atrocities took place in disregard of traditional practices of post-war ritual purification amplified the impact on the perpetrators and their home communities, because in the absence of the performance of cleansing rituals the impurity resulting from such acts was interpreted as having a lasting bearing on society. As a result, abductees' links to their home communities were severed, and they were forcefully taken from Acholi and parts of neighbouring Lango and Teso to be re-socialised into soldiers, wives and porters for the LRA.[82]

It remains unclear exactly how many people were abducted by the LRA. Registration of sorts by local councils and community volunteers commenced only in 1997, leaving the period of 1986 to 1997 largely unaccounted for. When registration did happen, it was haphazard, and the accuracy of figures has rightly been questioned.[83] However, among others, UNICEF and more recently an academic study based on data from eight reception centres in the northern districts of Gulu, Kitgum, Pader, Apac and Lira have gathered quantitative and qualitative data which have allowed a piecing together of a more detailed picture of the extent of the use of abduction and the realities of the abduction experiences.[84] An estimated 60,000–80,000 people were abducted, with adolescent males being the main target group, but females and males of all ages taken. An estimated 53% of abductees were children under the age of eighteen.[85] In this analysis we are particularly interested in the experiences of female abductees, many of whom ended up as mothers of children fathered by LRA rebels. Women and girls who joined the LRA carried out many of the traditional gender roles, such as cooking, cleaning and serving men. In this they replicated tasks that they were familiar with from the realities of the patriarchal society they had grown up in. But simultaneously, many also participated in fighting, and thus the abduction experience 'sometimes provided opportunities for these girls and women – such as achieving positions of power not previously possible and learning new skills, ... expand[ing] their possibilities'.[86]

While LRA activities were low-scale initially, from 1993–1994 onwards, the war between the LRA and the government's Ugandan People's Defence Force intensified, with Uganda's northern neighbour Sudan providing the

LRA with sanctuary within its borders, with military bases and supplies. This allowed the rebels to step up abductions in general and those of young women and girls in particular, because they could now establish camps for captive girls who supported the fighting forces. The conflict which, as described above, was marked by extreme brutality, including sexual abuse, mental, physical and sexual torture, disfigurement, mutilation and forced cannibalism was a conflict aimed at the civilian population. It targeted both individuals and families. Abductions, as well as the forced atrocities, affected abductees' families, neighbours and villages,[87] thereby deliberately threatening the supportive community networks in the form of organisational structures of Northern Ugandan society, its family and clan structures.

Despite its brutality, the LRA had a strict code of conduct that determined various aspects of behaviour, including fighting, eating, religious practice and sexual conduct.[88] Sex was only permitted for combatants, and it was organised in forced 'marriages', with distribution of wives being 'one of the LRA's only systems of privilege and remuneration'.[89] Most reports on females within the LRA have highlighted their role as sex slaves and 'forced captive wives',[90] but their involvement within LRA captivity was more nuanced than this picture suggests. A detailed study examining the civil war, post-conflict reintegration and related gender issues examined the roles of females within the LRA on the basis of surveys which threw light on the abduction experiences of the women. The data suggests that women served in a variety of roles, with the majority being in servile and supporting roles (as porters, water collectors and cooks), but that those who were abducted for any length of time were trained on weapons, mostly for defensive purposes. A small minority (around 11%) described their main role as combat. Moreover, women who had given birth were rarely used as fighters any more.[91]

The variation in the experiences in LRA captivity is confirmed in a recent analysis of the data collected in four reception centres and one rehabilitation centre in Northern Uganda, based on almost 9000 returnees' records. Data from these centres suggest that experiences of victimisation through walking long distances, hunger, thirst, carrying of heavy loads or being wounded hardly differed for male and female returnees, with such experiences consistently being reported lower by female victims, but only marginally so. In contrast, sexual abuse was reported by 56% of female returnees and by none of the male returnees. Females tended to have witnessed similar levels of atrocities – including watching captives die of starvation, killing of people, captives being forced to kill – with only witnessing of death during battle being significantly more common among male returnees than females. Equally importantly, the level of atrocities perpetrated, including looting, killing, abducting, fighting and destructing, was reported by 71% of female returnees compared with 79% of males,[92] again demonstrating a difference, but not a very significant one. Altogether these findings indicate differentiated experiences of male and female abductees, but this differentiation is less pronounced than the traditional gender roles in wars, as well as in peacetime rural Uganda, might have suggested.

Nevertheless, research confirms that females were frequently recruited to become 'wives' and mothers, and most women reported to have been sexually abused or forced to have sex with a man (mostly within the forced marriage). One survey among forced wives indicates that 25% were 'married' within nine days of abduction, 50% within two months, and 75% within a year.[93] The data further confirms that the rebels divided females into three groups: prepubescent girls; young adolescents; and older adolescents and adults who were assumed to have had sexual experience. These three groups were treated differently, with the prepubescent girls being kept as servants (*ting ting*) in order to be forcibly married later, while young adolescents were forcibly married soon after recruitment, and older adolescents and young adults rarely given as wives, as they were seen as potential carriers of sexual disease.[94]

From the numerous accounts of former abductees it is clear that the marriages were exploitative and coercive relationships without the consent of the women.[95] The experiences of the women varied considerably, with some describing treatment as abusive, others reporting to have been treated well.[96] However, the image of sexual liberalism in the form of extreme promiscuity, gang rapes or even forced infection with HIV/AIDs as described in the Rwandan genocide, was not a feature of the LRA system of enslavement.[97] Interview data suggest that LRA commanders assumed responsibility for the welfare of their 'wives', in turn receiving free services, including sexual; wives of high commanders, as well as pregnant women or young mothers, received preferential treatment, including better access to food, medicine and other goods.[98]

Surveys further suggest that female abductees on average stayed longer in captivity than males.[99] Based on the knowledge of the nature of activities during captivity, three main reasons could account for this. Firstly, being given to commanders as 'wives' would have made escape more difficult, especially if girls became pregnant or gave birth in captivity. Secondly, as described above, it was common practice for girls to be kept in camps for sustained periods of time. This encampment was a more controlled environment away from combat zones which made escape, surrender or capture by Ugandan government troops less likely. Thirdly, the situation of 'wives' in captivity, especially those women who had given birth, may have altered their outlook on the risks and benefits of escape and some no longer saw this as a viable or even desirable option.[100]

As in many of the cases of CBOW explored above, an appreciation of the situation of children conceived from foreign soldiers is closely linked to an understanding of their mothers' plight. This is no different in the case of the children fathered by LRA rebels, because although the needs and challenges faced by mothers and children are different and distinct – at times even diametrically opposed – they are still closely interwoven, because the experiences of the children are a function of the life circumstances of the mothers. Therefore, as in previous case studies, it is essential to explore the challenges faced by returning female abductees within their receptor communities and to investigate them in more detail in relation to the specific issues affecting their LRA-fathered children.

Returnees – women and girls

In the early twenty-first century, a more gender-sensitive approach to post-conflict reconstruction has led to increasing awareness of the distinct experiences of girls and women in fighting forces, especially in the context of child soldiering and forced recruitment of females. As a result of the very significant changes in war and civil war, post-war societies have been faced with the issue of integrating larger numbers of female ex-combatants and abductees than ever before. After years of ignoring women and girl returnees, leading to a lack of provision for their reintegration, resocialisation and psychosocial as well as other support needs, the early twenty-first century has seen a growing recognition of the necessity to understand better the experiences of girls and women in fighting forces, in order to aid successful post-conflict reintegration and reconstruction.

Many of these reintegration efforts take place in traditionally patriarchal societies where the women's roles are primarily following the traditional patterns of servitude, child bearing and child rearing, as well as subsistence farming. When female ex-combatants return to their home communities, they come back with the physical residues of bush war, including injuries, physical deformities, and diseases such as malaria, tuberculosis and parasites,[101] as well as the mental scars of memories of terror and the brutality of the atrocities witnessed and committed. Moreover, they re-join communities the structures and values of which bear little or no resemblance to the LRA experiences. In the bush the women – as described above – not only fulfilled their traditional roles but also, in many cases, experienced greater freedom and independence than in the traditional home setting and sometimes even ended up in commanding roles with authority within the fighting forces.[102] This caused significant reintegration problems, because the girls themselves found it difficult to settle back into traditional gender roles in the community which did not allow for freedom and similar levels of self-determination. Conversely, the mismatch between the girls' experiences and receptor community expectations further exacerbated community stereotypes of bush life having led to rebellious behaviour and alienation among female returnees.[103] Furthermore, traditional sub-Saharan African societies, not unlike the Balkans in the 1990s, Indochina in the 1960s and 1970s or Europe in the first half of the twentieth century, were guided by a strict moral code associated with the reproductive role of women. In the African context, this was linked to traditional clan and family values, as well as being part of the economic fabric of society, which was based on familial and clan interconnectedness. These moral codes, for reasons explored in more detail below, strictly regulated female sexual relations and resulted in any non-conformist sexual activities, such as pre-marital sex, extra-marital pregnancy and children born out of wedlock carrying stigma and having a significant impact on the women's social standing.

Ex-combatants who had been in intimate relationships – consensual or coercive – were subject to resentment and exclusion on their return, and this marginalisation was exacerbated if they returned as mothers of children fathered by the LRA rebels. This stigma associated with being mother of an LRA-fathered child was combined with the resentment of conception out of wedlock, amplified by a lack of knowledge of the exact details of children's paternity and coupled with the knowledge that the father belonged to the enemy.[104]

In order to understand the significance of CRSV for the returnees in the reintegration process, it is important to consider the basis of pre-colonial and in many cases also post-colonial social organisation in many African countries. Inter-related core aspects to be considered in this context are the kinship system, the role of (male) elders in the community, and the significance of land/property and by implication marriage, in creating and maintaining kinship ties and the related social security.

The kinship system provided, and especially in rural areas still provides, the basic framework for social organisation and economic co-operation between social groups and individuals within that social group. An individual has a status as defined in relation to the kinship group, for example, as a child, a parent, a sibling or a spouse. In other words, identity is relational, very much in contrast to the Western liberal concepts of autonomy and individuality.[105] The self and one's identity therefore require an understanding of the relationship of this individual with other members of the group, a proposition echoed and explored in an increasing body of research.[106] The formalisation of these relations comes in the form of kinship structures; and with status within the kinship group come certain rights and responsibilities, claims or entitlements. Thus the actions of the individual can have significant repercussions for the entire kinship group.[107]

The main way in which kinship ties were created and maintained was the transfer of property and services between members, which secured the economic well-being of the kinship group and by implication the individuals within it. Another significant pillar of the socio-economic structure was and remains marriage as a fundamental institution for the recruitment of new members of a kinship group, both through acquisition of a spouse as well as – by implication – through the creation of the framework for procreation. The significance of this recruitment has to be seen within the context of the subsistence agriculture and animal husbandry which formed the foundation of much of the economic activity in pre-colonial Africa in general and Uganda in particular. This required the deployment of large numbers of people for farming, and the livelihoods of families and kinship groups depended on the successful negotiation of social and economic alliances within and between kinship groups, and the transfer of goods, services and group members, all of which secured survival not just of the individual but of the entire kinship group.[108]

Given the system of kinship with its mechanisms of responsibilities and entitlements that has developed over time to create security for both individuals and group, it is hardly surprising to find that the responsibility for overseeing this social contract lay with the senior male members, the elders, who acted on behalf of the group. They negotiated within and between kinship groups and – among other responsibilities – negotiated marriages.[109]

While many people in early twenty-first-century industrialised nations would regard marriage as an affair between two consenting adults, in many other societies, even today, marriage is regarded as a socially approved relationship; and in large parts of the world, it is the socially approved setting within which the conception and birth of children takes place. This is certainly true for Africa. Here the expression of the conceptualisation of the link between marriage and children and the transfer of goods and services between kinship groups is tangible in the practice of bridewealth, a transfer of resources from the family of the groom to that of the bride. This has the dual function of validating the marriage and of compensating for a transfer of the bride's procreative capacity to that of the husband's family. In other words, bridewealth ensures that all the children born to the wife belong to the husband and his lineage, irrespective of whether or not he is the biological father. Conversely, if sufficient bridewealth has not been paid, the children belong to the maternal family until redeemed by the husband.[110] Thus, bridewealth is essential in determining the status of a child.

The worth of children in part stems from their economic and social roles performed from a very early age in a labour-intensive economy. As such, the children are part of a system of inter-generational dependence, in which they are being nurtured in their younger years in return for future support of the older generation later in life. As part of this contract, girls eventually take on the role of brides who help to link their own family with that of their future husbands. Aside from the procreative aspect, such a marriage also secures the woman's own economic well-being. Through marriage she gains the right to access the husband's resources, including land for farming and livestock. In Northern Uganda, prior to, and again since the end of wartime and post-war displacement, most people have lived and now again live in villages where residence and inheritance are patrilineal, where marriages can be polygamous and are almost always patrilocal. Not only this, spatial relations are an expression of social and kinship relations and represent belonging in more than a geographical sense: 'whom one is related to, one's age and gender, also govern one's place in space and regulate everyday life, including land distribution, judicial processes, inheritance, and marriage'.[111] In particular, a woman's economic activity in rural Northern Uganda, as a rule, is seen as an extension of her husband's (or another male relative's). A corollary of this is that unmarried women, often without land or livestock, face food and income insecurity.

The above-described significance of the reproductive role of women in society as a whole and the kinship group and family more specifically in part explain the strict moral codes of conduct which have long regulated pre-marital sex for girls. Although the economic and social transformation of the colonial and post-colonial period with its monetarisation of the economy and its greater emphasis on the individual have led to significant changes in bride-wealth practices, the underlying assumptions about the desirability of girls not to engage in pre-marital intimate relations has remained intact, as this still impacts on the eligibility of a girl for a respectable marriage. In a recent analysis of the changing context of sexual initiation in sub-Saharan Africa, researchers commented on the reluctance, even in the early twenty-first century, of unmarried young women to report experiences of premarital sex, as evident in the prevalence of so-called 'virgin' infections, namely among women who claim never to have had sex.[112] This suggests that, at least in rural areas of sub-Saharan Africa, traditional attitudes to premarital sex are still strong and that women have internalised those, even if they do not adhere to abstinence, as required by tradition. Yet, sub-Saharan African Demographic Health Surveys of the first decade of the twenty-first century show a clear disconnect between these traditional moral codes and sexual behaviour. In Uganda data show that 14% of males and 12% of females report having been sexually active before the age of 15, and 20% of never-married male and 19% of never-married female 15–19-year-olds having been sexually active in the previous year.[113] This reveals (both in rural and urban areas) changing attitudes among the younger generation, but also an adaptation of marriage negotiations and informal cohabitation.[114] Despite changes to many of those social norms[115] perhaps exacerbated by camp life and displacement, post-conflict return to villages has seen efforts to revive pre-conflict culture and its values, 'invoking high moral standards of life before the war and displacement'.[116] This also included clan-based negotiations of marriage and procreation, some of which affected CBOW. Among such rules related to kinship and procreation were those that regulated sexual relations within one clan (*jok* – incest) which are a taboo (*kwer*), just as intimate relations with another man's wife or an unmarried woman, both of which are classified as *luk* and outlawed in customary law. In Northern Uganda, children born outside wedlock are referred to as children of *luk* (*otino luk*), with the child being recognised as a member of the mother's particlan as a matter of course.[117] Yet, although the women's fertility rights belong to the particlan, a premarital pregnancy is regarded as undesirable because the *luk* interferes with the clan's custodial rights over the women's fertility.[118] Even leaving aside such custodial rights, in the aftermath of the LRA conflict the mere existence of LRA-fathered children born out of wedlock is a potent and constant reminder of the LRA-past of the women and in particular of their pre-marital sexual activity, and this in itself is sufficient to expose them and their children to stigmatisation.

Children born of the Lord's Resistance Army conflict

As elsewhere, the number of CBOW in Northern Uganda during the LRA conflict cannot be established with accuracy. This is hardly surprising, given that the number of abductees itself remains an approximation. Estimates for CBOW vary, but there is agreement that they are in their thousands.[119] Returning to the specific situation of female child soldiers during the LRA war, the widespread use of sexual violence against women and girls was a well-known feature of the bush warfare, and female returnees were generally presumed to have been sexually active in captivity. This carried significant stigma on their return. Their bush marriages were not regarded as validated, as no bridewealth had been paid. Therefore the girls' sexual activity was perceived as having taken place outside marriage.[120] HIV/AIDS was rampant in Northern Uganda, and although the LRA, as described above, had its own strictly enforced moral code regarding forced marriages and sexual conduct, the infection rate among returning girls was significant. Recent research suggests that it was comparable with infection rates among non-abductees of the same age group,[121] but receptor communities learnt little about the realities of LRA life, and therefore stereotypes and preconceptions, such as those concerning gang rapes and sexual promiscuity strongly influenced how the female abductees were perceived locally upon their return. Since HIV and STIs were associated with sexual impropriety and LRA experiences similarly were associated with such impropriety, the HIV/STI stigma was transferred to the returnees, irrespective of the actual level of infection rates. The situation was even more difficult if the women returned pregnant or with children born in captivity. As seen in other contexts, CBOW in post-LRA Uganda were readily associated with the circumstances of their conception, as *otino onwyalo ilum* (children born in the bush).[122] But within the concept of Langi or Acholi kinship, the status of these children, despite their existence having the negative connotation of having been conceived outside wedlock and having been conceived by a rebel father, was not linked to the father's lineage, because of the lack of bridewealth or post-conception *luk*.[123] The consequences of this lack of validation of their status within the kinship group will be explained in some detail below in the context of opportunities for these children. What is interesting to note, though, is that because of the patrilineal and patriarchal character of the social order, CBOW are still associated with their fathers,[124] even if within the traditional social organisation pattern they belong to the maternal side of their parentage.

Similar to the many other cases of CBOW in the twentieth century discussed earlier, the stigmatisation of LRA children operated on several levels: the association with the rebel father; the absence of the father; the fact that the children were clearly the 'product' of premarital sex, an act dismissed in local communities as morally and socially unacceptable; the fear of HIV/AIDS; the suspicion that the 'evil' brought to the local community by the rebels to whom the father belonged would somehow be perpetuated by the child – to name but a few elements of the supposed rationale underlying the stigma surrounding the children.[125]

Stigmatisation is not limited to the societal level. In its most profound manifestation it was present in the relationship between mother and child. As in the Rwandan case, women show different levels of resilience in the face of conflict-related traumatisation and this affects their relationship with their LRA-fathered children. In a study of the psychological impact of war and sexual abuse on adolescent girls,[126] based on cross-sectional self-reporting of 123 girls at three rehabilitation centres in Gulu and Kitgum, a participant group that reported similar war experiences as those discussed above, the physical, emotional, cognitive and behavioural signs and symptoms displayed and experienced by the ex-combatants were investigated. The research confirms that the majority of the girls suffered long-term adverse physical effects, including STIs, and ill health due to malnourishment and poor medical support while in captivity as well as consequences of injuries sustained in fighting and as a result of physical and sexual abuse. Many also showed PTSD symptomatology, a phenomenon confirmed by a later more extensive study of a larger cohort of ex-combatants whose mental health was assessed using the 'African Youth Psychological Assessment Instrument', a field-based measurement developed specifically for Northern Uganda.[127] While existing studies on the impact of war experiences on both boys and girls in Northern Uganda[128] still leave open a number of significant methodological questions,[129] not least the applicability of Western conceptualisation of PTSD and, as a corollary, the validity and reliability of instruments and scales developed out of this culturally sensitive context, research indicates a high degree of psychological distress both in former boy and girl soldiers.[130]

If the situation of returnees in general is difficult, that of returning child mothers of LRA-fathered children is even more precarious. As one UNICEF child protection officer stated: 'I can't think of a higher risk group of children anywhere. There is no forgiveness for them. There is no social fabric, no social protection.'[131] Therefore, it is not surprising that, in Uganda, as seen in other post-conflict contexts, vulnerable mothers attempt to keep their children's parentage secret, or at least try to keep their LRA past quiet and avoid confronting it at home and in the local community.[132] As a result, children often become aware of their biological heritage not through conversations with their mothers, but as a result of stigmatisation and discrimination which they experience, including name calling which related to their parents' LRA past.

Only one small-scale study to date has explored the situation of CBOW in Northern Uganda specifically.[133] Although its published findings are not representative, partly because of the small sample size of only 69 children, the outcomes are nevertheless interesting and indicative of the problems facing

LRA-fathered CBOW. Based on structured and unstructured interviews and focus-group discussions, the research described physical and mental health impacts of birth in captivity.[134] These included malnutrition on return as a result of food deprivation in captivity; need to catch up on immunisation which was not available for all but the most privileged LRA children; lack of education and traumatisation due to war experiences, as many had witnessed (or even had taken part in) fighting. All the children observed and interviewed were affected by lack of basic needs on arrival in the reception centres, and most continued to be adversely affected because of their mothers' economic insecurity.[135] In terms of psychosocial impact, the single most significant issue identified was the stigma attached to the names given to the children. Unlike in most other settings discussed in this volume, where CBOW were exposed to name-calling as a member of a group (as in one of a group of children who shared the provenance as son or daughter of the enemy or as conceived of rape), in Uganda, many mothers gave their children individual names reflecting the negative experiences, thus directly affecting the children's sense of self, their identity and by implication also their ability to integrate. Of the 69 children in the above-mentioned study 49 had been given names related to the experiences of the mothers such as *Komakech* (I am unfortunate), *Anenocan* (I have suffered) or *Odokorac* (things have gone bad).[136] As we have seen in the case of Rwandan children born of rape, mothers often perceive their children as a living reminder of the ordeal of their conception; this is further exacerbated by the continued referral to the child with a name reminiscent of that ordeal. Furthermore, the children themselves, as well as the local communities, are continually reminded of the background of conception and the unresolved status of the child within the kinship network. For these children this can lead to self-stigmatisation as their names are a constant reminder of the suffering they have brought to the mother and of her continued vulnerability.

The stigmatisation affecting the children is confirmed by many of the mothers; around one third report that the CBOW are treated differently to children who were not born in captivity, to the point of admitting that they felt life was better for them and their children in the LRA, because there they did not stand out and were not discriminated against.[137] Even in cases where the receptor family accepts the child, societal stigmatisation is often pervasive, as CBOW are symbolic of LRA atrocities.[138]

Field studies have indicated that a widely held belief existed in the rural local communities that any given name might be a factor in the character development of a child. Therefore, children with names of LRA commanders were widely perceived as being likely to develop character traits associated with such rebels, and it was not uncommon for names of CBOW being changed upon their return to the local community to prevent predisposing the children to such character developments.[139]

In cases where the name does not give away the LRA provenance, families often choose to withhold information about the child's biological origins in order to facilitate integration and prevent stigmatisation. But as noted in other post-conflict situations, in adolescence children often start questioning their own background. In Northern Uganda, too, they began enquiring about their identity, wondering about their fathers and 'a generation of mothers is struggling to find acceptance of these children'.[140]

Another aspect of name giving is of significance with respect to the children's belonging. In African societies 'not belonging' can be akin to 'slavery',[141] or more generically to some form of entrapment. The issue of belonging is a powerful one in African society and culture, often epitomised by an individual's name – and here in particular the clan name. Children born of war were not normally given clan names by their mothers or the mothers' clan elders, and therefore the children's belonging to the clan was not confirmed in the name,[142] and the group identity, including rights, obligations and privileges, were not extended to the children through naming.[143] Such privileges are closely linked to an additional 'stress factor' among female returnees and their children – the economically volatile situation of many rape survivors, especially where the breadwinning family members have been killed and the mothers have to rely on charity and hand-outs to feed themselves and their children.[144]

Although Uganda's constitution is one of the most gender neutral with regard to property rights in sub-Saharan Africa, including land rights,[145] affording equal rights to men and women without bias to gender or marital status, the disconnect between legislation and implementation accounts for a strong bias against women's rights to own or inherit productive resources including land. Legal pluralism has resulted in formal laws of marriage and inheritance being weakly defined in Uganda. It has been debated whether the erosion of customary land ownership has disadvantaged women's access to land as some scholars claim,[146] or whether customary law is actually biased against women and its erosion therefore is advantageous for them, as others argue.[147] However, what is less controversial is the fact that despite the considerable body of law existent in Uganda, women's property rights within the marriage, family and in case of inheritance are still largely a function of social norms and customary law. Due to gender inequalities associated with those social norms, especially regarding land ownership and inheritance more generally, LRA 'wives' as a rule cannot access any means of production by right and are reliant on the goodwill of their families and clans.[148] Therefore, many of them have to resort to subsistence farming and/or subsidiary occupations such as brewing, unskilled labour and petty business.[149] And considering the second generation (i.e. the children born of the LRA conflict), given that individuals inherit, as a rule, from either husbands or fathers, in the absence of clan privilege in their mother's clan and in the absence of a father, through whom they could gain access rights to their paternal clan, the prospect of eventual economic self-reliance of these children is slim.[150]

Scholars have disagreed about the level of psychological damage caused by the LRA experience and the success of reintegration, but the weight of evidence clearly supports the view that particularly women and children who integrated spontaneously, without the support of integration centres, suffered long-term psychological effects.[151] Generally, only groups who had benefitted from reintegration support were accepted by families and local communities.[152]

A regular coping strategy of returnees, which in part accounts for the differences in integration experiences of female ex-combatants, is the settlement in new communities away from their immediate family, clan or existing reference group. Numerous women, especially those who returned from the bush with children,[153] chose to form new alliances and move to different locations, preferably in towns where they would not be associated with the LRA. Their strategy is secrecy. Secrecy, however, is also a strategy employed by some women who return to their own families, when they attempt to downplay their bush experiences.[154] Economic hardship is a feature of the lives of the vast majority of female ex-combatants, especially those with children. Abduction experiences often result in educational deficits and reskilling was often most difficult for young mothers or pregnant returnees. As a result child mothers who were lacking the reintegration support network, and were unable to close the skills deficit, ended up reliant on charity, begging or prostitution.[155]

In the face of adverse factors impacting on the reintegration of female ex-combatants into local communities, returnees and their families and kinship groups often invoke religious and customary practices to help bridge the gap between former abductees and their homes in order to support the healing process.[156] The Acholi and Lango ethnic groups relied heavily on a number of rituals with healing effect that had the purpose of chasing away evil spirits utilising the power of clan leaders. These are often a combination of traditional ceremonies and more recently introduced religious practices, including prayers. In this context it is important to note that just like marriage, health is not merely an individual's but also a community concern. Therefore, coping with disease, both physical and mental, is traditionally a communal and frequently a public matter, and healing is often performed with involvement of the kinship group. Without going into detail about the complexities of recent developments, which have seen traditional cleansing and healing approaches in competition with newer cultural practices, a brief exploration of healing as precursor to and part of (re)integration is useful. Similar to our notion of physical and mental health, Northern Ugandans differentiate between 'normal' diseases – which have their causes in the 'natural world' and which can be treated successfully with sufferers responding to treatment and being 'cured' – and recurring symptoms and diseases, which are seemingly unresponsive to treatment and often perceived as having supernatural causes. They are spirit related, caused by spiritual agents, including ancestral spirits, clan or chiefdom spirit forces or the more powerful free spirit forces. Severe psychiatric disorders are perceived to be caused by such forces and consequently have to be healed by overcoming such forces; similarly – and of particular importance in the context of war and killing – *cen*, the vengeful ghosts of those who have died a violent death – have to be overcome by specific healing rituals.[157]

For women and their CBOW, the two contexts that required healing and cleansing were those relating to receiving someone back home into the community who had been away for a long time (abduction), and those relating to killing and coming upon a dead body. Ex-combatants, as other community members who returned after a long absence, would be received back with rituals such as 'stepping on the egg' (*nyono tong gweno*) or 'washing away the tear' (*lwoko pik wang*) ritual, or more generally *moyo kom*, a procedure that is believed to cleanse the body of bad spirits. These cleansing rituals go back to the belief that someone who had been away from home may have encountered bad spirits which, on return, could adversely affect the whole kinship group. But the stepping on the egg ceremony went beyond this cleansing; it was generally applied after someone had left after a disagreement and in these circumstances is performed as a gesture of welcome and commitment of both the returnee and the receptor community to live in harmony in the future.[158] In settings where the family or clan had already believed a returnee lost and had mourned for them, an additional ceremony of 'washing away the tear' would be performed to avert misfortune. It is significant that these rituals were applied to the returnees, and not to the LRA-fathered children. There were no rituals or ceremonies aimed directly at CBOW. As children of LRA fathers, they may not have been recognised as *bona fide* members of their mothers' families. Moreover, having not previously been part of the kinship group, they could not be welcomed *back*, and thus the ceremonies aimed at such reintegration were not applicable to CBOW. This is despite the fact that spiritual affliction of the 'vengeance ghost', the *cen*, haunting and LRA killer or perpetrator of other mistreatment is believed to have the capacity to be passed on to the children of former LRA members. Not addressing such *cen* could therefore impact on the kinship group. As such, the integration of LRA-fathered children did not follow any pattern of traditional reconciliation or welcome, and it appears that it was largely left to the mothers to negotiate the relations both with her children on the one hand and the clan on the other.[159]

How successfully mothers were able to effect the acceptance of their children has never been explored in detail, but findings of recent fieldwork give some indication about the challenges faced by mothers of LRA children in bringing them up as part of their home communities. A number of factors appear to be significant, not least maternal trauma. The impact of the LRA conflict on abductees and combatants has been explored in great detail, and there is widespread agreement that large numbers of former child soldiers present extensive PTSD symptomology.[160] Trauma and PTSD are demonstrably linked to openness to reconciliation and feelings of revenge, among others, in Ugandan ex-combatants, pointing to the fact that former child soldiers with PTSD were less open to reconciliation and that they were less likely to overcome feelings of revenge and hate.[161] Given the prevalence of PTSD among women who had experienced sustained sexual violence,[162] one would expect that the girl-mothers would experience significant emotional adjustment difficulties. Also, given what has been discussed above about the impact of rape-induced trauma on transgenerational trauma transmission, it would not be surprising to find poor prenatal and post-natal parental attachment and therefore the risk of poor mother–child relationships, rejection, abuse and neglect. Yet, while initial studies suggest that such trauma among formerly abducted child mothers played a large part in the formation of often challenging relations between them and their children, the nature and quality of those relations show considerable variation,[163] pointing to the fact that it will be essential to gain a better understanding of the factors that foster resilience in mothers and families and lead to good long-term outcomes for both mothers and children. The depth of impact that the bush experience had on the young mothers is nowhere more evident than in the naming of the children, which frequently associated the child with the trauma and reinforced the difficult attachment conditions. The difficulties are compounded by the economic hardships that frequently go hand-in-hand with community exclusion, educational deficit and ill health – factors that affect many survivors of civil war and displacement yet disproportionally disadvantage child mothers of LRA children.[164]

Despite these adverse circumstances, a growing body of empirical studies points to a different phenomenon, namely that trauma can result in psychological benefits,[165] and rather surprisingly, there is some evidence that women use motherhood as part of their coping strategy to overcome the trauma of rape.[166] Although this has been demonstrated primarily in the case of rape survivors bringing up children who were not the product of war rape, but conceived before and after the traumatic experiences, there is some sketchy evidence that some ex-combatants also try to 'give a positive meaning to the child born of rape' and construct their child 'as a life-saver, a gift from God or as a new family to replace the one that had been taken',[167] or as 'the key to my bright future'.[168]

This mixed impression of maternal responses to CBOW and the related consequences for the children themselves is symptomatic of the broader picture of relations between CBOW and their mothers, families, local environments and their life experiences more general. The final chapter and epilogue will address this broader phenomenon alongside an exploration of current attempts, at international level, to provide a framework for policies directed at the inclusion of CBOW in post-conflict reconstruction by addressing more directly their specific needs, as well as exploiting their potential as bridge-builders between enemies of the preceding conflict. More often than not, these initiatives involve the UN, as an organisation that not only has an interest in this question because on their watch some children were fathered by peacekeepers, but also as an institution which stands for upholding human rights and humanitarian law. It is this tension inherent in the UN being part of the problem while aspiring to become the instigator and facilitator of solutions which forms the background of the next chapter.

Notes

1. Data on Conflicts: www.prio.org/Data/. (accessed 12.12.2014).
2. Gwyn Campbell and Elizabeth Elbourne, *Sex, Slavery and Power* (Athens, OH: Ohio University Press, 2014); Joel Quirk, 'Wartime Enslavement And Forced Marriage in sub-Saharan Africa: Linking Historical Slave Systems and Modern Problems' (unpublished manuscript); J. Allain, *The Law and Slavery: Prohibiting Human Exploitation* (Leiden: Brill, 2015); Annie Bunting, 'Forced marriage in conflict situations: Researching and prosecuting old harms and new crimes', *Canadian Journal of Human Rights*, 1 (2012), 165–85.
3. www.unitedhumanrights.org/genocide/genocide_in_rwanda.htm. (accessed 12.12.2014).
4. See Mahmood Mamdani, *When Victims Become Killers: Colonialism, Nativism, and the Genocide in Rwanda* (Princeton: Princeton University Press, 2001), pp. 41–75.
5. Gerard Prunier, *The Rwanda Crisis: History of a Genocide* (New York: Columbia University Press, 1997), p. 9.
6. www.unitedhumanrights.org/genocide/genocide_in_rwanda.htm. (accessed 21.7.2014), www.bbc.co.uk/news/world-africa-13431486. (accessed 21.7.2014).
7. AERG report, http://allafrica.com/stories/200810040044.html. (accessed 21.7.2014).
8. www.amnesty.org/en/library/asset/AFR47/007/2004/en/53d74ceb-d5f7-11dd-bb24-1fb85fe8fa05/afr470072004en.pdf, p. 6. (accessed 2.12.2014).
9. Emily Wax, 'Rwandans are struggling to love the children of hate', *The Washington Post*, 28.3.2004, https://www.washingtonpost.com/archive/politics/2004/03/28/rwandans-are-struggling-to-love-children-of-hate/dd942c7b-9287-42cc-8763-bd0675c0b73f/?utm_term=.3a17cbf65ac6. (accessed 28.2.2017); other estimates speak of 20,000 children born of rape. http://foundationrwanda.org. (accessed 21.7.2014). See also J.E. Burnett, 'Situating sexual violence in Rwanda (1990–2001): Sexual agency, sexual consent and the political economy of war', *African Studies Review*, 55:2 (2012), 97–118.
10. Binafer Nowrojee, 'A lost opportunity for justice: Why did the ICTR not prosecute gender propaganda?', in Allen Thompson (ed.), *The Media and the Rwanda Genocide* (London: Pluto Press, 2007), pp. 362–74; here p. 365.
11. Marcel Kabanda, 'Kangura: The triumph of propaganda refined', in Allen Thompson (ed.), *The Media and the Rwanda Genocide* (London: Pluto Press, 2007), pp. 62–72; here p. 62.
12. *Kangura*, Issue 6, Genocide Archive Rwanda, https://repositories.lib.utexas.edu/bitstream/handle/2152/9315/unictr_kangura_006a.pdf, p. 24. (accessed 24.7.2014).
13. RTLM – *Radio Télévision Libre des Mille Collines*, government-supported radio station.

14 Summary Verdict of the Media Trial, reproduced by International Development Research Centre, http://web.idrc.ca/en/ev-108222-201-1-DO_TOPIC.html#ch25. (accessed 24.7.2014).
15 Lisa Sharlach, 'Gender and genocide in Rwanda: Women as agents and objects of Genocide 1', Journal of Genocide Research, 1 (1999), 387–99, here 393; Rachel Rinaldo, 'Women survivors of the Rwandan genocide face a grim reality', Inter Press Service, 6.4.2014, www.ipsnews.net/2004/04/rights-rwanda-women-survivors-of-the-rwandan-genocide-face-grim-realities/. (accessed 22.7.2014).
16 Peter K. Landesman, 'A woman's work', New York Times, 15.9.2002, www.nytimes.com/2002/09/15/magazine/a-woman-s-work.html. (accessed 22.7.2014).
17 Report on the situation of Human Rights in Rwanda, submitted by Mr Rene Degni-Segui, Special Rapporteur of the Commission on Human Rights, www1.umn.edu/humanrts/commission/country52/68-rwa.htm. (accessed 2.12.2014)
18 Nowrojee, 'A lost opportunity', pp. 62–3.
19 See chapter 5.
20 T. Meron, 'Rape as a crime under international humanitarian law', The American Journal of International Law, 87 (1993), 424–8, here 425.
21 Laura Smith-Spark, 'How did rape become a weapon of war?', BBC News, 8.12.2004, http://news.bbc.co.uk/1/hi/4078677.stm. (accessed 4.12.2014).
22 I. Skjelsbæk, 'Sexual violence and war: Mapping out a complex relationship', European Journal of International Relations, 7 (2001), 211–37, here 213.
23 Donatilla Mukamana and Petra Brysiewicz, 'The lived experiences of genocide rape survivors', Journal of Nursing Scholarship, 40 (2008), 379–84.
24 Heide Rieder and Thomas Elbert, 'Rwanda – lasting imprints of a genocide: Trauma, mental health and psychosocial conditions in survivors, former prisoners and their children', Conflict and Health (2013), 6–19.
25 T.L. Gard et al., 'The impact of HIV status, HIV disease progression, and post-traumatic stress symptoms on the health-related quality of life of Rwandan women genocide survivors', Quality of Life Research, 22 (2013), 2073–84; S.G. Russell et al., 'The legacy of gender-based violence and HIV/Aids in the post-genocide era: Stories from women in Rwanda', Health Care for Women International 37 (2016), 721–43.
26 E. Rehn and E.J. Sirleaf, Women, War and Peace: The Independent Experts' Assessment on the Impact of Armed Conflict on Women and Women's Role in Peacebuilding (New York: UNIFEM, 2002), pp. 9–10.
27 Landesman, 'A woman's work'.
28 F. Nduwimana, The Right to Survive: Sexual Violence, Women and HIV/AIDS (International Centre for Human Rights and Democratic Development, 2004), http://publications.gc.ca/collections/Collection/E84-13-2004E.pdf, pp. 20–6. (accessed 23.7.2014).
29 Amnesty International, Rwanda: "Marked for Death", Rape Survivors: Living with HIV/AIDS in Rwanda, 5.4.2014 (AI Index: AFR 47/007/2004). (accessed 23.7.2014).
30 Jennifer Park, 'Sexual violence as a weapon of war in international humanitarian law', International Public Policy Review, 3 (2007), 13–18, here 15; drawing on F. Hampson, 'Working paper on the criminalization, investigation and prosecution of acts of serious sexual violence', UN Doc. E/CN.4/Sub.2/2004/12,

available online: http://documents-dds-ny.un.org/docs/UNDOC/GEN/G04/154/40/pdf/G0415440.pdf?OpenElement (20.3.2006), specifically pp. 4–5.
31 See para. 417 in *Prosecutor v. Jean-Paul Akayesu*. Case no. ICTR-96-4-T. Decision of 2 September 1998; cited in Park, 'Sexual violence', p. 17 note 18.
32 Kelly D. Askin, 'Sexual violence in decisions and indictments of the Yugoslav and Rwandan tribunals: Current status', *The American Journal of International Law*, 93 (1999), 97–123; here 107. See also Anne-Marie L.M. De Brouwer, *Supranational Criminal Prosecution of Sexual Violence: The ICC and the Practice of the ICTY and the ICT* (Cambridge: Intersentia, 2005).
33 Wax, 'Rwandans'.
34 Cassandra Clifford, 'Rape as a weapon of war and it's [sic] long-term effects on victims and society', paper presented at 7th Global Conference Violence and the Contexts of Hostility, Budapest May 2008, p. 7, http://ts-si.org/files/BMJCliffordPaper.pdf. (accessed 24.7.2014).
35 Nowrojee, 'A lost opportunity'.
36 M. Mukangendo, 'Introduction', in Jonathan Torgovnik, *Intended Consequences: Rwandan children born of rape* (New York: Aperture, 2009).
37 Torgovnik, *Intended Consequences*.
38 See e.g. Marie Consolée Mukangendo, 'Caring for children born of rape in Rwanda', in R. Charli Carpenter (ed.), *Born of War, Protecting Children of Sexual Violence Survivors in Conflict Zones* (Bloomfield, CT: Kumarin Press, 2007), pp. 40–52.
39 James C. McKinley Jr., 'Legacy of Rwanda violence: The thousands born of rape', *New York Times News Service*, 23.9.1996.
40 M.A. Angelucci et al., *C'est ma taille qui m'a sauvé: Rwanda: de la tragedie à la réconstruction* (Rome: Cooperazione Italiana, Ministre Italienne de l'Enseignement Superieur, de la Recherche Scientifique, et de la Culture, et UNICEF, 1997); Heather B. Hamilton, 'Rwanda's women: The key to reconstruction', *The Journal of Humanitarian Assistance* (January 2000), http://reliefweb.int/report/rwanda/rwandas-women-key-reconstruction. (accessed 4.12.2014).
41 Wax, 'Rwandans'.
42 Nowrojee, 'A lost opportunity'.
43 J. Matloff, 'Rwanda copes with babies of mass rape', *Christian Science Monitor*, 87 (1995), 1, www.csmonitor.com/1995/0327/27014.html. (accessed 4.12.2014).
44 Janine Natalya Clark, 'A crime of identity: Rape and its neglected victims', *Journal of Human Rights*, 13 (2014), 146–69.
45 Ibid., 148.
46 Joshua Goldstein, *War and Gender: How Gender Shapes the War System and Vice Versa* (Cambridge: Cambridge University Press 2001), p. 365.
47 Anne-Marie De Brouwer et al. (eds), *The Men Who Killed Me: Rwandan Survivors of Sexual Violence* (Quebec: Douglas & McIntyre, 2012).
48 Eduard Klain, 'Intergenerational aspects of the conflict in Former Yugoslavia', in Yael Danielle (ed.), *International Handbook of Multigenerational Legacies of Trauma* (Berlin: Springer, 2010), pp. 279–96, here 289–90.
49 Torgovnik, *Intended Consequences*.
50 Dele Olojede, 'Genocide's child: Her son, her sorrow', *Newsday*, 2.5.2004, www.pulitzer.org/archives/6916. (accessed 4.12.2014).

51 Torgovnik's exhibition cited in Mark Feeney, 'Life after hell, in Rwanda: Seeing victims and children of rape', *The Boston Globe*, 3.9.2011.
52 De Brouwer et al., *The Men Who Killed Me*.
53 Human Rights Watch (ed.), *Shattered Lives: Sexual Violence During the Rwandan Genocide and its Aftermath*, September 1996, www.hrw.org/reports/1996/Rwanda.htm#P737_200522. (accessed 27.7.2014).
54 Patricia Weitsmann, 'Children born of war and the policy of identity', in R. Charli Carpenter (ed.), *Born of War: Protecting Children of Sexual Violence Survivors in Conflict Zones* (Bloomfield, CT: Kumarin Press, 2007), pp. 110–27, here pp. 112–13.
55 Ibid.
56 P. Clark, *The Gacaca Courts, Post-Genocide Justice and Reconciliation in Rwanda: Justice without Lawyers* (Cambridge: Cambridge University Press, 2010), p. 310.
57 Giorgia Doná, 'Being young and of mixed ethnicity', *Forced Migration Review*, 40 (2012), 16–17.
58 Doná, 'Being young', p. 17.
59 Robert Maxon, *East Africa: An Introductory History* (Morgantown: West Virginia Press, 2009), pp. 142–6.
60 A. Kasozi, *Social Origins of Violence in Uganda, 1964–1985* (Montreal / Quebec: McGill-Queen's Press, 1994), pp. 17–29, here pp. 22–9.
61 G.N. Uzoigwe, *Uganda: The Dilemma of Nationhood* (New York: NOK Publishers International, 1982), p. 217.
62 Chris Dolan, *Social Torture: The Case of Northern Uganda, 1986–2006* (New York: Berghahn, 2011), p. 41.
63 Nancy G. Wright, 'Uganda: History from 1971', in John Middleton (ed.), *Encyclopedia of Africa South of the Sahara* (New York: Charles Scribner's Sons, 1996), p. 306.
64 Adam Branch, *Displacing Human Rights: War and Intervention in Northern Uganda* (Oxford: Oxford University Press, 2011), p. 57.
65 J.R. Quinn, 'Getting to peace: Negotiations with the LRA in Northern Uganda', *Human Rights Review*, 10 (2009), 55–71, here 56.
66 Daniel G. Acheson-Brown, 'The Tanzanian Invasion of Uganda: A just war?', *International Third World Studies Journal and Review*, 12 (2001), 1–11.
67 Natasha M. Ezrow and Erica Frantz, *Dictators and Dictatorships: Understanding Authoritarian Regimes and Their Leaders* (New York: Continuum, 2011), p. 60; also Cass Cassidy, *Gaba Road* (Rothersthorpe: Paragon Publishing, 2012), p. 11ff.
68 Jacob Bercovitch and Richard Jackson, *International Conflict: A Chronological Encyclopedia of Conflicts and Their Management 1945–1955* (Washington: CQ Press, 1997).
69 Heike Behrend, *Alice Lakwena and the Holy Spirits: War in Northern Uganda 1985–97* (Oxford: James Currey Publishers, 1999), p. 24.
70 Branch, *Displacing Human Rights*, p. 63.
71 Svenker Finnström, *Living with Bad Surroundings: War, History, and Everyday Moments in Northern Uganda* (Durham, NC: Duke University Press, 2008), pp. 76–7.
72 Behrend, *Alice Lakwena*, p. 25.
73 Dolan, *Social Torture*, pp. 43–4.

74 Branch, *Displacing Human Rights*, pp. 62–3.
75 Behrend, *Alice Lakwena*, pp. 179–83.
76 Kevin C. Dunn, 'The Lord's Resistance Army', *Review of African Political Economy*, 31 (2004), 139–42, here 141.
77 'African Union Designates Lord's Resistance Army a Terror Group', *Voice of America*, 21 November 2011, www.voanews.com/content/african-union-designates-lords-resistance-army-a-terror-group-134338788/159205.html. (accessed 14.8.2014).
78 See Tim Allen, *Trial Justice: The International Criminal Court and the Lord's Resistance Army* (London: Zed Books, 2006), p. 49; see also Tim Allen and Koen Vlassenroot (eds), *The Lord's Resistance Army: Myth and Reality* (London: Zed Books, 2010).
79 Else De Temmerman, *Aboke Girls: Children Abducted in Northern Uganda* (Kampala: Fountain Publishers, 2001), p. 150.
80 Evelyn Amony, *I am Evelyn Amony: Reclaiming My Life from the Lord's Resistance Army*, ed. by Erin Baines (Madison: University of Wisconsin Press, 2016).
81 Phuong N. Pham, Patrick Vinck and Eric Stover, 'Returning home: Forced conscription, reintegration, and mental health status of former abductees of the Lord's Resistance Army in Northern Uganda', *BMC Psychiatry*, 9 (2009), 1–14.
82 See Richard Lane, 'Northern Uganda: Looking for peace', *The Lancet*, 370 (2007), 1991–2.
83 Allen, *Trial Justice*, p. 60.
84 Phuong N. Pham, Patrick Vinck and Eric Stover, 'The Lord's Resistance Army and forced conscription in Northern Uganda', *Human Rights Quarterly*, 30 (2008), pp. 404–11.
85 www.state.gov/r/pa/prs/ps/2012/03/186734.htm, published 23 March, 2012. (accessed 20.2.2013); Jeannie Annan, Christopher Blattman and Roger Horton, *The state of youth and youth protection in Northern Uganda* (Uganda: UNICEF, 2006).
86 Susan McKay and Dyan E. Mazurana, *Where are the Girls? Girls in Fighting Forces in Northern Uganda, Sierra Leone and Mozambique: Their Lives During and After War* (Rights & Democracy, 2004), p. 17, www.uwyo.edu/wmst/_files/mckay.../mckay_where_are_the_girls.pdf. (accessed 12.11.2014), www.essex.ac.uk/armedcon/story_id/000478.pdf. (accessed 2.9.2014).
87 Women's Commission for Refugee Women and Children (ed.), *Against All Odds: Surviving the War on Adolescents, Promoting the Protection and Capacity of Ugandan and Sudanese Adolescents in Northern Uganda* (New York, 2001), https://www.essex.ac.uk/armedcon/story_id/000611.pdf. (accessed 2.9.2014); Amnesty International (ed.), *Uganda: 'Breaking God's Command': The Destruction of Childhood by the Lord's Resistance Army* (New York, 1997), www.amnesty.org/en/library/asset/AFR59/001/1997/en/e3d1420e-ea53-11dd-965c-b55c1122d73f/afr590011997en.pdf. (accessed 3.9.2014).
88 Erin Baines, 'Forced marriage as a political project: Sexual rules and relations in the Lord's Resistance Army', *Journal of Peace Research*, 51 (2014), 4–17.
89 Jeannie Annan et al., 'Civil war, reintegration, and gender in Northern Uganda', *Journal of Conflict Resolution*, 55 (2011), 877–908, here 883.
90 Amnesty International, *Uganda: 'Breaking God's Command'*, pp. 15–20.
91 Ibid., pp. 19–20. Recent, as yet unpublished, research by Eunice Apio has thrown

new light on the LRA camp structure and social norms within the camps. See Eunice Apio, 'Children Born of War in Northern Uganda: Kinship, Marriage, and the Politics of Post-Conflict Reintegration in Lango Society' (Ph.D. dissertation, University of Birmingham, 2016).

92 Sofie Vindevogel et al., 'Forced conscription of children during armed conflict: Experiences of former child soldiers in Northern Uganda', *Child Abuse and Neglect*, 35 (2011), 551–62, here 556.
93 Annan et al., 'Civil war, reintegration, and gender', p. 884.
94 See also Sophie Kramer, 'Forced marriage and the absence of gang rape: Explaining sexual violence by the Lord's Resistance Army in Northern Uganda', *The Journal of Politics and Society* (2012), 11–49.
95 Recent fieldwork suggests an even more differentiated picture with 'widowed' captives having significantly larger room for manoeuvre in their choice of bush 'husbands'. See Apio, 'Children born of war in Northern Uganda', pp. 147–51.
96 Robby Muhumuza, *Girls Under Guns: A Case Study of Girls Abducted by Joseph Kony's Lord's Resistance Army (LRA) in Northern Uganda* (Kampala, Uganda: World Vision 1995).
97 Kramer, 'Forced marriage and the absence of gang rape'.
98 Amnesty International, *Uganda: 'Breaking God's Command'*, p. 18.
99 Vindevogel, 'Forced conscription', 556; see also Anett Pfeiffer and Thomas Ebert, 'PTSD, depression and anxiety among former abductees in Northern Uganda', *Conflict and Health*, 5 (2011), 1–7, here 2.
100 Eric Awich Ochen, 'Children and young mothers' agency in the context of the experiences of formerly abducted people in Northern Uganda', *Child Abuse and Neglect*, 42 (2015), 183–94.
101 McKay and Mazurana, *Where Are the Girls?*, p. 67.
102 Jeannie Annan et al., 'Women and Girls at War: 'Wives', Mothers and Fighters in the Lord's Resistance Army', PRIO (Unpublished manuscript), www.prio.org/ (accessed 3.9.2014), p. 2.
103 Dyan E. Mazurana et al., 'Girls in fighting forces and groups: Their recruitment, participation, demobilization, and reintegration', *Peace and Conflict: Journal of Peace Psychology*, 8 (2002), 97–123; here 116–19.
104 Eunice Apio, 'Uganda's forgotten children of war', in R. Charli Carpenter (ed.), *Born of War: Protecting Children of Sexual Violence Survivors in Conflict Zones* (Bloomfield, CT: Kumarian Press, 2007), pp. 94–109; here p. 103.
105 Okot p'Bitek, *Artist the Ruler: Essays on Art, Culture and Values* (Nairobi: East African Educational Publishers, 1986), pp. 19–20, 68.
106 C.L. p'Chong and 'Okot p'Bitek, 'The cultural matrix of the Acholi in his writings', in E. Breitinger (ed.), *Uganda: The Cultural Landscape* (Kampala: Fountain Publishers, 2000), pp. 83–96. See also S. Wilson, *Research is Ceremony: Indigenous Research Methods* (Nova Scotia: Fernwood Publishing, 2008); Linda Tuhiwai Smith, *Decolonizing Methodologies: Research and Indigenous Peoples* (New York: St. Martin's Press, 1992).
107 B. Rwezaura, 'The concept of the child's best interest in the changing economic and social context of sub-Saharan Africa', *International Journal of Law and the Family*, 8 (1994), 82–114, here 85–9.
108 M. Gluckman, 'Property rights and status in African traditional law', in

M. Gluckman (ed.), *Ideas and Procedures in African Customary Law* (Oxford: Oxford University Press, 1969), p. 252.
109 See B.A. Rwezura, 'The changing community obligations to the elderly in contemporary Africa', *Journal of Social Development in Africa*, 4 (1989), 2–24.
110 Peter Atekyereza, 'Socio-cultural change in Uganda: Emerging perceptions on bride wealth', *Journal of Cultural Studies*, 3 (2001), 360–84.
111 Erin Baines and Lara Rosenoff Gauvin, 'Motherhood and social repair after war and displacement in Northern Uganda', *Journal of Refugee Studies* (2014), Epub ahead of print 4 March 2014. DOI: 10.1093/jrs/feu001 (http://jrs.oxford journals.org/content/early/2014/03/04/jrs.feu001, p. 6; leaning on A. Apoko, 'At home in the village: Growing up in Acholi', in L.K. Fox (ed.), *East African Childhood* (Nairobi: Oxford University Press, 1967), pp. 45–75 and F.K. Girling, *The Acholi of Uganda* (London: Her Majesty's Stationery Office, 1960).
112 Barbara S. Mensch, Monica J. Grant and Ann K. Blanc, 'The changing context of sexual initiation in sub-Saharan Africa', *Population and Development Review*, 32 (2006), 699–727, here 707.
113 Aoife M. Doyle et al., 'The sexual behaviour of adolescents in sub-Saharan Africa: Patterns and trends from national surveys', *Tropical Medicine and International Health*, 17 (2011), 796–807, here 798.
114 Grace Kyomuhendo Bantebya et al., 'Adolescent girls in the balance: Changes and continuity in social norms and practice around marriage and education in Uganda' (2014), www.odi.org/sites/odi.org.uk/files/odi-assets/publications-opinion-files/9180.pdf. (accessed 12.1.2015).
115 Ben Mergelsberg, 'The displaced family: Moral imaginations and social control in Pabbo, Northern Uganda', *Journal of Eastern African Studies*, 6 (2012), 64–80.
116 Ibid., 73.
117 Richard T. Curley, *Elders, Shades, and Women: Ceremonial change in Lango, Uganda* (Berkeley: University of California Press, 1973).
118 Apio, 'Children born of war in Northern Uganda'.
119 See Jeanie Annan and Moriah Brier, 'The risk of return: Intimate partner violence in Northern Uganda's Armed Conflict', *Journal of Social Science and Medicine*, 1 (2010), 152–59; see also www.newvision.co.ug/D/8/14/676382. (accessed 11.10.2014).
120 Baines, 'Forced marriage', 5–7.
121 Sheetal Patel et al., 'Comparison of HIV-related vulnerabilities between former child soldiers and children never abducted by the LRA in Northern Uganda', *Conflict and Health*, 7 (2013), 17–31.
122 Eunice Apio, data from unpublished field research March 2013–March 2014; notes shared with author.
123 For details of retrospective legitimisation and validation of a child's lineage see Baines and Rosenoff Gauvin, 'Motherhood and social repair', 15.
124 Father Carlos Rodriguez, *Seventy Times Seven: The Implementation and Impact of the Amnesty Laws in Acholi* (Association of Religious Leaders' Peace Initiative, Caritas Gulu, Justice and Peace Commission, 2002), p. 18.
125 Annette Weber, 'Abducted and abused: Renewed conflict in Northern Uganda', *Human Rights Watch*, 15 (2003), https://www.hrw.org/report/2003/07/15/abducted-and-abused/renewed-war-northern-uganda. (accessed 22.10.2015).

See also Beth Stewart, *We Are All the Same: Experiences of Children Born into LRA Captivity*, JRP Field Note, 23.12.2015, http://justiceandreconciliation.com/publications/field-notes/2015/we-are-all-the-same-experiences-of-children-born-into-lra-captivity/. (accessed 27.5.2016).

126 Kennedy Amone-P'Olak, 'Psychological impact of war and sexual abuse on adolescent girls in Northern Uganda', *Intervention*, 3 (2005), 33–45.

127 Amone-P'Olak, K. et al., 'Cohort profile: Mental health following extreme trauma in Northern Ugandan cohort of War Affected Youth Study (The WAYS Study)' *SpringerPlus* 2 (2013), 300. http://link.springer.com/article/10.1186/2193-1801-2-300. (accessed 14.3.2017); T.S. Betancourt et al., 'A qualitative study of psychosocial problems of war-affected youth in Northern Uganda', *Journal of Transcultural Psychiatry*, 46 (2009), 238–56; T.S. Betancourt et al., 'Measuring local instrument validity and reliability: A field-based example from Northern Uganda', *Journal of Social Psychology and Psychiatric Epidemiology*, 44 (2009), 685–92.

128 K. Amone-P'Olak, 'The impact of war experiences and physical abuse on formerly abducted boys in Northern Uganda', *South African Psychiatry Review*, 10 (2007), 76–82; K. Amone-P'Olak, 'Psychological impact of war and sexual abuse on adolescent girls in Northern Uganda', *Intervention* 3 (2005), 33–45.

129 Theresa S. Betancourt et al., 'Research Review: Psychosocial adjustment and mental health in former child soldiers–a systematic review of the literature and recommendations for future research', *Journal of Child Psychology and Psychiatry*, 54 (2013), 17–36.

130 Amone-P'Olak, 'Impact on formerly abducted boys', 80; Amone-P'Olak, 'Psychological impact on adolescent girls', 41.

131 Euan Denholm, 'Uganda: Former child soldiers excluded in adulthood', *Amnesty International News*, 14.10.2005, www.amnesty.org/en/news-and-updates/feature-stories/uganda-former-child-soldiers-excluded-adulthood-20051014. (accessed 16.12.2014).

132 Allen Kiconco, 'Understanding Former "Girl Soldiers": Central Themes in the Lives of Formerly Abducted Girls in post-Conflict Northern Uganda (Ph.D. dissertation, University of Birmingham, 2015), pp. 130–56.

133 Eunice Apio (All Saints University Lira and University of Birmingham), Allen Kiconco (University of Birmingham) and Elizabeth Bramley (SOAS, University of London) have carried out extensive field studies relating, among others topics, to the integration of child mothers and the experiences of children born of war in Northern Uganda. I am grateful to all three for sharing their field notes, some of which have been used in this chapter's analysis. A further project is currently undertaken under the Justice and Reconciliation Project, and a first set of field notes with initial findings relating to the experiences of children born in LRA captivity has now been published. Stewart, *We Are All the Same*.

134 Apio, 'Uganda's forgotten children', pp. 94–109.

135 Ibid., 100. Apio's findings in Lango were further supported by Kiconco's qualitative interviews in the Kitgum area in Acholi.

136 Ibid., 101.

137 Ibid., 103.

138 See Grace Akello, Annemiek Richters and Ria Reis, 'Reintegration of former child soldiers in Northern Uganda', *Intervention*, 4 (2006), 229–43, 239–40.

139 Bramley Fieldnotes, E3 and F1; in author's possession.
140 C.M. Mukangendo, 'Rwanda: Coping with children born of rape', published on www.people.umass.edu/chali/childrenbornofwar/mukangendo%20Working%20Paper.pdf. (accessed 11.10.2014).
141 Suzanne Miers and Igor Kopytoff, 'African slavery as an institution of marginality', in Suzanne Miers and Igor Kopytoff (eds), *Slavery in Africa: Historical and Anthropological Perspectives* (Madison: University of Wisconsin Press, 1977), pp. 3–81.
142 See E. Bramley, 'Naming Practices in the Lango Region of Northern Uganda and their Impact on the Integration of Children Born of the Conflict with the Lord's Resistance Army' (Undergraduate dissertation, University of Birmingham, 2014), p. 5.
143 Children and Youth as Peacebuilders, 'Watiko Goom: We have hope', www.childrenyouthaspeacebuilders.ca/programs.watikogoom.html. (accessed 16.12.2014)
144 Helen J. Liebling-Kalifani, 'Research and intervention with women war survivors in Uganda: Resilience and suffering as the consequences of war', in H. Bradby and G. Lewando-Hundt (eds), *Global Perspectives on War, Gender and Health: The Sociology and Anthropology of Suffering* (Farnham: Ashgate, 2010), pp. 69–90. See also Stewart, *We Are All the Same*, pp. 42–4.
145 Margaret Rugadya et al., *Gender and the Land Reform Process in Northern Uganda: Assessing Gains and Losses for Women in Uganda*, Land Research Series No. 2, 2004, www.mokoro.co.uk/files/.../gender_and_land_reform_process_uganda. (accessed 10.1.2015).
146 Aili Mari Tripp, 'Women's movements, customary law, and land rights in Africa: The case of Uganda', *African Studies Quarterly*, 7 (2004), 1–19.
147 e.g. P. Kameri-Mbote, 'Gender issues in land tenure under customary law', United Nations Development Programme–International Land Coalition Workshop: Land rights for African development: from knowledge to action. Nairobi, 31 October–3 November, 2005 (2005), www.capri.cgiar.org/pdf/brief_land-05.pdf. (accessed 11.1.2015).
148 Cheryl Doss et al., 'Women, marriage and asset inheritance in Uganda', Working Paper 184, April 2011, Department of Economics, Yale University, www.chronicpoverty.org/publications/details/women-marriage-and-asset-inheritance-in-uganda. (accessed 16.12.2014).
149 A. Kiconco, 'Understanding Former "Girl Soldiers": Central Themes in the Lives of Formerly Abducted Girls in post-Conflict Northern Uganda (Ph.D. dissertation, University of Birmingham, 2015).
150 Fieldnotes Kiconco, CM32, CM03, CM09, CM20, CM50.
151 Kennedy Amone-P'Olak et al., 'Cohort profile: Mental health following extreme trauma in a Northern Ugandan cohort of War-Affected Youth Study (The WAYS Study)', *SpringerPlus*, 2 (2013), 1–11.
152 Annan et al., 'Women and Girls at War'.
153 Fieldnotes Kiconco, InterviewMale01, Laroo, Gulu, 7.2.2013; interview CM14.
154 Susan McKay, 'Reconstructing fragile lives: Girls' social reintegration in Northern Uganda and Sierra Leone', *Gender & Development*, 12 (2004), 19–30, here 26.
155 Kiconco, 'Understanding Former "Girl Soldiers"', pp. 167–8.

156 For an insightful analysis of the complex societal processes around integration of LRA rape victims see Holly Porter, 'After Rape. Justice and Social Harmony in Northern Uganda' (Ph.D. thesis, London School of Economics, 2015), http://etheses.lse.ac.uk/717/1/Porter_After_rape_2013.pdf. (accessed 21.2.2016).

157 Without author, *Gender and Generation in Acholi Traditional Justice Mechanisms*, JRP Field Note, November 2012, www.justiceandreconcoliation.com/wp-content/uploads/2012/Gender-amd-Generation-in-Acholi-Traditional-Mechanisms-Web.pdf. (accessed 12.1.2015).

158 For details about the purpose and procedure see T. Harlacher, 'Traditional Ways of Coping with Consequences of Traumatic Stress in Acholiland Northern Ugandan Ethnography from a Western Psychological Perspective' (Ph.D. dissertation, University of Freiburg, 2009), p. 188.

159 Without author, *Gender and Generation*, pp. 5–6.

160 e.g. Kennedy Amone-P'Olak et al., 'War experiences, general functioning and barriers to care among former child soldiers in Northern Uganda: The WAYS study', *Journal of Public Health*, 36 (2014), 568–76; Theresa S. Betancourt et al., 'Sierra Leone's former child soldiers: A longitudinal study of risk, protective factors, and mental health', *Journal of the American Academy of Child & Adolescent Psychiatry*, 49 (2010), 606–15.

161 Ch.P. Bayer, F. Klasen and A. Hubertus, 'Association of trauma and PTSD symptoms with openness to reconciliation and feelings of revenge among former Ugandan and Congolese Child Soldiers', *Journal of the American Medical Association*, 298 (2007), 555–9; here 559.

162 Amone-P'Olak, 'Psychological impact on adolescent girls', 38.

163 Stewart, *We Are All the Same*, 21–4.

164 Allen Kiconco and Eunice Otuko Apio, 'Psychosocial Consequences of Being a Child of a Child Soldier: Issues of (Re)integration in Northern Uganda Post Conflict Society' (Unpublished paper, Conference 'Child and War: Past and Present', University of Salzburg, 2013).

165 V.S. Helgeson, K.A. Reynolds and P.L. Tomich, 'A meta-analytic review of benefit finding and growth', *Journal of Consulting and Clinical Psychology*, 7 (2006), 797–816.

166 M. Zraly, S.E. Rubin and D. Mukamana, 'Motherhood and resilience among Rwandan genocide-rape survivors', *Ethos* 41 (2013), 411–39.

167 Elisa Van Ee and Rolf J. Kleber, 'Growing up under a shadow: Key issues in research on and treatment of children born of rape', *Child Abuse Review*, 22 (2013), 386–97; here 391.

168 Stewart, *We Are All the Same*, 22.

7

Unintended consequences ...

In April 2015, *The Wall Street Journal* reported that France was investigating allegations of sexual assault by its peacekeepers in the Central African Republic.[1] This was the beginning of a sequence of harrowing revelations of alleged abuses by peacekeepers from the UN Multidimensional Integrated Stabilization Mission in the Central African Republic culminating in an independent review of peacekeepers' abuses detailing extensive and repeated sexual exploitation and abuse (SEA) by French SANGARIS forces.[2] This was a stark reminder that conflict-related sexual violence (CRSV) is neither limited to barbaric genocidal conflicts such as those described in previous chapters, nor is it limited to irregular armed groups of dubious military or paramilitary ethos in unregulated conflicts untouched by considerations of international law. In the reported case, soldiers from a country with military traditions that claim to instil ethical behaviour into their troops during training were faced with misconduct allegations; this indicates that even in operations which are tasked with protecting the local population, and in particular the more vulnerable groups including women and children, civilians might still not be protected adequately against CRSV. It also points towards the fact that the quite extensive engagement of the UN aimed at just this protection against sexual violence in conflict and post-conflict scenarios has shortcomings that need to be addressed urgently.

Since the UN, in 1948, authorised the deployment of an international observer mission to the Middle East, the organisation to date has been involved in 71 so-called peace support operations (PSOs), a term referring to a broad range of UN peacekeeping operations. In April 2016, a total of 103,510 uniformed personnel, including almost 90,000 troops, more than 12,500 police and around 1,800 military observers from 123 countries served in sixteen peacekeeping operations, primarily in Africa, the Middle East and Asia, as well as in Haiti.[3] Although not explicitly addressed by the UN Charter of 1945, peacekeeping has evolved as one of the main tools employed by the security sector. The concept has been developed over the years to be utilised alongside conflict prevention, peace making and peace enforcement as part of the post-conflict processes of peace building and prevention of relapse into conflict.[4] From the early 1990s onwards, there has been a significant increase in PSOs in support of interactions between peacekeepers and local populations; in the first fifteen years of the twenty-first century, the number of personnel deployed in such operations rose to unprecedented levels. Not only this, there has also been a significant shift in the troop-contributing countries (TCCs). The so-called middle powers, such as Canada, Sweden or Norway, no longer supply the majority of forces;[5] instead, among the top fifteen troop contributors we find: Bangladesh, Pakistan, India, Ethiopia, Rwanda, Nepal, Senegal, Ghana, Nigeria, Egypt, China, Morocco, Tanzania, South Africa and Burkina Faso. Most of these countries are not only relatively new to large-scale engagement in PSOs, but many also have questionable human rights records and transparency, and democratic credentials in their home countries have raised questions in some of these TCCs.

Despite their significant contributions and sacrifices (since 1948 there have been 3,471 fatalities in peacekeeping, peacebuilding and political missions),[6] peacekeepers have increasingly been associated with SEA of the vulnerable populations they had been mandated to project. Hence on the one hand, there has been an ever-extending engagement of peacekeeping missions to protect civilian populations and safeguard them from mass sexual violence that had often accompanied the foregoing conflicts in volatile and fragile regions; on the other hand, these very missions have been tarnished by reports of rape, paedophilia, prostitution and other forms of SEA in a variety of countries, including Angola, Bosnia and Herzegovina, Cambodia, the DRC, East Timor, Kosovo, Liberia, Mozambique, Sierra Leone and Somalia.[7]

The final chapter of this volume will explore the issue of intimate contacts between peacekeepers and local populations. The focus will be on relations between uniformed personnel and local women, whether they are exploitative or consensual, before considering the life courses of children fathered by UN personnel on PSOs. As in the case of CBOW investigated in earlier chapters, it is essential to understand the circumstances of conception, and in particular the situation and experiences of the mothers, in order to grasp the challenges of their children. Like other CBOW, 'peace babies' are fathered by foreign soldiers (or personnel associated with foreign forces) and born to local mothers; but their conception takes place in situations that differ from war and armed conflict, and also from amicable or inimical occupations. Yet, the children conceived in such relationships share some of the experiences and challenges explored for other CBOW in earlier parts of the book.

Peace support operations: special responsibilities for 'special forces'?

The UN as an organisation is tasked with the maintenance of peace and security, a tenet which should underscore the entirety of its operations, including peacekeeping missions, and should guide all its personnel, including all its soldiers, at all levels. Given this UN ethos, sexual misconduct and the exploitation and abuse of civilians are not only morally reprehensible, but also damaging to the credibility of the UN itself as an organisation created to support and protect. As the UN Secretariat put it, referring to the severe sexual transgressions of its staff: 'Wherever crimes are committed by persons participating in a United Nations operation, there will be an impact on the trust that the United Nations seeks from the local community, ... Without trust of the community mandates will not receive full co-operation and may fail or take longer to achieve.'[8] In other words, SEA violate the trust between the peacekeepers and the vulnerable civilian population, thus weakening the fabric on which the missions are built and on which they rely for ultimate success. Moreover, any abuse of power on the part of peacekeepers is particularly disconcerting given the volatility of post-conflict regions where peacekeepers are posted and specifically given the vulnerability of the civilian populations in the affected areas. As such, SEA perpetrated by peacekeepers attacks the very essence of the PSO deployment by counteracting the ethical principles underlying the missions. Even consensual relations, as will be discussed below, have the potential of being a disruptive force in post-conflict peacekeeping. They are often based on power relations which deny the local women genuine choice and, especially where the relationships result in children and where peacekeepers absolve themselves from their paternal responsibilities, they result in increased economic and social volatility and vulnerability for mothers and, by implication, for the peace babies themselves.

Sexual exploitation and abuse by UN personnel

The first concerns about SEA at the hands of peacekeepers were voiced in the early 1990s, when reports emerged about improprieties during the UN operations in Mozambique (ONUMOZ) to be followed soon afterwards by accounts of a significant rise in prostitution and human trafficking in the wake of peacekeeping missions in Bosnia and Herzegovina (UNMIBH),[9] Cambodia (UNAMIC, UNTAC)[10] and Somalia (UNOSOM I and II).[11] Since then, almost all UN PSOs have been associated with sexual misconduct of UN personnel of different magnitude and severity. These include missions in West Africa (Liberia, Sierra Leone and Guinea-Bissau), the DRC, Eritrea and East Timor. Extensive coverage of the issues has included reporting by the media, as well as the UN themselves, and the issue has been the subject of significant academic activity too.[12] During the first wave of UN-directed allegations of SEA those reports were often met by a 'boys will be boys' attitude among the UN leadership.[13] In Cambodia, for example, where reportedly the number of prostitutes during the time of the UNTAC mission rose from 6,000 in 1992 to a high of 25,000, where brothels and massage parlours proliferated, child prostitution rose and where growing infection rates of HIV and other sexually transmitted diseases caused alarm, little action was taken on the part of the UN. This was despite the fact that the civilian population had raised the issue of UNTAC personnel's inappropriate behaviour with their military leadership. Tacit acceptance prevailed of the notion that the sexual appetites of the fit young men had to be met and their 'needs' had to be fulfilled.[14]

Similarly, in Bosnia and Kosovo, NATO and UN peacekeeping personnel were widely understood to be important clients for sexual services, and the increased demands were met through 'trafficking' women into sexual servitude. In the words of a regional human rights officer in Bosnia in 2001 and 2002, 'the slave trade in Bosnia largely exists because of the U.N. peacekeeping operation. Without the peacekeeping presence, there would have been little or no forced prostitution in Bosnia'.[15] Although this claim has been refuted by a UN spokesman, who stated that almost four fifth of clients of Bosnian prostitutes were local men, there is no doubt that peacekeepers fuelled the trade and made it more profitable, not least because their disposable income far exceeded that of local men.[16] In this case, too, there was no immediate response on the part of the UN leadership, and the sex trade, including supply trafficking, remained an unintended yet permanent feature of the UN mission.

SEA are wrong in any context, no matter who the victims are, who the perpetrators are and where and when the offences are committed. However, the offences committed by peacekeepers against the population they are tasked with protecting are even more harmful because of the specific context of peacekeeping missions. They take place in volatile post-conflict situations. Many of the regions where PSOs operate, especially in recent years, have experienced genocidal wars in which civilian populations have been targeted deliberately and where war strategies included ethnic cleansing and systematic and genocidal rape. Furthermore, civilians have often suffered displacement and women are frequently sole providers for their households. The result is a situation where civilians are particularly vulnerable and therefore any abuse of trust and power, especially in the form of SEA, is likely to be even more damaging than in less volatile environments.

It was not until 2002 that the UN began treating this SEA seriously and started addressing the issue in a comprehensive way. An Inter-Agency Standing Committee Task Force on Protection from Sexual Exploitation and Abuse in Humanitarian Crises, composed of a number of UN and nongovernmental entities, was established in March 2002. Initiated with the goal of devising and implementing a coherent approach to the prevention of SEA across all agencies, its purpose was to develop agreed definitions of SEA, to advise the UN on specific measures and to provide guidelines for investigations. This development was a direct precursor of the issuance by the Secretary General, in October 2003, of a Bulletin 'Special Measures for Protection from Sexual Exploitation and Abuse', which detailed what has since become known as the 'zero-tolerance policy'.[17] While this bulletin among others defined and prohibited SEA and laid down some responsibilities for senior staff in facilitating the implementation of the zero-tolerance policy, the more significant change in attitude and policy happened in the wake of the so-called 'Zeid report', commissioned by the Secretary General with the aim to provide a 'Comprehensive Strategy to Eliminate Future Sexual Exploitation and Abuse in United Nations Peacekeeping Operations'.[18] This not only led to a Statement of Commitment on the part of the UN and 34 non-UN entities on 'Eliminating Sexual Exploitation and Abuse by UN and Non-UN Personnel',[19] but also, in July 2007, to the adoption of a new model memorandum of understanding between TCCs and the UN, which included specific provisions on SEA.[20] Most significantly, in December 2007 the United Nations General Assembly adopted two resolutions on criminal accountability (Resolution 62/63)[21] and on victim support (Resolution 62/214), the 'Comprehensive Strategy on Assistance and Support to Victims of Sexual Exploitation and Abuse by United Nations Personnel and Related Personnel'.[22] More will be said about the challenges of developing, and even more acutely of implementing, a successful strategy on SEA, but there is no doubt that – no matter how imperfect the UN response to SEA has been and continues to be – the provisions of the first decades of the twenty-first century have been ground-breaking. They were radical, not only in their acknowledgement of the problem and their genuine desire to tackle SEA but also in the stipulation that soldiers should be accountable for their actions and should shoulder the responsibility for acts of SEA. They were also pioneering in addressing the issue of children conceived in relationships between peacekeepers and local women. In its Comprehensive Strategy, the UN, for the first time, acknowledged that CBOW are among those directly affected by SEA. Alongside complainants[23] and victims,[24] children 'who are found by a competent national authority to have been born as a result of acts of sexual exploitation and abuse by United Nations staff or related personnel' deserve and are entitled to support.

Having created the legal framework within which to address SEA, both in terms of prevention and mitigation, from 2008 onwards efforts have focused more strongly on enhancing prevention of SEA, and agreement was reached to support pilot countries on prevention efforts, develop a tools repository,[25] enhance training efforts, develop guidance on complaints mechanism, investigations and victim assistance, and to develop a managerial compliance mechanism.

The merits and demerits of the UN approach and the challenges faced in the combat of SEA in peacekeeping missions have been discussed in some detail elsewhere,[26] and here we will focus on two significant strands of the debate of relevance for the subsequent analysis of the situation of peace babies and their mothers. The key shortcomings of the UN response to SEA, as identified by the debates of the early twenty-first century – seemingly contradictory – lie in diametrically opposed directions. One concern is that the zero-tolerance approach goes too far in regulating sexual conduct of UN staff and, as a consequence, of the civilian population who might entertain relations with UN personnel. By doing so, the argument goes, it is damaging to the very population they are trying to protect. A second concern is that, at the same time, the UN does not (and cannot) go far enough in its policies of enforcement of zero tolerance and thus is ineffectual and similarly harmful to the local population under their protection.

As to the first of these critiques, it has been pointed out with some justification that, while the intention of protecting vulnerable populations from exploitation and abuse is laudable, the all-embracing definition of (almost) all sexual activity of peacekeepers with local populations as coercive and harmful 'radiates a crusading urgency' which 'erases the agency of the purported victims and the material realities of their lives'.[27] The problem lies in the simplistic view of UN internal research, supported by part of the feminist academic discourse which sees consensual sex in conditions of inequality as exploitative by construct,[28] that sexual relations in themselves are coercive. A corollary of this is that sexual relations between peacekeepers and local populations are either sexual exploitation (in cases where they are consensual, because the underlying socio-economic realities and power relations deprive the local civilian of genuine choice) or sexual abuse (coercive sex without consent). This one-dimensional assessment, while acknowledging the material realities of poverty, post-conflict volatility and lack of opportunity, completely negates any agency on the part of the civilian. Thus, by treating both (consensual) survival prostitution and abusive (non-consensual) sex in the form of forced prostitution, sexual slavery or rape similarly and by outlawing both without taking into account the perceptions of the local population and the choices of the supposed victim, their survival can be rendered even more precarious. As one researcher put it, young women in these survival prostitution economies 'are unlikely to see themselves as victims of sexual exploitation', instead they see this 'sexual labour' as a coping strategy for themselves and their families, linked to hope for a better life.[29] Despite the fact that these relationships are clearly borne out of distributional injustices and in that sense are 'unequal', young women and their families regard them as 'privileges'.[30] As such, the zero-tolerance policy of the UN to some critics is 'overinclusive' in its prohibition of sexual relations and thereby deprives women who are engaged in survival sex economies of their livelihoods.

However, frequently the perceived privilege turns into a distinct liability in case of pregnancies and maternity, because in most cases peacekeepers, as most soldiers discussed in earlier case studies, have been reluctant to take on paternal responsibilities, and thus the economic hardships of the peace babies' mothers are further exacerbated.[31] As will be discussed below, this approach of characterising (almost) all sex between local civilians and peacekeepers as harmful has significant consequences also for the children conceived in such relationships, as it *de facto* deprives their mothers of support options, if the fathers do not fulfil their paternal obligations.

At the other end of the spectrum, criticism levelled at the UN has focused on the ineffectiveness of much of the legal framework in preventing SEA. In the period immediately following the publication of the Bulletin in 2003, in spite of its extensive prohibitions, SEA excesses among peacekeepers, specifically in the DRC, were so severe that they triggered the subsequent intensification of UN efforts leading, among others, to the commissioning of the Zeid Report. Yet, despite wide-spread awareness of the problem of SEA, despite a recognition on the part of the UN that these excesses had to be prevented and where they did occur had to be mitigated by punishment of the perpetrators and support of the victims, peacekeeper perpetrators have still benefitted from almost complete impunity. In other words, in spite of an increasingly strong rhetoric, there is little evidence of a similarly significant increase in accountability. The reasons for this have been related to what one commentator described as 'discordance between politics and law on the internal-external divide'.[32] SEA perpetrated by UN peacekeepers, in the public and media narrative are often perceived as a 'UN concern', diverting the attention away from the individual offender and from the national forces to which he belongs – frequently not even identifying either. As a result, a disjuncture exists between the reality of legal and moral responsibility for off-duty crimes of soldiers operating under UN flag and public perception of responsibility and accountability. This lies at the heart of much of the criticism of the fact that despite UN good will and ample legal process perpetrators of SEA still enjoy near-complete impunity for two main reasons.

Firstly, the UN lack competence over disciplinary and criminal matters: the model memorandum between UN and TCCs lays down that TCCs have exclusive responsibility for disciplining and sanctioning their military contingents, and therefore the UN is required to refer complaints about SEA to the individual TCCs. Although the UN can make recommendations to the TCC, these are not binding. As the offences by construct are committed exterritorialy, persecution is often difficult, because evidence collected in the host country (the country where the offence has taken place) is not always permissible in local courts. Furthermore, idiosyncrasies of operating in different legal settings may result in certain types of offences not being prosecutable.[33]

This leads to a second, related problem of TCCs' responsibility. Under the provision of the revised model memorandum, TCCs are now required to provide an assurance to the UN that they exercise the same jurisdiction to offences of peacekeepers abroad as they would with regard to other crimes, and that the crimes are passed to the appropriate local authorities for action.[34] However, given the lack of enforcement powers on the part of the UN, this assurance is entirely dependent on the good will of the TCCs, and past experience demonstrates that prosecution of sexual misconduct of peacekeepers by their home legal systems is patchy at best. Although the revised memorandum gives the UN the right and duty to carry out initial preliminary investigations, it has to transfer the case to the TCCs, who then have a duty to follow up and report back to the UN. Furthermore, the UN is now also permitted to authorise investigations in case the TCCs is unable or unwilling to do so, which should safeguard the collection of initial evidence and facilitate follow up.

Although TCCs are further required to share information about the progress and outcome of misconduct investigations, the response rate had been hovering well below the 30% mark until 2012 and only rose significantly for the first time in 2013.[35] This reinforces the impression that the UN has limited (though increasing) success in enforcing prosecution. Yet, as all the statistics published by the UN on compliance with the reporting requirements have been aggregated without clear indication of which countries show high compliance levels and which show low levels or non-compliance, incentives for proactive persecution have been low.[36]

These structural problems are exacerbated by issues which have been described in other case studies on CRSV, namely the widespread underreporting of crimes because of the stigma, fear, trauma and isolation engendered by such crimes. If anything, this problem is even more difficult to overcome in post-conflict societies where suspects and investigators are foreign and are likely to lack any meaningful interest in rigorous investigation.

In response to the Zeid Report, the United Nations General Assembly's Special Committee on Peacekeeping Operations recommended the appointment of a group of legal experts in order to advise on how best to overcome these and other obstacles to criminal accountability. The two principal impediments to be addressed have been identified as the jurisdiction to investigate and prosecute and the disparities in national criminal laws.[37] Although the Report of Legal Experts leaves the exclusive jurisdiction of the TCCs unchallenged with respect to military contingents, it nevertheless suggests a greater role of the host countries with regard to other categories of personnel, including investigation and prosecution of criminal offences of UN officials, staff and experts on missions. These officials have functional immunity; in other words they are immune from prosecution or liability for any actions undertaken in their official capacity and can only be investigated or prosecuted for actions undertaken in private capacity. The UN has the right to waive such immunities,[38] but is unlikely to do so, especially in the case of host countries where reasonable doubt exists about impartiality and proper functioning of the justice systems of the host states; and this is typically the case in countries where peace missions are situated. Compromises might be hybrid tribunals in the host states which have international elements (such as in Cambodia, East Timor or Sierra Leone).[39] Falling short of this official collaboration at tribunal stage the Zeid Report recommended that the prosecutions should be supported by investigators of non-TCCs in gathering evidence in accordance with the national laws of the host countries so as to allow follow up in case of evidence of misconduct.[40]

In one other respect, the report of legal experts breaks new ground. In their view, peacekeeping crimes, by virtue of the abuse of power implicit in such a crime, turn 'ordinary' crimes (i.e. crimes under national jurisdiction) into international crimes which ought to be afforded international jurisdiction.[41]

This is a very significant departure from current practice and understanding, because it recognises the severity of the impact of crimes committed by peacekeepers, not just on the individual victim but also on the credibility of the peacekeeping operation as a whole.

A major obstacle to prosecution remains the disparity in domestic criminal law. One concern is that some of the most typical forms of SEA that peacekeepers are known to have engaged in are not explicitly reflected in international humanitarian law treaties. As a result, domestic criminal law statutes may view these offences very differently. For instance, TCCs will have different ages of consent for sexual relations, and will vary in their approach to prostitution. Similarly, attitudes towards gender equality vary greatly, and sexual exploitation of women and young persons is not uniformly recognised as a crime by TCCs.

It is against the background of the legal framework of PSOs and the realities on the ground that children fathered by peacekeepers are being integrated into volatile post-conflict communities. As will be explored in more detail below, the international community's responses to SEA and also the problematic nature of the zero-tolerance policies on the part of the UN have repercussions for the perceptions of local communities. More significantly, they also determine the options open to children of peacekeepers and their mothers in terms of securing livelihoods for themselves in a post-peacekeeping environment, when like many CBOW and their mothers before them, they become 'the ones they left behind'.

'Peace babies'

As indicated above, SEA among peacekeepers have been widely reported and studies both within and beyond the UN have recognised this issue as a serious and wide-spread problem. In contrast, and similar to CBOW previously, children fathered by peacekeepers, whether in consensual or coercive relations, have found very little scholarly or political attention. Although the UN was and is well aware of the problem of the so-called peace babies, it is no coincidence that the issue was first considered widely in response to revelations by the media, who have been reporting about children of peacekeepers regularly in the last decade. The issue first hit the media headlines in 2006, when an Australian journalist reported about an internal UN investigation that found 'a culture of cover-up': babies fathered by peacekeepers and born to local Timorese women had been kept secret because of a 'fear of shame and embarrassment' and these babies were abandoned by the peacekeepers and the UN without financial support. The newspaper article, based on a review and evaluation of Gender-Related Activities of United Nations Peacekeeping Operations, not only detailed the issue of prostitution (both female and male) and child prostitution, but also described the situation of mothers of peacekeeper babies.[42] Even in this first tentative story many of the challenges described for CBOW in other contexts and conflicts are in evidence, too. Mothers of the babies fathered by peacekeepers experienced stigmatisation and ostracisation. In most cases, the children were abandoned by the fathers, with the mothers left to provide for them. The article further stipulated that the conservative and deeply religious Timorese society with patriarchal power structures provided an environment unlikely to encourage women to report abuse or abandonment.[43]

The UN investigation – though acknowledging the tendency to under-report sexual violence and pregnancies arising out of relationships with peacekeepers – recorded around 20 so-called 'peace babies'. Since then, it has become clear that children fathered by peacekeepers are a lot more numerous. More than 6,000 children were registered in Libera who had been fathered by peacekeepers from the Economic Community of Western African States Monitoring Group (ECOMOG) between 1990 and 1998, and many of whom had been abandoned by both their fathers and their mothers and lived on the streets.[44] No numbers are known relating to other peacekeeping operations. However, it has been reported – reminiscent of the images from the evacuation of GIs at the time of the Fall of Saigon, when desperate GI girlfriends with their GI children tried to get on board helicopters and boats – that UN peacekeepers' departures led to similar scenes of despair. When ECOMOG peacekeepers were leaving the country at the end of their tour of duty, women whose children had been fathered by those soldiers reportedly lined the route to the airport in search of support for their children and themselves.[45]

If research on CBOW has been described as being in its infancy, research relating to peace babies has not even commenced in any meaningful way. Evidence is entirely anecdotal and often relies on journalistic findings. However, the above described circumstances of peace operations allow some conclusions about the life courses of peace babies even on the basis of this very limited specific evidence base. Peacekeeping operations provide a distinct social, economic and historical context to the women's lives and – by implication – to the lives of the babies fathered by peacekeepers. While this is culturally sensitive, the situations in host countries of peacekeeping missions are similar by construction. All PSOs bring with them the kind of peacekeeping economies described above, which provide both opportunity for formal but even more so informal (mostly service) economies. The opportunities are (almost) always based on inequalities at various levels. The relative security of the peacekeeper contrasts with the relative insecurity of the local population; the relative wealth of the peacekeepers contrasts with the poverty of the local civilians; and as a result relations between the two groups are based on a stark power differential. The choices which arise for women with regard to the engagement in voluntary and consensual, yet often still exploitative, relations have to be seen in this context. Moreover, most families and local communities, even when they benefit from the women's sexual labour through partaking in her financial compensation or additional food or other remuneration, ostracise women engaging in prostitution as violators of social and cultural norms. A study of (in)security in PSOs investigated the nature of sexual relations in the PSO context on the basis of interviews with peacekeepers. It found that peacekeepers who had used the sexual services of local women were well aware of sensitivities around prostitution in the local communities, although their discourse constructed those sexual relations as 'natural' and the local women as 'predatory'.[46] This was evident in the fact that they used prostitutes discreetly, for instance by supplying them with phones to allow them to be contacted inconspicuously to avoid ostracisation. The discretion became an impossibility as soon as sexual encounters led to pregnancies. Most reports on the circumstances of mothers of peacekeepers' children indicate that their economic and social insecurities were adversely affected by motherhood, for three reasons. Firstly, they were deprived of their income stream because sexual labour, at least temporarily, was no longer an option for them. Secondly, the mother of the peacekeeper's child had to provide for not just herself (and whomever she had been supporting through prostitution) but also her child. Thirdly, the peacekeepers' children alongside their mothers, according to many anecdotal reports, suffered from stigmatisation. Birth outside marriage, in many post conflict-societies currently hosting peacekeeping missions, is still frowned upon,[47] and the prevalence of HIV/AIDS among peacekeepers and those who provide sexual services for them leads to additional stigmatisation and discrimination similar to that described for victims of the Rwandan genocide.[48]

However, the situation of peace babies may be more diverse, complex and even contradictory than that of the children of genocidal rape. It has been suggested that in some situations, the social stigma attached to being born out of wedlock and even more so to being born as a child of a sex worker may be counterbalanced by being a 'peace baby'.[49] This can be a result of being born as mixed-race with lighter skin colour, which in some societies is still seen as a sign of racial superiority. Furthermore, the association with the peacekeeping forces was and is not negative *per se*, and this could impact positively on the children's experiences as they grow up. Conversely, however, paternity disputes and the mere existence of children fathered by 'foreigners' have been known to have led to resentment of local men vis-à-vis peacekeepers in a way that is reminiscent of the experiences described for children of the Second World War. These diverse facets indicate clearly that the evidence base is insufficient to allow a clear verdict about the experiences of children fathered by peacekeepers and to gauge the impact that being born of war has on peace babies within the complex web of stigma, identity and childhood adversities. Such an understanding, however, is essential for any effective targeting of support for children of peacekeepers as envisaged in the Zeid Report and the Comprehensive Strategy.

The above considerations apply to children fathered by peacekeepers irrespective of whether they were conceived in consensual or coercive circumstances. As was mentioned at the beginning of this chapter, the UN departed from the traditional policies of national militaries, which almost always worked on the premise of non-responsibility of the military for the actions of their soldiers' off-duty actions in the case of sexual misconduct, not only with respect to the responsibilities for the (violated) women but also, in case of pregnancies, with respect to the children. In its zero-tolerance strategy and, building on this, in the Comprehensive Strategy 2008, the UN adopted a policy that not only dealt with the support to be given to those who were sexually exploited and abused by those employed by or under contract of the UN, but also with support to be given to children fathered by peacekeepers in such exploitative and abusive relationships. Assistance and support to be offered and provided comprised 'medical care, legal services, support to deal with the psychological and social effects of the experience, and immediate material care such as food, clothing, emergency and safe shelter as necessary'.[50] Similarly, children born as a result of sexual exploitation or abuse are entitled to assistance in accordance with individual needs, addressing 'the medical needs, legal, psychological and social consequences directly arising from sexual exploitation and abuse, in the best interest of the child'.[51] This is a significant step towards securing provisions for CBOW, and although very few children currently benefit from such support, in recent years there have been examples of the UN actively working with mothers to help them establish paternity for the peacekeepers' children.[52]

While the UN has acknowledged the existence of peacekeeper babies, seems genuinely willing to assist them, and has developed a strategy of doing so within the limits of its powers, the organisation cannot and does not take responsibility for CBOW and their mothers. This responsibility lies with the fathers, and the UN's role is that of a facilitator of paternity and child support claims, as outlined in the Comprehensive Strategy. It is at this point that intentions and reality diverge. The implementation of the Comprehensive Strategy's victim support programme is entirely dependent on the collaboration of the TCCs. Under the revised memorandum of understanding TCCs are required to seek to facilitate paternity claims provided by the UN or the relevant authorities in the host countries. But it has rightly been remarked that some TCC's might not have an interest in enforcing this provision and indeed will reconsider their involvement in peacekeeping operations if their soldiers face the prospects of child maintenance in other countries.[53] The UN itself recognised the limitations to the implementation of victim support in a report in 2009, when the Secretary General commented on challenges and outlined lessons learnt and 'the way forward'.[54] The focus remained on prevention activities, including training, plus additional staff to help implement conduct and discipline polices, but the report also contained suggestions for provision of better complaints services and the setting up of victim assistance mechanisms. However, the notable absence is any mention of the provision for children fathered by peacekeepers and their mothers.

UN policies, even if they were more effectual, suffer from another shortcoming, which is closely linked to the above described over-inclusiveness of the organisation's 'zero-tolerance' approach. As is clear from the 'Sexual Exploitation and Abuse Victims Assistance Guide',[55] the UN focus is on the establishment of reliable victim assistance mechanisms based on existing local services; and with regard to children fathered by peacekeepers, the emphasis is on facilitation of paternity and child support claims and on support for caregivers with the aim of enabling them to be 'socially and economically stable'.[56] This assistance, however, is only available to victims of SEA. Children fathered in consensual relationships and their mothers are not entitled to UN support in their attempts to have their children's paternity established, to trace the fathers and fight for child support. Mothers of these children are in the same situation as all other mothers whose children were fathered by men of a different nationality, and their only option is to attempt a child support claim through private international law,[57] or ultimately by resorting to the Hague Convention on the International Recovery of Child Support and Other Forms of Family Maintenance.[58] Given the volatility of the 'typical' post-conflict society in which peacekeepers operate, it is highly unlikely that the mothers of peacekeeper babies would have access to legal representation that would allow them to pursue such claims. Moreover, the Hague Convention on the International Recovery of Child Support has not been signed and ratified widely, and it is likely that in the vast majority of cases the requirements of the countries of residence of mother and father being party to the Convention is not fulfilled.

The result is that while in principle the UN has set out to establish a support system for a narrow group of victims of abuse, it is all but powerless to implement is. At the same time, it is hard to envisage a situation in which individual victims – whether victims of SEA or their children – would have a realistic prospect of consistently enforcing the rights afforded to them by the UN Comprehensive Policy. This difficulty is borne out by the very small number of paternity claims to date.[59]

Notes

1 Sam Schechner and Drew Hinshaw, 'France investigates allegations of sexual assault by its peacekeepers in Central African Republic', *The Wall Street Journal*, 29.4.2015, www.wsj.com/articles/france-investigates-allegations-of-sexual-assault-by-its-peacekeepers-in-central-african-republic-1430344621. (accessed 30.4.2015).

2 Marie Deschamps, Hassan B. Jallow and Yasmin Sooka, 'Taking action on sexual exploitation and abuse by un peacekeepers. Report of an independent review of on sexual exploitation and abuse by international peacekeeping forces in the Central African Republic', www.un.org/News/dh/infocus/centafricrepub/Independent-Review-Report.pdf. (accessed 27.5.2016). Operation SANGARIS is the French military intervention in the Central African Republic. It is not a UN PSO but an intervention based on a UN SC Resolution 2127, which initiated the *Mission inter-*

nationale de soutien à la Centrafrique sous conduite africaine, an African Union peacekeeping mission and sanctioned military support by France.

3 Factsheet, United Nations Peacekeeping Operations, 30.4.2016, p. 2, www.un.org/en/peacekeeping/resources/statistics/factsheet.shtml. (accessed 27.5.2016).

4 Capstone Doctrine, www.effectivepeacekeeping.org/sites/effectivepeacekeeping.org/files/04/DPKO-DFS_Capstone%20Document.pdf, p. 19. (accessed 14.3.2015). See also Norrie MacQueen, *Peacekeeping and the International System* (London: Routledge, 2006).

5 Arturo C. Sotomayor, *The Myth of the Democratic Peacekeeper: Civil–Military Relations and the United Nations* (Washington: Johns Hopkins University Press, 2013), p. 1.

6 United Nations Peacekeeping, Fatalities by Year, www.un.org/en/peacekeeping/fatalities/documents/stats_1.pdf, p. 2. (accessed 27.5.2016); see also James R. Rogers and Caroline Kennedy, 'Dying for peace: Fatality trends for United Nations peacekeeping personnel', *International Peacekeeping*, 2 (2014), 658–72.

7 Chiyuki Aoi et al. (eds), *Unintended Consequences of Peacekeeping Operations* (New York: United Nations University Press, 2007).

8 'Criminal accountability of United Nations Officials and experts on mission', Note by Secretariat, A/62/329, 11 September 2007, paras. 11–12, www.un.org/en/ga/search/view_doc.asp?symbol=A/62/329. (accessed 7.3.2017).

9 Martina Vandenberg, *Hopes Betrayed: Trafficking of Women and Girls to Post-Conflict Bosnia and Herzegovina for Forced Prostitution* (New York: Human Rights Watch, 2002); O. Simic, 'Accountability of UN civilian police involved in trafficking of women in Bosnia and Herzegovina', *University for Peace and Conflict Monitor* (online), www.monitor.upeace.org/pdf/bosnia.pdf, pp. 4–5. (accessed 7.3.2017).

10 Kien Serey Phal, 'The lessons of the UNTAC experience and the ongoing responsibilities of the international community in Cambodia', *Pacifica Review*, 2:7 (1995), 129, 133.

11 Natalia Lupi, 'Report by the Enquiry Commission on the behavior of Italian peacekeeping troops in Somalia', *Yearbook of International Humanitarian Law*, 1 (1998), 375.

12 UNHCR and Save the Children UK, 'Note for implementing and operation partners on sexual violence and exploitation: The experience of refugee children in Guinea, Liberia and Sierra Leone', 2002, www.savethechildren.org.uk/sites/default/files/docs/sexual_violence_and_exploitation_1.pdf (accessed 7.3.2017); Paul Higate, 'Gender and peacekeeping case studies: The DRC and Sierra Leone', 2004, Institute for Security Studies, www.africaportal.org/dspace/articles/gender-and-peacekeeping-case-studies-drc-and-sierra-leone. (accessed on 15.3.2017); 'U.N. investigates alleged sexual abuse by peacekeepers in Eritrea', 2005, www.reliefweb.int/rw/rwb.nsf/db900SID/ACIO-6BFN5E?OpenDocument. (accessed 7.3.2017); Anne Barker, 'UN takes step to prevent sex abuse in East Timor', ABC PM, 2006, www.abc.net.au/pm/content/2006/s1728448.htm. (accessed 7.3.2017). 'Investigation by the Office of Internal Oversight Services into allegations of sexual exploitation and abuse in the United Nations Organization mission in the Democratic Republic of the Congo', UN doc., A/59/661, 5 January 2005 (OIOS MONUC Investigation); 'Cote d'Ivoire: French peacekeeping force opens inquiry into sex abuse claims', IRIN, 20.5.2005, www.irinnews.org/report.

aspx?reportid=54555. (accessed 7.3.2017); 'DRC-Nigeria: 11 policemen suspended over sex abuse allegations in DR Congo', IRIN, 27.9.2005 www.irin news.org/report.aspx?reportid=56514. (accessed 7.3.2017); Kate Holt and Sarah Hughes, 'UN staff accused of raping children in Sudan', *Daily Telegraph*, 2.1.2007, www.telegraph.co.uk/news/worldnews/1538396/UN-staff-accused-of-raping-children-in-Sudan.html. (accessed 7.3.2017); 'UN troops face child abuse claims', *BBC News*, 30.11.2006, http://news.bbc.co.uk/1/hi/world/americas/6195830.stm; Reed Lindsay, 'U.N. peacekeepers accused of rape', *The Washington Times*, 17.12.2006, www.washingtontimes.com/news/2006/dec/17/20061217-122119-4767r/. (accessed 7.3.2017).

13 Sarah Martin, *Must Boys Be Boys? Ending Sexual Exploitation & Abuse in UN Peacekeeping Missions* (Washington, DC: Refugees International, 2005).
14 Angela MacKay, 'Sex and the peacekeeping soldier: The new UN resolution', *Peace News*, Issue 2443, 2001, www.peacenews.info/issues/2443/mackay.html. (accessed 25.2.2015).
15 Keith J. Allred, 'Human trafficking and peacekeepers', in Cornelius Friesendorf (ed.), *Strategies against Human Trafficking: The Role of the Security Sector* (Vienna and Geneva: National Defence Academy and Austrian Ministry of Defence and Sports, DCAF 2009), pp. 299–328, here p. 307. Also Daniel Pallen, 'Sexual slavery in Bosnia: The negative externality of the market for peace', *Swords and Ploughshares*, 13 (2003), 27–43.
16 Keith J. Allred, 'Peacekeepers and prostitutes: How deployed forces fuel the demand for trafficked women and new hope for stopping it', *Armed Forces & Society*, 33 (2006), 5–23, here 19, note 12.
17 Secretary General's Bulletin, 'Special measures for protection from sexual exploitation and sexual abuse', 9.10.2003, www.un.org/en/ga/search/view_doc.asp?symbol=ST/SGB/2003/13. (accessed 1.3.2015).
18 United Nations General Assembly, 'A Comprehensive Strategy to Eliminate Future Sexual Exploitation and Abuse in United Nations Peacekeeping Operations', UN doc. A/59/710, 24.3.2003, http://daccess-dds-ny.un.org/doc/UNDOC/GEN/N05/247/90/PDF/N0524790.pdf?OpenElement. (accessed 23.4.2015), hereinafter cited as 'Zeid Report'.
19 'Eliminating Sexual Exploitation and Abuse by UN and Non-UN Personnel', Tools Repository, Section 4 item 2, www.un.org/en/pseataskforce/tools.shtml. (accessed 23.4.2015).
20 'Report of the Special Committee on Peacekeeping Operations and its Working Group on the 2007 Resumed Session', 12.6.2007. UN. Doc. A61/19 (Part III), annex (hereinafter cited as 'model memorandum'). See also United Nations Peacekeeping Law Reform Project, 'UN peacekeeping and the Model of Forces Agreement', Background Paper Prepared for the Experts' Workshop, 26.8.2010, London, Hosted by the New Zealand High Commission, www.essex.ac.uk/plrp/documents/model_sofa_peliminay_report_august_2010.pdf, p. 23. (accessed 10.4.2015).
21 'Criminal Accountability of United Nations Officials and Experts on Mission', Resolution adopted by the General Assembly on 6 December 2007, http://daccess-dds-ny.un.org/doc/UNDOC/GEN/N07/467/55/PDF/N0746755.pdf?OpenElement. (accessed 30.4.2015).

22 'Comprehensive Strategy on Assistance and Support to Victims of Sexual Exploitation and Abuse by United Nations Personnel and Related Personnel', Resolution adopted by the General Assembly on 21 December 2007, www.un.org/en/ga/search/view_doc.asp?symbol=A/RES/62/214. (accessed 16.3.2017).
23 Complainants are defined as 'Persons who allege, in accordance with established procedures, that they have been, or are alleged to have been, sexually exploited or abused by United Nations staff or related personnel, but whose claim has not yet been established through a United Nations administrative process or Member States' processes'.
24 Victims are defined as 'Persons whose claims that they have been sexually exploited or abused by United Nations staff or related personnel have been established through a United Nations administrative process or Member States' processes'.
25 See www.un.org/en/pseataskforce/tools.shtml. (accessed 2.4.2015).
26 Carla Ferstman, 'Criminalizing sexual exploitation and abuse by peacekeepers', United States Institute of Peace, Special Report 335 (Washington, 2013); Martin, *Must Boys be Boys?*; Anthony J. Miller, 'Legal aspects of stopping sexual exploitation and abuse in UN peacekeeping operations', *Cornell International Law Journal*, 39 (2006), 71; Elizabeth F. Defeis, 'UN peacekeepers and sexual abuse and exploitation: An end to impunity', *Washington University Global Studies Law Review*, 7 (2008), 185. Marsha Henry, 'Sexual exploitation and abuse in UN peacekeeping missions: Problematising current responses', in Sumi Madhok, Anne Phillips and Kalpana Wilson (eds), *Gender, Agency and Coercion* (Basingstoke: Palgrave Macmillan, 2013), pp. 122–42; Róisín Burke, 'Shaming the state: Sexual offences by UN military peacekeepers and the rhetoric of zero tolerance', in Heathcote and Otto (eds), *Rethinking Peacekeeping*, pp. 70–95; Seun Abiola and Nkateko Jannet Chauke, 'The impact of peacekeeping operations: Successful United Nations initiatives in response to sexual exploitation and abuse: fact file 2', *Conflict Trends*, 2 (2014), 30–3.
27 Dianne Otto, 'Making sense of zero tolerance policies in peacekeeping sexual economies', in V. Munro and C. Stychin (eds), *Sexuality and the Law: Feminist Engagements* (Abingdon: Routledge, 2007) 259–82; here 263.
28 See for instance C.A. MacKinnon, *Are Women Human? And Other International Dialogues* (Cambridge, MA: Harvard University Press, 2006), pp. 247–58.
29 Otto, 'Making sense of zero tolerance policies', p. 265.
30 UNHCR and Save the Children UK, *Sexual Violence and Exploitation: The Experience of Refugee Children in Liberia, Guinea and Sierra Leone*, Report of Assessment Mission carried out from 22 October to 30 November 2001 (2002), www.unhcr.org/3c7cf89a4.pdf, p. 9. (accessed 13.4.2015).
31 See e.g. Gabriele Simm, *Sex in Peace Operations* (Cambridge: Cambridge University Press, 2013), p. 12. Also Zeid Report, para. 10.
32 Michiko Kanetake, 'The UN zero tolerance policy's whereabouts: On the discordance between politics and law on the internal–external divide', *Amsterdam Law Forum*, 4:4 (2012), 51–61.
33 UNCHR, 'Working Paper on Accountability of International Personnel Taking Part in Peace Support Operations Submitted by Francois Hampson', E/CN.4/Sub.2/2005/42, 7.7.2005.
34 'Model memorandum', Article 7.

35 United Nations Conduct and Discipline Unit, 'Statistics', https://cdu.unlb.org/Statistics/UNFollowupwithMemberStatesSexualExploitationandAbuse.aspx. (accessed 30.4.2015).
36 Ferstman, 'Criminalizing', 5.
37 'Ensuring the Accountability of United Nations Staff and Experts on Mission with Respect to Criminal Acts Committed in Peacekeeping Operations', Report of the Group of Legal Experts on ensuring the accountability of United Nations staff and experts on mission with respect to criminal acts committed in peacekeeping operations, UN doc. A60/980, www.un.org/en/ga/search/view_doc.asp?symbol=A/60/980. (accessed 30.4.2015).
38 For details see documentations of 'Code Blue Campaign' of the Aids Free World, a campaign aimed at ending impunity for UN personnel, among others, by seeking to remove immunity for sexual offences. *Factsheet: Privileges and Immunities of the United Nations*, www.codebluecampaign.com/fact-sheets-materials/2015/5/13/immunity. (accessed 27.5.2016).
39 'Ensuring the Accountability', paras. 33–7.
40 Zeid Report, para. 33.
41 Report of legal experts, paras. 69–76.
42 Sofi Ospina, 'A review and evaluation of gender-related activities of UN peacekeeping operations and their impact on gender relations in Timor-Leste', www.peacekeepingbestpractices.unlb.org/PBPS/Pages/PUBLIC/ViewDocument.aspx?docid=797&cat=22&scat=0&menukey=_7_10. (accessed 13.4.2015).
43 Linsdey Murdoch, 'UN legacy of shame in Timor', *The Age*, 22.7.2006, www.theage.com.au/news/world/uns-legacy-of-shame-in-timor/2006/07/21/1153166587803.html?page=fullpage. (accessed 13.4.2015).
44 Jonathan Paye-Layleh, 'Liberia's peacekeeping legacy', *BBC Newschannel*, 24.1.2005, http://news.bbc.co.uk/1/hi/world/africa/4195459.stm. (accessed 22.10.2015).
45 Elisabeth Rehn and Ellen Johnson Sirleaf, 'Women, war and peace: The independent experts' assessment on the impact of armed conflict on women and women's role in peace-building' (New York: UNIFEM, 2002), www.unwomen.org/en/digital-library/publications/2002/1/women-war-peace-the-independent-experts-assessment-on-the-impact-of-armed-conflict-on-women-and-women-s-role-in-peace-building-progress-of-the-world-s-women-2002-vol-1, p. 16. (accessed on 16.3.2017).
46 Paul Higate and Marsha Henry, 'Engendering (in)security in peace support operations', *Security Dialogue*, 35 (2004), 481–98, here 491. For an excellent analysis of the counter-narratives of the powerful yet vulnerable peacekeeper versus the vulnerable yet powerful local population see Kathleen M. Jennings, 'Service, sex and security: Gendered peacekeeping economies in Liberia and the Democratic Republic of the Congo', *Security Dialogue* (2014), 1–18.
47 See e.g. Bally Mutuyami, Ashish Kumar Sen and Saikat Datta, 'The peacekeeper's child', *Outlook*, 8.8.2011, www.outlookindia.com/article/the-peacekeepers-child/277848. (accessed 25.4.2015); Paul Higate, 'Peacekeepers, masculinities and sexual exploitations', *Men and Masculinities*, 10 (2007), 99–119, here, 100.
48 United States General Accounting Office, *U.N. Peacekeeping: United Nations faces Challenges in Responding to the Impact of HIV/AIDS on Peacekeeping Operations*

Unintended consequences 243

(Washington, 2001), p. 3. See also Muawuya Zakarule Adam Gombe, 'How Nigerian soldiers fathered "ECOMOG kids"', 22.12.2010, http://zakariahdg.blogspot.co.uk/2010/12/how-nigerian-soldiers-fathered-ecomog.html. (accessed 30.4.2015). It should be pointed out that there is strong evidence that, as a rule, peacekeepers do not pose a significant threat to host countries in terms of HIV transmission. Contrary to common misperceptions, most peacekeepers do not come from countries with higher HIV prevalence than the host countries. See Massimo Lowicki-Zucca, Sarah Karmin and Karl-Lorenz Dehne, 'HIV among peacekeepers and its likely impact on prevalence on host countries' HIV epidemics', *International Peacekeeping*, 16 (2009), 352–63, here 361.

49 Higate and Henry, 'Engendering (in)security', 492, note 17.
50 Comprehensive Strategy, [6]–[7].
51 Ibid., [8].
52 Amy Bracken, 'Haitian moms demand UN help for the babies their peacekeepers left behind', *Public Radio International*, 29.8.2014, www.pri.org/stories/2014-08-28/un-peacekeepers-destabilize-haiti-babies-they-left-behind. (accessed 2.4.2015).
53 Olivera Simić and Melanie O'Brien, 'Peacekeeper babies': An unintended legacy of United Nations peace support operations', *International Peacekeeping*, 21 (2014), 345–63, here, 353.
54 'Implementation of the United Nations Comprehensive Strategy on Assistance and Support to Victims of Sexual Exploitation and Abuse by United Nations Staff and Related Personnel', 27.9.2009, UN doc. A/64/176, particularly sections IV–VI, https://cdu.unlb.org/LinkClick.aspx?fileticket=HVcYeR36fGw%3D&tabid=93&mid=480. (accessed 1.5.2015).
55 ECHA/ECPS UN and NGO Task Force on Protection from Sexual Exploitation, 'SEA Victim Assistance Guide Establishing Country-Based Mechanisms for Assisting Victims of Sexual Exploitation and Abuse by UN/NGO/IGO Staff and Related Personnel', April 2009.
56 Ibid., pp. 7–8.
57 For detailed analysis see Simić and O'Brien, 'Peacekeeper babies', 354–5.
58 www.hcch.net/index_en.php?act=conventions.text&cid=131.
59 R. Siva Kumar, 'UN offers DNA tests to address sexual abuse claims', *News Everyday*, 16.6.2015, www.newseveryday.com/articles/19355/20150616/un-offers-dna-tests-address-sexual-abuse-claims.htm. (accessed 22.10.2015).

Epilogue
Children born of war: lessons learnt?

CBOW are a global phenomenon. It is likely that the scale of this phenomenon will never be fully comprehended, as there are many reasons that account for the fact that data about children fathered by foreign soldiers and born to local mothers will remain inaccurate and incomplete. Despite this reservation with regard to exact figures, the analysis of the chosen case studies – the Second World War and its post-war occupations, the Vietnam War, the Bosnian Wars, sub-Saharan African conflicts and UN peacekeeping missions – leaves no doubt about some baseline conclusions.

In all the conflict and post-conflict scenarios, relationships between foreign soldiers and local women developed, often in very large numbers and frequently in spite of efforts by military leadership to prevent such relations. Evidence unequivocally demonstrates that in all those scenarios children were born as a result of such relations. As is clear from the detailed explorations above, the experiences of the mothers of CBOW are diverse and complex; and as a result, the experiences of the children are similarly diverse and complex. Life courses of CBOW as described above in the different conflicts reveal some similarities but also differences. But just as variance can be observed between the different geopolitically and culturally distinct experiences across the different case studies, there is also variance in the experiences of children within each specific conflict. A recent journal portrait of children fathered by Soviet soldiers in the final days of the Second World War and during the post-war occupations exhibits this forcefully.[1] Some of the *Russenkinder* (Russians' children), a term these CBOW adopted for themselves, not just for the purpose of this article but as a term that signifies their link to the Russian father, describe stigmatisation, ostracisation and discrimination; others emphasise their loving homes and the absence of any discrimination at school or in the local communities. Individual circumstances, in these instances, overrode geopolitical and cultural preconditions.

While firm assessments require significantly more detailed research – in particular, longitudinal studies exploring psychosocial as well as economic, cultural, and political factors – the initial exploration of the extremely diverse conflicts chosen for analysis here allows some preliminary conjectures beyond the almost self-evident but important consideration of variance. Across all conflicts, several factors stand out. At the core of the childhood experiences, as was to be expected, was the child's relationship with the mother (or in her absence the primary caregiver). Therefore, the way in which the mother was and is affected by being the mother of a CBOW determines how the child experiences being a CBOW. As is evident from all the case studies, mothering, and by implication the childhood of CBOW, is affected profoundly by economic, cultural and social circumstances. In all the countries and conflicts which were investigated, significant numbers of mothers whose children had foreign soldier fathers lived in particularly challenging economic conditions; often their hardship was exacerbated by single motherhood, by social exclusion and, especially where they had been subjected to sexual violence, by ill health. Economic insecurity, maternal (physical and mental) ill health and the stigma associated with single motherhood and extra-marital birth were superimposed on the children who, in addition to encountering these adversities, often had to struggle with the 'walls of silence' surrounding their biological origin.[2] They felt exclusion and discrimination, but could not understand the reasons. Almost universally, despite the often existential economic hardships and intense childhood adversities the single most significant issue expressed by CBOW as profoundly affecting their lives was the question of identity. And almost without exception, the pivotal issue was the absent father which affected the conceptualisation of the CBOW's social identity, as a son or daughter, as a member of a local, regional or even national community. This fact points to an interesting phenomenon, namely that even in increasingly individualistic societies identity is intensely affected by affiliation to a group; for CBOW, this affiliation and with it a sense of belonging, is disturbed by the fact that the father is (almost always) unknown, and often believed to be an enemy. The way in which this lack of affiliation impacts on the children varied. In some cases, in particular where membership of a community has a more strongly transactional character, the lack of attachment to a kinship group can result in curtailment of access to resources and a significant impact on identity, which is often constructed as relational to other members of this kinship group. In other societies where, for instance, the emphasis is more strongly on smaller family units than on belonging to a larger group, the impact may be more in the form of the 'otherness' of the specific situation of growing up as a child of an (abstract and absent) enemy among groups of friends in 'normal' families. What many CBOWs, irrespective of their individual circumstances, have in common, is the desire to find the missing link that obscures some aspects of what we would, in short-hand, refer to as identity.

Over centuries, national militaries ignored the fact that their soldiers engaged in intimate contacts with local women during war and occupation. If any note was taken, then this was in the form of facilitating (or even forcing) soldiers' departures when long-term liaisons became known or, even more significantly, if soldiers were known to have caused pregnancies. As a rule, national governments did not accept responsibilities for their soldiers' conduct and, as a rule, they did not accept the consequences by way of supporting their soldiers' illegitimate children or those children's mothers. Historically, some notable exceptions to this general pattern existed. The French, as explored in the case of the Second World War and mentioned in the context of Vietnam and Indochina more generally, claimed their soldiers' offspring for the French Nation, irrespective of racial provenance. As a result, large numbers of children fathered by French soldiers and born to German mothers were adopted into French families after the Second World War; similarly, CBOW in Indochina who had French fathers were encouraged (or forced) to resettle in France and became French citizens by right. A second example is that of GI children of the Vietnam War: the United States facilitated their exit from Vietnam through the evacuation of Operation Babylift, as well as their resettlement following the American Homecoming Act. These acts remain the exception, and in both cases one has to ask about the motivation of such policies. Was the impetus for these policies what has become known in international humanitarian law as the principle of the 'best interest of the child'? This has to be doubted. In the French case, little or no consideration for the welfare of the children is in evidence in the aftermath of either the Second World War or the Indochina Wars. The overriding consideration was one of concern for the nation and of securing for France those who were – in contemporary French legal thinking – members of the French nation. Similarly, while without doubt some consideration of child welfare played a role in the American policies to allow Vietnamericans to emigrate to the United States in 1975 and after 1987, the questions arise: why Vietnamese children, and why at those particular points in time? After all, American GIs had left behind scores of children all over the globe during their deployments throughout the twentieth century, and the group of children supported through the award of citizenship was limited to this specific cohort who were not necessarily significantly more vulnerable than children left in Korea, the Philippines or other localities. Political expediency mixed with public pressure may be the answer. As the analysis above has shown humanitarianism in this case was mixed with a significant degree of political calculation.

It is no secret that political change requires political will. Military and governmental policies are unlikely to be determined by humanitarian considerations for women and children in a foreign country if this thinking has to compete with questions of military preparedness and a nation's ability to respond to threats of national security. The latter will always take precedence, but there are increasing signs of a realisation among the leadership of at least regular forces that ethical behaviour, in particular vis-à-vis the civilian population, does not have to counteract the Forces' ability to fight well. In 1943, the Chief of Chaplains of the US Army, commenting on the US troops' sexual morality, remarked: 'We are in a war to preserve moral values, not to destroy them; to defend the dignity of human beings, not to animalize them; to make this country a decent place to live in, not to turn it into a barnyard or a pig sty'.[3] Clearly, as the above exploration of military–civilian relations in international and civil wars has shown, this attitude is still far from commonplace. But the initiative of the then Foreign Secretary of the UK William Hague, in 2013, to address the problem of sexual violence in conflict and the subsequent 'Global Summit to End Sexual Violence in Conflict' in June 2014[4] indicate that governments are beginning to take more seriously their obligation to protect vulnerable civilians in conflicts. Similarly, the UN with its zero-tolerance policy and its Comprehensive Strategy, aimed at the prevention of sexual violence and abuse, is proactive in attempting to tackle the increasing problem of CRSV, at least for those areas within its sphere of influence.

As has been evident in all the case studies, the long-term impact of GBV has been a significant aspect contributing to the challenges faced by those CBOW whose mothers had been victims of sexual abuse. But the experiences of CBOW conceived in consensual relations similarly point to significant childhood adversities. The critical deficit is not merely that of being part of a fatherless generation (a fate they frequently share with other children growing up in post-conflict situations), but the difficulty in learning anything at all about their fathers. This gap in knowledge about their biological origin appears to be an overriding concern for many CBOW, especially as they get older. In recent years some countries, including the United States and Germany, have recognised the importance of facilitating access for children to their fathers' military records to allow the CBOW to locate their fathers and thereby solve some of the mysteries surrounding their own identity. Recently, a German politician summarised the concerns when stating the significance of channelling the existing 'knowledge surrounding the taboo of children born of war and occupation into useful political, social legal and humanitarian measures'.[5] She identified several key demands frequently expressed by CBOW in the political and societal discourse. Some of these related specifically to mitigating the impact of living as a CBOW across all age groups and thus also addressing 'historic' cases; others dealt primarily with contemporary concerns relating to children's rights today. Among the former are demands for access to archives and information about the biological origin of CBOW; support for CBOW, nationally and internationally, to facilitate paternity claims; and a consistent policy regarding nationality rights. Regarding the latter, the key concern is a consistent implementation of children's rights, such as those explored in Chapter 5 above. But as that analysis demonstrated, children's rights frequently conflict with human rights of their mothers. On the other hand, going back to the observation at the beginning of this chapter, the children's fate is determined most profoundly by the mothers' circumstances. Therefore, the most promising approach towards mitigating the adversities challenging the lives of CBOW is to tackle the challenges that their mothers are faced with. This includes the prejudices and stigma they encounter, but also the economic hardships and disadvantages as a result of discrimination or ill health. Only in this way can one hope that more CBOW will echo the desires of the Bosnian girl born out of war rape, cited above, who aspires to give her situation a 'sense of purpose' and to become a 'force for the good' at the intersection of her parents' still divided community.⁶ Only in this way can we hope to find more mothers echoing Marianne V., one of the victims of the post-war gang rapes in Germany who confidently told those who pitied her in the early post-war years: 'I am not poor, I am rich. I have a child'.⁷ Only in this way can we hope to hear echoes of the voice of one Austrian child born of war, who self-assuredly proclaims: 'I am proud to be a child born of the occupation'.⁸

Notes

1 Mathias Mesenhöller, 'Wir Russenkinder', *GEO Magazin* (May 2015), 116–34.
2 Ibid., 118; Ute Baur-Timmerbrink, *Wir Besatzungskinder: Töchter und Söhne alliierter Soldaten erzählen* (Berlin: Ch. Links-Verlag, 2015), p. 13.
3 WMR Arnold to Charles I Carpenter, 12.8.1943, National Archives and Records Administration, RG247-1-355 (726).
4 www.gov.uk/government/topical-events/sexual-violence-in-conflict. (accessed 14.5.2015).
5 Mechthild Rawert, 'Wir Besatzungskinder können BrückenbauerInnen sein', 24.3.2015, www.mechthild-rawert.de/inhalt/2015-03-24/wir_besatzungskinder_k_nnen_br_ckenbauerinnen_sein. (accessed 14.5.2015).
6 See above chapter 5, p. 170.
7 'Ich bin nicht arm, ich bin reich. Ich habe ein Kind'. Mesenhöller, 'Wir Russenkinder', 130.
8 'Ich bin stolz, Besatzungskind zu sein.' See Ingrid Bauer, '"Ich bin stolz, ein Besatzungskind zu sein." Zeitgeschichtliche Forschungen als Impulse für Empowerment? Befunde mit Blick auf die einstige US-Zone in Österreich', in Barbara Stelzl-Marx and Silke Satjukow (eds), *Besatzungskinder: Die Nachkommen alliierter Soldaten in Österreich und Deutschland* (Wien: Böhlau Verlag, 2015), pp. 183–206.

Bibliography

Archival sources

France

Archives Nationales Fontainebleau
Archives Nationales Paris
Centre des Archives Diplomatique

Germany

Archiv des Diakonischen Werkes der Evangelischen Kirche Deutschlands, Berlin
Bayerisches Hauptstaatsarchiv (BayHStA), München
Bundesarchiv Koblenz
Bundesarchiv Berlin-Lichterfelde
Bundesarchiv Militärarchiv, Freiburg
Landesarchiv Baden-Württemberg: Hauptstaatsarchiv Stuttgart (HStAStg)
Landesarchiv Baden-Württemberg: Staatsarchiv Freiburg

Netherlands

Nederlands Instituut voor Oorlogsdocumentatie (NIOD)

United Kingdom

National Archives – Public Record Office, Kew

United States

National Archives at College Park, Maryland
Social Welfare History Archive University of Minnesota, Minneapolis

Published sources

Ahram, A., 'Sexual and ethnic violence and the construction of the Islamic State', *Political Violence @ a Glance*, 18.9.2014, http://politicalviolenceataglance.org/2014/09/18/sexual-and-ethnic-violence-and-the-construction-of-the-islamic-state/. (accessed 11.2.2015).
Allain, J., *The Law and Slavery: Prohibiting Human Exploitation* (Leiden: Brill, 2015).
Allen, B., *Rape Warfare: The Hidden Genocide in Bosnia-Herzegovina and Croatia* (Minneapolis: University of Minnesota Press / Amnesty International, 1996).
Allen, K.M., 'Operation Babylift: An adoptee's perspective', *Humanist*, 69 (2009), 21.
Allen, T., *Trial Justice: The International Criminal Court and the Lord's Resistance Army* (London: Zed Books, 2006).
Allen, T. and K. Vlassenroot (eds), *The Lord's Resistance Army: Myth and Reality* (London: Zed Books, 2010).
Allied Museum (ed.), *It Started with a Kiss: German–Allied Relations after 1945* (Berlin: Jaron Verlag, 2005).
Allred, K.J., 'Peacekeepers and prostitutes: How deployed forces fuel the demand for trafficked women and new hope for stopping it', *Armed Forces & Society*, 33 (2006), 5–23.
Allred, K.J., 'Human trafficking and peacekeepers', in C. Friesendorf (ed.), *Strategies against Human Trafficking: The Role of the Security Sector* (Vienna and Geneva: National Defence Academy and Austrian Ministry of Defence and Sports, DCAF 2009), pp. 299–328.
Allukian Jr., M. and P.L. Atwood, 'Public health and the Vietnam War', in B.S. Levy and V.W. Sidel (eds), *War and Public Health* (Washington: American Public Health Association, 2000), pp. 215–37.
Alston, P., 'The best interest principle: Towards a reconciliation of culture and human rights', *International Journal of Law and the Family*, 8 (1994), 1–25.
Amone-P'Olak, K., 'Psychological impact of war and sexual abuse on adolescent girls in Northern Uganda', *Intervention* 3 (2005), 33–45.
Amone-P'Olak, K., 'The impact of war experiences and physical abuse on formerly abducted boys in Northern Uganda', *South African Psychiatry Review*, 10 (2007) 76–82.
Amone-P'Olak, K. et al., 'Cohort profile: Mental health following extreme trauma in a Northern Ugandan cohort of War-Affected Youth Study (The WAYS Study)', *SpringerPlus*, 2 (2013), 1–11.
Amone-P'Olak, K. et al., 'War experiences, general functioning and barriers to care among former child soldiers in Northern Uganda: The WAYS study', *Journal of Public Health*, 36 (2014), 568–76.
Amony, E., *I am Evelyn Amony: Reclaiming My Life from the Lord's Resistance Army*, ed. by Erin Baines (Madison: University of Wisconsin Press, 2016).
Andvig, C., 'Child soldiers: Reasons for variation in their rate of recruitment and standards of welfare', NUPI paper 704 (Oslo: Norwegian Institute for International Affairs, 2006).
Anette Brauerhoch, 'Fräuleins und GIs: Besonderheiten einer historischen Situation', *Forschungs Forum Paderborn*, http://kw.uni-paderborn.de/fileadmin/mw/Brauerhoch/downloads/FF-Brauerhoch.pdf.
Angelucci, M.A. et al., *C'est ma taille qui m'a sauvé: Rwanda: de la tragedie à la réconstruc-*

tion (Rome: Cooperazione Italiana, Ministre Italienne de l'Enseignement Superieur, de la Recherche Scientifique, et de la Culture, et UNICEF, 1997).

Annan, J. and M. Brier, 'The risk of return: Intimate partner violence in Northern Uganda's armed conflict', *Journal of Social Science and Medicine*, 1 (2010), 152–9.

Annan, J., Ch. Blattman and R. Horton, *The state of youth and youth protection in Northern Uganda* (Uganda: UNICEF, 2006).

Annan, J. et al., 'Civil war, reintegration, and gender in Northern Uganda', *Journal of Conflict Resolution*, 55 (2011), 877–908.

Anon, *Eine Frau in Berlin* (Geneva: Kossodo, 1959).

Aoi, C. et al. (eds), *Unintended Consequences of Peacekeeping Operations* (New York: United Nations University Press, 2007).

Apio, E. 'Bearing the burden – the children born of the Lord's Resistance Army, Northern Uganda', http://google.co.uk/url?sa=t&rct=j&q=&esrc=s&source=web&cd=2&ved=0CCUQFjAB&url=http%3A%2F%2Fmhpss.net%2F%3Fget%3D54%2F1367708997–ChildrenofFormerlyAbductedGirls-Uganda-Opio-2008.pdf&ei=xU5jVPbANOOasQSc9oGYAg&usg=AFQjCNHxO8Dd8_S3V-GB2mbE6gsvTeC5tw&bvm=bv.79189006,d.cWc. (accessed 31.10.2016).

Apio, E., 'Uganda's forgotten children of war', in R. Ch. Carpenter (ed.), *Born of War: Protecting Children of Sexual Violence Survivors in Conflict Zones* (Bloomfield, CT: Kumarian Press, 2007), pp. 94–109.

Apio, E., 'Children born of war in Northern Uganda: Kinship, marriage, and the politics of post-conflict reintegration in Lango society' (Ph.D. dissertation, University of Birmingham, 2016).

Apoko, A., 'At home in the village: Growing up in Acholi', in L.K. Fox (ed.), *East African Childhood* (Nairobi: Oxford University Press, 1967), pp. 45–75.

Appy, C.G., *Working-Class War: American Combat Soldiers and the Vietnam War* (Chapel Hill: University of North Carolina Press, 1993).

Argibay, C.M., 'Sexual slavery and the comfort women of World War II', *Berkeley Journal of International Law*, 21 (2003), 375–89.

Aries, Ph., *Centuries of Childhood* (Bungaz: The Chaucer Press, 1962).

Arrowsmith, R., *All the Way to the USA: Australian WWII War Brides* (self-published, 2013).

Arthur, M.M.L., 'The neglected virtues of comparative-historical methods', in Ieva Zake and Michael De Cesare (eds), *New Directions in Sociology: Essays on Theory and Methodology in the 21st Century* (Jefferson/NC: McFarland, 2011), 172–92.

Askin, K.D., 'Sexual violence in decisions and indictments of the Yugoslav and Rwandan tribunals: Current status', *The American Journal of International Law*, 93 (1999), 97–123.

Aslam, M., *Gender-Based Explosions: The Nexus Between Muslim Masculinities, Jihadist Islamism and Terrorism* (New York: United Nations University Press, 2012).

Atekyereza, P., 'Socio-cultural change in Uganda: Emerging perceptions on bride wealth', *Journal of Cultural Studies*, 3 (2001), 360–84.

Audoin-Rouzeau, S., *L'Enfant de l'ennemi 1914–1918* (Paris: Aubier 1995).

Aßmann, A.-L. et al., 'Stigmatisierungserfahrungen deutscher Besatzungskinder des Zweiten Weltkrieges', *Trauma und Gewalt* 9 (2015), 294–303.

Baden, A.L. et al., 'Reclaiming culture: Reculturation of transracial and international adoptees', *Journal for Counselling and Development*, 90 (2012), 387–99.

Baines, E., 'Forced marriage as a political project: Sexual rules and relations in the Lord's Resistance Army', *Journal of Peace Research*, 51 (2014), 4–17.

Baines, E. and L. Rosenoff Gauvin, 'Motherhood and social repair after war and displacement in Northern Uganda', *Journal of Refugee Studies* (2014), 282–300.

Baldwin, F.D., 'No sex please, we're American', *Warrior Scout*, 24.4.2014.

Bantebya, G.K. et al., 'Adolescent girls in the balance: Changes and continuity in social norms and practice around marriage and education in Uganda' (2014), www.odi.org/sites/odi.org.uk/files/odi-assets/publications-opinion-files/9180.pdf. (accessed 28.2.2017).

Barker, A., 'UN takes step to prevent sex abuse in East Timor', ABC PM, 2006, www.abc.net.au/pm/content/2006/s1728448.htm. (accessed 28.2.2017).

Barstow, A. (ed.), *War's Dirty Secret: Rape, Prostitution, and other Crimes Against Women* (Cleveland, OH: The Pilgrim Press, 2000).

Bartels, S. et al., 'Patterns of sexual violence in Eastern Democratic Republic of Congo: reports from survivors presenting to Panzi Hospital in 2006', *Conflict and Health*, 4: 9 (2010), 48–52.

Bartholet, E., 'International adoption: The human rights position', *Global Policy*, 1 (2010), 91–100. http://ssrn.com/abstract=1446811. (accessed 2.1.2015).

Barton, A, 'Unearthing the roots of adoption', *The Globe and Mail*, Vancouver, 31.7.2007. www.theglobeandmail.com/life/parenting/unearthing-the-roots-of-adoption/article4266097/. (accessed 14.3.2017).

Bartov, O., *The Eastern Front, 1941–1945: German Troops and the Barbarisation of Warfare* (London: Macmillan, 1985).

Bartov, O., *Hitlers Wehrmacht. Soldaten, Fanatismus und die Brutalisierung des Krieges* (Reinbek: Rohwolt Verlag, 1995).

Bass, T.A, *Vietnamerica: The War Comes Home* (New York: Soho Press Inc., 1997).

Bastick, M., K. Grimm and R. Kunz, *Sexual Violence in Armed Conflict: Global Overview and Security Implications for the Security Sector* (Geneva Centre for the Democratic Control of Armed Forces, 2007).

Bauer, I., 'The GI war bride – place holder for the absent? (De)constructing a stereotype of post-World War II Austrian History, 1945–55', *Homme: Zeitschrift für Feministische Geschichtswissenschaft*, 7 (1996), 107–21.

Bauer, I., '"Ich bin stolz, ein Besatzungskind zu sein": Zeitgeschichtliche Forschungen als Empowerment? Befunde mit Blick auf die einstige US-Zone in Österreich', in B. Stelzl-Marx and S. Satjukow (eds), *Besatzungskinder: Die Nachkommen alliierter Soldaten in Österreich und Deutschland* (Wien: Böhlau-Verlag, 2015), pp. 183–206.

Bauer, I. and R. Huber, 'Sexual encounters across (former) enemy borderlines', *Contemporary Austrian Studies*, 15 (2007), 65–101.

Baur-Timmerbrink, U., *Wir Besatzungskinder: Söhne und Töchter alliierter Soldaten erzählen* (Berlin: Chr.-Links Verlag, 2015).

Bayer, Ch.P., F. Klasen and A. Hubertus, 'Association of trauma and PTSD symptoms with openness to reconciliation and feelings of revenge among former Ugandan and Congolese child soldiers', *Journal of the American Medical Association*, 298 (2007), 555–9.

Beardsley, E.H., 'Allied against sin: American and British responses to venereal disease in World War I', *Medical History*, 20 (1976), 189–202.

Bibliography

Bećirbašić, B. and D. Secic, 'Invisible casualties of war', *Institute for War and Peace Reporting*, 2005.

Beckermann, R. *Jenseits des Krieges: Ehemalige Wehrmachtssoldaten erinnern sich* (Wien: Döcker, 1998).

Beevor, A., *The Fall of Berlin 1945* (Harmondsworth: Penguin, 2003).

Behlau, W. (ed.), *Distelblüten: Russenkinder in Deutschland* (Ganderkesee: Countour, 2015).

Behrend, H., *Alice Lakwena and the Holy Spirits: War in Northern Uganda 1985–97* (Oxford: James Currey Publishers, 1999).

Bell, B., 'Occupation children shunned in post-war German and Austria', *BBC News online*, 6.6.2015, http://bbc.co.uk/news/world-europe-32972893. (accessed 31.10.2016).

Bell, J., 'Anonyma: A woman in Berlin', *Sight and Sound*, 20 (2010), 54–5.

Benhadj, R., *Mirka* (Paris: DD Production, 2000).

Benndorf, M., *Von der Geschichte befreit: Bevrijd uit de geschiedenis* (Goch: Pagina Verlag, 2014).

Bercovitch, J. and R. Jackson, *International Conflict: A Chronological Encyclopedia of Conflicts and Their Management 1945–1955* (Washington: CQ Press, 1997).

Bessel, R. and D. Schumann (eds), *Life after Death: Approaches to a Cultural and Social History of Europe during the 1940s and 1950s* (New York: Cambridge University Press, 2003).

Besson, S., 'Das Grundrecht auf Kenntnis der eigenen Abstammung', *Zeitschrift für Schweizerisches Recht*, 1 (2005), 39–71.

Besson, S., 'The principle of non-discrimination in the Convention on the Rights of the Child', *International Journal of Children's Rights*, 13 (2005), 433–61.

Besson, S., 'Enforcing the child's right to know her origins: Contrasting approaches under the Convention on the Rights of the Child and the European Convention on Human Rights', *International Journal of Law, Policy and the Family*, 21:2 (2007), 137–59.

Betancourt, T.S. et al., 'A qualitative study of psychosocial problems of war-affected youth in Northern Uganda', *Journal of Transcultural Psychiatry*, 46 (2009), 238–56.

Betancourt, T.S. et al., 'Measuring local instrument validity and reliability: A field-based example from Northern Uganda', *Journal of Social Psychology and Psychiatric Epidemiology*, 44 (2009), 685–92.

Betancourt, T.S. et al., 'Sierra Leone's former child soldiers: A longitudinal study of risk, protective factors, and mental health', *Journal of the American Academy of Child & Adolescent Psychiatry*, 49 (2010), 606–15.

Bharath, D., 'Reunited with their rescuer; in April 1975 Betty Tisdale helped evacuate 2,919 children at Saigon orphanage', *The Orange County Register*, 23.5.2010.

Bjørnlund, M., '"A fate worse than dying": Sexual violence during the Armenian genocide', in D. Herzog (ed.), *Brutality and Desire: War and Sexuality in Europe's Twentieth Century* (Houndmills: Palgrave Macmillan, 2009), pp. 16–58.

Bland, L., 'In the name of protection: The policing of women in the First World War', in J. Brophy and S. Smart (eds), *Women-in-Law: Explorations in Law, Family, and Sexuality* (London: Routledge, 1985), pp. 23–49.

Bock, G. 'Racism and sexism in Nazi Germany: Motherhood, compulsory sterilization, and the state', *Signs*, 8 (1983), 400–21.

Bonnet, C., 'Le Viol des femmes survivantes de genocide au Rwanda', in R. Verider, E. Decaux and J.-P. Chretien (eds), *Rwanda: Un genocide du XXieme siècle* (Paris: L'Harmatten, 1995), pp. 17–29.

Borgersrud, L., *Staten of krigsbarna: En historisk undersøkelse av statsmyndighetenes behandling av krigsbarna i de første etterkrigsårene* (Oslo: University of Oslo, Department of Culture Studies, 2004).

Bos, P.R., 'Feminists interpreting the politics of wartime rape: Berlin, 1945; Yugoslavia, 1992–1993', *Journal of Women in Culture and Society*, 31 (2006), 996–1025.

Bowlby, J., *Maternal Care and Mental Health* (Geneva: WHO, 1952).

Bowlby, J., *Attachment and Loss: Vol 1. Attachment* (New York: Basic Books, 1969).

Bowlby, J., *A Secure Base: Clinical Applications of Attachment Theory* (London: Routledge, 1988).

Bracken, A., 'Haitian moms demand UN help for the babies their peacekeepers left behind', *Public Radio International*, 29.8.2014, http://pri.org/stories/2014-08-28/un-peacekeepers-destabilize-haiti-babies-they-left-behind. (accessed 31.10.2016).

Bradby, H. and G. Lewando-Hundt (eds), *Global Perspectives on War, Gender and Health: The Sociology and Anthropology of Suffering* (Farnham: Ashgate, 2010).

Bramley, E., 'Naming Practices in the Lango Region of Northern Uganda and their Impact on the Integration of Children Born of the Conflict with the Lord's Resistance Army' (Undergraduate dissertation, March 2014, University of Birmingham).

Branch, A., *Displacing Human Rights: War and Intervention in Northern Uganda* (Oxford: Oxford University Press, 2011).

Breitinger, E. (ed.), *Uganda: The Cultural Landscape* (Kampala: Fountain Publishers, 2000).

Brockopp, J.E. (ed.), *Islamic Ethics of Life: Abortion, War, and Euthanasia* (Columbia, SC: University of South Carolina Press 2003).

Brownmiller, S., *Against our Will: Men, Women, Rape* (New York: Simon and Schuster, 1975).

Bryant, T., *Himmlers Kinder: Zur Geschichte der SS-Organisation "Lebensborn e.v." 1935–1945* (Wiesbaden: Marix-Verlag 2011).

Buisson, P., *1940–1945: Années érotiques: Vichy ou les infortunes de la vertu* (Paris: Albin Michel, 2008).

Bunster-Burotto, X., 'Surviving beyond fear: Women and torture in Latin America', in J. Nash and H. Safe (eds), *Women and Change in Latin America* (South Hardley: Bergin & Garvey, 1986), pp. 297–325.

Bunting, A., 'Forced marriage in conflict situations: Researching and prosecuting old harms and new crimes', *Canadian Journal of Human Rights*, 1 (2012), 165–85.

Burds, J., 'Sexual violence in Europe in World War II, 1939–1945', *Politics and Society*, 37 (2009), 35–73.

Burke, J.W., *The Big Rape* (New York: Popular Library, 1953).

Burke, R., 'Shaming the state: Sexual offences by UN military peacekeepers and the rhetoric of zero tolerance', in Gina Heathcote and Dianne Otto (eds), *Rethinking Peacekeeping, Gender Equality and Collective Security* (Basingstoke: Palgrave Macmillan, 2014), pp. 70–95.

Burnett, J.E., 'Situating sexual violence in Rwanda (1990–2001): Sexual agency, sexual consent and the political economy of war', *African Studies Review*, 55:2 (2012), 97–118.

Buske, S., *Fräulein Mutter und ihr Bastard: Eine Geschichte der Unehelichkeit in Deutschland 1900–1970* (Göttingen: Wallstein, 2004).

Buss, D.E., 'Knowing women: Translating patriarchy in international criminal law', *Social and Legal Studies*, 23 (2014), 73–92.

Campbell, G. and E. Elbourne, *Sex, Slavery and Power* (Athens, OH: Ohio University Press, 2014).

Carpenter, R. Ch. 'Surfacing children: Limitations of genocidal rape discourse', *Human Rights Quarterly*, 22 (2000), 428–77.

Carpenter, R. Ch. (ed.), *Born of War: Protecting Children of Sexual Violence Survivors in Conflict Zones* (Bloomfield, CT: Kumarian Press, 2007).

Carpenter, R. Ch., *Forgetting Children Born of War: Setting the Human Rights Agenda in Bosnia and Beyond* (New York: Columbia University Press, 2010).

Carrier, N.H. and J.R. Jeffrey (eds), *External Migration: A Study of the Available Statistics, 1815–1950* (London: HMSO, 1953).

Cassidy, C., *Gaba Road* (Rothersthorpe: Paragon Publishing, 2012).

Chambers, J., *The Oxford Companion to American Military History* (Oxford: Oxford University Press, 2000).

Chang, E.N., 'Engagement abroad: Enlisted men, US military policy and the sex industry', *Notre Dame Journal of Law, Ethics & Public Policy*, 15 (2001), 621–53.

Chang, I. *The Rape of Nanking: The Forgotten Holocaust of World War II* (New York: Basic Books, 1996).

Children's Aid Society (ed.), *The Children's Aid Society of New York: Its History, Plan and Results / Compiled from the Writings and Reports of Charles Loring Brace, and from the Records of the Secretary's Office* (New York: Children's Aid Society, 1893).

Chludzinski, K., 'The fear of colonial miscegenation on the British colonies of South East Asia', *The Forum, Cal Poly's Journal of History*, 1 (2009), 54–64.

Choi, C. (ed.), 'The comfort women: Colonialism, war, and sex', *Special Issue of East Asia Culture Critique*, 5:1 (1997).

Chung, C.S., 'Korean women drafted for military sexual slavery by Japan', in H. Keith (ed.), *The Stories of the Korean Comfort Women* (New York: Cassell, 1995), pp. 11–30.

Chung, H.-K., 'Your comfort versus my death: Korean comfort women', in A. Barstow (ed.), *War's Dirty Secret: Rape, Prostitution, and other Crimes Against Women* (Cleveland, OH: The Pilgrim Press, 2000), pp. 13–25.

Clark, J.N., 'A crime of identity: Rape and its neglected victims', *Journal of Human Rights*, 13 (2014), 146–69.

Clark, P., *The Gacaca Courts, Post-Genocide Justice and Reconciliation in Rwanda: Justice without Lawyers* (Cambridge: Cambridge University Press, 2010).

Clifford, C., 'Rape as a Weapon of War and its [sic] Long-Term Effects on Victims and Society', paper presented at 7th Global Conference Violence and the Contexts of Hostility, Budapest May 2008.

Clinton, C., *Public Women and the Confederacy* (Milwaukee: Marquette University Press, 1999).

Cockburn, P., 'US finally ends trade embargo', *The Independent*, 4.2.1994.

Cohen, D.K., 'Explaining rape during civil war: Cross-national evidence (1980–2009)', *American Political Science Review*, 107 (2013), 461–77.

Cohen, D.K. and R. Nordås, 'Sexual violence in armed conflict: Introducing the SVAC dataset, 1989–2009', *Journal of Peace Research*, 51 (2014), 418–28.

Cohen, H., *Equal Rights for Children* (Totowa NJ: Rowman & Littlefield, 1980).
Copelon, R., 'Surfacing gender: Reconceptualizing crimes against women in time of war', in A. Stiglmayer (ed.), *Mass Rape: The Way against Women in Bosnia-Herzegovina* (Lincoln: University of Nebraska Press, 1994), pp. 197–218.
Coulter, D.J., 'Montessori and Steiner: A pattern of reverse symmetries', *Montessori Life* 15 (2003), 24–5.
Cramer, C. and P. Richards, 'Violence and war in agrarian perspective', *Journal of Agrarian Change*, 11 (2011), 277–97.
Crews, D. and A.C. Gore, 'Transgenerational epigenetics: Current controversies and debates' (2014), http://utexas.edu/research/crewslab/pdfs/Crews_Gore_Chapter_Final.pdf. (accessed 31.10.2016).
Crossland, D., 'Lebensborn children break their silence: Nazi Program to breed master race', *SpiegelOnlineInternational*, 7.11.2006, www.spiegel.de/international/nazi-program-to-breed-master-race-lebensborn-children-break-silence-a-446978.html. (accessed 31.10.2016).
Culbert, D., '"It started with a kiss": German–Allied love affairs after 1945', *History Today*, 56 (2006), 2–3.
Cunningham, H., *Children and Childhood in Western Society Since 1500* (London: Longman, 1995).
Curley, R.T., *Elders, Shades, and Women: Ceremonial Change in Lango, Uganda* (Berkeley: University of California Press, 1973).
Damme, C., 'Infanticide: The worth of an infant under the law', *Medical History*, 22 (1978), 1–24.
Danico, M.Y. (ed.), *Asian American Society: An Encyclopedia* (Los Angeles-London-New Dehli: Sage, 2014).
Danielle, Y. (ed.), *International Handbook of Multigenerational Legacies of Trauma* (Berlin: Springer, 2010).
Daniel-Wrabetz, J., 'Children born of war rape in Bosnia-Herzegovina and the Convention on the Rights of the Child', in R. Ch. Carpenter (ed.), *Born of War: Protecting Children of Sexual Violence Survivors in Conflict Zones* (Bloomfield, CT: Kumarian Press, 2007), pp. 21–39.
Davenport, O, 'US race prejudice dooms 1000 British babies', *Reynolds News*, 9 Feb. 1947.
De Bonis, S., *Children of the Enemy: Oral Histories of Vietnamese Amerasians and their Mothers* (Jefferson: McFarland & Co, 1994).
De Brouwer, A.-M.L.M., *Supranational Criminal Prosecution of Sexual Violence: The ICC and the Practice of the ICTY and the ICT* (Cambridge: Intersentia, 2005).
De Brouwer, A.-M. et al. (eds), *The Men Who Killed Me: Rwandan Survivors of Sexual Violence* (Quebec: Douglas & McIntyre, 2012).
De Jong, L., *Het Koninkrijk der Nederlanden in de Tweede Wereldoorlog*, vol. 5, part 1 (The Hague: Martinus Nijoff, 1972).
De Temmerman, E., *Aboke Girls: Children Abducted in Northern Uganda* (Kampala: Fountain Publishers, 2001).
De Wit, T., 'Sexual Violence in the Democratic Republic of Congo' (Bachelor thesis, Utrecht University, 2012).
Defeis, E.F., 'UN peacekeepers and sexual abuse and exploitation: An end to impunity', *Washington. University Global Studies Law Review*, 7 (2008), 185.

Bibliography

Dekel, R., and H. Goldblatt, 'Is there intergenerational transmission of trauma? The case of combat veterans' children', *American Journal of Orthopsychiatry*, 78 (2008), 281–329.

Delić, A., 'Kvalitet Života i Dugoročne Psihičke Posljedice u Žena sa Iskustvom Ratnog Silovanja' (Master's thesis, Tuzla University, 2015).

Delva J.G., 'UN Haiti peacekeepers face outcry over alleged rape', *Reuters*, US edition, 5.9.2011.

DeMonaco, M.K., 'Disorderly departure: An analysis of the United States policy toward Amerasian immigration', *Brooklyn Journal of International Law*, 15 (1989), 641–710.

Denéchère, Y., 'Des adoptions d'État: Les enfants de l'occupation française en Allemagne, 1945–1952', *Revue d'histoire modern & contemporaine*, 2 (2010), 159–79.

Denholm, E., 'Uganda: Former child soldiers excluded in adulthood', *Amnesty International News*, 14.10.2005, www.amnesty.org/en/news-and-updates/feature-stories/uganda-former-child-soldiers-excluded-adulthood-20051014. (accessed 16.12.2014).

Denov, M., *Child Soldiers: Sierra Leone's Revolutionary United Front* (Cambridge: Cambridge University Press, 2010).

Deschamps, M., H.B. Jallow and Y. Sooka, 'Taking action on sexual exploitation and abuse by un peacekeepers. Report of an independent review of sexual exploitation and abuse by international peacekeeping forces in the Central African Republic', http://un.org/News/dh/infocus/centafricrepub/Independent-Review-Report.pdf. (accessed 31.10.2016).

Detrick, S., *A Commentary on the United Nations Convention on the Rights of the Child* (The Hague: Martinus Nijhoff Publishers, 1999).

DeVries, M.W., 'Temperament and infant mortality among the Masai of East Africa', *The American Journal of Psychiatry*, 141 (1984), 1189–94.

Diederichs, M., 'Stigma and silence: Dutch women, German soldiers and their children', in K. Ericsson and E. Simonsen (eds), *Children of World War II: The Hidden Enemy Legacy* (Oxford: Berg, 2005), 151–66.

Diederichs, M., *Wie geschoren wordt moet stil zitten: De omgang von Nederlandse meisjes met Duitse militairen* (Den Haag: Boom, 2006).

Diederichs, M., '"Moffenkinder": Kinder der Besatzung in den Niederlanden', *Historical Social Research*, 34 (2009), 304–20.

Diederichs, M., *Kinderen van Duitse militairen in Nederland 1941–46: Een verborgen leven* (Soesterberg: Uitjeverij Aspekt, 2012).

Dolan, C., *Social Torture: The Case of Northern Uganda, 1986–2006* (New York: Berghahn, 2011).

Doná, G., 'Being young and of mixed ethnicity', *Forced Migration Review*, 40 (2012), 16–17.

Don-wan, K. (director), *63 Years On* (2008), http://imdb.com/title/tt1619828/combined.

Dorn, W. and D.J.H. Bell, 'Intelligence and peacekeeping: The UN operation in the Congo, 1960–1964', *International Peacekeeping*, 2 (1995), 11–33.

Doss, C. et al., 'Women, Marriage and Asset Inheritance in Uganda', Working Paper 184, April 2011, Department of Economics, Yale University, http://chronicpoverty.org/publications/details/women-marriage-and-asset-inheritance-in-uganda. (accessed 31.10.2016).

Doyle, A.M. et al., 'The sexual behaviour of adolescents in sub-Saharan Africa: Patterns and trends from national surveys', *Tropical Medicine and International Health*, 17 (2011), 796–807.
Drabble, M., 'A beastly century', *American Scholar*, 70:1 (2001), 160.
Drakulić, S.S., 'Women hide behind a wall of silence', *The Nation*, 13 (1993).
Drixler, F., *Mabiki: Infanticide and Population Growth in Eastern Japan, 1660–1950* (Berkeley: University of California Press, 2013).
Drolshagen, E.D., *Wehrmachtskinder: Auf der Suche nach dem nie gekannten Vater* (Munich: Droemer Verlag, 2005).
Du Long, P., *The Dream Shattered: Vietnamese Gangs in America* (Richmond: Northeastern University Press, 1997).
Dunn, K.C., 'The Lord's Resistance Army', *Review of African Political Economy*, 31 (2004), 139–42.
Dunson, D.H., *Child, Victim, Soldier: The Loss of Innocence in Uganda* (Michigan: Orbis Books, 2008).
Dupuis, E., *Befreiungskind* (Wien: Edition Liaunigg, 2015).
Durbach, A. and L. Chappell, 'Leaving behind the age of impunity: Victims of gender violence and the promise of reparations', *International Feminist Journal of Politics*, 16 (2014), 3–62.
Eck, H., 'Die Französinnen unter dem Vichy Regime: Frauen in der Katastrophe?' in G. Duby and M. Perot (eds), *Geschichte der Frauen*, vol. 5 (Frankfurt: Fischer, 1997), pp. 223–55.
Edmonds, A.O., *The War in Vietnam* (London: Greenwood, 1998).
Edwards, W., *Comfort Women: A History of Japanese Forced Prostitution During the Second World War* (CreateSpace Independent Publishers, 2013).
Eichstaedt, P., *First You Kill Your Family: Child Soldiers of Uganda and the Lord's Resistance Army* (London: Lawrence Hill Books, 2009).
Ellam, D., 'Our escape from Saigon', *The Sunday Mirror*, 28.3.2010, 36–7.
Ellingsen, D., *En registerbasert undersökelse*, Statistics Norway, Rapport Nr. 2004/19, 2004.
Emerson, G., *Winners and Losers: Battles, Retreats, Gains, Losses, and Ruins from the Vietnam War* (New York: W.W. Norton & Company, 1985).
Engelen, B., 'Warum heiratete man einen Soldaten? Soldatenfrauen in der ländlichen Gesellschaft Brandenburg-Preußens im 18. Jahrhundert', in S. Kroll and K. Krüger (eds), *Militär und ländliche Gesellschaft in der frühen Neuzeit* (Münster: Lit-Verlag, 2000), pp. 251–73.
Engle, K., 'The grip of sexual violence: Reading UN Security Council Resolution on Human Security', in G. Heathcote and D. Otto (eds), *Rethinking Peacekeeping, Gender Equality and Collective Security* (Basingstoke: Palgrave, 2014), pp. 23–47.
Ericsson, K. and E. Simonsen, *Krigsbarn i fredstids* (Oslo: Universitetsforlaget, 2005).
Ericsson, K. and E. Simonsen (eds), *Children of World War II: The Hidden Enemy Legacy* (Oxford: Berg, 2005).
Eriksson, M., P. Wallensteen and M. Sollenberg, 'Armed conflict, 1989–2002', *Journal of Peace Research*, 40 (2003), 593–607.
Erjavec, K. and Z. Volčić, 'Living with the sins of their fathers: An analysis of self-representation of adolescents born of war rape', *Journal of Adolescent Studies*, 25 (2010), 359–86.

Bibliography

Espirutu, Y.L., 'Possibilities of a multiracial Asian America', in T. Williams-León and C.L. Nakashima (eds), *The Sum of Our Parts: Mixed-Heritage Asian Americans* (Philadelphia: Temple University Press, 2001), pp. 25–33.

Evans, R., *In Defence of History* (London: Granta Books, 1997).

Eyferth, K., 'Eine Untersuchung der Neger-Mischlingskinder in Westdeutschland', *Vita Humana*, 2 (1959), 102–14.

Eyferth, K., U. Brandt and W. Hawel, *Farbige Kinder in Deutschland: Die Situation der Mischlingskinder und die Aufgabe ihrer Eingliederung* (Munich: Juventa, 1960).

Ezrow, N.M. and E. Frantz, *Dictators and Dictatorships: Understanding Authoritarian Regimes and Their Leaders* (New York: Continuum, 2011).

Farwell, N., 'War rape: New conceptualizations and responses', *Affilia*, 19 (2004), 389–403.

Feeney, M., 'Life after hell, in Rwanda: Seeing victims and children of rape', *The Boston Globe*, 3 September 2011.

Fehrenbach, H., *Race After Hitler* (Princeton: Princeton University Press, 2005).

Feigelman, W. and A.R. Silverman, 'The long-term effects of transracial adoption', *Social Services Review*, 8 (1984), 588–602.

Ferstman, C., 'Criminalizing sexual exploitation and abuse by peacekeepers', United States Institute of Peace, Special Report 335 (Washington, 2013).

Finnström, S., *Living with Bad Surroundings: War, History, and Everyday Moments in Northern Uganda* (Durham, NC: Duke University Press, 2008).

Firpo, C., 'Crises of whiteness and empire in Colonial Indochina: The removal of abandoned Eurasian children from the Vietnamese milieu, 1890–1956', *Journal of Social History*, 43 (2010), 587–613.

Fischer, E., *Die USA im Vietnamkrieg: Kriegsverbrechen amerikanischer Soldaten* (Hamburg: Diplomica Verlag, 2009).

Fischer, S., 'Occupation of the womb: Forced impregnation as genocide', *Duke Law Journal*, 46 (1996), 91–134.

Fishman, S., *We Will Wait: Wives of French Prisoners of War, 1940–1945* (New Haven: Yale University Press, 1992).

Fortin, J., *Children's Rights and Developing Law* (London: Butterworth, 2003).

Fox, L.K. (ed.), *East African Childhood* (Nairobi: Oxford University Press, 1967).

Fraiberg, S., E. Adelson and V. Shapiro, 'Ghosts in the nursery: A psychoanalytic approach to the problems of impaired infant-mother relationships', *Journal of the American Academy of Child & Adolescent Psychiatry*, 14 (1975), 387–421.

Frankenstein, L., *Soldatenkinder: Die unehelichen Kinder ausländischer Soldaten mit besonderer Berücksichtigung der Mischlinge* (Munich: Wilhelm Steinbach, 1954).

Freeman, M., *The Rights and Wrongs of Children* (London: F. Pinter, 1983).

Freeman, M.D.A., *The Moral Status of Children: Essays on the Rights of the Child* (The Hague: Martinus Nijhoff Publishers, 1997).

Freundlich, M. and J.K. Lieberthal, 'The gathering of the first generation of adult Korean adoptees', *Perceptions of International Adoption* (Evan B. Donaldson Adoption Institute, 2002).

Funcke, D., 'Der unsichtbare Dritte: Ein Beitrag zur psychohistorischen Dimension der Identitätsfindung am Beispiel der Spendersamenkinder', *Zeitschrift Psychotherapie & Sozialwissenschaft*, 11 (2009), 61–98.

Gaines, J., 'Orphans ... survivors ... successes', *The Boston Globe*, 19.2.1995.

Gaines, J., '2 decades after the U.S. carried out "Babylift" in South Vietnam, you should see them now', *St. Louis Post Dispatch*, 26.2.1995.

Gard, T.L. et al., 'The impact of HIV status, HIV disease progression, and post-traumatic stress symptoms on the health-related quality of life of Rwandan women genocide survivors', *Quality of Life Research*, 22 (2013), 2073–84.

Gardiner, J., *Over Here: The GIs in Wartime Britain* (London: Collins and Brown, 1992).

Garraio, J., 'Verschweigen, feministische Begeisterung, deutscher Opferdiskurs und romantische Trivialisierung: Die vielen Leben des Tagebuches Eine Frau in Berlin', paper presented at Em Trânsito – Übergänge. Grenzen überschreiten in der Germanistik, Faculdade de Letras da Universidade de Coimbra, 28–29 October 2011.

Gebhardt, M., *Als die Soldaten kamen* (Munich: Deutscher Taschenbuch Verlag, 2015).

Gedda, G., 'US to seek release of thousands of Viet Cong prisoners to resettle here', *Schenectady Gazette*, 12.9.1984, 10.

Gelfand, V., *Das Deutschland-Tagebuch 1945–1946* (Berlin: Aufbau-Verlag, 2005).

Gerlach, C., *Kalkulierte Morde: die Deutsche Wirtschafts- und Vernichtungspolitik in Weißrussland 1941 bis 1944* (Hamburg: Hamburger Edition, 1999).

Gertjejanssen, W.J., 'Victims, Heroes, Survivors: Sexual Violence on the Eastern Front During World War II' (Ph.D. thesis, University of Minnesota, 2004).

Ghiglieri, M.P., *The Dark Side of Man: Tracing the Origins of Male Violence* (Cambridge, MA: Perseus Books, 2000).

Gibbons, J.L. and K.S. Robati, *Intercountry Adoption: Policies, Practices, and Outcomes* (London: Ashgate, 2012).

Gingerich, T. and J. Leaning, *The Use of Rape as a Weapon of War in the Conflict in Darfur, Sudan* (Boston, MA: Program on Humanitarian Crises and Human Rights, François-Xavier Bagnoud Center for Health and Human Rights, Harvard School of Public Health, and Physicians for Human Rights, 2005).

Girling, F.K., *The Acholi of Uganda* (London: Her Majesty's Stationery Office, 1960).

Glaesmer, H., 'Traumatische Erfahrungen in der älteren deutschen Bevölkerung', *Zeitschrift für Gerontologie und Geriatrie*, 47:3 (2014), 194–201.

Glaesmer, H. et al., 'Die Kinder des Zweiten Weltkrieges in Deutschland: Ein Rahmenmodell für psychosoziale Forschung', *Trauma und Gewalt*, 6 (2012), 318–28.

Gluckman, M. (ed.), *Ideas and Procedures in African Customary Law* (Oxford: Oxford University Press, 1969).

Goedde, P., *GIs and Germans: Culture, Gender and Foreign Relations, 1945–1949* (New Haven: Yale University Press, 2003).

Goldstein, A.T., *Recognizing Forced Impregnation as a War Crime under International Law* (New York: Center for Reproductive Law and Policy, 1993).

Goldstein, J., *War and Gender: How Gender Shapes the War System and Vice Versa* (Cambridge: Cambridge University Press 2001).

Goodhart, M., 'Sins of the fathers: War rape, wrongful procreation, and children's human rights', *Journal of Human Rights*, 6 (2007), 307–24.

Gottschall, J., 'Explaining wartime rape', *The Journal of Sex Research*, 41 (2004), 129–36.

Grant, L., 'Anyone here been raped and speak English?', *The Guardian*, 8.8.1993, p. 10.

Bibliography

Grbavica, 2006, http://imdb.com/title/tt0464029/. (accessed 31.10.2016).
Greene, G., *The Quiet American* (London: Vintage, 1955).
Greer, G., 'Rape, the oldest and the newest war crime', International Planned Parenthood Federation, 20.6.2008, www.ippf.org/NR/exeres/AD977915-0C90-4BFB-90EE-27D4DEBC704B.htm. (accessed 17.8 2014).
Grieg, K., 'The war children of the world', *War and Children Identity Project* (Bergen: War and Children Identity Project, 2001).
Gries, R., 'Les enfants d'État: Französische Besatzungskinder in Deutschland', in B. Stelzl-Marx and S. Satjukow (eds), *Besatzungskinder. Die Nachkommen alliierter Soldaten in Österreich und Deutschland* (Wien: Böhlau-Verlag, 2015), pp. 380–407.
Grossmann, A., 'Eine Frage des Schweigens: Die Vergewaltigung deutscher Frauen durch Besatzungssoldaten. Zum historischen Hintergrund von Helke Sanders Film BeFreier und Befreite', *Frauen und Film*, 54/55 (April 1994), 15–28.
Grossmann, A., 'A question of silence: The rape of German women by cccupation soldiers', *October*, 72 (1995), 42–63.
Guibilini, A. and F. Minerva, 'After-birth abortion: Why should the baby live?' *Journal of Medical Ethics* 39 (2013) 261–3.
Gullace, N.F., 'Sexual violence and family honor: British propaganda and international law during the First World War', *The American Historical Review*, 102 (1997), 714–47.
Gulzow, M. and C. Mitchell, '"Vagina dentata" and "incurable venereal disease" legends from the Viet Nam War', *Western Folklore*, 39 (1980), 306–16.
Gupta, O.D., 'Unerwünschte Kinder des Feindes', *Süddeutsche Zeitung*, 9.2.2015, http://sueddeutsche.de/politik/besatzungskinder-nach-zweitem-weltkrieg-unerwuenschte-kinder-des-feindes-1.2342768. (accessed 31.10.2016).
Gutman, R., *A Witness to Genocide* (New York: Macmillan, 1993).
Hagemann, K. and R. Pröve, *Landsknechte, Soldatenfrauen und Nationalkrieger: Militär, Krieg und Geschlechterordnung im historischen Wandel* (Frankfurt / New York: Campus Verlag, 1998).
Hallin, D.C., *The Uncensored War: The Media and Vietnam* (Berkeley: University of California Press, 1989).
Hamilton, H., *Children of the Occupation: Japan's Untold Story* (New Brunswick: Rutgers University Press, 2012).
Hamilton, H.B., 'Rwanda's women: The key to reconstruction', *The Journal of Humanitarian Assistance* (January 2000), 2–3.
Hamilton, W., *Children of the Occupation, Japan's Untold Story* (New Brunswick: Rutgers University Press, 2013).
Hancock, W.K. and M.M. Gowing, *British War Economy* (London: HMSO, 1949).
Harding, L., 'Row over naming of rape author', *The Guardian*, 4.10.2003, www.theguardian.com/world/2003/oct/05/historybooks.germany. (accessed 2.2.2015).
Harlacher, T., 'Traditional Ways of Coping with Consequences of Traumatic Stress in Acholi and Northern Ugandan Ethnography from a Western Psychological Perspective' (Ph.D. thesis, University of Freiburg, 2009).
Harris, R., 'The "child of the barbarian": Rape, race and nationalism in France during the First World War', *Past and Present*, 141 (1993), 170–206.
Harrison, M., 'The British army and the problem of venereal disease in France and Egypt during the First World War', *Medical History*, 39 (1995), 133–58.

Harrison, M., 'Sex and citizen soldier: Health, morals and discipline in the British army during the Second World War', *Clio Medica/The Wellcome Series in the History of Medicine*, 55 (1999), 225–49.

Harris-Rimmer, S., '"Orphans" or veterans? Justice for children born of war in East Timor', *Texas International Law Journal*, 42 (2007), 223–344.

Harris-Short, S., 'International human rights law: Imperialist, inept, and ineffective? Cultural relativism and the UN Convention on the Rights of the Child', *Human Rights Quarterly*, 25 (2003), 130–81.

Hayslip, L.L., *When Heaven and Earth Changed Places* (London: Penguin, 2003).

Heathcote, G. and D. Otto (eds), *Rethinking Peacekeeping, Gender Equality and Collective Security* (Basingstoke: Palgrave, 2014).

Heiber, H. (ed.), *Reichsführer!... Briefe an und von Himmler* (Stuttgart: Deutsche Verlagsanstalt, 1968).

Heidenreich, G., *Das endlose Jahr: Die langsame Entdeckung der eigenen Biographie – ein Lebensbornschicksal* (Frankfurt: Fischer-Verlag, 2002).

Heinemann, E., 'The hour of the woman', in H. Schissler (ed.), *The Miracle Years: A Cultural History of West Germany 1945–1948* (Princeton: Princeton University Press, 2001), pp. 21–56.

Heinemann, I., 'Rasse, Siedlung, deutsches Blut': Das Rasse- und Siedlungshauptamt der SS und die rassenpolitische Neuordnung Europas* (Göttingen: Wallstein Verlag, 2003).

Helgeson, V.S., K.A. Reynolds and P.L. Tomich, 'A meta-analytic review of benefit finding and growth', *Journal of Consulting and Clinical Psychology*, 7 (2006), 797–816.

Hellmann, J., *American Myth and the Legacy of Vietnam* (New York: Columbia University Press, 1986).

Henke, K.D., *Die amerikanische Besatzung Deutschlands* (Munich: Oldenbourg, 1995).

Henry, M., 'Sexual exploitation and abuse in UN peacekeeping missions: Problematising current responses', in S. Madhok, A. Phillips and K. Wilson (eds), *Gender, Agency and Coercion* (Basingstoke: Palgrave Macmillan, 2013), pp. 122–42.

Heywood, C., *A History of Childhood: Children and Childhood in the West from Medieval to Modern Times* (Cambridge: Polity, 2001).

Higate, P., 'Gender and peacekeeping case studies: The DRC and Sierra Leone', 2004, Institute for Security Studies, www.africaportal.org/dspace/articles/gender-and-peacekeeping-case-studies-drc-and-sierra-leone. (accessed 15.3.2017).

Higate, P., 'Peacekeepers, masculinities and sexual exploitations', *Men and Masculinities*, 10 (2007), 99–119.

Higate, P. and M. Henry, 'Engendering (in)security in peace support operations', *Security Dialogue*, 35 (2004), 481–98.

Hintjens, H.M., 'Explaining the 1994 genocide in Rwanda', *The Journal of Modern African Studies*, 37 (1999), 241–86.

Hirschfeld, M., *The Sexual History of the World War* (New York: The Panurge Press, 1934).

Hodes, M. (ed.), *Sex, Love, Race: Crossing Boundaries in North American History* (New York: New York University Press, 1999).

Hodgkin, R. and P. Newell, *The Implementation Handbook for the Convention on the Rights of the Child* (New York: UNICEF, 2002).

Hodgson, D., 'The international legal protection to the child's right to a legal identity and statelessness', *International Journal of Law Policy and the Family*, 7 (1993), 255–70.

Hoffmann, G., *NS-Propaganda in den Niederlanden: Organisation und Lenkung der Publizistik unter deutscher Besatzung 1940–1945* (München: Verlag Dokumentation, 1972).
Holt, K. and S. Hughes, 'UN staff accused of raping children in Sudan', *Daily Telegraph*, 2.1.2007, www.telegraph.co.uk/news/worldnews/1538396/UN-staff-accused-of-raping-children-in-Sudan.html. (accessed 31.10.2016).
Holt, M.I., *The Orphan Trains: Placing Out in America* (Lincoln and London: University of Nebraska Press, 1992).
Horne, J., 'Corps, lieux et nation: La France et l'invasion de 1914', *Annales*, 55 (2000), 73–109.
Howard, T., 'The idle GI and liberated France are mighty tired of each other', *Newsweek*, 19.11.1945, 56–7.
Hügel-Marschall, I., *Daheim Unterwegs: Ein deutsches Leben* (Frankfurt: Fischer, 2001); English translation *Invisible Women: Growing up Black in Germany* (New York: Peter Lang Publishing, 2008).
Hughes, S., 'Wartime Rape Survivors Losing Hope of Justice', *BBC News Europe*, 1.4.2014.
Human Rights Watch, *Sexual Violence and its Consequences Among Displaced Persons in Darfur and Chad* (New York: Human Rights Watch, 2004).
Husić, S., 'The legacy of wartime rape in Bosnia', *Infosud: Human Rights Tribune*, 25.2.2008.
Huth-Bocks, A.C., A.A. Levendosky and G.A. Bogat, 'The effects of domestic violence during pregnancy on maternal and infant health', *Violence and Victims*, 17 (2002), 169–85.
Huth-Bocks, A.C. et al., 'The impact of maternal characteristics and contextual variables on infant–mother attachment', *Child Development*, 75 (2004), 480–96.
Imber, M., 'The First World War, sex education, and the American Social Hygiene Association's Campaign against venereal disease', *Journal of Educational Administration and History*, 16 (1984), 47–56.
Irsigler, F. and A. Lassotta, *Bettler und Gaukler, Dirnen und Henker. Außenseiter in einer mittelalterlichen Stadt: Koln 1300–1600* (Munich: Deutscher Taschenbuch Verlag, 1989).
Jaleel, R., 'Weapons of sex, weapons of war: Feminism, ethnic conflict and sexual violence in public international law during the 1990s', *Cultural Studies*, 27 (2013), 115–35.
Jansson, K. 'Soldaten und Vergewaltigung im Schweden des 17. Jahrhunderts', in B. Krusenstjern and H. Medick (eds), *Zwischen Alltag und Katastrophe: Der Dreißigjährige Krieg aus der Nähe* (Göttingen: Vandenhock & Ruprecht, 1999), pp. 195–225.
Janus, L., *The Enduring Effects of Prenatal Experience* (London: Jason Aronson Inc. Publishers 1977).
Jarratt, M., *War Brides: The Stories of the Women Who Left Everything Behind to Follow the Men They Loved* (Stroud: The History Press, 2007).
Jeffery, K., '"Hut Ab", " Promenade with Kamerade for Schokolade" and the Flying Dutchman: British soldiers in the Rhineland, 1918–1929', *Diplomacy and Statecraft*, 16 (2006), 455–73.
Jenkins, B.M., *Building an Army of Believers* (Santa Monika: RAND, 2007).
Jennings, K.M., 'Service, sex and security: Gendered peacekeeping economies in Liberia and the Democratic Republic of the Congo', *Security Dialogue* (2014), 1–18.

Johnson, D., 'Red Army troops raped even Russian women as they freed then from camps', *The Telegraph*, online edition www.telegraph.co.uk, 24.1.2002, www.telegraph.co.uk/news/worldnews/europe/russia/1382565/Red-Army-troops-raped-even-Russian-women-as-they-freed-them-from-camps.html. (accessed 16.7.2015).

Jones, O., 'Sex, culture, and the biology of rape: Toward explanation and prevention', *California Law Review*, 87 (1999), 821–941.

Juffer, F. and M.H. Van IJzendoorn, 'A longitudinal study of Korean adoptees in the Netherlands: Infancy to middle childhood', in K.J.S. Bergquist et al. (eds), *International Korean adoption: A Fifty-Year History of Policy and Practice* (Binghampton, NY: Haworth Press, 2007), pp. 263–76.

Juffer, F. and M.H. Van IJzendoorn, 'Adoptees do not lack self-esteem: A meta analysis of studies of self esteem of transracial, international and domestic adoptees', *Psychological Bulletin*, 133 (2007), 1067–83.

Kabanda, M., 'Kangura: The triumph of propaganda refined', in A. Thompson (ed.), *The Media and the Rwanda Genocide* (London: Pluto Press, 2007), pp. 62–72.

Kaime, T., 'The Convention on the Rights of the Child and the cultural legitimacy of children's rights in Africa: Some reflections', *African Human Rights Journal*, 5 (2005), 221–38.

Kaiser, D.E, *American Tragedy: Kennedy, Johnson, and the origins of the Vietnam War* (Cambridge: Belknap Press, 2000).

Kaiser, H., *WWII Voices: American GIs and the French Women Who Married Them* (CreateSpace Independent Publishing Platform, 2012).

Kaiser, M. et al. 'Depression, somatization and posttraumatic stress in children born of occupation after World War II in comparison with a general population sample', *The Journal of Nervous and Mental Disease*, 203:10 (2015), 1–7.

Kameri-Mbote, P., 'Gender issues in land tenure under customary law', United Nations Development Programme–International Land Coalition Workshop: Land rights for African development: from knowledge to action. Nairobi, 31.10.2005 to 3.11.2005 (2005).

Kanetake, M., 'The UN zero tolerance policy's whereabouts: On the discordance between politics and law on the internal-external divide', *AmsterdamLawForum*, 4:4 (2012), 51–61.

Kaps, J., *Martyrium und Heldentum ostdeutscher Frauen* (self-published, 1954).

Kapstein, E.B., 'The baby trade', *Foreign Affairs*, 82:6 (2003), 115–25.

Karnow, S., *Vietnam: A History* (New York: Viking Press, 1983).

Karovic, B., 'One Bosnian man's search for his father, the rapist', *Newsweek*, 16.3.2015, http://newsweek.com/2015/03/20/one-bosnian-mans-search-his-father-rapist-313985.html. (accessed 31.10.2016).

Kasozi, A., *Social Origins of Violence in Uganda, 1964–1985* (Montreal / Quebec: McGill-Queen's Press, 1994).

Kater, M.H., *Hitler Youth* (Cambridge, MA: Harvard University Press, 2004).

Ketwig, J., *... and a Hard Rain Fell: A GI's True Story of the War in Vietnam* (New York: Macmillan, 2008).

Kiconco, A., 'Understanding Former "Girl Soldiers": Central Themes in the Lives of Formerly Abducted Girls in post-Conflict Northern Uganda (Ph.D. dissertation, University of Birmingham, 2015).

Kiconco, A. and E.O. Apio, 'Psychosocial Consequences of Being a Child of a Child

Soldier: Issues of (Re)Integration in Northern Uganda Post Conflict Society' (Unpublished paper, Conference 'Child and War: Past and Present', University of Salzburg, 2013).

Kidder, A., 'A Disappearing Boundary? The Changing Distinction Between Combatant and Civilians from the First World War to the Present Day' (Honors thesis, Colby College, 2010).

Kidder, T., *My Detachment: A Memoir* (London: Random House Digital, Inc., 2006).

Kim, D.S., 'Intercountry Adoptions: A Study of Self-Concept of Adolescent Korean Children Who Were Adopted by American Families' (Ph.D. thesis, University of Chicago, 1976).

Kim, E.H. and E.-Y. Yu (eds), *East to America: Korean American Life Stories* (New York: The New York Press, 1996).

Kim, E.J., *Adopted Territory: Transnational Korean Adoptees and the Politics of Belonging* (Durham, NC: Duke University Press, 2010).

Kirchner, W., *Eine anthroposiphische Studie an Mulattenkindern in Berlin unter besonderer Berücksichtigung der sozialien Verhältnisse* (Berlin: self-publication, 1952).

Kissinger, H., *Ending the Vietnam War: A history of America's Involvement in and Extrication from the Vietnam War* (London: Simon and Schuster, 2003).

Klain, E., 'Intergenerational aspects of the conflict in Former Yugoslavia', in Yael Danielle (ed.), *International Handbook of Multigenerational Legacies of Trauma* (Berlin: Springer, 2010), pp. 279–96.

Kleinau, E., 'Occupation children in German post-war history – of the pitfalls of biographical research and dealing with the networks of those affected', in H. Glaesmer and S. Lee (eds), *Interdisciplinary Perspectives on Children born of War: From World War II to Current Conflict Settings*, Conference reader, 2015, pp. 103–10, http://medpsy.uniklinikum-leipzig.de/medpsych.site.postext.rueckblick,a id,1412.html. (accessed 28.2.2017).

Kleinschmidt, J., 'Amerikaner und Deutsche in der Besatzungszeit – Beziehungen und Probleme', in Haus der Geschichte Baden-Württemberg, Landeszentrale für politische Bildung Baden-Württemberg (eds), *Besatzer – Helfer – Vorbilder: Amerikanische Politik und deutscher Alltag in Württemberg-Baden 1945 bis 1949* (Baden-Württemberg: LpB, 1996).

Kleinschmidt, J., '"German Fräuleins": Heiraten zwischen amerikanischen Soldaten und Deutschen in der Besatzungszeit 1945–1949', *Frauen in der einen Welt*, 4 (1992), 42–58.

Klemesrud, J., 'Vietnamese War Brides', *New York Times*, 13.9.1971.

Knauth, P., 'Fraternisation: The word takes on a brand-new meaning in Germany', *Life*, 2.7.1945, 26.

Koekebakker, J. *Onze kinderbescherming in oorlog en vrede* (Purmerend: Muusses, 1945).

Koepf, P.H., 'An unexpected freedom', *The Atlantic Times*, 1.4.2009.

Kohen, D.K., 'Explaining rape during civil wars: cross-national evidence 1980–2009', *American Political Science Review*, 107 (2013), 461–77.

Koo, K.L., 'Confronting disciplinary blindness: women, war and rape in the international politics of security', *Australian Journal of Political Science*, 37 (2002), 525–36.

Koonz, C., *Mothers in the Fatherland: Women, Family and Nazi Politics* (London: St. Martin's Press, 1986).

Kositza, E., 'Gedanken zu Miriam Gebhardts "Als die Soldaten kamen"', *Sezession in*

Netz, 7.4.2015, http://sezession.de/49105/gedanken-zu-miriam-gebhardt-als-die-soldaten-kamen.html. (accessed 28.2.2017).

Kramer, H. (ed.), *Die Gegenwart der NS-Vergangenheit* (Berlin: Philo, 2000).

Kramer, S., 'Forced marriage and the absence of gang rape: Explaining sexual violence by the Lord's Resistance Army in Northern Uganda', *The Journal of Politics and Society* (2012), 11–49.

Krenn, M.L., Review of T.A. Bass. *Vietnamerica: The War Comes Home*, H-Pol, H-Net Reviews. May 1997.

Kuby, E., *Die Russen in Berlin* (Bern / München: Scherz, 1965); English translation *The Russians in Berlin* (London: Heinemann, 1968).

Kumar, R.S., 'UN offers DNA tests to address sexual abuse claims', *News Everyday*, 16.6.2015, http://newseveryday.com/articles/19355/20150616/un-offers-dna-tests-address-sexual-abuse-claims.htm. (accessed 31.10.2016).

Kumin, J., 'Orderly departure from Vietnam: Cold War anomaly or humanitarian intervention?', *Refugee Survey Quarterly*, 27 (2008), 104–17.

Kundrus, B., 'Nur die halbe Geschichte: Frauen im Umfeld der Wehrmacht zwischen 1939 und 1945 – ein Forschungsbericht', in R.-D. Müller and H.-E. Volkmann (eds), *Die Wehrmacht: Mythos und Realität* (Munich: Oldenbourg Verlag, 1999), 719–38.

Kunitz, D., '"Kind des Feindes?" Eine Untersuchung zu den Identitätsbildern der deutschen "Besatzungskinder" des Zweiten Weltkrieges' (Master's thesis, Leipzig University, 2014).

Kutler, S. (ed.), *Encyclopedia of the Vietnam War* (New York: Scribner Book Company, 1996).

Kwiet, K., *Reichskommissariat Niederlande: Versuch und Scheitern nationalisozialistischer Neuordnung* (Stuttgart: Deutsche Verlagsanstalt, 1968).

Lamb, D., 'Children of the Vietnam War', *Smithsonian Magazine*, June 2009, http://smithsonianmag.com/people-places/Children-of-the-Dust.html?c=y&story=fullstory. (accessed 12.12.2014).

Landesman, P.K., 'A woman's work', *New York Times*, 15.9.2002, www.nytimes.com/2002/09/15/magazine/a-woman-s-work.html. (accessed 22.7.2014)..

Landler, M., 'Result of secret Nazi breeding program: ordinary folk', *New York Times*, 7.11.2006, www.nytimes.com/2006/11/07/world/europe/07nazi.html?pagewanted=all. (accessed 4.6.2016).

Lane, R., 'Northern Uganda: Looking for peace', *The Lancet*, 370 (2007), 1991–2.

Lathrop, A., 'Pregnancy resulting from rape', *Journal of Obstetric, Gynecological, & Neonatal Nursing*, 27 (1998), 25–31.

Lawson, E.D., 'Development of patriotism in children: A second look', *The Journal of Psychology*, 55 (1963), 279–86.

Leaning, J. and T. Gingerich, *The Use of Rape as a Weapon of War in the Conflict in Darfur, Sudan* (Program on Humanitarian Crises and Human Rights, Harvard School of Public Health, 2005).

LeBlanc, L., *The Convention on the Rights of the Child: UN Lawmaking on Human Rights* (Lincoln: University of Nebraska Press, 1995).

Lee, N.Y., 'The Construction of US Camptown Prostitution in South Korea: Transformation and Resistance' (Ph.D. dissertation, University of Maryland, 2006).

Lee, R.M., 'The transracial adoption paradox: History, research, and counseling implications of cultural socialization', *The Counseling Psychologist*, 31 (2003), 711–44.

Lee, R.M. et al., 'Cultural socialization in families with internationally adopted children', *Journal of Family Psychology*, 20 (2006), 571–80.
Lee, S., 'A forgotten legacy of the Second World War: GI children in post-war Britain and Germany', *Contemporary European History*, 20 (2011), 157–81.
Lee, S. and I.C. Mochmann, 'Kinder des Krieges im 20. Jahrhundert', in B. Stelzl-Marx and S. Satjukow (eds), *Besatzungskinder: Die Nachkommen alliierter Soldaten in Österreich und Deutschland* (Wien: Böhlau-Verlag, 2015), 15–38.
Leepson, M. and H. Hannaford, *Webster's New World Dictionary of the Vietnam War* (New York: Macmillan, 1999).
Leiby, M.L., 'Wartime sexual violence in Guatemala and Peru', *International Studies Quarterly*, 53 (2007), 445–68.
Leitenberg, M., *Deaths in Wars and Conflicts in the 20th Century* (Ithaca, NY: Cornell University, Peace Studies Program, 2006).
Lemke Muniz de Faria, Y.C., *Zwischen Fürsorge und Ausgrenzung: Afrodeutsche "Besatzungskinder" im Nachkriegsdeutschland* (Berlin: Metropol, 2002).
Lemke Muniz de Faria, Y.C., 'Germany's "brown babies" must be helped! Will you? U.S. adoption plans for African-German children, 1950–1955', *Callaloo*, 26 (2003), 342–62.
Lemkin, R., *Axis Rule in Occupied Europe: Laws of Occupation, Analysis of Government, Proposals for Redress* (Washington DC: Carnegie Endowment for International Peace, 1944).
Levy, B.S. and V.W. Sidel (eds), *War and Public Health* (Washington: American Public Health Association, 2000).
Liebel, M., 'Working class children as social subjects: The contribution of the working children's organisation to social transformation', *Childhood*, 10 (2003), 265–83.
Liebling-Kalifani, H.J., 'Research and intervention with women war survivors in Uganda: Resilience and suffering as the consequences of war', in H. Bradby and G. Lewando-Hundt (eds), *Global Perspectives on War, Gender and Health: The Sociology and Anthropology of Suffering* (Farnham: Ashgate, 2010), pp. 69–90.
Lilienthal, G., *Der 'Lebensborn e.V.': Ein Instrument nationalsozialistischer Rassenpolitik* (Frankfurt: Fischer, 2003).
Lilly, R., *Taken by Force: Rape and American GIs in Europe During World War II* (London: Palgrave Macmillan, 2007).
Lindsay, R., 'U.N. peacekeepers accused of rape', *The Washington Times*, 17.12.2006, www.washingtontimes.com/news/2006/dec/17/20061217-122119-4767r/. (accessed 31.10.2016).
Lindsey, R., 'From atrocity to data: Historiographies of rape in the Former Yugoslavia and the gendering of genocide', *Patterns of Prejudice*, 36 (2002), 79–87.
Lipman, J.K., 'The face is the road map: Vietnamese Amerasians in U.S. political and popular culture, 1980–1988', *Journal of Asian American Studies*, 14 (2011), 33–68.
Little, K.L., 'The psychological background of white-coloured contacts in Britain', *The Sociological Review*, 35 (1943), 12–28.
Littlewood, R., 'Military rape', *Anthropology Today*, 13 (1997), 7–17.
Lončar, M. et al., 'Psychological consequences of rape on women in 1991–1995 war in Croatia and Bosnia and Herzegovina', *Croatian Medical Journal*, 47 (2006), 67–75.
Loscher, G. and J.A. Scanlan, *Calculated Kindness: Refugees and America's Half-Open Door, 1945 to the Present* (London: Collier Macmillan Publishers, 1986).

Lovelock, K., 'Intercountry adoption as a military practice: A comparative analysis of intercountry adoption and immigration policy and practice in the United States, Canada, and New Zealand in the post W.W. II period', *International Migration Review*, 34 (2000), 907–23.

Lowicki-Zucca, M., S. Karmin and K.-L. Dehne, 'HIV among peacekeepers and its likely impact on prevalence on host countries' HIV epidemics', *International Peacekeeping*, 16 (2009), 352–63.

Lunch, W.L. and P.W. Sperlich, 'American public opinion and the war in Vietnam', *The Western Political Quarterly*, 32 (1979), 21–44.

Lupi, N., 'Report by the Enquiry Commission on the behavior of Italian peacekeeping troops in Somalia', *Yearbook of International Humanitarian Law*, 1 (1998), 375.

Lynn II, John A., *Women, Armies and Warfare in Early Modern Europe* (Cambridge: Cambridge University Press, 2008).

Lyons-Ruth, K. and D. Block, 'The disturbed caregiving system: Relations among childhood trauma, maternal caregiving, and infant affect and attachment', *Infant Mental Health Journal*, 17 (1996), 257–75.

Machakanja, P., 'Reintegration of child soldiers: A case of Southern Sudan', in S.B. Maphonsa, L. DeLuca and A. Keasley (eds), *Building Peace from Within* (Pretoria: Africa Institute of South Africa, Pretoria, 2014), pp. 88–90.

MacKay, A., 'Sex and the peacekeeping soldier: The new UN resolution', *Peace News*, Issue 2443, 2001, http://peacenews.info/node/3602/sex-and-peacekeeping-soldier-new-un-resolution. (accessed 31.10.2016).

MacKinnon, C.A., 'Rape, genocide, and human rights', in Stiglmayer, A. (ed.), *Mass rape: The War Against Women in Bosnia Herzegovina* (Lincoln: University of Nebraska Press, 1994), 182–96.

MacKinnon, C.A., *Are Women Human? And Other International Dialogues* (Cambridge, MA: Harvard University Press, 2006).

MacQueen, N., *Peacekeeping and the International System* (London: Routledge, 2006).

Magnusen, A. and D.G. Petrie, *Orphan Train* (New York: Dial Press, 1978).

Mahlzahn, M., *Germany 1945–1949: A Sourcebook* (London: Routledge, 1991).

Main, M. and E. Hesse, 'Parents' unresolved traumatic experiences are related to infant disorganized attachment status: Is frightened and/or frightening parental behavior the linking mechanism?', in M.T. Greenberg et al. (eds), *Attachment in the Preschool Years: Theory, Research, and Intervention* (Chicago: University of Chicago Press, 1990), pp. 161–82.

Mally, L., *The Culture of the Future: The Proletkult Movement in Revolutionary Russia* (Berkeley: University of California Press, 1990).

Mamdani, M., *When Victims Become Killers: Colonialism, Nativism, and the Genocide in Rwanda* (Princeton: Princeton University Press, 2001).

Man, J., *Ghengis Khan: Life, Death and Resurrection* (London: Bantam Press, 2004).

Marie Kaier et al., 'Psychosoziale Konsequenzen des Aufwachsens als Besatzungskind in Deutschland: Psychologische Hintergründe eines quantitativen Forschungsprojektes', in B. Stelzl-Marx and S. Satjukow (eds), *Besatzungskinder: Die Nachkommen alliierter Soldaten in Österreich und Deutschland* (Wien: Böhlau-Verlag, 2015), pp. 39–61.

Maroger, K., *Les Racines du Silence* (Paris: Anne Carrière, 2008).

Martin, M., 'Französische Besatzungszeit', paper given at the 2012 Franco-German meeting of *Coeurs sans Frontieres*, www.coeurssansfrontieres.com/de/kolloquium/franzoesisch-deutsches-treffen-2012/franzoesische-besatzungszeit/. (accessed 12.10.2014).

Martin, S., *Must Boys Be Boys? Ending Sexual Exploitation & Abuse in UN Peacekeeping Missions* (Washington, DC: Refugees International, 2005).

Masson, J., 'Intercountry adoption: A global problem or a global solution?' *Journal of International Affairs* 55 (2001), 141–66.

Matloff, J., 'Rwanda copes with babies of mass rape', *Christian Science Monitor*, 87 (1995), 1.

Mause, L.D. (ed.), *The History of Childhood* (Ann Arbor: University of Michigan Press, 1974).

Maxon, R., *East Africa: An Introductory History* (Morgantown: West Virginia Press, 2009).

Mazurana, D.E. et al., 'Girls in fighting forces and groups: Their recruitment, participation, demobilization, and reintegration', *Peace and Conflict: Journal of Peace Psychology*, 8 (2002), 97–123.

McAllister, J., *No Exit: America and the German Problem, 1943–1954* (Ithaca: Cornell University Press, 2002).

McGinnis, H. et al., *Beyond Culture Camp: Promoting Healthy Identity Formation in Adoption* (New York: Evan B. Donaldson Adoption Institute, 2009).

McIntosh, R., 'The making of modern childhood', in R. McIntosh, *Boys in the Pits – Child Labour in the Coal Mines* (Montreal: McGill-Queens University Press, 2000), pp. 14–41.

McKay, S., 'Reconstructing fragile lives: Girls' social reintegration in Northern Uganda and Sierra Leone', *Gender & Development*, 12 (2004), 19–30.

McKay, S., 'Girls as "weapons of terror" in Northern Uganda and Sierra Leonean rebel fighting forces', *Studies in Conflict and Terrorism*, 28 (2005), 385–97.

McKay, S. and D.E. Mazurana, *Where Are the Girls? Girls in Fighting Forces in Northern Uganda, Sierra Leone and Mozambique: Their Lives During and After War* (Montreal: Rights & Democracy, 2004).

McKelvey, R.S., *The Dust of Life: America's Children Abandoned in Vietnam* (Seattle and London: University of Washington Press, 1999).

McKelvey, R.S. and J.A. Webb, 'Long-term effects of maternal loss on Vietnamese Amerasians', *Journal of the American Academy of Child & Adolescent Psychiatry*, 32 (1993), 1013–18.

McKelvey, R.S. and J.A. Webb, 'Premigratory expectations and post-migratory mental health', *Journal of the American Academy of Child & Adolescent Psychiatry*, 35 (1996), 470–3.

McKelvey, R.S., J.A. Webb and A.R. Mao, 'Premigratory risk factors in Vietnamese Amerasians', *American Journal of Psychiatry*, 150 (1993), 470–3.

McKinley, J.C. Jr., 'Legacy of Rwanda violence: The thousands born of rape', *New York Times*, 23.9.1996.

McKinnon, C.A., 'Rape, genocide, and women's human rights', in A. Stiglmayer (ed.), *Mass Rape: The Way Against Women in Bosnia-Herzegovina* (Lincoln: University of Nebraska Press, 1994), pp. 183–96.

Meinen, I., 'Wehrmacht und Prostitution im besetzten Frankreich', *Einblicke*:

Forschungsmagazin der Carl von Ossietzly Universität Oldenburg, 31, http://presse.uni-oldenburg.de/einblicke/30/meinen.htm (October 1999). (accessed 31.10.2016).

Meinen, I., *Wehrmacht und Prostitution im besetzten Frankreich* (Bremen: Edition Temmen, 2002).

Melvin, K., *Sorry 'Bout That: Cartoons, Limericks and other Diversions of GI Vietnam* (Tokyo: The Wayward Press, 1966).

Melvin, K., *Be Nice: More Cartoons and Capers of GI Vietnam* (Tokyo: The Wayward Press, 1968).

Mensch, B.S., M.J. Grant and A.K. Blanc, 'The changing context of sexual initiation in Sub-Saharan Africa', *Population and Development Review*, 32 (2006), 699–727.

Mergelsberg, B., 'The displaced family: Moral imaginations and social control in Pabbo, Northern Uganda', *Journal of Eastern African Studies*, 6 (2012), 64–80.

Meron, T., 'Rape as a crime under international humanitarian law', *The American Journal of International Law*, 87 (1993), 424–8.

Merritt. R.L., *Democracy Imposed: US Occupation Policy and the German Public 1945–1949* (New Haven: Yale University Press, 1995).

Mertus, J. and J.A. Benjamin, *War's Offensive on Women: The Humanitarian Challenge in Bosnia, Kosovo, and Afghanistan* (Bloomfield, CT: Kumarian Press, 2000).

Mesenhöller, M., 'Wir Russenkinder', *GEO Magazin* (May 2015), 116–34.

Meznaric, S., 'Gender as an ethno-marker: Rape, war and identity in the Former Yugoslavia', in V. Moghadan (ed.), *Identity Politics and Women: Cultural Reassertion and Feminism in International Perspective* (Boulder, CO: Westview, 1994), pp. 76–97.

Middleton, J. (ed.), *Encyclopedia of Africa South of the Sahara* (New York: Charles Scribner's Sons, 1996).

Miers, S. and I. Kopytoff (eds), *Slavery in Africa: Historical and Anthropological Perspectives* (Madison: University of Wisconsin Press, 1977).

Miller, A.J., 'Legal aspects of stopping sexual exploitation and abuse in UN peacekeeping operations', *Cornell International Law Journal*, 39 (2006), 71.

Min, P.G., 'Korean "comfort women": The intersection of colonial power, gender, and class', *Gender & Society*, 17 (2003), 938–57.

Mochmann, I.C., 'Developing a methodology for the research field of "children born of war"', European Survey Research Association Conference, Warsaw, 29.6.2009–3.7.2009.

Mochmann, I.C, 'Using participatory methods in hidden populations: Experiences from an international research project', European Survey Research Association Conference, Lausanne, 18–22.7.2011.

Mochmann, I.C. and A. Øland, 'Der lange Schatten des Zweiten Weltkriegs: Kinder deutscher Wehrmachtsoldaten und einheimischer Frauen in Dänemark', *Historical Social Research*, 34 (2009), 282–303.

Mochmann, I.C. and S.U. Larsen, 'Kriegskinder in Europa', *Aus Politik und Zeitgeschichte*, 18–19 (2005), 34–8.

Mochmann, I.C. and S.U. Larsen, 'The forgotten consequences of war: The life course of children fathered by German soldiers in Norway and Denmark during WWII – some empirical results, *Historical Social Research*, 33 (2008), 347–63.

Mochman, I.C. and S. Lee, 'The human rights of children born of war: Case analyses of past and present conflicts', *Historical Social Research/Historische Sozialforschung*, 35 (2010), 268–98.

Mochmann, I.C. and I.K. Haarvardsson, 'The legacy of war time rape: Mapping key concepts and issues', *PRIO Paper* (Oslo: Peace Research Institute 2012).

Mochmann, I.C., S. Lee and B. Stelzl-Marx (eds), 'Special focus. Children born of war: Second World War and beyond', *Historical Social Research*, 34:3 (2009), 263–372.

Modell, J., *Kinship with Strangers: Adoption and Interpretations of Kinship in American Culture* (San Francisco; Berkeley: University of California Press, 1994).

Moe, B.A., *Adoption: A Reference Handbook* (Santa Barbara: ABC-Clio, 2007).

Moghadan V. (ed.), *Identity Politics and Women: Cultural Reassertion and Feminism in International Perspective* (Boulder, CO: Westview, 1994).

Moon, K.H.S., *Sex Among Allies: Military Prostitution in U.S.-Korean Relations* (New York: University of Columbia Press, 1997).

Moorehead, C., *Dunant's Dream: War in Switzerland and the History of the Red Cross* (London: Harper Collins, 1998).

Morris, J.M., 'Occupation babies: Mixed-race Japanese children', *Wonders and Marvels*, http://wondersandmarvels.com/2015/02/occupation-babies-mixed-race-japanese-children.html. (accessed 31.10.2016)

Moss, G.D. (ed.), *A Vietnam Reader: Courses and Essays* (Englewood Cliffs, N.J.: Prentice Hall, 1991).

Muel-Dreyfus, F. and K.A. Johnson, *Vichy and the Eternal Feminine: A Contribution to a Political Sociology of Gender* (Durham, NC: Duke University Press, 2001).

Mühlhäuser, R., 'Between extermination and Germanization: Children of German men in the "Occupied Eastern Territories, 1942–1945"', in Kjersti Ericsson and Eva Simonssen (eds), *Children of World War II* (Oxford: Berg, 2005), pp. 167–89.

Mühlhäuser, R., '"Diskriminiert als sei es ein Negerbastard": Der Nationalsozialistische Blick auf die Kinder deutscher Soldaten und einheimischer Frauen in den besetzten Gebieten der Sowjetuion (1942–1945)', *Werkstattgeschichte*, 51 (2009), 43–55.

Mühlhäuser, R., *Eroberungen: Sexuelle Gewalttaten und intime Beziehungen deutscher Soldaten in der Sowjetunion 1941–1945* (Hamburg: Hamburger Edition HIS Verlagsgesellschaft, 2010).

Muhumuza, R., *Girls under Guns: A Case Study of Girls Abducted by Joseph Kony's Lord's Resistance Army (LRA) in Northern Uganda* (Kampala: World Vision 1995).

Mukamana, D. and P. Brysiewicz, 'The lived experiences of genocide rape survivors', *Journal of Nursing Scholarship*, 40 (2008), 379–84.

Mukangendo, M.C., 'Caring for children born of rape in Rwanda', in R.C. Carpenter (ed.), *Born of War: Protecting Children of Sexual Violence Survivors in Conflict Zones* (Bloomfield, CT: Kumarin Press, 2007), pp. 40–52.

Mukangendo, M.C., 'Rwanda: Coping with children born of rape', published on http://people.umass.edu/charli/childrenbornofwar/Mukangendo%20Working%20Paper.pdf. (accessed 31.10.2016).

Mullins, C.W., '"He would kill me with his penis": Genocidal rape in Rwanda as a state crime', *Critical Criminology*, 17 (2009), 15–33.

Munin, J., 'A political economic history of the Liberian State: Forced labour and armed militarization', *Journal of Agrarian Change*, 11 (2011), 357–76.

Muñoz-Rojas, D. and F. Jean-Jacques, 'The roots of behaviour in war: Understanding and preventing IHL violations' (ICRC Resource Center, 2005).

Murdoch, L., 'UN legacy of shame in Timor', *The Age*, 22.7.2006, http://theage.com.au/news/world/uns-legacy-of-shame-in-timor/2006/07/21/1153166587803.html?page=fullpage. (accessed 31.10.2016).

Muth, K., *Die Wehrmacht in Griechenland – und ihre Kinder* (Leipzig: Eudora Verlag, 2008).

Naimark, N.M., *The Russians in Germany: A History of the Soviet Zone of Occupation, 1945–1949* (Cambridge, MA: Harvard University Press, 1995).

Nash, J., and H. Safe (eds), *Women and Change in Latin America* (South Hardley: Bergin & Garvey, 1986).

Ndulo, M., 'The United Nations responses to the sexual abuse and exploitation of women and girls by peacekeepers during peacekeeping missions', *Berkeley Journal for International Law*, 27 (2009), 127–61.

Nduwimana, F., *The Right to Survive: Sexual Violence, Women and HIV/AIDS*, International Centre for Human Rights and Democratic Development, 2004, http://publications.gc.ca/collections/Collection/E84-13-2004E.pdf. (accessed 31.10.2016).

Newman, E., 'The "New Wars" debate: A historical perspective is needed', *Security Dialogue*, 35:2 (2004), 173–89.

Nicholson, Baroness E., 'Red light on human traffic', *Society Guardian*, 1 July 2004, http://theguardian.com/society/2004/jul/01/adoptionandfostering.europeanunion. (accessed 31.10.2016).

Nixon, J.L., *A Family Apart* (New York: Bantam Books, 1987).

Nordås, R. and D.K. Cohen, 'Sexual violence in African conflicts', *Centre for the Study of Civil War Policy Brief* 1/201, http://file.prio.no/publication_files/cscw/Nordas-Cohen-Sexual-Violence-Militias-African-Conflicts-CSCW-Policy-Brief-01-2012.pdf. (accessed 31.10.2016).

Nowrojee, B., 'A lost opportunity for justice: Why did the ICTR not prosecute gender propaganda?', in A. Thompson (ed.), *The Media and the Rwanda Genocide* (London: Pluto Press, 2007), pp. 362–74.

Nowrojee, B., *Shattered Lives: Sexual Violence During the Rwandan Genocide and its Aftermath* (New York: Human Rights Watch, 1996).

Nozaki, Y., 'The "comfort women" controversy: History and testimony', *The Asia-Pacific Journal: Japan Focus* (2005). n.p. http://apjjf.org/-Yoshiko-Nozaki/2063/article.html. (accessed 28.2.2017).

Oberman, M., 'A brief history of infanticide and the law', in Margaret G. Spinelli (ed.), *Infanticide: Psychosocial and Legal Perspectives on Mothers who Kill* (Arlington: American Psychiatric Press Inc., 2002), pp. 3–18.

O'Brien, K.J., 'The uncounted casualties of war: Epigenetics and the intergenerational transference of PTSD symptoms among children and grandchildren of Vietnam veterans in Australia' (eprint, 2007), http://eprints.qut.edu.au/13794/1/13794.pdf. (accessed 31.10.2016).

Ochen, E.A., 'Children and young mothers' agency in the context of the experiences of formerly abducted people in Northern Uganda', *Child Abuse and Neglect*, 42 (2015), 183–94.

O'Donovan, K., 'A right to know one's parentage?', *International Journal of Law, Policy and the Family*, 2 (1988), 27–45.

Olojede, D., 'Genocide's child: Her son, her sorrow', *Newsday* 2.5.20014, www.pulitzer.org/winners/dele-olojede. (accessed 31.10.2016).

Olsen, K., *Krigens barn: De norske krigsbarna og deres mødre* (Oslo: Aschehoug, 1998).

Olsen, K., *Vater: Deutscher – Das Schicksal der Norwegischen Lebensbornkinder und ihrer Mütter von 1940 bis heute* (Frankfurt: Campus Verlag, 2002).

Olsen, K., 'Under the care of the Lebensborn', in K. Ericsson and E. Simonsen (eds), *Children of World War II: The Hidden Enemy Legacy* (Oxford: Berg, 2005), pp. 25–34.

Olujic, M.B., 'Embodiment of terror: Gendered violence in peacetime and wartime in Croatia and Bosnia-Herzegovina', *Medical Anthropology Quarterly*, 12 (1998), 31–50.

Omerdić, M., 'The position of the Islamic community on the care for children of raped mothers', in Mirsad Tokaca (ed.), *The Plucked Buds* (Sarajevo: Commission for Gathering Facts on War Crimes in Bosnia and Herzegovina, 2002), pp. 428–32.

Oreskovic, J. and T. Maskew, 'Red thread of slender reed: Deconstructing Prof. Bartholet's mythology of international adoption', *Buffalo Human Rights Law Review*, 14 (2008), 71–128.

Orlowski, H.V. et al., 'Psychologie der Vermissung am Beispiel der Kinder von vermissten deutschen Soldaten des Zweiten Weltkriegs', *Zeitschrift für Psychosomatische Medizin und Psychotherapie*, 59:2 (2013), 189–97.

Ospina, S., 'A review and evaluation of gender-related activities of UN peacekeeping operations and their impact on gender relations in Timor-Leste', www.peacewomen.org/sites/default/files/dpko_timorlesteevaluation_2006_0.pdf. (accessed 31.10.2016).

Otto, D., 'Making sense of zero tolerance policies in peacekeeping sexual economies', in V. Munro and C. Stychin (eds), *Sexuality and the Law: Feminist Engagements* (Abingdon: Routledge, 2007), pp. 259–82.

P'Bitek, O., *Artist the Ruler: Essays on Art, Culture and Values* (Nairobi: East African, 1986).

p'Chong, C.L. and O. p'Bitek, 'The cultural matrix of the Acholi in his writings', in E. Breitinger (ed.), *Uganda: The Cultural Landscape* (Kampala: Fountain Publishers, 2000), pp. 83–96.

Palacios, J. et al., 'Family context for emotional recovery in internationally adopted children', *International Social Work*, 52 (2009), 609–20.

Pallen, D., 'Sexual slavery in Bosnia: The negative externality of the market for peace', *Swords and Ploughshares*, 13 (2003), 27–43.

Papineni, P., commenting on C. Kiklahan and N. Ewigman, 'Rape as a weapon of war in modern conflicts', *British Medical Journal*, 340 (2010), 3270.

Park, J., 'Sexual violence as a weapon of war in international humanitarian law', *International Public Policy Review*, 3 (2007), 13–18.

Parra-Aranguren, G., 'Explanatory report to the Hague Convention of 29 May 1993 on protection of children and co-operation in respect of intercountry adoption', http://hcch.net/upload/expl33e.pdf. (accessed 31.10.2016).

Pascoe, P., 'Miscegenation law, court cases, and ideologies of "race" in 20th century America', in M. Hodes (ed.), *Sex, Love, Race: Crossing Boundaries in North American History* (New York: New York University Press, 1999).

Patel, S. et al., 'Comparison of HIV-related vulnerabilities between former child soldiers and children never abducted by the LRA in Northern Uganda', *Conflict and Health*, 7 (2013), 17–31.

Paul, C., *Zwangsprostitution: Staatlich errichtete Bordelle im Nationalsozialismus* (Berlin: Edition Hentrich, 1994).

Paye-Layleh, J., 'Liberia's peacekeeping legacy', *BBC News Channel*, 24.1.2005, http://news.bbc.co.uk/1/hi/world/africa/4195459.stm. (accessed 31.10.2016).

Penny, S., 'Reporting of mass rape in the Balkans: Plus ça change, plus c'est la même chose? From Bosnia to Kosovo', *Civil Wars*, 2 (1999), 74–110.

Pfau, A.E., *Miss Your Lovin: GI, Gender and Domesticity in WWII*, available at www.gutenberg-e.org/pfau/. (accessed 31.10.2016).

Pfeiffer, A. and T. Ebert, 'PTSD, depression and anxiety among former abductees in Northern Uganda', *Conflict and Health*, 5 (2011), 1–7.

Pham, P.N., P. Vinck and E. Stover, 'The Lord's Resistance Army and forced conscription in Northern Uganda', *Human Rights Quarterly*, 30 (2008), 404–11.

Pham, P.N., P. Vinck and E. Stover, 'Returning home: Forced conscription, reintegration, & mental health status of former abductees of the Lord's Resistance Army in Northern Uganda', *BMC Psychiatry*, 9 (2009), 1–14.

Phelps, A.A., 'Gender-based war crimes: Incidence and effectiveness of international criminal prosecution', *William & Mary Journal of Women and Law*, 12 (2006), 499–520.

Picaper, J.-P. and L. Norz, *Enfants maudits* (Paris: Edition de Syrtes, 2004).

Picker, H., *Hitlers Tischgespräche im Führerhauptquartier* (München: Goldmann, 1979).

Plassmann, M., 'Wehrmachtsbordelle: Anmerkungen zu einem Quellenfund im Universitätsarchiv Düsseldorf', *Militärgeschichtliche Zeitschrift*, 62 (2003), 157–73.

Platt, A., *The Child Savers* (Chicago: University of Chicago Press, 1969).

Plattner, D., 'Protection of children in international humanitarian law', *International Committee of the Red Cross-ICRC*, 1984.

PLoS Medicine Editors, 'Rape in war is common, devastating, and too often ignored', *PLoS Med*, 6:1 (2009), np.

Plummer, B.G., 'Brown babies: Race, gender and policy after World War II', in B.G. Plummer (ed.), *Window on Freedom: Race, Civil Rights and Foreign Affairs 1945–1988* (Chapel Hill: University of North Carolina Press, 2003).

Pohl, D., *Die Herrschaft der Wehrmacht: Deutsche Militärbesatzung und einheimische Bevölkerung in der Sowjetunion* (Oldenbourg: Wissenschaftsverlag, 2008).

Polenberg, R., *One Nation Divisible: Race, Class and Ethnicity in the United States Since 1938* (New York: Penguin, 1980).

Pommerin, R., *Sterilisierung der Rheinlandbastarde: Das Schicksal einer farbigen Minderheit 1918–1937* (Düsseldorf: Droste, 1979).

Porter, H., 'After Rape: Justice and Social Harmony in Northern Uganda' (Ph.D. thesis, London School of Economics, 2015), http://etheses.lse.ac.uk/717/1/Porter_After_rape_2013.pdf. (accessed 21.2.2016).

Pötsch, H., 'Rearticulating the experience of war in Anonyma: *Eine Frau in Berlin*', *Nordlit*, 30 (2012), 15–33.

Pratt, M. and L. 'Sexual terrorism: Rape as a weapon of war in Eastern Democratic Republic of Congo. An assessment of programmatic responses to sexual violence in North Kivu, South Kivu, Maniema, and Orientale Provinces' (USAID, 2004), http://pdf.usaid.gov/pdf_docs/Pnadk346.pdf. (accessed 20.5.2016).

Prentice, E.A., 'No peace for GI babies', *The Times*, 24.12.2002, p. 11.

Prunier, G., *The Rwanda Crisis: History of a Genocide* (New York: Columbia University Press, 1997).
Purdy, L.M., *In Their Best Interest? The Case Against Equal Rights for Children* (Ithaca: Cornell University Press, 1992).
Quinn, J.R., 'Getting to peace: Negotiations with the LRA in Northern Uganda', *Human Rights Review*, 10 (2009), 55–71.
Quirk, J., 'Wartime enslavement and forced marriage in sub-Saharan Africa: Linking historical slave systems and modern problems' (unpublished manuscript).
Qureshi, S., 'Progressive development of women's human rights in international humanitarian law and within the UN system', *Journal of Political Studies*, 19 (2012), 111–24.
Raedts, P., 'The Children's Crusade of 1212', *Journal of Medieval History*, 3 (1977), 279–323.
Rains, O., L. Rains and M. Jarratt (eds), *Voices of the Left Behind* (Toronto: Project Roots, 2004).
Ranard, D.E. and D.F. Gilzow, 'The Amerasians', *In America* (June 1989), http://files.eric.ed.gov/fulltext/ED323751.pdf (accessed on 16.3.2017).
Ranard, D.E. and D. Gilzow, 'The Amerasians: A 1990 update', *In America* (October 1990), http://files.eric.ed.gov/fulltext/ED323751.pdf (accessed on 16.3.2017).
Reese, W.J., 'The origins of progressive education', *History of Education Quarterly*, 41 (2001), 1–24.
Reeves, E., 'Rape as a continuing weapon of war in Darfur: Reports, bibliography of studies, compendium of incidents', *Sudan, Research Analysis and Advocacy*, http://sudanreeves.org/2012/03/04/rape-as-a-continuing-weapon-of-war-in-darfur-reports-bibliography-of-studies-a-compendium-of-incidents/. (accessed 31.10.2016).
Rehn, E. and E.J. Sirleaf, *Women, War and Peace: The Independent Experts' Assessment on the Impact of Armed Conflict on Women and Women's Role in Peacebuilding* (New York: UNIFEM, 2002).
Reynolds, D., *Rich Relations: The American Occupation of Britain 1942–1945* (London: Harper Collins, 1996).
Rhoades, M.K., 'Renegotiating French masculinity: Medicine and venereal disease during the Great War', *French Historical Studies*, 29 (2006), 293–327.
Richmond, A, *Colour Prejudice in Britain: A Study of West Indian Workers in Liverpool 1941–1951* (London: Routledge and K. Paul, 1954).
Rieder, H. and T. Elbert, 'Rwanda – lasting imprints of a genocide: Trauma, mental health and psychosocial conditions in survivors, former prisoners and their children', *Conflict and Health* (2013), 6–19.
Rinaldo, R., 'Women survivors of the Rwandan genocide face a grim reality', *Inter Press Service*, 6.4.2014, http://ipsnews.net/2004/04/rights-rwanda-women-survivors-of-the-rwandan-genocide-face-grim-realities/. (accessed 31.10.2016).
Ringdal, N.J., *Love for Sale: A World History of Prostitution* (New York: Grove Press, 2004).
Rispler-Chaim, V., 'The right not to be born: Abortion of the disadvantaged fetus in contemporary fatwas', in J.E. Brockopp (ed.), *Islamic Ethics of Life: Abortion, War, and Euthanasia* (Columbia, SC: University of South Carolina Press 2003), pp. 87–8.
Robertson, E. et al. 'Antenatal risk factors for postpartum depression: A synthesis of recent literature', *General Hospital Psychiatry*, 26 (2004), 289–95.

Rodriguez, Father C., *Seventy Times Seven: The Implementation and Impact of the Amnesty Laws in Acholi*, Association of Religious Leaders' Peace Initiative, Caritas Gulu, Justice and Peace Commission (2002).

Roeger, M., 'Children of German soldiers in Poland', in L. Westerlund (ed.), *The Children of German Soldiers* vol. 2 (Helsinki: Painopaikka Nord Print, 2011), pp. 261–72.

Roeger, M., 'Occupation children in West and Eastern Europe', paper presented at the conference *War Children in the Post-War Period: A West-East Perspective on Child Policies, Child Experiences and War Childhood Remembrance Cultures in Europe since 1945*, 14.12.2012 at the Ludwig-Boltzmann-Institut, Wien.

Rogers, J.R. and C. Kennedy, 'Dying for peace: Fatality trends for United Nations peacekeeping personnel', *International Peacekeeping*, 2 (2014), 658–72.

Ronen, Y., 'Redefining the child's right to identity', *International Journal of Law, Policy and the Family*, 18 (2004), 144–77.

Root, M.P.P. (ed.), *Racially Mixed People in America* (London: Sage Publishers, 1992).

Rose, S.O., 'Girls and GIs: Race, sex, and diplomacy in Second World War Britain', *International History Review*, 19 (1997), 146–60.

Rose, S.O., 'Sex, citizenship, and the nation in World War II Britain', *The American Historical Review*, 103 (1998), 1147–76.

Rose, S.O., *Which People's War? National Identify and Citizenship in Wartime Britain 1939–1945* (Oxford: Oxford University Press, 2003).

Rosen, D.M. *Armies of the Young: Child soldiers in War and Terrorism* (Chapel Hill: Rutgers University Press, 2005).

Rosen, D.M., *Child Soldiers: A Reference Handbook* (Santa Barbara: ABC-Clio, 2012).

Ross, J., 'Epigenetics: The controversial science behind racial and ethnic health disparities', *National Journal*, 20.3.2014.

Rostan, P., *Inconnu, Présumé Français* (Jour2Fête & Filmover Production, 2011).

Rotabi, K.S. and K.M. Bunkers, 'Intercountry adoption reform based on the Hague Convention on Intercountry Adoption: An update on Guatemala in 2008', *Social Work and Society News Magazine* 11/2008, 12–19.

Roy, C.B., 'Child trafficking new form of slavery. Interview with Emma Nicholson', *Arab Times*, 25.6.2003, http://arabtimesonline.com/NewsDetails/tabid/96/smid/414/ArticleID/160266/t/Child-trafficking-new-form-of-slavery/Default.aspx. (accessed 27.2.2015).

Rublack, U., 'Metze und Magd: Frauen, Krieg und die Bildfunktion des Weiblichen in deutschen Städten der frühen Neuzeit', *Historische Anthropologie*, 3 (1995), 412–32; translated into English as 'Wench and maiden: Women, war and the pictorial function of the feminine in German cities in the early modern period', *History Workshop Journal*, 44 (1997), 1–21.

Rugadya, M. et al., *Gender and the Land Reform Process in Northern Uganda: Assessing Gains and Losses for Women in Uganda*, Land Research Series, no. 2, 2004, https://s3.amazonaws.com/landesa_production/resource/481/Rugadya_Gender-and-the-land-reform-process-in-Uganda_2004.pdf?AWSAccessKeyId=AKIAICR3ICC22CMP7DPA&Expires=1477944352&Signature=u8rEpFOHm1KtMxYXgTSecnbbzKU%3D. (accessed 31.10.2016).

Russell, S.G. et al., 'The legacy of gender-based violence and HIV/Aids in the post-genocide era: Stories from women in Rwanda', *Health Care for Women International*, 37 (2016), 721–43.

Rwezaura, B., 'The concept of the child's best interest in the changing economic and social context of sub-Saharan Africa', *International Journal of Law and the Family*, 8 (1994), 82–114.
Rwezaura, B.A., 'The changing community obligations to the elderly in contemporary Africa', *Journal of Social Development in Africa*, 4 (1989), 2–24.
Saada, E., *Les Enfants de la Colonie: Les Métis de l'Empire français entre sujétion et citoyenetté* (Paris: Editions La Découverte, 2007).
Saada, E., *Empire's Children: Race, Filiation, and Citizenship in the French Colonies* (Chicago: University of Chicago Press, 2012).
Sachs, D., *The Life We Were Given: Operation Babylift, International Adoption and the Children of War in Vietnam* (Boston: Beacon Press, 2010).
Sajor, I.L. (ed.), *Common Grounds: Violence Against Women in War and Armed Conflict Situations* (Asian Center for Women's Human Rights, 1998).
Salganik, M.J., 'Commentary: Respondent-driven sampling in the real world', *Epidemiology*, 23 (2012), 148–50.
Salganik, M.J. and D.D. Heckathorn, 'Sampling and estimation in hidden populations using respondent-driven sampling', *Sociological Methodology*, 34 (2004), 193–240.
Salzmann, T.A., 'Rape camps as a means of ethnic cleansing: Religious, cultural and ethical responses to rape victims in the Former Yugoslavia', *Human Rights Quarterly*, 20 (1998), 348–78.
San, S., 'Where the girls are: The management of venereal disease by United States military forces in Vietnam', *Literature and Medicine*, 23 (2004), 66–84.
Sander, H., *Freier und BeFreite: Krieg, Vergwaltigung, Kinder* (Munich: Verlag Antje Kunstmann, 1992).
Sandke, C., 'Der Lebensborn: Eine Darstellung der Aktivitätendes Lebensborn e.V. im Kontext der nationalsozialistischen Rassenideologie' (Master's thesis, Leipzig University, 2005), pp. 32–4.
Satjukow, S., *Besatzer: Die Russen in Deutschland 1945–1994* (Göttingen: Vandenhoek & Ruprecht, 2008).
Satjukow, S., 'Besatzungskinder: Nachkommen deutscher Frauen und alliierter Soldaten seit 1945', *Geschichte und Gesellschaft*, 37 (2011), 559–91.
Satjukow, S. and R. Gries, *'Bankerte!' Besatzungekinder in Deutschland nach 1945* (Frankfurt: Campus Verlag 2015).
Satjukow, S. and B. Stelzl-Marx, 'Besatzungskinder in Vergangenheit und Gegenwart', in B. Stelzl-Marx and S. Satjukkow (eds), *Besatzungskinder: Die Nachkommen alliierter Soldaten in Österreich und Deutschland* (Wien: Böhlau Verlag, 2015), pp. 11–14.
Schäfers, N. and R.F. Stiegler, 'Besatzungskinder', *Kriesenjahre und Aufbruchsstimmung: Die Nachkriegszeit in Deutschland 1945–1965*, Internetportal Westfälische Geschichte: Aufwachsen in Westfalen. http://lwl.org/westfaelische-geschichte/portal/Internet/input_felder/langDatensatz_ebene4.php?urlID=896&url_tabelle=tab_websegmente. (accessed 31.10.12016).
Scharlach, L., 'Rape as genocide: Bangladesh, the Former Yugoslavia, and Rwanda', *New Political Science*, 22 (2000), 89–102.
Schechner, S. and D. Hinshaw, 'France investigates allegations of sexual assault by its peacekeepers in Central African Republic', *The Wall Street Journal*, 29.4.2015, http://wsj.com/articles/france-investigates-allegations-of-sexual-assault-by-its-peacekeepers-in-central-african-republic-1430344621. (accessed 28.2.2017).

Schechter, D.S. et al., 'Mother–daughter relationships and child sexual abuse: A pilot study of 35 days', *Bulletin of the Menninger Clinic*, 66 (2002), 39–60.

Schechter, D.S. et al., 'Psychobiological dysregulation in violence-exposed mothers: Salivary cortisol of mothers with very young children pre- and post-separation stress', *Bulletin of the Menninger Clinic*, 68 (2004), 319–36.

Scheidt, C.E. et al., *Narrative Bewältigung von Trauma und Verlust* (Stuttgart: Schattauer Verlag, 2014).

Schellstede, S.C. and S.M. Yu, *Comfort Women Speak: Testimony by Sex Slaves of the Japanese Military. Includes New United Nations Human Rights Report* (New York: Holmes & Meier Publishers, 2000).

Schissler, H. (ed.), *The Miracle Years: A Cultural History of West Germany 1945–1948* (Princeton: Princeton University Press, 2001).

Schmidlechner, K., 'Kinder und Enkelkinder britischer Besatzungssoldaten in Österreich', in B. Stelzl-Marx and S. Satjukow (eds), *Besatzungskinder: Die Nachkommen alliierter Soldaten in Österreich und Deutschland* (Wien: Böhlau-Verlag, 2015), pp. 238–58.

Schmidlechner, K.M., *Frauenleben in Männerwelten: Kriegsende und Nachkriegszeit in der Steiermark* (Wien: Döcker, 1997).

Schmitz-Köster, D., *Deutsche Mutter bist du bereit – Alltag im Lebensborn* (Berlin: Aufbau-Verlag, 2002).

Schott, C., *Kindesannahme – Adoption – Wahlkindschaft, Rechtsgeschichte und Rechtsgeschichten* (Frankfurt: Wolfgang Metzner Verlag, 2009).

Schwerdtfeger, K.L., 'Intergenerational transmission of trauma: Exploring mother–infant prenatal attachment' (Master's thesis, Kansas State University, Manhattan, KS, 2004).

Schwerdtfeger, K.L. and B.S.N. Goff, 'Intergenerational transmission of trauma: Exploring mother–infant prenatal attachment', *Journal of Traumatic Stress*, 20 (2007), 39–57.

Seager, J., *The State of Women in the World Atlas* (London: Penguin, 1997).

Seegers, L., 'Absente Väter der Nachkriegszeit: Vater-Los – Der gefallene Vater in der Erinnerung von Halbwaisen in Deutschland nach 1945', in J. Brunner (ed.), *Mütterliche Macht und väterliche Autorität: Elternbilder im deutschen Diskurs* (Göttingen: Wallstein Verlag 2008), pp. 128–51.

Seifert, R., *War and Rape: Analytical Approaches* (London: Women's International League for Peace and Freedom, 1992).

Seifert, R., 'Krieg und Vergewaltigung: Ansätze einer Analyse', in A. Stiglmayer (ed.), *Massenvergewaltigungen: Krieg gegen die Frauen* (Freiburg/Br.: Kore Verlag, 1994), pp. 85–108; translated into English as R. Seifert, 'War and rape: A preliminary analysis', in A. Stiglmayer (ed.), *Mass Rape: The War against Women in Bosnia-Herzogovina* (Lincoln: University of Nebraska Press, 1994), 54–72.

Selman, P., 'The rise and fall of intercountry adoption in the 21st century', *International Social Work*, 52 (2009), 575–94.

Seto, D., *No Place for a War Baby: The Global Politics of Children Born of Wartime Sexual Violence* (Farnham: Ashgate, 2013).

Sharlach, L., 'Gender and genocide in Rwanda: Women as agents and objects of Genocide 1', *Journal of Genocide Research*, 1 (1999), 387–99.

Shawcross, W., *Sideshow: Kissinger, Nixon and the Destruction of Cambodia* (New York: Simon and Schuster, 1979).
Sheehan, P., 'An orgy of denial in Hitler's bunker', *The Sydney Morning Herald*, 17.5.2003, www.smh.com.au/articles/2003/05/16/1052885399546.html. (accessed 28.2.2017).
Sheppard, B., *War in the Wild East: The German Army and Soviet Partisans* (Cambridge, MA: Harvard University Press, 2004).
Shonkoff, J.P. and S.J. Meisels (eds), *Handbook of Early Childhood Intervention* (Cambridge: Cambridge University Press, 2000).
Shoten, I., *Jugun Ianfu (The Wartime Comfort Women)* (1995); translated into English as, *Comfort Women: Sexual Slavery in Japanese Military during World War II* (New York: Columbia University Press, 2000).
Shukert, E.B. and B.S. Scibetta, *War Brides of World War II* (California: Presidio Press, 1988).
Sieg, R., *Mischlingskinder in Westdeutschland: Festschrift für Frédéric Falkenburger* (Baden-Baden: Verlag für Kunst und Wissenschaft, 1954).
Siek, S., 'The difficult identities of Germany's brown babies', *Spiegel Online International*, 13.10.2009 www.spiegel.de/international/germany/germany-s-brown-babies-the-difficult-identities-of-post-war-black-children-of-gis-a-651989.html. (accessed 31.10.2016).
Simić, O., 'Accountability of UN civilian police involved in trafficking of women in Bosnia and Herzegovina', *University for Peace and Conflict Monitor* (online), http://monitor.upeace.org/pdf/bosnia.pdf, pp. 4–5. (accessed 31.10.2016).
Simić, O. and M. O'Brien, 'Peacekeeper babies': An unintended legacy of United Nations peace support operations', *International Peacekeeping*, 21 (2014), 345–63.
Simm, G., *Sex in Peace Operations* (Cambridge: Cambridge University Press, 2013).
Simms, B., *Unfinest Hour: Britain and the Destruction of Bosnia* (London: Penguin, 2001).
Simonsen, E., 'Into the open – or hidden away? The construction of war children as a social category in post-war Norway and Germany', *NORDEUROPAforum*, 2 (2006), 25–49.
Skelsbæk, I., 'Sexual violence and war: Mapping out a complex relationship', *European Journal of International Affairs*, 7 (2001), 211–37.
Skjelsbæck, I., 'Victim and survivor: Narrated social identities of women who experienced rape during the war in Bosnia-Herzegovina', *Feminism and Psychology*, 16 (2006), 373–403.
Skjelsbæk, I., 'The elephant in the room: An overview of how sexual violence came to be seen as a weapon of war' (Oslo: PRIO Report, 2010).
Skjelsbæk, I., 'Conceptualizing sexual violence perpetrators', in M. Bergmo, A. Butenschø Skre and E.J. Wood (eds), *Understanding and Proving International Sex Crimes* (Beijing: Torkel Opsahll Academic Publishers, 2012), pp. 495–509.
Skjelsbæck, I., *The Political Psychology of War Rape* (Abingdon: Routledge, 2012).
Smith, H., 'Rape victims: Babies pay the price of war', *Observer*, 16.4.2000.
Smith-Spark, L., 'How did rape become a weapon of war?', *BBC News*, 8.12.2004, http://news.bbc.co.uk/1/hi/4078677.stm. (accessed 31.10.2016).
Smolin, D.M, 'Intercountry adoption as child trafficking', *Valparaiso Law Review*, 39 (2005), 281–325.
Smolin, D.M., 'Child laundering: How the adoption system legitimizes and incentivizes

the practices of buying, trafficking, kidnapping and stealing children', *Wayne Law Review*, 52 (2006), 113–200.

Soh, C.S., *The Comfort Women: Sexual Violence and Postcolonial Memory in Korea and Japan* (Chicago: University of Chicago Press, 2008).

Solomon, A., *Far From the Tree: Parents, Children and the Search for Identity* (London: Random House, 2013).

Solomos, J., *Race and Racism in Britain*, 3rd edn (Basingstoke: Palgrave Macmillan, 2003).

Šoštarić, M., *War Victims and Gender-Sensitive Truth, Justice, Reparations and Non-Recurrence in Bosnia and Herzegovina* (Utrecht: Impunity Watch, 2012).

Sotomayor, A.C., *The Myth of the Democratic Peacekeeper: Civil–Military Relations and the United Nations* (Washington: Johns Hopkins University Press, 2013).

Spinelli, M.G. (ed.), *Infanticide: Psychosocial and Legal Perspectives on Mothers who Kill* (Arlington: American Psychiatric Press Inc., 2002).

Spinney, L., 'Born scared: How your parents' trauma marks your genes', *New Scientist*, 2 (2010), 46–9.

Spreen, M., 'Rare populations, hidden populations, and link-tracing designs: What and why?' *Bulletin de Methodologie Sociologique*, 36 (1992), 34–58.

Srncik, G., 'Besatzungskinder: Ein Weltproblem', *Arbeiter-Zeitung*, 3.11.1955.

Stambolis, B. (ed.), *Vaterlosigkeit in vaterarmen Zeiten: Beiträge zu einem historischen und gesellschaftlichen Schlüsselthema* (Landsberg: Beltz Juventa, 2013).

Starr, J.R., *Fraternisation with the Germans in World War II*, Office of the Chief Historian, US European Command, Planning for the Occupation of Germany, Occupation Forces in Europe Series, 1945–46 (Frankfurt: US European Command, 1947).

Statistisches Bundesamt (ed.), *Statistische Berichte*, Wiesbaden, 'Die unehelichen Kinder von Besatzungsangehörigen im Bundesgebiet und Berlin (West)', Arb-Nr. VI/29/6, 1956, Tables 1–19.

Steiger, H.T.T, 'Changes in Lango marriage customs', *Uganda Journal*, 7:4 (1940), 145–63.

Stelzl-Marx, B., 'Die unsichtbare Generation: Kinder sowjetischer Besatzungssoldaten in Österreich und Deutschland', *Historical Social Research*, 34 (2009), 352–72.

Stelzl-Marx, B., *Stalins Soldaten in Österreich: Die Innensicht der sowjetischen Besatzung 1945–1955* (Wien / München: Böhlau Verlag, 2012).

Stelzl-Marx, B. and S. Satjukow (eds), *Besatzungskinder: Die Nachkommen alliierter Soldaten in Österreich und Deutschland* (Wien: Böhlau-Verlag, 2015).

Sternberg, T.H. et al., 'Communicable diseases', in US Army Medical Department (ed.), *History of the Office of Medical History: Preventive Medicine in WWII, Volume V*, http://history.amedd.army.mil/booksdocs/wwii/communicablediseasesV5/chapter10.htm. (accessed 6.6.2014).

Stewart, B., *We Are All the Same: Experiences of Children Born into LRA Captivity*, JRP Field Note, 23.12.2015, http://justiceandreconciliation.com/publications/field-notes/2015/we-are-all-the-same-experiences-of-children-born-into-lra-captivity/. (accessed 31.10.2016).

Stiglmayer, A. (ed,), *Mass Rape: The War Against Women in Bosnia-Herzegovina* (Lincoln: University of Nebraska Press, 1994).

Stouffer, S., *The American Soldier: Studies in Social Psychology in World War II* (Princeton: Princeton University Press, 1949).

Strauß, S., 'Wo bist du? Besatzungskinder: Die Suche nach dem Vater', *Berliner Zeitung*, 27.10.2013, www.berliner-zeitung.de/berlin/besatzungskinder--die-suche-nach-dem-vater-wo-bist-du--3640012. (accessed 28.2.2017).
Stur, H.M., *Beyond Combat: Women and Gender in the Vietnam War Era* (Cambridge: Cambridge University Press, 2011).
Sturdevant, S.P. and B. Stoltzfus, *Let the Good Times Roll: Prostitution and the US Military in Asia* (New York: New Press, 1993).
Sullivan, S., 'Born under a bad sign', *Newsweek*, 23.9.1996.
Sun, S., 'Where the girls are: The management of venereal disease by United States military forces in Vietnam', *Literature and Medicine*, 23 (2004), 66–87.
Swillen, G., *Koekoekskind: Door de vijand verwekt 1940–1945* (Antwerpen: De Bezige Bij 2009).
Tanaka, Y. *Japan's Comfort Women: Sexual Slavery and Prostitution During World War II and the US Occupation* (London & New York: Routledge, 2002).
Tanaka, Y., 'Introduction', in M.R. Henson (ed.), *Comfort Woman: A Filipina's Story of Prostitution and Slavery under the Japanese Military* (Lanham, MD; Rowman & Littlefield, 1999), pp. vii–xxi.
Tavecchia, G. et al., 'Estimating population size and hidden demographic parameters with state-space modeling', *The American Naturalist*, 173 (2009), 722–33.
Taylor, R., *Orphans of War: Work with Abandoned Children of Vietnam 1967–1975* (London: Collins, 1988).
Templeton, I., 'What's so German About it? Cultural Identity in the Berlin Hip Hop Scene' (D.Phil. thesis, University of Stirling, 2005).
Thane, P. and T. Evans, *Sinners? Scroungers? Saints? Unmarried Motherhood in Twentieth-Century England* (Oxford: Oxford University Press, 2012).
Thomas, D.K. and R.E. Ralph, 'Rape in war: Challenging the tradition of impunity', *SAIS Review*, 14 (1994), 81–99.
Thompson, A. (ed.), *The Media and the Rwanda Genocide* (London: Pluto Press, 2007).
Thompson, L.V., 'Lebensborn and the eugenics policy of the Reichsführer-SS', *Central European History*, 4 (1971), 54–77.
Thorne, C.G. (ed.), *Border Crossings: Studies in International History* (Oxford: Wiley Blackwell, 1988).
Thornhill, R. and C. Palmer, *A Natural History of Rape* (Cambridge, MA: MIT Press, 2000).
Thurber, C., 'Militias as sociopolitical movements: Lessons from Iraq's armed Shia groups', *Small Wars & Insurgencies*, 25 (2014), 900–23.
Tiefenbrun, S.W., 'Child soldiers, slavery, and the trafficking of children', *Fordham International Law Journal*, 31 (2007), 417–86.
Titmuss, R.M., *Problems of Social Policy* (London: HMSO, 1950).
Toeka, T., 'Grim prospects of DRC's female child soldiers', *International Justice ICC*, 296 (2011).
Tokaca, M. (ed.), *The Plucked Buds* (Sarajevo: Commission for Gathering Facts on War Crimes in Bosnia and Herzegovina, 2002).
Torgovnik, J., *Intended Consequences: Children Born of Rape* (New York: Aperture, 2009).
Travis, A., 'Britain will ease way for adoption', *The Guardian*, 4.1.1993, 9.
Travis-Robyns, S.R., '"What is winning anyway?" Redefining veteran: A Vietnamese American woman's experience', in L.T. Võ and M. Sciachitano (eds), *Asian-American*

Women: The Frontiers Reader (Lincoln: University of Nebraska Press, 2004), pp. 125–49.

Tripp, A.M., 'Women's movements, customary law, and land rights in Africa: The case of Uganda', *African Studies Quarterly*, 7 (2004), 1–19.

Tucker, S.C. (ed.), *The Encyclopedia of the Vietnam War: A Political, Social and Military History*, 2nd edn (Santa Barbara: ABC-Clio, 2011).

Tuhiwai Smith, L., *Decolonizing Methodologies: Research and Indigenous Peoples* (New York: St. Martin's Press, 1992).

Turner, F., *Echoes of Combat: The Vietnam War in American Memory* (New York: Anchor Books, 1996).

Tynes, R.M., 'Child Soldier Use: The Diffusion of a Tactical Innovation' (Ph.D. thesis, State University of New York at Albany 2011).

Uhlenius, P., 'The hidden children of German soldiers and Soviet prisoners of war', in L. Westerlund (ed.), *Children of German Soldiers: Children of Foreign Soldiers in Finland 1940–1948*, vol. 1 (Helsinki: Painopaikka Nord Print, 2011), 153–9.

UN Sub-Commission on the Promotion and Protection of Human Rights, 'Systematic Rape, Sexual Slavery and Slavery-Like Practices During Armed Conflict: Final Report', submitted by Gay J. McDougall, Special Rapporteur, 22.6.1998, E/CN.4/Sub.2/1998/13, http://unhcr.org/refworld/docid/3b00f44114.html. (accessed 31.10.2016).

UN PSEA Taskforce, *To Serve with Pride*. 2009, http://un.org/en/pseataskforce/video_english.shtml. (accessed 31.10.2016).

UNHCR and Save the Children UK, 'Note for implementing and operation partners on sexual violence and exploitation: The experience of refugee children in Guinea, Liberia and Sierra Leone', 2002, www.savethechildren.org.uk/sites/default/files/docs/sexual_violence_and_exploitation_1.pdf. (accessed 31.10.2016).

United Nations (ed.), 'Addressing Conflict-Related Sexual Violence: An analytical Inventory of Peacekeeping Practice' (New York, 2010), www.resdal.org/wps/assets/04dananalyticalinventoryofpeacekeepingpracti.pdf. (accessed 31.10.2016).

United Nations, 'United Nation Comprehensive Strategy on Assistance and Support to Victims of Sexual Exploitation and Abuse by United Nations Staff and Related Personnel' A/RES/62/214, 21.12.2007, www.un.org/en/ga/search/view_doc.asp?symbol=A/RES/62/214. (accessed 16.3.2017).

United Nations Security Council, 'Women, Peace and Security', Resolution 1820 (2008) www.un.org/press/en/2008/sc9364.doc.htm. (accessed 31.10.2016).

UNOCHA, 'Sexual Violence in Armed Conflict: Understanding the Motivations', Discussion paper of the UN OCHA Research Meeting, 26.6.2008, www.peacewomen.org/assets/file/Resources/UN/ocha_svinarmedconflictmotivations_2009.pdf. (accessed 31.10.2016).

Uzoigwe, G.N., *Uganda: The Dilemma of Nationhood* (New York: NOK Publishers International, 1982).

Valverde, K.-L.C., 'From dust to gold: The Vietnamese Amerasian experience', in Maria P.P. Root (ed.), *Racially Mixed People in America* (London: Sage Publishers, 1992), pp. 144–61.

Van den Dries. L. et al., 'Fostering security? A meta-analysis of attachment in adopted children', *Children and Youth Services Review*, 31 (2009), 410–21.

Van Ee, E. and R.J. Kleber, 'Child in the shadowlands', *The Lancet*, 380:9842 (2012), 642–3.
Van Ee, E., and R.J. Kleber, 'Growing up under a shadow: Key issues in research on and treatment of children born of rape', *Child Abuse Review*, 22 (2013), 386–97.
Vandenberg, M., *Hopes Betrayed: Trafficking of Women and Girls to Post-Conflict Bosnia and Herzegovina for Forced Prostitution* (New York: Human Rights Watch, 2002).
Verdier, R.E.D., E. Decaux and J.-P. Chretien (eds), *Rwanda: Un genocide du XXieme siècle* (Paris: L'Harmatten, 1995).
Vikman, E., 'Ancient origins: Sexual violence in warfare, Part I', *Anthropology & Medicine*, 12 (2005), 21–31.
Vindevogel, S. et al., 'Forced conscription of children during armed conflict: Experiences of former child soldiers in Northern Uganda', *Child Abuse and Neglect*, 35 (2011), 551–62.
Virgili, F., 'Enfants de Boches: The war children of France', in Kjersti Ericsson and Eva Simonssen (eds), *Children of World War II* (Oxford: Berg, 2005), 21–31.
Virgili, F., *La France virile: Des femmes tondues à la Libération* (Paris: Payot, 2000).
Virgili, F., *The Shorn Women: Gender and Punishment in Liberation France* (Oxford: Berg, 2002).
Virgili, F., *Naître ennemi: Les Enfants de couples franco-allemands nés pendant la Seconde Guerre mondiale* (Paris: Payot, 2009).
Vittachi, V.T., *Between the Guns: Children as a Zone of Peace* (London: Hodder and Stoughton, 1993).
Võ, L.T. and M. Sciachitano (eds), *Asian-American Women: The Frontiers Reader* (Lincoln: University of Nebraska Press, 2004).
Voges, W. (ed.), *Methoden der Biographie- und Lebenslaufforschung*, vol. 1. (Heidelberg: Springer-Verlag, 2013).
Von Lehndorff, H., *Ostpreußisches Tagebuch: Aufzeichnungen eines Arztes aus den Jahren 1945–1947* (München: Deutscher Taschenbuch Verlag, 1997).
Von Nogent, G., *Dei Gesta per Francos*, translated as *The Deeds of God Through the Franks* (tr. by Robert Levine, 1997), http://gutenberg.org/ebooks/4370.
Waldemar Oelrich, 'Die unehelichen Besatzungskinder der Jahrgänge 1945 bis 1954 in Baden-Württemberg', *Statistische Monatshefte Baden-Württemberg*, 2 (1956), 38–9.
Walkowitz, J.R., *Prostitution and Victorian Society: Women, Class, and the State* (Cambridge: Cambridge University Press, 1982).
Wältermann, D., 'The functions and activities of the Lebensborn Organisation within the SS, the Nazi regime, and Nazi ideology', *The Honors Journal*, 2 (1985), 5–23.
Warburton, A., 'EC investigative mission into the treatment of Muslim women in the former Yugoslavia: Report to Foreign Ministers', www.liverpool.ac.uk/library/sca/colldescs/owen/boda/sp7a.pdf. (accessed 31.10.2016).
Ward, M. et al., *Japanese War Brides in America: An Oral History* (Santa Barbara: Praeger, 2009).
Watson, A.M.S., 'Children born of wartime rape: Rights and representations', *International Feminist Journal of Politics*, 9 (2007), 20–34.
Watson, C., 'Birth control and abortion in France since 1939', *Population Studies*, 5 (1951/52), 261–86.
Watson-Smyth, K., 'GI babies abandoned during Second World War reunite to trace their unknown fathers', *The Independent*, 8.7.2000.

Wax, E., 'Rwandans are struggling to love the children of hate', *The Washington Post*, 28.3.2004. www.washingtonpost.com/archive/politics/2004/03/28/rwandans-are-struggling-to-love-children-of-hate/dd942c7b-9287-42cc-8763-bd0675c0b73f/?utm_term=.3a17cbf65ac6. (accessed 28.2.2017).

Weber, A., 'Abducted and abused: Renewed conflict in Northern Uganda', *Human Rights Watch*, 15 (2003), https://hrw.org/report/2003/07/15/abducted-and-abused/renewed-war-northern-uganda. (accessed 31.10.2016).

Weissbach, L.S. 'Child labor legislation in Nineteenth-Century France', *The Journal of Economic History*, 37 (1977), 268–71.

Weitsmann, P., 'Children born of war and the policy of identity', in R. Charli Carpenter (ed.), *Born of War: Protecting Children of Sexual Violence Survivors in Conflict Zones* (Bloomfield, CT: Kumarin Press, 2007), pp. 110–27.

Werner, E., 'Protective factors and individual resilience', in J. P. Shonkoff and S.J. Meisels (eds), *Handbook of Early Childhood Intervention* (Cambridge: Cambridge University Press, 2000), pp. 97–116.

Westerlund, L. (ed.), *Children of German Soldiers: Children of Foreign Soldiers in Finland 1940–1948*, vol. I (Helsinki: Painopaikka Nord Print, 2011).

Westerlund, L. (ed.), *The Children of Foreign Soldiers in Finland, Norway, Denmark, Austria, Poland and Occupied Soviet Karelia: Children of Foreign Soldiers in Finland 1940–1948*, vol. II (Helsinki: Painopaikka Nord Print, Helsinki 2011).

Wietsma, A., *Tuan Papa – Mijnheer de Vader – Suir Daddy: De vergeten kinderen van Nederlandse militairen in Indonesië* (Hellwig Productions, 2010).

Willbanks, J.H., *Vietnam War Almanac* (New York: Checkmarck Books, 2010).

Williams, C.J., 'Bosnia's orphans of rape: Innocent legacy of hatred', *The Times*, 24.7.1993. http://articles.latimes.com/1993-07-24/news/mn-16356_1_bosnian. (accessed 28.2.2017).

Williams-León, T. and C.L. Nakashima (eds), *The Sum of Our Parts: Mixed-Heritage Asian Americans* (Philadelphia: Temple University Press, 2001).

Willoughby, J., 'The sexual behavior of American GIs during the early years of the Occupation of Germany', *Journal of Military History*, 62 (1998), 155–74.

Wilson, S., *Research is Ceremony: Indigenous Research Methods* (Nova Scotia: Fernwood Publishing, 2008).

Winfield, P. *Melancholy Baby: The Unplanned Consequences of the G.I.s' Arrival in Europe for World War II* (Westport: Bergin & Garvey, 2000).

Winfield, P., *Bye Bye Baby: The Story of the Children the GIs Left Behind* (London: Bloomsbury, 1992).

Wingfield-Hayes, R., 'Japan revisionists deny World War II sex slave atrocities', *BBC News online*, www.bbc.co.uk/news/world-asia-33754932, 3.8.2015. (accessed 31.10.2016).

Wood, E., 'Multiple perpetrator rape during war', in M.A.H. Horvath and J. Woodhams (eds), *Handbook of the Study of Multiple Perpetrator Rape: A Multidisciplinary Response to an International Problem* (New York: Routledge, 2013), pp. 132–59.

Wood, E.J., 'Armed groups and sexual violence: When is wartime rape rare?', *Politics and Society*, 37 (2009), 131–62.

Wood, S.K, 'A woman scorned for the "least condemned" war crime: Precedent and problems with prosecuting rape as a serious war crime in the International Criminal Tribunal for Rwanda', *Columbia Journal of Gender and the Law*, 13 (2004), 274–327.

Yahyavi, T., M. Zarghami and U. Marwah, 'A review on the evidence of transgenerational transmission of posttraumatic stress disorder vulnerability', *Revista Brasiliera de Psyquiatra*, 36 (2014), 89–94.

Yang, H., 'Re-remembering the Korean military comfort women', in E.H. Kim and C. Choi (eds), *Dangerous Women: Gender and Korean Nationalism* (New York: Routledge 1998), 123–39.

Yarborough, T., *Surviving Twice: Amerasian Children in Vietnam* (Washington: Potomac Books, 2006).

Yehuda, R. et al., 'Parental posttraumatic stress disorder as a vulnerability factor for low cortisol trait in offspring of holocaust survivors', *Archives of General Psychiatry*, 64 (2007), 1040–8.

Yoshiaki, Y., *Comfort Women: Sexual Slavery in the Japanese Military During World War II* (New York: Columbia University Press, 2000).

Yoshida, R., 'Mixed-race babies in lurch. Facts of occupation life: Abandoned kids from GI–Japanese liaisons', *The Japan Times*, 10.9.2008, http://japantimes.co.jp/news/2008/09/10/national/mixed-race-babies-in-lurch/#.VcsmxPnz57V. (accessed 31.10.2016).

Yuh, J.Y., *Beyond the Shadow of Camptown: Korean Military Brides in America* (New York: New York University Press, 2004).

Zahra, T., *Kidnapped Souls: National Indifference and the Battle for the Children in the Bohemian Lands* (Ithaca: Cornell University Press, 2008).

Zahra, T., *The Lost Children* (Cambridge, MA: Harvard University Press, 2011).

Zarkov, D. and M. Glasius (eds), *Narratives of Justice in and out of the Courtroom. Former Yugoslavia and Beyond* (Heidelberg: Springer, 2014).

Zeiger, S., *Entangling Alliances: Foreign War Brides and American Soldiers in the Twentieth Century* (New York: New York University Press, 2010).

Zhou, M. and C.L. Bankston, *Growing up American: How Vietnamese Children Adapt to Life in the United States* (New York: Russell Sage Foundation, 1998).

Ziemele, I., *Commentary on the United Nations Convention on the Rights of the Child, Article 7: The Right to Birth Registration, Name and Nationality, and the Right to Know and Be Cared for by Parents* (The Hague: Martinus Nijhoff Publishers, 2007).

Ziemke, E.F., *The US Army in the Occupation of Germany 1944–1946* (Washington, DC: Center of Military History, United States Army 1990).

Zink, H., *The United States in Germany, 1944–1955* (Princeton: D. Van Nostrand Company, 1957).

Zornado, J.L, *Inventing the Child: Culture, Ideology, and the Story of Childhood* (New York: Garland, 2001).

Zraly, M., S.E. Rubin and D. Mukamana, 'Motherhood and resilience among Rwandan genocide-rape Survivors', *Ethos*, 41 (2013), 411–39.

Index

Note: page numbers in *italic* refer to figures.

abortion, 27, 56, 64, 71, 154, 156, 159, 164, 195
adoption, 38, 123–6, 157–8, 167
 of French fathered children in Germany, 84, 85
 of GI children, 74, 75, 78, 80–3
 Nazi *Lebensborn e.V.* programme, 57–9, 62, 66–7, 163, 173
adoption, international and interracial, 13, 81–2, 123–34, 138–9, 141, 158, 167
 critics of 'Baby Trade', 12–13, 126, 127, 128–9
 Operation Babylift (1975), 8, 12–13, 112–13, 122–3, 124, 129–34, 174, 246
Africa, sub-Saharan
 bridewealth and luk payments, 15, 207, 208, 209
 concepts of childhood, 14, 195, 197, 206, 207, 209, 211
 and human rights legislation, 9, 15–16
 infanticide in, 163, 195
 kinship groups, 14, 15, 205–10, 212, 213–14
 mixed legal spaces, 14, 16, 212
 moral codes on female sexuality, 203, 204, 205–6, 208–9
 traditional lineage-making, 15, 31–2, 198, 206–9
 see also individual countries
African Charter on the Rights and Welfare of the Child, 171
Algeria, 9, 24

Ali D'adulhakk, 159–60, 170
Allied Museum, Berlin, 51
American Civil War, 27
Amin Dada, General Idi, 200
Anonyma: Eine Frau in Berlin (book and film), 51–2
Ariès, Philippe, 35
Austria, post-war occupation of (1945–1955), 3, 7, 8–9, 28, 53, 70, 73, 85, 123
 life courses of CBOW, 11, 72, 175
 Soviet Zone, 26, 71, 72

Babylift, Operation (1975), 8, 12–13, 112–13, 122–3, 124, 129–34, 174, 246
Bangladesh, 9, 29, 154, 159
Belgium, 57, 58, 59, 66–7, 189
biogenetics, 167
Bosnian War (1992–1995)
 Ali D'adulhakk's 'Fatwa on Children Born by Raped Women', 159–60, 170
 CBOW during, 2, 3–4, 153–60, 161, 163, 165, 166, 168–71
 and CRC, 9, 151–2, 161–3, 165, 168, 171–2
 CRSV as integral part of war tactics/strategy, 1–2, 7, 13–14, 27, 33, 152–4, 161, 191
 ethnically motivated CRSV, 3–4, 13, 21, 27, 29, 33, 151, 152, 153–60, 165
 ICTY, 2, 152, 192, 193–4
 infanticide during, 157, 163

Index

nationality and citizenship issues, 166
  Serb 'rape camps', 3, 7, 13, 21, 165
  UN peacekeeping operations, 228, 229
A Boy from a War Movie (Semsudin Gegic film), 169
Brace, Charles Loring, 125
Brownmiller, Susan, *Against Our Will: Men, Women and Rape*, 30–1, 34
Buck, Pearl, 124
Burundi, 26, 188, 198
Butler, Ethel, 81–2

Cambodia, 3, 116, 227, 228–9
Canada, 3, 26, 70, 73
care systems, 66, 69, 75, 79, 80, 81, 83, 125–6, 132, 157–8
Carpenter, Charli, *Born of War* (essay collection), 2, 5, 154, 175
Central African Republic, 25, 26, 156, 187, 226
Chad, 21
Channel Islands, 57, 59
Chevalier, Jacques, 59–60
childhood, concepts of, 10, 35, 36, 160, 164
  'social construct' theory, 35, 161
  sub-Saharan Africa, 14, 195, 197, 206, 207, 209, 211
  Western notions, 14, 15, 35–6, 161
Children and War: Past and Present (international conference), 5
children born of rape, 1–5, 7, 29–30, 33, 34–5, 167–8, 187, 230
  in Bosnian War, 2, 3–4, 13–14, 153–60, 163, 164, 168–71, 192
  of the LRA conflict, 4, 7, 14–15, 165, 204–5, 206, 209–15
  of post-war occupation soldiers, 70–1, 85
  in Rwandan genocide, 4, 14, 190, 192–3, 194–8
  during Second World War, 56–7, 71–2, 165
children born of war (CBOW)
  adverse health outcomes, 11, 64, 65, 68, 156–7, 195, 211, 245, 248
  claims to fathers' nationality, 8, 83–4, 247
  definitions and categorisations of, 10, 24–6
  distinct French approach to, 83–5, 173–4, 246

  as expedient political pawns, 12–13, 36, 78–86, 121–2, 126, 130–1, 134, 136–7, 139–40, 160, 173–4, 246
  fathered by American GIs in WW2 period, 73, 74–5, 76–83, 123–4
  fathered by UN peacekeepers, 3, 16, 25–6, 215–16, 230, 231, 234–8
  idealisation/fantasies of the father, 28, 69, 72, 89, 92
  of LRA conflict, 4, 14, 15, 165, 198, 204–5, 206, 209–15
  mixed-race offspring of GIs in Asia, 3, 12, 25, 112–13, 124, 125, 129, 133, 134–41
  mixed-race offspring of GIs in Europe, 74–5, 76, 77, 79–83, 123, 124
  as not recent phenomenon, 2, 21–3
  post-conflict integration of, 7, 14–16, 29, 35, 76–86, 87–93, 136–8, 158–60, 170–1, 194–8, 206, 208–15
  psychosocial challenges, 11, 83, 85, 87, 131, 141, 170–1, 175, 210–11, 212–13, 237, 244–5
  responses of local communities to, 11, 13, 69, 129, 131, 159–60, 164, 194–8, 205–15, 244, 245
    see also stigmatisation and discrimination
  Russenkinder (of Soviet soldiers, 1945–55), 9, 71, 72, 87–9, 88, 90, 244
  of Rwandan conflict, 4, 192, 194–5, 196–8
  search for their fathers, 72, 89–91, 92, 133, 172, 174, 247
  as secondary victims of rape, 196
  secrecy and taboo, 65, 67, 69, 72, 87, 89, 213, 245
  socio-economic challenges, 11, 39, 67–8, 86, 121, 137–8, 157, 169–70, 195–7, 211–13, 215, 245, 247–8
  visibility of biological origin, 8, 12, 74–5, 79–80, 82–3, 92–3, 112–13, 121
  of Wehrmacht soldiers, 3, 5, 24, 57–67, 89, 92, 165, 173, 174
  of Western occupation soldiers in Germany, 3, 8–9, 11–12, 53, 70, 77–87, 89–92
  as widely ignored reality, 1, 2, 4, 5, 14, 52, 153, 154
    see also mothers of CBOW

children born of war (CBOW), life courses of
  of Babylift children, 130–1, 132, 133–4
  Bosnian War, 155–60, 168–71
  children of peacekeeping forces, 236–7
  children of post-war occupations, 11–12, 53, 72, 77–93, 175
  conceptualisation of factors affecting, 67–8, 68, 121–2
  LRA children, 209–15
  nature of parents' relationship, 6, 23, 26, 28–9, 247
  Rwandan conflict, 194–5, 196–8
  Second World War, 11, 64–9, 68, 69, 74–5, 86–93, 174–5
  Vietnam War, 112–13, 121–3, 130–41
Children's Crusade (1212), 25
children's rights issues, 2, 4, 5, 9, 13–14, 16, 35–8, 39–40
  'best interest of the child' concept, 14, 37, 38, 126, 127, 161, 167–8, 171–2, 173, 174, 237, 246
  Declaration of Geneva (1924), 37, 161, 171
  importance of local culture, 15–16, 163–4, 176, 198
  international humanitarian law (IHL), 10, 13–14, 36, 37–9, 160, 161–8, 171–2, 175–6
  in pre-CRC conflicts, 172–5
  rights of mother conflicting with, 14, 164, 166–8, 172, 247
  and struggle for women's rights, 36–7, 171
  Western/Northern legal traditions, 14, 15
  see also Convention on the Rights of the Child, UN (CRC, 1989)
child soldiers, 25, 32, 39, 187, 205
  female sex slaves, 4, 7, 14–15, 25, 27, 28, 187, 202, 203, 204, 209, 214–15
Christian missionary ideas, 125
Clark, Janine Natalya, 195, 196
class prejudices, 11, 63, 74, 137
Cold War, 8, 12, 75, 113–15
conflict-related sexual violence (CRSV)
  academic research and studies, 2, 5, 10–11, 151
  biosocial theory, 34–5
  Bosnian Wars, 1, 3–4, 7, 13–14, 21, 27, 33, 151–60, 161, 165, 166, 193–4
  as crimes against humanity and war crimes, 2, 13, 152–3, 154–5, 193–4
  ethnically motivated, 3–4, 13, 14, 27, 29, 33–4, 151, 152, 153–60, 165, 190–1, 192–7
  forced pregnancy, 21, 33, 152, 153–60, 161, 164, 194
  forced prostitution, 27, 34, 53, 55, 63–4, 152, 154, 229, 231
  Hague Regulations, 192
  increased attention to, 1–2, 29, 192
  instrumentalisation of women in warfare, 31, 33, 190–1, 192
  as integral part of war (strategic rape theory), 1–2, 7, 13–14, 27, 29–30, 33–4, 152–4, 191, 192–3
  international humanitarian law (IHL), 13–14, 15–16, 31, 192
  in LRA conflict, 4, 7, 14, 15, 165, 202, 203, 204, 206, 209–15
  motivations for, 29–35
  post-war occupation soldiers, 70–1
  and pre-twentieth-century conflicts, 21, 22–3, 29
  psychosocial consequences of, 33–4, 154–5, 193, 194, 195–6, 210, 212–13, 214–15
  rape as 'crime of identity', 195–6
  'Rape of Nanjing' (1937–38), 63–4
  in Rwanda, 1, 4, 7, 14, 21, 27, 29, 33, 152, 190–1, 192–3, 194–7
  Second World War, 7, 27, 28, 30, 51–2, 54–7, 69–70, 71–2, 76
  socio-cultural theories, 30–5
  spread of HIV/AIDS, 192–3, 194, 196, 209, 210
  Tanzanian soldiers in Uganda, 200
  by UN peacekeepers, 3, 16, 21, 26, 28, 35, 226, 227, 228–30, 232–4
  war rape victims as war heroes, 159–60
consensual/non-violent relationships, 2, 6, 23, 26, 28, 51, 172, 200, 247
  in conditions of inequality, 119, 231, 235–6
  post-war occupation soldiers, 8–9, 70, 71, 72, 73–85
  and pre-twentieth-century conflicts, 21, 22, 23
  UN peacekeeping operations, 228, 231, 235–6, 238
  Vietnam War, 118, 119

Index

Convention on the Rights of the Child, UN (CRC, 1989), 9, 14, 37–8, 40, 160, 161–76
   Bosnian War, 151–2, 161–3, 165, 168, 171–2
   enforcement/implementation, 14, 15–16, 163, 167–8, 175–6
   guiding principles/substantive provisions, 38–9, 161, 162tab, 163–72, 176, 247
Coomaraswamy, Radhika, 31
Crimean War, 27
Croatia, 157, 166

Darfur, 21, 154
The Daughter from Danang (documentary film), 112
Democratic Republic of Congo (DRC), 9, 25, 26, 27, 32, 187, 228, 232
Denmark, 11, 58, 64, 65, 66
discrimination and stigmatisation *see* stigmatisation and discrimination
Distelblüten (thistle blossom), 87–9
Drabble, Margaret, 6

East Timor, 3, 228, 234–5
Enfants maudits (Jean-Paul Picaper and Ludwig Norz), 65
Eyferth, Klaus, 82

feminist literature, 31, 231
First World War, 3, 24, 27, 36, 37, 52
Ford, Gerald, 115–16, 122
fostering arrangements, 124, 125
France, 9, 24–5, 59–62, 83–5, 168
   children fathered by French soldiers, 8, 83–5, 160, 173–4, 246
   children of Wehrmacht soldiers, 3, 57, 59–60, 61–2, 64, 65–6
   femmes tondues in, 65–6, 86
   Indochina Wars, 8, 84, 113, 160, 173–4, 246
   Vichy, 60, 61
Fröbel, Friedrich, 35
Fulbright, Senator, 117

gender-based violence (GBV) *see* conflict-related sexual violence (CRSV)
Geneva Convention, Fourth (1949), 154, 162, 192, 193
   Additional Protocol II (1977), 152, 154, 162, 192
Genocide Convention, 162
Germany, colonial rule in Africa, 189

Germany, Nazi
   CBOW of Wehrmacht soldiers, 3, 57–67, 89, 92, 165, 173
   child soldiers in Second World War, 25
   Lebensborn e.V. programme, 57–9, 62, 66–7, 163, 173
   policy on CBOW, 56–9, 61–2, 66–7
   racial ideology, 54–9, 61–2, 66–7, 173
   'Rhineland Bastards' in 1930s, 79–80
   and sexuality, 55
   sexual slavery in concentration camps, 27
   SS, 56, 57, 58, 60, 62
   WW2 military brothels, 27, 34, 53, 55, 60–1
Germany, post-war occupation of (1945–1955), 3, 7, 8–9, 11, 25, 26, 27, 28
   CBOW data, 70, 76–7, 83, 86
   constitutional discourse of late 1940s, 78–80
   German–Allied love affairs, 51, 70, 75–82
   legal frameworks in USA and Germany, 77–81
   life courses of CBOW, 11–12, 53, 72, 77–93, 175
   mixed-race GI children, 76, 77, 79–83, 124
   rape by occupation soldiers, 70–1
   Soviet occupation soldiers, 26, 71–2, 87–9, *88*, *90*, 244
   Western occupation soldiers, 73, 75–82, 83–6, 124, 246
GI-Trace network, 87
'Global Summit to End Sexual Violence in Conflict' (London, June 2014), 2, 247
Gottschall, Jonathan, 30
Grammer, Mabel A., 81–2
Grbavica (Jasmila Zbanic film), 168–9
Great Britain, 9, 85–6, 158
   American presence in (WW2), 25, 26, 28, 70, 73–5, 81, 82–3, 124
   CBOW in care system, 83
   WW2 'good-time girls', 73, 74, 75, 86
Greece, 67, 89, 92
Greene, Graham, *The Quiet American*, 119
Grieg, Kai, 3
Gutman, Roy, 152

Habyarimana, President, 189
Hague, William, 247

Hague Convention on Intercountry Adoption (HCIA, 1993), 126–7, 128
Hague Convention on the International Recovery of Child Support, 238
Haiti, 26
Himmler, Heinrich, 56, 57, 61
Hitler, Adolf, 58, 59, 61
HIV/AIDS, 192–3, 194, 196, 209, 210, 229, 236
Holt, Bertha and Harry, 124, 125, 126, 130
Horizon 2020 doctoral Training Network, 5
Husic, Sabiha, 170–1

identity issues, 5, 6, 7–8, 65–6, 68, 69, 75, 172, 174–5
   absent father as pivotal, 65, 66, 68–9, 72, 92, 175, 245, 247
   of adopted individuals, 131–2, 133–4
   affiliation to a group, 245
   CBOW of Rwandan rape victims, 197–8
   and children's rights, 166–71, 176
   of LRA children, 211–12
   name-calling and name-giving, 91, 137, 165–6, 194, 209, 210, 211, 212
   as relational in kinship system, 206
   right to know biological parents, 166–8, 171–2, 174
   Vietnamerican, 138, 139
Immigration and Nationality Act (McCarran Walter Act) (US, 1952), 121
Indochina Wars, 8, 25, 27, 72, 84, 113, 119, 160, 173–4, 246
   see also Vietnam War (1955–1975)
Indonesia, 9, 24, 27
Industrial Revolution, 36
infanticide, 157, 163–4, 195
Intended Consequences (Jonathan Torgovnik documentary), 194, 196
International Criminal Court, Rome Statute, 152–3, 154, 155
international humanitarian law (IHL)
   and children's rights, 10, 13–14, 36, 37–9, 160, 161–8, 171–2, 175–6
   and cultural sensitivity, 15, 163–4, 176
   customary international law, 193
   enforcement/implementation, 14, 15–16, 163, 167–8, 175–6
   impact of Rwandan genocide, 191–2, 193, 194
   sub-Saharan legal frameworks, 14, 15–16, 212
   see also children's rights issues; Convention on the Rights of the Child, UN (CRC, 1989)
International Research Network on Children Born of War, 5
International Union for Child Welfare, Geneva, 80
Islam, 32, 159–60, 170

Japan, 25, 27, 34, 53, 63–4, 70, 121, 164
Jebb, Eglantyne, 37
Jewish CBOW, 53
Johnson, Lyndon B., 114, 115

Kagame, President Paul, 189, 192
Kapstein, Ethan, 'The baby trade', 129
Kennedy, John F., 113–14, 115
Kony, Joseph, 201
Korean War, 9, 75, 117, 119, 121, 173
   and children, 25, 124, 125, 132, 133

Lakwena, Alice Auma, 201
Lamarck, Jean-Baptiste, 156
Larsen, Stein Ugelvik, 4
League of Nations, 36, 37, 161
Leduc, Nicholas, 131
Lee, Richard, 131
Le Ly Hayslip, 118, 120
Liberia, 26, 228, 235
Lord's Resistance Army (LRA) conflict, Northern Uganda (1988–2006), 7, 14–15, 25, 187–8, 201–15
   children born of, 4, 14, 15, 165, 198, 204–5, 206, 209–15
   CRSV during, 4, 7, 14, 15, 165, 202, 203, 204, 206, 209–15
   female child soldiers as sex slaves, 4, 7, 14–15, 25, 27, 28, 202, 203, 204, 209, 214–15

Mai Thi Hiep (Heidi Bob), 112
Mazowiecki Report, 154
McNaughton, John, 114
Melvin, Ken, 117–18
mental health and well-being, 138–9, 141, 156, 210, 211, 245
   children of Wehrmacht soldiers, 64, 65

healing rituals in Uganda, 213–14
and identity issues, 8, 65, 169–71, 175, 176
transgenerational issues, 5, 155–7, 192, 196, 197, 215
see also psychological perspective; trauma
military–civilian relations, gendered
agency of women, 51–2, 231
differing relations within single conflict, 24–5, 51–2
five broad patterns of, 26–7
friendly 'business arrangements', 26–7, 70, 76
love affairs, 26, 28, 51, 70, 71, 72, 75–82
marriage promises, 22, 23
military and governmental policies, 11, 12, 53, 55–67, 72, 73–85, 112–13, 116–21, 134, 173–4, 245–7
and nature of conflict, 27–8
peacekeeping forces and local women, 3, 16, 21, 25–6, 27, 28, 35, 215–16, 226, 227, 228–37
post-war occupation soldiers, 8–9, 70–84
and pre-twentieth-century conflicts, 21–3
Second World War, 51–3, 54–62, 173
and shift in nature of warfare, 1, 3–4, 7, 11, 13, 27, 29, 33–4, 152–3, 191–4, 201–3
US military policies in Vietnam, 12, 113, 116–21, 134, 173
see also conflict-related sexual violence (CRSV); consensual/non-violent relationships
Miss Saigon (musical), 112
Montessori, Maria, 35
morality and deviance, gendered discourse on, 11, 21–2, 92, 157, 165
'good-time girl' perceptions, 73, 74–5, 86
post-war German-American romances, 73, 75–6, 77
relationships with WW2 German soldiers, 59, 62–3, 64–6, 86
in sub-Saharan Africa, 190–1, 196, 205–6, 208–9
in Vietnam, 117–18, 119, 137
see also stigmatisation and discrimination

mothers of CBOW
agency of, 15, 231
economic hardships of, 39, 86, 137–8, 157, 169–70, 195–7, 211–13, 215, 231, 236, 245, 247–8
healing rituals in Uganda, 213–14
love affairs in Soviet Zone, 72
of peacekeeping babies, 230, 231, 234–8
rape-related health complications, 33–4, 156, 193, 195–6, 210
reintegration into post-conflict societies, 14–16, 157–8, 196, 205–15, 235, 236, 245, 247–8
rejection of their children, 66, 89, 135, 136, 138, 157–9, 165, 168, 169, 170–1, 195, 235
relationships with their children, 91, 155–7, 163–4, 165, 169–71, 194–5, 196–7, 210, 211, 215, 245
responses of local communities to, 11, 22, 23, 33–4, 157–8, 159–60, 164, 165, 205–15, 235–6, 245
see also stigmatisation and discrimination
settlement in new communities, 213
under-age, 15, 202, 210, 213, 215
Mozambique, 228
Mrazek, Robert, 135
Museveni, Yoweri, 201

Nadig, Friederike, 78
Netherlands, 9, 11, 24, 26, 27, 70, 73
children of Wehrmacht soldiers, 57, 58–9, 62, 63, 65, 66
WW2 *Moffenmeiden*, 62–3, 66, 86
Ngo Dinh Diem, 113–14
Nigeria, 25, 27, 187
Nixon, Richard, 114–15, 122
Norway, 3, 5, 11, 24, 57–9, 62, 64–5, 66, 165, 174
Nyiramasuhuku, Pauline, 191

Obote, Milton, 200–1
orphanages, 124–5, 130
Orphan Train Movement, 125–6

patriarchal social orders, 21–2, 31, 32, 205–10, 235
CBOW and perpetrator father, 165, 195, 197, 207, 209–10, 212
sub-Saharan Africa, 15, 31–2, 195, 197, 202, 205–10, 212

peacekeeping operations, UN, 153,
    226–32, 234–8
  children born of, 3, 16, 25–6, 215–16,
    230, 231, 234–8
  home legal systems and SEA, 232–3,
    234
  SEA by peacekeepers, 3, 16, 21, 26,
    28, 35, 226, 227, 228–34
  troop-contributing countries (TCCs),
    227, 232–4, 237
  zero-tolerance policies on SEA,
    229–34, 237, 247
Peace Research Institute Oslo, 5
Philippines, 63, 134, 246
Poland, 57, 58, 67
Post-Traumatic Stress Disorder (PTSD),
  155, 156, 210, 214–15
prostitution, 22, 27, 59–61, 137, 196
  camptown system in Asia, 116–17,
    119, 121
  child, 38, 39
  'comfort women', 27, 34, 53, 63–4
  Dutch *Moffenmeiden*, 62–3, 66, 86
  forced, 27, 34, 53, 55, 63–4, 152,
    154, 229, 231
  survival, 59–60, 61, 70, 76, 231,
    235–6
  during UN peacekeeping operations,
    228–9, 231, 234, 235–6
psychological perspective, 68–9, 69
  'African Youth Psychological
    Assessment Instrument', 210
  internalisation of guilt, 169–70, 197
  in Mochmann's methodology, 67–8,
    68, 121–2
  pre-natal formation of the 'self', 155–6
  Vietnamericans, 138, 140, 141
  wartime rape perpetrators, 30–2
  see also identity issues; mental health
    and well-being; stigmatisation
    and discrimination; trauma

race and ethnicity
  African-American GIs in WW2 period,
    73–6, 79–83, 124
  Afro-Amerasians in Vietnam, 12, 137,
    140
  Asian stereotypes in US culture,
    117–18, 139
  critics of Babylift, 130–1
  ethnically motivated CRSV, 3–4, 13,
    14, 27, 29, 33–4, 151, 152,
    153–60, 165, 190–1, 192–7
  and European colonial rule, 9, 24, 27,
    79–80, 83, 173, 189, 198–200

identity experiences of interracial
    adoptees, 131–4, 138, 139
  Lee's 'transracial adoption paradox',
    131
  mixed-race CBOW of WW2, 74–5, 76,
    77, 79–83, 92–3, 124
  mixed-race children of French
    colonies, 83–4
  Nazi racial ideology, 54–9, 61–2,
    66–7, 173
  'Rhineland Bastards' in 1930s, 79–80
  in Rwanda, 188–91, 197–8
  segregation/racism in USA, 73–4, 79,
    120–1, 122
  in Uganda, 198–200, 201
  Vietnamericans' integration into US,
    13, 113, 131, 139–41
rape see children born of rape; conflict-
    related sexual violence (CRSV);
    gender-based violence (GBV)
Reagan Administration, 139–40
research data and methodology, 3–12,
    13, 15, 53, 65, 87, 244–5
  lack of reliable CBOW data, 3–4, 5, 10,
    70–1, 244
  Mochmann's conceptualisation, 67–8,
    68, 121–2
Rwandan genocide (1994), 187–9, 188
  100 days (6 April–16 July 1994),
    189–90, 191, 192–3
  children born of, 4, 192, 194–5,
    196–8
  CRSV during, 1, 4, 7, 14, 21, 27, 29,
    33, 152, 190–1, 192–3, 194–7
  ethnic issues, 188–91, 197–8
  ICTR, 2, 152, 190–1, 192, 193, 194
  impact on international law, 191–2,
    193, 194
  spread of HIV/AIDS, 192–3, 194, 196

Save the Children, 37
Schultz, George, 136
Second World War (1939–1945)
  Allied forces stationed in Europe, 70,
    73–5, 86–7, 174
  CBOW data, 3, 11, 52–3, 58, 61, 62,
    64, 65, 66, 67
  CBOW 'telling their stories', 11–12, 53
  children fathered by British soldiers,
    174
  children fathered by French soldiers, 8,
    160, 173–4, 246
  children fathered by Wehrmacht
    soldiers, 3, 5, 24, 57–67, 89, 92,
    165, 173, 174

Index

CRSV during, 7, 27, 28, 30, 51–2, 54–7, 69–70, 71–2, 76
demographic changes caused by, 73, 76, 78
Eastern Front, 54–7, 173
German military brothels, 27, 34, 53, 55, 60–1
German occupation of France, 24–5, 59–62
GI brides, 74, 77, 120
life courses of CBOW, 64–9, *68*, *69*, 89–93, 174–5
Nazi policy on CBOW, 56–9, 61–2, 66–7
'ownership' of soldiers' children, 11, 77–85, 173–4
Pacific War, 27, 34, 53, 63, 64
rapes by German soldiers in Soviet Union, 30, 54–7
Red Army mass rapes of German women, 27, 28, 51–2, 54, 69–70, 71–2
US policies towards GI offspring, 73, 74–5, 77–8
Seifert, Ruth, 31
sexuality
  inequalities of gendered power relations, 30–1, 119, 231
  as regimented in Third Reich, 55
  sexual desire as factor in wartime rape, 34
  sub-Saharan African moral codes, 205–6, 208–9
sexually transmitted infections (STIs), 52, 59, 60, 64, 71, 116, 173, 229
  HIV/AIDS, 192–3, 194, 196, 209, 210, 229, 236
  racial prejudice and, 74, 117
  in sub-Saharan conflicts, 195, 196, 204, 209, 210
Sierra Leone, 4, 9, 25, 27, 228
Simms, Brendan, 158
Sirik Matak, Prince, 116
slavery, sexual, 27, 28, 119, 152
  female child soldiers in Uganda, 4, 7, 14–15, 25, 27, 28, 202, 203, 204, 209, 214–15
  WW2 'comfort women', 27, 34, 53, 63–4
Somalia, 14, 26, 175, 187, 228
South Sudan, 25, 187
Soviet Union, 9, 26, 36, 67
  'Eastern Front' in Second World War, 54–7, 173
  post-WW2 Soviet occupation soldiers, 26, 71–2, 87–9, *88*, *90*, 244
  Red Army mass rapes of German women, 27, 28, 51–2, 54, 69–70, 71–2
Sri Lanka, 3
Steiner, Rudolf, 35
stigmatisation and discrimination, 5, 11, 14, *68*, *69*, 160, 164, 165–6, 175, 176, 245, 247–8
  CBOW in Bosnia, 157–8, 168–71
  CBOW of American GIs in Asia, 8, 112, 123–4, 135, 136–8
  CBOW of WW2 German soldiers, 63, 64–6, 67, 69, 86, 89–93
  children of Soviet soldiers, 72, 87–9, *88*, *90*, 244
  CRC principle of non-discrimination, 37, 38, 165–6
  female LRA returnees, 15, 206, 209
  'good-time girl' perceptions, 73, 74–5, 86
  Grammar's 'Brown Baby Plan', 81–2
  LRA children, 209–13
  mixed-race GI children in Europe, 74–5, 81–2
  mothers of CBOW fathered by peacekeepers, 235, 236
  post-war German-American romances, 73, 75–6, 77
  relationships with WW2 German soldiers, 59, 62–3, 64–6, 86
  Rwandan rape victims, 195–8
  self-stigmatisation, 74, 169–70, 196, 211
  and underreporting of CBOW/rape, 70, 76, 83, 233
Sudan, 25, 26, 27, 187, 202–3
Switzerland, 168
Syria, 25, 27

Tanzania, 200
Taylor, Rosemary, 125, 133
Thirty Years' War, 22, 23
Tiernan, Audrey, 135
Tisdale, Betty, 130
Topham, Kristin, 130
Tran, William, 138
trauma, 32, *68*, *69*, 132, 133, 170–1, 175
  CBOW discovery of origins, 8, 66, 69, 89, 169, 174–5, 210
  CBOW of WW2 German soldiers, 67, 69

trauma (*cont.*)
  inflicted through rape, 33–4, 164, 168–9, 193, 194–7, 205, 210, 215, 233
  of LRA children, 211, 212–13, 214–15
  maternal, 91, 155–8, 164, 169–70, 194–7, 210, 214–15
  psychological benefits from, 215
  transgenerational transmission, 5, 155–7, 192, 196, 197, 215

Uganda, 15, 16, 198–201, 202, 212
  LRA terror in Acholi region, 201–2, 203–4
  religious healing rituals, 213–14
  significance of kinship, 15, 205–10, 212, 213–14
  see also Lord's Resistance Army (LRA) conflict, Northern Uganda (1988–2006)
UNICEF, 127, 157, 158
United Nations (UN)
  Bulletin on SEA (2003), 229–30, 232
  'Comprehensive Strategy' (December 2007), 16, 35, 40, 230, 236, 237, 247
  'Declaration on the Rights of the Child' (1959), 37, 161, 171
  OCHA, 30
  Report of Legal Experts, 233–4
  SC Resolutions on CRSV, 33, 152, 153
  'Sexual Exploitation and Abuse Victims Assistance Guide', 238
  Special Rapporteurs, 31, 154
  Standing Committee Task Force on SEA, 229
  'Universal Declaration of Human Rights' (1948), 37, 161
  Women, Peace and Security (SC Resolution 1325, 2000), 153
  Zeid Report, 230, 232, 233, 236
  see also Convention on the Rights of the Child, UN (CRC, 1989); peacekeeping operations, UN
United States of America (USA)
  adoption legislation, 124, 125, 126
  Amerasian Immigration Act (1982), 135, 139, 140
  American Homecoming Act (1986/87), 8, 12, 13, 113, 129, 134–6, 138, 139–40, 174, 246
  non-signatory of CRC, 14, 38, 175
  Office for Refugee Resettlement, 140–1
  policies towards GI offspring in Vietnam, 12, 112–13, 116, 120, 121–5, 129–41, 174
  see also Babylift, Operation (1975)
  policies towards GI offspring in WW2 period, 73, 74–5, 77–8
  presence in Great Britain (WW2), 25, 26, 28, 70, 73–5, 81, 82–3, 124
  racial segregation/racism in, 73–4, 79, 120–1, 122
  Vietnamericans' integration into, 13, 113, 131, 139–41
  Vietnamese community in, 13, 113, 139–41
  war brides legislation, 120–1
  see also Vietnam War (1955–1975)

vagina dentate myth, 117
Van Tien Dung, 115
venereal disease (VD) *see* sexually transmitted infections (STIs)
Vietnam, communist, 8, 12, 112, 129, 135, 136–8
Vietnam War (1955–1975)
  camptown system for prostitution, 116–17, 121
  CBOW as visible, 8, 12, 112–13, 121
  course of, 113–16, 122, 129
  fall of Saigon, 12, 112, 113, 115, 129, 135, 136, 158
  'friendly business arrangements' during, 27
  GI children (*Bui Doi*), 3, 8, 12, 25, 112–13, 121–3, 129, 130–41, 165, 174, 246
  image of deceitful local woman, 117–18
  military attitude to GI girlfriends, 12, 116–21, 134
  Rest and Recuperation (R&R) programme for GIs, 118–19
  Tet Offensive (1968), 114, 115
  US public opinion, 114, 115, 122, 135
  Vietnamese-American marriages, 116, 119, 120, 134
  young US military cohort, 119–20
Virgili, Fabrice, 65–6

The War and Children Identity Project, 3, 4
warfare
  changing nature of, 1, 3–4, 7, 11, 13,

27, 29, 33–4, 152–3, 191–4,
      201–3
combat roles of girls and women, 25,
      202, 203, 205
command and control structures,
      32–3
in early modern times, 21, 22, 23

instrumentalisation of women, 31, 33,
      190–1, 192
irregular forces, 53, 152, 173, 187,
      191
women as pivotal in travelling armies,
      21, 22
Weise, Knut, *88*, *89*, *90*

EU authorised representative for GPSR:
Easy Access System Europe, Mustamäe tee 50,
10621 Tallinn, Estonia
gpsr.requests@easproject.com

www.ingramcontent.com/pod-product-compliance
Lightning Source LLC
Chambersburg PA
CBHW071402300426
44114CB00016B/2153